ON WAR AND DEMOCRACY

ON WAR AND DEMOCRACY

CHRISTOPHER KUTZ

PRINCETON UNIVERSITY PRESS
Princeton & Oxford

First paperback printing, 2020
Paperback ISBN 978-0-691-20236-5

The Library of Congress has cataloged the cloth edition as follows:
Kutz, Christopher.
On war and democracy / Christopher Kutz.
pages cm
Includes bibliographical references and index.
ISBN 978-0-691-16784-8 (hardcover : alk. paper)
1. Democracy—Philosophy. 2. War—Moral and ethical aspects.
3. Politics and war. 4. Agent (Philosophy).   I. Title.
JC423.K87 2016
321.8—dc23   2015018418

British Library Cataloging-in-Publication Data is available

This book has been composed in Granjon LT Std

For Oliver, Madeleine, and Jessica

CONTENTS

PERMISSIONS

The following chapters have appeared, in similar form, as published articles.

CHAPTER 2   "Democratic Security," in *Security: A Multidisciplinary Normative Perspective*, ed. Cecilia Bailliet (Martinus Nijhoff, 2009).

CHAPTER 3   "The Difference Uniforms Make: Collective Violence in Criminal Law and the Law of War," *Philosophy and Public Affairs* 33 (2005): 148–180.

CHAPTER 4   "Fearful Symmetries," in *Just and Unjust Warriors*, ed. David Rodin and Henry Shue (Oxford University Press, 2008).

CHAPTER 5   "Against Political Luck," in *Reading Bernard Williams*, ed. Daniel Callcut (Routledge, 2009).

CHAPTER 6   "Secret Law and the Value of Publicity," *Ratio Juris* 22 (2009): 197–217.

CHAPTER 7   "Torture, Necessity, and Existential Politics," *California Law Review* 95 (2007): 235–176.

CHAPTER 8   "Democracy, Defense and the Threat of Intervention," in *The Morality of Defensive War*, ed. Cécile Fabre and Seth Lazar (Oxford: Oxford University Press, 2014).

CHAPTER 11   "Democratic Norm Death," *Ethics & International Affairs* (Winter 2014): 425–449.

CHAPTER 12   "Justice in Reparations: The Problem of Land and the Value of Cheap Talk," *Philosophy & Public Affairs* 32 (2004): 277–312.

ACKNOWLEDGMENTS

I owe so many thanks to so many readers and interlocutors that it is difficult to know where to start. I am grateful to the University of California at Berkeley, which has been my chief intellectual home since 1998, and to my colleagues in the Jurisprudence and Social Policy Program. I continue to remark on the miracle of UC Berkeley: a public university that combines a commitment to democratic access with one to vaulting intellectual ambition. I am also grateful to Columbia and Stanford Law Schools, which were temporary homes during the book's gestation, and Sciences-Po, Paris, where two marvelous years provided a crucial oblique view on many of my arguments. Audiences at Princeton, Yale, Vanderbilt, Oxford, Stanford, Delft, Toronto, and Osgoode Hall have all provided terrific commentary and criticism.

At the risk of forgetting many individuals, I would like to thank the following people for extremely constructive comments on talks or drafts: Charles Beitz, Gabriel Beringer, Mark Bevir, Peter Cane, Joshua Cohen, Ariel Colonomos, Richard Craswell, Meir Dan-Cohen, Tom Dannenbaum, Mary Dudziak, Cécile Fabre, Barbara Fried, Stephen Galoob, Michael Gross, Andrew Guzman, Kinch Hoekstra, Kate Jastram, Sanford Kadish, Paul Kahn, Niko Kolodny, Martin Krygier, Seth Lazar, David Lieberman, Katerina Linos, David Luban, Daniel Markovits, Larry May, Melissa McCall, Jeff McMahan, Jamie O'Connell, Gloria Origgi, Robert Post, Eric Rakowski, Jessica Riskin, David Rodin, Samuel Scheffler, Scott Shapiro, Henry Shue, Jonathan Simon, David Sklansky, Sarah Song, Kevin Stack, Annie Stilz, Jerry Vildostegui, Jay Wallace, and Mikhail Xifaras. I am especially grateful to the members of this group who participated in a workshop on this manuscript in Fall 2014 at Berkeley, and to Sarah Song and Amatullah Alaji-Sabrie for organizing it. I owe special thanks to my deans and chairs at Berkeley, whose support made the book possible. I am further grateful to Amatullah Alaji-Sabrie and Kavitha Iyengar for invaluable help with final preparation of the manuscript.

I would like to mention several particular intellectual debts here. I owe one to Michael Walzer, whose book *Just and Unjust Wars*—in its insistence that the problem of war be confronted simultaneously concretely, through lived and historical example, and abstractly, through philosophical reflection—inspires every page. (The pervasiveness of that influence is why specific footnotes are more scant.) The others are to two departed teachers and colleagues. First, Bernard Williams's voice echoed in my head throughout the writing of this book, in his insistence that philosophical thought must address life if it is to hope to be interesting. The second is Sandy Kadish, who more than anyone created at Berkeley Law a haven for philosophical thought about morality and law, and whose guidance, kindness, and generosity have been a model for me.

The people at Princeton University Press have been a pleasure to work with, including my editor, Rob Tempio, and my copyeditor, Molan Goldstein.

Finally, I owe my deepest thanks for all manner of advice and support to Allen Galson, Myra Jehlen, Karon Johnson, Robert Kutz, Ruth Kutz, Carl Riskin, and Jessica Riskin; and to Oliver and Madeleine Riskin-Kutz, who are the point of it all.

1

INTRODUCTION:
WAR, POLITICS, DEMOCRACY

We live in an era of belligerent democracy, an unhappy sequel to the peaceful democratic transitions that unfolded across Latin America and Eastern Europe at the end of the twentieth century. Democratic aspirations are increasingly voiced across the Mediterranean in the new century—leading more often than not to civil conflict rather than electoral transitions.[1] We live also in an era of democratic wars, when democratic states pursue violent conflict in the name of peaceable ends, ranging from disarmament to democratization to securing access to natural resources.

Despite Churchill's famous quip—"Democracy is the worst form of government, except for all those other forms that have been tried from time to time"[2]—democracy is seen as a source of both domestic and international flourishing. Democracy, understood roughly for now as a political system with wide suffrage in which power is allocated to officials by popular election, can solve or help solve a host of problems with stunning success. It can solve the problem of revolutionary violence that condemns autocratic regimes, because mass politics can work at the ballot box rather than the streets. It can help solve the problem of famine, because the systems of free public communication and discussion that are essential to democratic politics are the backbone of the markets that have made democratic societies far richer than their competitors. It can help solve the problem of environmental despoliation, which occurs when those operating polluting factories (whether private citizens or the state) do not need to answer for harms visited upon a broad public. And democracy has been famously thought to help solve the problem of war, in the guise of the idea of the "peace amongst democratic nations"—an idea emerging with Immanuel Kant in the Age of Enlightenment and given new energy with the wave of democratization at the end of the twentieth century.

The "democratic peace" thesis, which holds that mature democracies rarely fight each other, has been a comforting mainstay of political thought, especially in the United States. As a modern correlation, it has held up

reasonably well, notwithstanding some important counterexamples, notably the American Civil War.[3] But closer scrutiny has also brought to light
further doubts about any broader, happy connection between war and
democracy. Indeed, as political scientists Edward Mansfield and Jack
Snyder have shown, emerging democracies are more likely than other
kinds of states to go to war, often as a means of securing internal support and legitimacy. And mature democracies have shown great willingness to go to war against nondemocracies, whether as part of colonialist
and imperialist agendas or for reasons of local or regional self-defense.[4]
Democracy and war, it seems, are anything but adversaries. This is not
news, especially in the United States. Indeed, the "pro-democracy" or
"freedom" agenda of George W. Bush's neoconservatism came to be identified around the world as an expression of martial imperialism.

Discussions of the democratic peace thesis and the real purposes or
effects of American "democracy promotion" are empirical questions. They
are vital to politicians and international relations scholars. This book, too,
is about the relations between democracy and war. But I ask principally
what philosophers call *normative* questions, among them: How should we,
as citizens, think about our responsibility for killing done in our name? Do
democracies face special constraints in the kinds of weapons or tactics they
can use, independently of the conventional law of war? Do democracies
have a right or even an obligation to aid other peoples in achieving democratic governance through force rather than example? Does the legal requirement that combatants be uniformed in order to be able to kill in war have
any rationale beyond protecting civilians? What responsibilities do democratic revolutionaries have to property holders under the ancien régime?

Still, it has been more than twenty years since the last great wave of
pro-democratic revolutions, in Eastern Europe and Latin America—not
long in political time, perhaps, but long enough for awareness of the risk
that democracy will wilt under the malfunctioning, corruption, and pa-
ralysis of so many of the older democracies. In the United States, the Arab
Spring coincided with the spectacle of a deadlocked government, seemingly unable to summon the collective forces needed to challenge the worst
economic crisis in nearly a century. Europe's experiment in fiscal union
staggers from crisis to crisis, for lack of concerted political will. The contrast between the initial hopes of the crowds of Cairo and Tunis and the
cynicism of Europe and America makes clear the gap between the ideal of
democracy and its messy reality.

As an ideal, democracy remains unchallenged, even unchallengeable.
Twenty years ago, Francis Fukuyama declared "the end of history," by

which he meant that a history of grand ideological conflict had ended with the collapse of the Soviet empire, leaving only one governing philosophy in place: democratic liberalism, meaning popular control of political institutions, private property rights, and a market-dominated system of resource allocation.[5] Fukuyama was soon mocked for his declaration: even as the Cold War became a memory, geopolitical conflict continued through decades defined by the resurgent tribalism and postnationalism of the Balkans and Africa, as well as the broader contest between the forces of capitalist globalization and antimarket Islamic fundamentalism. But even if history has not ended, Fukuyama's central claim remains strong: within Western thought, democracy has no extant challenger. On the broader global playing field, its only remaining challengers are fundamentalism and—perhaps—Chinese-style managerial capitalism. The distance kept by revolutionary Arab demonstrators from fundamentalism, especially in Egypt, makes the former an unwise bet; as to the latter, whether or not China can continue to suppress pro-democratic movements internally, its model represents a holding action at best, not a likely export.

Hegemony is an ugly word, but it well describes the role of democratic ideology within American political theory, if not political practice. Political theorists compete with one another to offer more radical or fundamental forms of democracy for consumption and endorsement.[6] Legitimacy is defined in theoretical terms as the right to rule; the only evident source of that right is democracy, in one or another institutional form. Put another way, the only acceptable answer to the question put by a citizen, "who are you to tell me what to do?" is an answer that says, "We (the rulers) are you— you chose us, or accepted the procedure that gave us this authority. You are responsible for the conditions of your own rule."[7] We can entertain, as a theoretical possibility, the benevolent dictator who says, "I'm in charge just because I can run your life better than you would yourself," but we entertain it only as a foil for the clearly correct answer, that the right to rule rests on the will of the governed. In the circumstances of politics—when it is a collective being ruled—the will of the governed is also collective. And this is the essence of democratic legitimacy: rulers rule on the basis of what Jean-Jacques Rousseau called the general will of the community they rule. Anything else is enslavement to the will of another.

The idea of democratic legitimacy, resting on a kernel of collective will, is obviously powerful, though it is pliant enough to serve as both banner and critique of many of the political pathologies we know today, from paralyzed legislatures to populist demagogues. The underlying idea that rule must be legitimated to each person ruled is what separates political modernity from feudal and caste systems. But, even apart from its vagueness, it suffers from two problems. The first is that it is too static: the value of democracy, on this understanding, exists when there is a correspondence between the authority claimed by the governors and the content of the will of the governed. When such a correspondence exists, confirmed by electoral institutions, then rules and norms are legitimate, because they express a people governing itself. The problem with this view is that it allows us to fix the label "democratic," which involves little more than viewing a spectacle of mass politics, on the basis of a moment of annual or quadrennial activity.[8] Whatever the defects of our actual democratic practice, I seek a way of understanding the form of collective self-determination that is at least potentially at play at the margins of democracy. By margins of democracy, I mean periods of revolution and wartime emergency rule, as well as in the forms of civic organization and resistance that contend with organized, institutional forms.

The heart of this book is therefore built around an alternative understanding of democracy, one that is simultaneously more modest and, I believe, more promising. The understanding I propose is one that focuses on our agency when we act together to build, defend, transform, and sometimes tear down the institutions of our common political life. I call this understanding *agentic democracy*. Agentic democracy is, in the view I develop here, much less a matter of formal institutions of democratic choice and representations, such as elections and parliaments, and much more a matter of how we think about and work with one another in establishing democratic political institutions. We act as democratic agents not just when we vote or debate in the public square but also before it is even possible to vote or to debate in public. Eastern European intellectuals, meeting in a café to lay the groundwork for a challenge to communist rule, were acting as democrats: thinking about how they might make mass politics safe for others to join in protest. Soldiers defending their homeland from invasion, not because they were ordered to do so, but because they think of themselves as defending their land, their way of life, can equally be acting as democrats. The crucial component of democracy, on my view, is a matter of our mutual orientation in collective action: how individuals conceive of their actions in relation to each other, and in relation to a broader set of goals involving building or defending open political institutions.

A further advantage of understanding democracy in terms of agency is that it can help to make sense of the particular phenomenon of collective violence, a phenomenon that has been central to the ways in which some—though hardly all—democracies understand themselves. Such a self-understanding was famously true of Revolutionary France. It also plays a major role in American self-consciousness.[9] The quintessentially Wilsonian assertion of democratic ideals in global life has been the major thread of world politics since World War I. In that respect, while I speak of a conception of democracy in general terms, it is a conception tailored to the particular contours of American politics. The account I provide is deliberately grounded on the American practice of war, so that we can understand the tangled and intimate connection between the violence of war and the prospect of democratic self-government.

Of course, the connection between a theory of the state and a theory of violence is linked by more than US history. Weber's definition of the state as the body successfully claiming a monopoly on violence presupposes the violence that lies at the origin of the state—if not as a matter of conceptual necessity, then as a matter of undisputed history.[10] Without violence (whether celebrated or shrouded in myths of origin), the circumstances of politics would not exist: a defined territory, a unifying system for resolving disputes between mine and thine, and common allegiance.

Still, one might have thought democratic politics to be hostile to violence as a matter of principle. Violence, at least political violence, denies the voice and integrity of others, rejects their standing as equals in a shared dialogue about common causes and meanings—the essence of democratic self-government. And, indeed, democratic states have achieved, over time, an outstanding record of rejecting violence in favor of dialogue, within their domestic spheres. But the global record is less reassuring, whether as a product of colonialism, ideological conflict, or—most recently—a missionary conception of democracy, with the aim of seeding it as widely as possible. Democracies have the same instincts of self-defense as other regimes, as well as the same expansive capacity to understand the interests worth defending through resort to violence. Whether the trigger for war is naked colonialism, more subtle calculations of balances of power, the entanglements of treaties with democratic allies, or a universalist rhetoric of the defense of human rights, democracies use war as a regular instrument of liberal foreign policy.

And yet the criminal law of the modern state is virtually defined by the limits it places on private violence. With the exception of the homeowner's right of self-defense, there rests almost no license to its recourse. The restrictions of private law find their mirror in the law of nations: since the Kellogg-Briand Pact of 1928, and further codified in the United Nations Charter, the right to war as a privilege of princes has been equally abrogated, save only in self-defense of territory or material interest.[11] One might well define the project of public international law as achieving for the international system something like the monopoly on violence exercised at the domestic level. Of course, the legal abolition of the right to nondefensive war has entailed nothing like its actual abolition, any more than its domestic abolition. If, in both cases, violence is now exercised in the face of the law, many actors are undeterred by law's sanction. Whether justified by tortured legal argument or simply executed in the teeth of the prohibition, violence, both private and political, persists.

At the international level, the ambivalence of political violence lies in more than the gap between the abolitionist ideal and the reality of its exercise. It lies also in the labored modern history of the doctrine of humanitarian intervention and its broader cousin, the responsibility to protect.[12] The doctrines are expansions of the right of national self- or other-defense, now including defense of persons and not just of the state. Both have been and still are seen as a threat to the absolutism of the UN Charter's Article 2(4), which generally prohibits the use of force in international relations, even if these doctrines also give voice to an ideal of the protection of human dignity in their own form, existing only when exercised by the international community, or some substantial-enough subset to claim legitimacy. It lies in the broad construal, accepted by international lawyers, of the right of military self-defense, extending beyond the right to defend territory to the right to protect one's nationals, wherever they are threatened, and the right to protect all the assets of national security, including electronic systems. And it lies in Additional Protocol II to the Geneva Convention (not universally accepted, to be sure), which grants the privilege of belligerency to insurgents fighting wars "of national liberation."[13] These doctrines and exceptions acknowledge that violence has the power to create and protect.

The ambivalence regarding mass violence is a problem at the heart of democratic theory as well. The ambivalence exists primarily across time, before and after the formation of what counts, in institutional terms, as a democracy. If democratic legitimacy resides, at first approximation, in the exercise of a universal franchise, then no acts preceding the exercise of franchise can claim *democratic* legitimacy. Thus, to justify its own origins, democratic theory must reach back into time to link a group defined by its aspirations to its future status as popular assembly. I adverted above to the need for a conception of democracy at the revolutionary margins of new institutions. The difficulty is that few or no rebellions or liberatory movements can actually define themselves in democratic terms, and hence can help themselves to democratic legitimacy only on terms of future credit. Put another way, the justification of the lives they take in revolutionary violence comes in the classical form: by the end it achieves, not the process of its justification.

There are, indeed, distinctions among revolutionary movements: those having wider or narrower popular support, with more or less dialogue-based ways of building that support; those giving greater or less attention to distinguishing noncombatants; and those having greater or less independence from international interests. But it is fair to say, using history as our guide, that few revolutionary movements are likely to be fully respectful of the laws of war, grounded in essentially democratic politics—and triumphant. Historically, the democratic ambitions (both successful and failed) of the American, French, and Russian revolutions were largely dependent on the military mobilization and crowd violence that swept out the anciens régimes. At the other extreme stand the Velvet Revolutions of Eastern Europe, particularly in Poland and Czechoslovakia. Those revolutions, it is true, owe a great deal to popular mobilization, democratic rhetoric, and—in Poland—genuine exercises in democratic votes. But even in these cases, success owed as much to the exogenous collapse of Soviet military control in the face of American defense spending as to the internal democratic practice of the revolutionaries. More generally, while contemporary revolutions—especially revolutions capable of winning the critical support of the democratic powers—will voice a democratic rhetoric, and will show their legitimacy through mass protest and mobilization, their eventual legitimation comes after the risks have been run. Thus, if we are inclined to take revolutions as epitomes of popular will, then an interest in historical adequacy entails a conception of democracy adequate to the way in which popular will can manifest itself in violence as well as in its polls. An interest in normative adequacy means that we need to elaborate a set of critical terms, internal to democratic agency, to restrain that violence. Such is my aim here.

Thus, I argue that we must maintain our guard against the seductions of a particular understanding of democracy and its romance of collective agency. Democracy celebrates the politics of cooperation: the fusion of individual wills in crafting a common space. Put another way, it is the value of politics as such—the fusion of goals and wills in pursuit of a common system of civil life—that provides the legitimacy of nonstate actors who are on the road to building democratic institutions. In earlier work, I have provided my own analysis of how we fuse our goals and wills to act together—and so to become responsible as individuals for what we do together.[14] I would today revise that analysis in some respects and will offer some of that revision in the course of the book. The basic idea of collective action has remained constant, however: acting together, at bottom, involves a mutual orientation around the goals and interests of another. Sometimes this orientation is hierarchical, as when a subordinate follows the commands of a superior (or a superior issues those commands); sometimes it is collateral, as when we resolve together what we will do. The capacity to treat each other as collateral authorities, and so to join our wills together, is if not uniquely human, at least a distinctive feature of our humanity.[15] In politics, therefore, we reveal our humanity.

This is the source of the conceptual threat posed by democracy. The very celebration of collective agency can lead to an overly permissive attitude towards collective violence. Seen no longer as an instrument of the king but instead an expression of popular will, democratic wars can seem to sanctify themselves. They offer a new form of holy war, I argue, one grounded in the comparative virtue of the democratic belligerent. But, I also argue, the temptation of democratic war rests on a misconception of democracy and the value of political agency: it takes democratic agency as something to be maximized rather than respected, as a value transferable from one state to another. Properly understood, democratic values should be seen as constraints on both the forms and ends of collective violence, not as a new source of war's legitimacy. This is the normative program of the book.

Before launching the normative argument, however, it is worth looking quickly over the history of the theory of war. We can tell two general stories of the history of the ethics of war. Around the fifteenth century, with the preceding rise of a system of mutually recognized absolute sovereignty, begins to emerge a de-moralized picture of war as essentially a prerogative of the sovereign, who is not to be judged by any further terrestrial body but only in the forum of victory. This is the traditional subject of the *jus ad bellum*: the question of whether a state has a right (in justice) to engage in war, as self-defense or vindication of its rights. The second strand, known as the *jus in bello*, concerns the question of how to fight a war justly— that is, using means and choosing targets that are legitimate, irrespective of whether the war as a whole is just.[16] This second strain emerges in the medieval chivalric tradition, then gaining force with the professionalized militaries of the eighteenth century, is a professional ethic of the warrior. Both strands crystallize in the eighteenth century, the first in the work of Emer de Vattel, the writer primarily responsible for the idea of "regular war" (*la guerre reglée*), or wars whose legitimacy comes from their form rather than the justice of their cause. Vattel's work, which marks the essential break from a philosophical-theological tradition to a less normative "legal science," sets the scene for the theory of war that dominated thought from the Treaty of Utrecht to the end of the Cold War. This is the idea of a regular war, or war in due form: a war waged between two public sovereigns, each asserting a right (to punish, to defend, and so on).[17] When a war is regular, though one may raise questions of justice concerning each side, actual judgment is withheld, and the two parties are permitted to contest until victory separates the righteous from the unrighteous.

The two strands, taken together, amount to a theory of war as a sort of reverse vacuum capsule: a morality of individual conduct is sealed inside, operating within an effective vacuum of international morality from without. Such a morality could barely claim to govern the period of Great Power warfare between sovereigns intent on maintaining geographical parity. And the ostensibly humanitarian rules of conduct did nothing to shield soldiers from trench gas in the First World War, or to shield civilians from area bombing in the Second. The great break in this tradition followed World War II, with the UN Charter and its restriction of war to self-defense, and the concomitant emergence of a conception of international human rights (which intersects in complex ways with international humanitarian law). While this intellectual and legal formation tilted again during the period of decolonization of the 1960s and 1970s, providing (within the Additional Protocols) protection and combatant privileges for nonstate actors, the system of state-centered legitimate violence remained generally intact. And the system, at least conceptually, has one great advantage: it permits a uniform set of humanitarian norms to apply to soldiers and civilians alike, with—in principle—gains in the reduction of suffering. Whatever the metaphysics of justice, the shift away from a view of soldiers and civilians as guilty of war making, and their location, instead, in a moral context seen as fully reciprocal, can offer them protection when they are most vulnerable.

Of course, any particular constellation of norms, laws, and historical understandings is unstable. It is remarkable that the regular war constellation endured as long as it did, though the seemingly endless and pervasive character of what lawyers and treaties refer to as "non-international armed conflict"—including the conflicts with al-Qaeda and ISIS—have largely put to rest any stable conception of regular war, understood as a conflict essentially involving two uniformed, hierarchically ordered, and politically directed hosts.[18] But the instability now comes from new sources. The first source is the rise, connected intimately with the politics of the

Middle East, of non-state-based violence, directed at both civilian and military targets. The second is the militarization of human rights norms, under the aegis of humanitarian intervention. The first source has given rise to military conflicts embedded within a transnational conflict of basic values: religion and tradition versus modernity and markets. While the Cold War was, of course, also transnational and ideological, it was fundamentally state based, and so the techniques of diplomacy and mutually advantageous trade could have some purchase over the conflict, as could the basic logic of deterrence. (Neither the USSR nor the US was, in the end, willing to gamble its own existence.) Conflicts between states and stateless (e.g., al-Qaeda) or semi-stateless (e.g., Hamas) forces take place out of the context of reciprocal threat and promise that can sustain a weak modicum of restraint. The end of reciprocity as a condition of war's constraint, as Mark Osiel has put it, entails on its own a need to rethink the foundations of humanitarian law.[19] To take one notorious example, the treatment of captives is a problem of principle as well as practice—one side, lacking a system of jails or justice, treats captives as objects of ransom (in a retreat to an older tradition), while the other finds itself tempted to discard in its entirety a legal regime crafted for a hierarchical and ordered military foe fighting a declared war in which victory or surrender is easily foreseen.[20]

The rise of a muscular conception of human rights norms, backed by the willingness of nations and international organizations to deploy force, has also complicated the context of war. The change can, of course, be exaggerated. While there is a traditional rhetoric of absolute respect for the rights of sovereigns in their internal sphere, the rule is usually immediately qualified with an exception. Hugo Grotius, the Dutch thinker usually considered to be the modern father of public international law, echoing the earlier Spanish writers Francisco Suárez and Francisco de Vitoria, wrote:

> Though it is a rule established by the laws of nature and of social order, and a rule confirmed by all the records of history, that every sovereign is supreme judge in his own kingdom and over his own subjects, in whose disputes no foreign power can justly interfere. Yet where a Busiris, a Phalaris or a Thracian Diomede provoke their people to despair and resistance by unheard of cruelties, having themselves abandoned all the laws of nature, they lose the rights of independent sovereigns, and can no longer claim the privilege of the law of nations.[21]

Even Emer de Vattel, who offers the conceptual high-water mark of the Westphalian system of independent states,[22] allows a qualified right of intervention against a flailing prince inflicting injury on his own people: "But, if the prince, by violating the fundamental laws, gives his subjects a legal right to resist him . . . every foreign power has a right to succour an oppressed people who implore their assistance."[23] The rhetorical tradition has, of course, a mirror in the practice of European states of interference in each other's affairs, frequently on the grounds of protecting religious minorities.

While the most robust conceptions of Westphalian sovereignty, including Vattel's, claim more rhetorically than realistically that the essence of nationhood lies in rights of noninterference,[24] it is undeniable that conceptions of state autonomy have weakened through a growing tradition of ostensible, and sometimes actual, humanitarian interventions. It is a tradition with admirable ideals, if not always admirable integrity, encompassing the Great Powers' interventions between Greece and Turkey in the 1820s and Hitler's "protection" of the Sudeten Germans of Czechoslovakia, as well as the (so far) better-judged interventions of NATO in Kosovo and Libya[25] and of UN forces in East Timor.[26]

That said, the postmillennial politics of humanitarian intervention, under the rubric of the "responsibility to protect," or R2P, has caused a fundamental shift in post-WWII international conflicts. While the doctrine of R2P is, on its terms, limited to the prevention of civilian massacres—and while the practice remains extremely selective in its targets—the framework of international intervention has shifted now to encompass the question of the prospects for reform in the targeted state. The effect is a gradual moralization of international politics, a breaking of a fragile consensus around limiting the use of force to circumstances of strict self-defense. Many democratic idealists have been heartened by this shift, replacing the political realists' self-interested assessments of the costs and benefits of international interventions with a richer cosmopolitan and moral framework—even as they strive to separate their position from the neoconservative emphasis on exporting democracy. The experience of Iraq has chastened neoconservative ambitions to remake the Middle East; and the politics of the Arab Spring, the rise of ISIS, and the continuing humanitarian disaster of Syria have further complicated the region. As a result, the conceptions of sovereignty and the triggers for intervention seem to have changed decisively within democratic thought.

These are the traditional issues of the *jus ad bellum* of Just War Theory. My focus will be largely, if not relentlessly, critical. I will take it as a given that war and other forms of political violence can be justified, if rarely—that, for example, de Gaulle and Churchill were right while Pétain and

Halifax were wrong in their decision to accept war. And whether or not the American, French, Chinese, South African, and Russian revolutions each took the best path to improving the well-being of the citizens concerned, I will take it that in at least some of these cases, violent resistance was an appropriate response to colonial, feudal, or racist domination. I also accept that lethal force is justified sometimes, under special conditions, in law enforcement domestically and in counterterrorism internationally. But I will leave my endorsements here. States are perfectly well equipped to develop their own defenses of the resort to war; they need no contemporary philosophical handmaidens for the task. While the just war tradition has attempted, by and large, to wrestle state violence into principled lines, it is fair to say that in its modern tradition, since Alberico Gentili and Grotius at least, it has been accepting of violence as an ordinary and permissible way of settling interstate disputes, whether flowing from an essentially theological conception of sovereign privileges or from a political perspective. The comfort of the just war tradition with war (if not all wars) is easily documented.[27] Indeed, the tradition's Grotian conception of war as just punishment for injury done by another state has been an enormously pernicious force, in licensing a degree of violence that goes beyond the real justificatory core of any appeal to violence: self-defense. For the justifications of self-defense end far short of the frontiers of actual wars, whose end points satisfy a range of concerns not linked directly to state survival.

Taking up a critical stance, then, entails two distinct but related tasks. The first is making sense of a political community's claim to be able to deploy violence in its name and for its ends, while restricting private violence among its members. This distinction between public and private violence (or between war and crime, in modern discussions) is fundamental to the nature of the state, sovereignty, and the conception of violence in human affairs. If a permission to use violence is seen to depend now on democratic credentials, then the link between democracy and force must be made clear. The second task will occupy much of the book's discussion: defining the limits of violence, not just in relation to the generic justification of self-defense, but also in relation to the justifications presented by democracy itself. Indeed, this is the operating conceit of the book as a whole: the respect for our personhood that animates democracy demands a humility in the face of conflict, rather than the imperial assertiveness that has characterized so much democratic rhetoric, from the French Revolution to the Second Iraq War. Here, I argue, is the pacific promise of agentic democracy: recognizing the value of our own collective activity entails respecting the agency of others.

More concretely, our capacity for collateral authority and hence for collective action enables everything from shared harvests and hunts to shared musical expression and ritual to shared deliberation and the construction of social institutions. Such a capacity need not be exercised in accordance with democratic norms, but it nonetheless lies at the root of democracy. Before the general will is bent towards democracy, it is still general, still collective, registering in an active demos, an agentic community. Active community is built on a foundation of shared, intersecting, and competing loyalties. It defines not a people, not a state, and not a full community (in any communitarian sense), but it does reflect a body of people doing politics—in success or failure. The neo-Roman republican tradition resuscitated by Quentin Skinner and Phillip Pettit reflects a model of the ideal, in both its individual and collective form. What is appealing about neo-republicanism is the way in which a thin ideal of nondomination can be thickened into a quite comprehensive guide for the development of political institutions.

If active community and the capacity for collective action define the basis for democracy, its structure is given by law. Law is the skeleton of complex social institutions, the framework that makes possible the coordination over great spaces and times of plans for self-organization.[28] Since the egalitarian balance of voice in a democracy is such an idealization, so distant from the messy imbalances of real power and privilege, democracies rest uniquely on law to maintain their character. This is the law not only of elections but of governmental structure and the balance of institutional power. But, in a striking parallel to the role of violence, the role of law in democracies is equally Janus-faced. If law makes democracy possible, democracy can seem to make law unnecessary by offering a separate claim to legitimacy hostile to the proceduralism inherent in democracies. Democracy, we might say, poses most strongly the question of the relation of legality and legitimacy to each other. Clearly they are not identical; legitimacy depends on, but exceeds, legality. This is the insight of legal philosophers H.L.A. Hart and—quite differently—Carl Schmitt.[29] Legitimacy is instantiated, operationalized, and preserved through legality. Legality provides the "what" of legitimacy—the structure of the subject. But obviously legal forms can be abused, honored in name but not in principle, and so subvert legitimacy. More tendentiously, refusing to treat legal principles as (sometimes) evolving standards and instead insisting on their rigidity can undermine legitimacy by divorcing the form of government from its function (protecting public welfare). This is the point of those who insist on emergency delegations. But there are, of course, particular aspects of public life that depend on having sharp lines drawn (in a liberal democratic state, they include a commitment to democratic processes; basic human rights, including the right against torture and the right against undocumented detention; and free speech).

The more basic point is that the basis of the legitimacy of a state arises from the beliefs of its occupants—it is those beliefs, acceptances, and willingness to cooperate that give law its normativity and authority. That legitimacy, in both its normative and sociological sense, comes from community—from the consolidation of a group of people, living together, around a common set of norms. Community, in turn, is a product of collective agency, of individuals orienting their values and actions around one another, taking emotional and behavioral cues from the groups as a whole as well as from leaders within that group.

Let me also be clear that this is a conception of war and democracy worked out in real time, as I tried to think through the issues presented by American foreign policy and the events of the world. I have generally tried to preserve the real-time quality of the meditations and arguments that follow, rather than attempt to smooth it into an illusion of a timeless synoptic view. I do so because philosophical reflection cannot detach itself from the political and moral contexts in which it is birthed. Thus, for example, the discussion of secret law does not cover many of the most recent revelations of the work of the Foreign Intelligence Surveillance Court, accounts of whose efficacy (or lack thereof) are emerging with the revelations of Edward Snowden. Similarly, my critique of drone warfare focuses on a policy that waxes and wanes in relation to the internal politics of Yemen, Pakistan, and Afghanistan. Nonetheless, the insights I offer provide, I hope, a guide to future thought on remote warfare, including that those forms will surely be conducted by fully autonomous war systems.

I turn now to outline how agentic democracy can guide us toward understanding the ethics of collective violence.

I begin, in chapter 2, "Democratic Security," with an account of the ideas of legitimacy and security, and the way in which perceiving them as too tightly linked with the specific values of democracy can impoverish all three concepts. Democracy is one route to legitimacy (for a particular institution), and an especially important one for comprehensive governing institutions, but its value is one in the constellation of political values necessary for a decent state. An overfocus on democracy, moreover, destabilizes competing notions of security and stability. The chapter also introduces the foil of the agentic conception: a *telic* conception (drawing on the idea of democracy as a goal, or *telos*). The telic conception of democracy is one that focuses on the ambition of establishing democratic institutions, rather than respecting democratic agency. I argue that if we take up a broader conception of legitimacy, and see democracy as a form of action rather than the only argument for legitimacy, the temptations to export democracy will be tempered.

Chapter 3, "Citizens and Soldiers," deepens the understanding of the relation among sovereignty, citizen, and state. Here I take up the role of state authority and the privilege of violence. Traditionally, to be a soldier is to bear the king's uniform, to share in an essentially collective identity. That identity has normative consequences: it makes one vulnerable to attack and gives one the privilege to kill. Once, we could see that identity as founded in the king's stamp. Now, in the wake of the democratic revolution, the identity is grounded in a conception of democratic will. A consequence of the democratic conception is that uniforms should be less privileged—or at least their significance is instrumental to the aim of protecting civilians and must be weighed against the other values at stake.

Chapter 4, "A Modest Case for Symmetry," addresses a consequence of the democratic conception of the combatant's privilege: such an argument undermines the case for moral symmetry—the status of a combatant depends on the nature of the end for which he fights, and this requires a substantive evaluation, albeit a limited one (we need a meta-ethics of violence). But there are subordinate, instrumental, and epistemic grounds for thinking that a symmetric approach is preferable. This again means emphasizing the limits of democracy in explicating the *jus in bello*, and showing why we must preserve the force of traditional, nondemocratic concerns of reprisal and reciprocity lest the entire restrictive regime collapse.

In chapter 5, "Leaders and the Gambles of War," I look to a pathology affecting political leaders in general, and democratic leaders in particular. Many leaders make the most serious decisions at issue, those of war and peace, with a conception of "political luck"—the idea that good outcomes can retrospectively justify the decisions (this is not the same as "the end justifies the means"). Democratic leaders, buoyed by a conception of the arc of history bending in their favor, have been especially prone to such gambles. But this conception of retrospective justification is incoherent in its own terms, and it leads to irrational decision making; it is also inconsistent with the values of democracy.

Chapters 6 and 7 then shift focus from the constraints and impulses behind the decision to go to war, to questions about how democracies should manage the wars they fight. Both chapters are products of reflection, stimulated by revulsion, at the turn taken by the United States in the Second Iraq War and the continuing conflict with al-Qaeda, and now with ISIS. Chapter 6, "War, Democracy, and Publicity," looks to the revelations during the George W. Bush administration of its system of secret legal guidance, through confidential memorandums providing interpretations of statutory and constitutional restrictions that had the effect of eviscerating their limitations. The purpose was to provide internal justification for what was later revealed to be a system of interrogatory torture, warrantless surveillance, and now remote killing. I argue that it is in law's nature to be public, as part of the link between law and legitimacy and, more broadly, as the way a democratic people must be able to understand its own character. The inclination towards secrecy is a hallmark of tyranny, of the delegitimized state.

Chapter 7, "Must a Democracy Be Ruthless?" concerns how one must think about principles in times of crisis and in emergencies—as having a natural limit. The connection between torture and constitutional dictatorship has to do with the relation of principle to necessity. There is a particular issue about how to conceive these trade-offs in a system rooted in democratic values. The anti-trade-off principle is, in part, about the nature of certain architectonic principles and their relation to teleological (institutionally molded) values.

Next, chapter 8, "Humanitarian Intervention and the New Democratic Holy Wars," and chapter 9, "Democratic States in Victory," look to further consequences of the telic conception of democracy for the theory of war: a tendency to lower the threshold of external sovereignty to justify humanitarian intervention, and a permission for more extensive post-victory reconstruction efforts following even defensive wars. Once, victorious nations enjoyed broad rights to transform the conquered. Now, the rights of victors are minimized. What can now justify the victor's rights? Has the ideal of pro-democratic humanitarian intervention led to too great an interest in the power of the conquering state? I argue that restoring the agentic conception of democracy can properly chastise democratic states contemplating military intervention.

I set out the current and next stage of the democratic conception of war in chapters 10, "Drones, Democracy, and the Future of War" and 11, "Democracy and the Death of Norms." Do democracies operate under different constraints than other states? The *jus in bello* is defined independently and legitimated in terms of harm prevention most naturally, but perhaps the nature of a democratic state, its commitment to process (and, underlying that, a principle of individuality), requires a stronger commitment to a more robust set of restrictions on killing in war. The forms of justification available to a democratic community are limited by the procedural norms a democracy imposes on itself, namely a commitment to make use of forms addressing the interests of each. Targeted killing, in some respects, best fits a democratic demand. One of the most striking features of the turn towards targeted and remote killing is its apparent contradiction, the simultaneous depersonalization of killing and the personalization of the killed. For all the talk of the illegality of extra-judicial killing, it receives (according to public documents) relatively more legalistic scrutiny than other kinds of warfare.

The book concludes with chapter 12, "Looking Backward," which examines the claims of democratic citizens after violent change, whether caused by revolution or defeat in war. What principles govern political transitions in which property is taken? How do we compare the claims of property holders against the claims of those who need food, justice, and an egalitarian distribution of resources? My answer: property holders take a lower priority and should receive symbolic rather than actual repayment. This is a consequence of taking seriously a collective conception of community, one extending as much over time as over territory, with a proper weighting of the interests of the living over the dead.

2

DEMOCRATIC SECURITY

As I suggest in the introduction, the story of contemporary political philosophy in recent years, as well as the practice of international development politics, has involved the convergence of liberal and democratic values. Democratic institutions have come to be seen both as shields of human well-being and rights domestically and as means of avoiding violent international conflict. Moreover, this convergence has both conceptual and empirical roots. Conceptually, democratic institutions both ground and express respect for human capacities of expression, deliberation, and sociability. Empirically, as the work of Amartya Sen and Jean Drèze has shown,[1] democratic institutions provide bulwarks against forms of corruption and tyranny that themselves have terribly pernicious effects on human welfare. Since Immanuel Kant's essay "On Perpetual Peace," and with its 1990s resuscitation by Bruce Russett, the contentious but suggestive work concerning the proclivity of democratic states to resolve conflict without war has been another empirical anchor.[2] The result is that democratic values, and conceptions of state legitimacy rooted in democracy, have come to have a nearly hegemonic force in contemporary theory.

My aim is not to question the strength of the connection between democracy and security and welfare in this regard. Rather, it is to point out that along with these profound connections between the two run connections pointing in the opposite direction, between democracy and *in*security. Understanding the full spectrum of the relation between these two values is important in two respects: first, by providing a basis for qualifying the resort to the rhetoric of democracy; and second, by restoring a broader range of values to political theory with which it might operate in modern thought.

My plan in this chapter is as follows. In section 2.2, I will discuss the important conceptual shift from a discourse centered on national security to one centered on human security—a shift that transforms the locus of normative concern from state to subject and opens the field of legitimacy from a sovereignty-based conception to a rights-based conception. In section 2.3, I discuss the way in which the governing concept of human security has become paired with democratization in recent work, such that the two are seen as working in tandem. I also discuss briefly the constitutive and instrumental contributions of democracy to human security. Section 2.4 challenges the yoking of democracy to security, looking at the ways in which themes and values associated with democracy can present obstacles to human security. Sections 2.5 through 2.7 take up the broader theme of this chapter, of the need, on the one hand, to see the value of democratic institutions as partial contributors to a broader conception of legitimacy in international affairs; and on the other, to understand democracy's value in terms of a people's own actions, not exportable institutions.

2.2. FROM NATIONAL SECURITY TO HUMAN SECURITY

We are in the midst of an important shift in how we organize claims of political justification, from a notion of national security to one of human security. The shift is partly rhetorical but also conceptual: it reflects a shift away from a state-centered organization of moral interests, to a person-centered view. As such, it changes the locus of normative concern in a fundamental way, from concern for an abstraction—the state—conceived as extending across time and independent of the identities of particular persons, to the interests of persons conceived independently of the states to which they belong. The shift began as a concerted effort of progressive development experts who wished to co-opt the persuasive force of national security claims for a broader agenda focusing on overall social welfare. But the shift has conceptual significance of its own and has led to an impressive research agenda.

I will begin with the traditional realists' notion of national security; then I show how the progressive shift of national security to the more encompassing notion of *human* security has brought about a natural bridge to the concept of democracy. Conceptually, claims of national security focus on two factors: the security of borders from outside interference, whether by states or individuals; and internal political order, understood in terms of the continuity of an existing regime. The language of Chapter VII of the UN Charter implicitly invokes both considerations in the responsibility of the Security Council to "maintain or restore international peace and security."[3] This Janus-like focus on order and borders is simply a consequence of understanding of the state as a territorially defined political entity. Generic risks are considered threats to national security to the extent they implicate either borders or orders, and many things beyond foreign armies and terrorist threats can present such risks—the concept of national security is reasonably capacious. For instance, epidemic disease and environmental catastrophe, whether human- or naturally caused, can disrupt internal political order (or, at the limit, present a so-called existential threat to the continuing viability of the state) or threaten borders with an uncontrolled flow of refugees from neighboring states. Similarly, an underemployed or undereducated workforce can be seen as a threat to national security through its effects on domestic economic power and, so, on the international muscle the state is able to exert.

While claims of national security are naturally made by those whose advantages are conferred by the existing state order (and territorial organization), especially the members of a political elite, the concept of national security need not be self-serving. The normative interests of a state are derived from the interests of its citizens, but they are not, as I noted above, identical with the interests of its current set of citizens. Arguably, a state's interests extend both backward in time, in safeguarding traditions, and forward in time, towards generations as yet unborn. To the extent custom or political organization is seen as having intrinsic value as the exemplar of a distinctive culture, either may ground a legitimate claim for preservation independent of the claims of its members. More to the point, territorial integrity and political order are primary contributors to the goodness of the lives of current citizens. One need not accept a Hobbesian autocrat to accept his premise that civil order is a precondition of a life lived beyond mere survival. The moral stakes in national security are substantial indeed.

At the same time, national security has two significant drawbacks: one conceptual and one rhetorical. The conceptual drawback is linked to its advantage, namely the logical space between the interests of peoples and the interests of the states to which they happen to belong. While high degrees of inequality and exploitation may threaten civil order, civil order is demonstrably compatible with extensive inequality. More generally, the interests of persons are more sensitive to disruption than the interests of the state as a whole and, so, focus on the latter category of threats lets more pervasive forms of social harm go unchallenged.

The rhetorical drawback is a direct consequence of the force of the concept of national security. Because national security values are tied to questions of existential threat, a discourse of national security *dominates* other forms of reason and justification that might be offered to advance alternative policy goals. Threats to national security command resources and overcome objections made on behalf of subsidiary values, including values of both welfare and dignity. As a consequence of the Hobbesian (or Schmittian) logic of national security discourse, efforts to maintain the preconditions of political order can entail sacrifices to the substantive values of the political order—values like the rule of law and constitutional commitments to substantive freedoms. This might be reckoned the paradox of national security: threats to national security can appear to justify eviscerating the qualities that make the nation state worth preserving, under the guise of emergency powers or executive prerogatives.[4]

The rival concept of *human security* has been offered as a way to correct the conceptual problems with an excessive focus on state welfare and to co-opt the rhetorical force of national security discourse. The term came to prominence in the 1994 UN Human Development Report, where it named a set of concerns to be monitored and fostered by the international community. While human security is, in that sense, an oppositional concept, it has substantial positive content. At the most general level, it shifts the locus of normative concern from the state to the individual, thus rendering salient the significance of disease, poverty, hunger, and vulnerability to environmental damage even when those risks do not threaten the foundations of political order. From the perspective of human security, state security is valuable only instrumentally, as one tool among many for promoting the interests of persons. Claims made on behalf of the state must be redeemed in the currency of personal well-being.

There are two more conceptual advantages to the idea of human security, apart from the breadth of its concerns, and the focus on personal well-being and dignity. First, by breaking the tight link between individual and state security, the concept of human security is better able to reckon with the non- and supra-state-level concerns that are proper focuses of policy at both the national and international level. To take the most obvious concern, while global climate change will affect states disparately, the nature of the threat requires coordinated international action. If the costs of global climate change are seen exclusively through the lens of national security, collective action problems loom large, for the threat to any given state's security may not be enough to justify costly responses. When seen transnationally, however, as affecting individuals, interstate response can be warranted. Similarly, questions of access to energy, and to sustainable nutrition, again require an awareness of borderless risks and coordinated international policies, with potentially large transfers of wealth and technology. A state-based perspective will fall short.

Most basically, a focus on human security implicates no state in particular; states are relevant only instrumentally, in virtue of the protections they offer their subjects. National security concerns, by contrast, presuppose the perspective of the particular state whose security is in question and implicate other states in virtue of the threat they pose. In practice, this means that national security concerns come to be identified with the interests and claims of strong states, whose interests are most affected by other actors in their geostrategic neighborhood. As a result, resources and attention simply fail to move in the direction of isolated states: non-oil- or non-drug-producing states in Africa or Latin America simply fail to move US policy, for example, except on the basis of much lower-ranking humanitarian concerns. A focus on human security corrects this bias towards the strong, by looking to the incidence of humanity. Policy makers guided by human security concerns thus look south and east rather than north and west, towards regions lacking the strong state institutions that ground national security. And they look towards international aggregations of power, such as the World Trade Organization (WTO), as both causes of and possible cures for human insecurity.

The second advantage consists in the implicit dynamic dimension of human security. To be sure, national security is a forward-looking concept, but the object to be protected from risk is essentially static: the state. Threats to the state are one-off: an attack pierces a border, unrest undermines state or civil authority, a foreign armory reduces international leverage, et cetera. By contrast, a focus on human security looks not to the lives of persons conceived statically, in terms of a present set of interests, but to individuals' capacities to cope with the vicissitudes of fortune. Human security, that is, focuses on reducing volatility through institutions that protect access to food, medical care, shelter, and employment. Such institutions, which John Rawls calls the "basic structure" of a society, form an integrated fabric of social protection, not simply a defensive perimeter around the state. A corollary of this point is that human security cannot be reduced to any crude form of utilitarianism, because individual security can be threatened as directly by welfare-maximizing state policies that shift resources without attention to individual claims as surely as it can be threatened by nonstate dangers. A focus on human security is thus philosophically dense, by virtue of the institutions we call upon to protect it.

Now, the expansiveness and density of human security, which I have called a virtue of the concept, might also be thought a vice. If part of the point of introducing human security is to capture the dominating quality of national security discourse, that rhetorical advantage is lost to the degree the concerns become ill-focused, assimilable to a generic policy goal of social welfare maximization. To put the point another way, one might well be suspicious that a rhetoric of human security is simply a repackaging of welfare economics, with the units of welfare conceived as whole lives rather than life-slices. Certainly, the emergence of the discourse in the UNDP reports, and in the work of Sen in particular, points to the welfarist foundations of the concept.[5]

My point is not to decry welfarism in social policy, to be sure. Rather, the point is that if human security is to have comparable suasive force, we must be able to pick out a set of normative demands, and thus institutions meeting those demands, that can command appropriate priority. But while human security is not necessarily more protean than other basic concepts of political justification, its capaciousness makes it hard to see how it can meet this demand—to be something other than a portmanteau for the range of concerns already canvassed by sophisticated, distributionally sensitive welfare economics.

2.3. FROM HUMAN SECURITY TO DEMOCRACY

One response to the concern that human security sweeps too broadly has been to link it tightly to a particular set of institutions: democratic institutions.[6] Spurred by the contemporary 1990s discussions of the so-called democratic peace—or the thesis that democracies tend to avoid military conflicts with one another—the discourses of human security and democratization have come to run together. In part this is a matter of happy coincidence: if the democratic-peace thesis is at least partly correct (as it seems to be, notwithstanding substantial debate about the basis and limits of the thesis), then democratic institutions might be thought to have a strongly instrumental relation to human security concerns.[7] Obviously, interstate war threatens human security like nothing else. But internally as well, democratic institutions can promote civil understanding, or at least modi vivendi, among different groups, simply by offering paths to resources and power without resort to violence.[8]

The more interesting set of instrumental connections, however, stems not from the stabilizing effects of democratic governance per se, but from the support of the ancillary institutions typical of democracies—notably, a free press, free speech, and market-based distribution of resources. As to the first, Sen and Drèze have argued that famines are rare in states with free presses, for the reason that a free press protects against the sort of corruption and rent-seeking that tip the balance from a problem of food access to mass privation.[9] A free press also provides early warning of health and environmental risks, independently of government channels. Next, institutions of free speech, like democratic competitions, also enable monitoring of governmental misconduct, while party competition creates rival sources of power, breaking up governmental monopolies over resources. Third, while market systems can, of course, generate great inequality and unrest, they also prevent governmental aggregations of power and hence can mitigate the victimization of vulnerable or disfavored groups by the state. Finally, the informal institutions of democracy—the barter and truck of political organization, conversation about elections—nurture a reserve of social capital that can be drawn upon for a range of welfare-enhancing ends.

These contingent, instrumental connections between democracy and security are important. But equally important are the constitutive connections between the two. Democracy can be conceived simply as one decision procedure among many, competing with dictatorships, aristocracies, and anarchies on the basis of its capacity to deliver maximum welfare. Indeed, classical conceptions of democracy famously treat it as an erratic and essentially irrational decision procedure at that, with decision making relegated to those least capable of exercising rational choice.[10] But since at least the Enlightenment (and with traces in medieval and early modern political theory), democracy has been conceived in more ambitiously moralized terms: as a way of allocating decisional authority in accordance with individuals' equal moral worth. Democracy, in other words, is the political manifestation of a moral ideal, one that insists that the proper unit of respect is the individual, taken one at a time, and without regard to rank or station. The ideal of democracy runs hand in hand with the rhetoric of human security, and in sharp contrast to the rhetoric of national security, insofar as both claim to honor the same set of ideals. We might thereby come to take the connection's intimacy for granted by recognizing a fused concept: that of *democratic security*.

2.4. THE LIMITS OF DEMOCRATIC SECURITY

We should, I have suggested, be impressed by the robustness of the connections between democracy and human security. Democratic institutions represent a convergence of moral and political thought, bringing together a range of ideals within a relatively coherent set of practices. We should therefore expect such happy coincidences. But I want now to offer some cautions as well. If the demand for democratic decision making is one lesson of the Enlightenment, the plurality of values is another—the resistance of values like liberty, most famously, but also dignity, recognition, honor, and excellence, to being reduced to some common coin.[11] I turn now to the problems posed by plurality. I do not mean to question the robustness of these connections, both instrumental and intrinsic. It is precisely because democracy has become such a powerful value in modern thought, to the extent that it displaces complementary but occasionally rival political values, that we must seek the limits of those connections as well.

First, however, a brief note about my use of the term "democracy." I have been deliberately nonspecific about what form of political regime counts as a democracy, and what institutions are democratic. At a certain level of generality or idealization, there is little dispute: democratic regimes are those in which political power is fundamentally directed through a mass electorate, reflecting a universal franchise, by means of the aggregation of expressed political preferences. Furthermore, it is a constitutive feature of democracy that preferences are weighted equally, a duke's no more than a squire's, in the aggregation of those preferences.

In practice, of course, derogations from the ideal do not necessarily forfeit a claim to the democratic label. A franchise restricted by sex, race, class, or literacy is distasteful and clearly imperfect in its democratic pedigree, but a state with such a system might still merit the label of a democracy, at least in contrast to dictatorial or oligarchic regimes. More vexing are the questions whether systems with universal franchise but massive informal intimidation of voters, or limited rights of assembly, or irregular elections, or without free presses, can be called democratic. And harder yet are questions about the compatibility of technocratic or administrative governance with some features of democratic decision making; or whether systems of constitutional restraint, entrenched citizen rights, and judicial review are either demanded by or even consistent with democratic ideals. I do not want here to wade into those swamps. All I need for the present discussion is the loose ideal of decision making by mass electorate.

Now, there are a number of quite obvious misconnections between human security and democracy that I should like to get out of the way. Both, alas, are risks fully on the modern scene. I will call these the problem of outcomes and the problem of pretexts.

The problem of outcomes is simply "What if the bad guys win?" Since democracy is a procedural concept, not a substantive one, there is no guarantee that the victors in democratic competition will, in fact, honor the ends of human security. While those who wish to retain power in subsequent elections will presumably try to ensure adequate levels of well-being for those voters, actual electoral calculations can be more cynical. Resources can be exploited unsustainably to boost the standard of living for the electorate immediately, threatening their food security later. Populist land or industrial reforms can cripple productivity. Leaders can start wars to gin up nationalist fervor. And with victories in hand, democratic leaders can impose a range of restrictions on the press, or on personal liberties (liberty of conscience is a favorite target), all of which have the effect of reducing political voice, increasing cultural marginalization, or otherwise negatively affecting security. At the limit, leaders can be voted in who take their genuine democratic mandate as a justification for restricting the effective franchise, eliminating elections or vastly increasing the power of the head of state.

The problem of pretexts is different, although also generated typically by cynicism on the part of participants in the democratic process: the values of democracy itself can be an occasion for highly nondemocratic interventions. Domestically, the preservation of "free and fair elections" can result in spurious charges of voter fraud or media manipulation, interfering with the communicative channels of democracy. Internationally, as we have seen too well, a "democracy-exporting" agenda can lead to foreign wars of "democratic liberation," or to other interference with foreign political processes, in the name of improving their democratic responsiveness. While in some cases this interference may be in good faith, in other cases it is patently a pretext for expanding the zone of influence of the exporting state. Of course, the use of pretexts in international realpolitik is not novel. But access to the legitimizing frame of democracy makes the pretext harder to displace, putting it in line with other pretextual traditions, notably the Christianization of the New World and the *mission civilisatrice* of France.

My purpose is not to belabor these points but simply to indicate that democratic processes are consistent with a great deal of mischief, all of which can undermine the otherwise positive instrumental connections. All ideologies are subject to opportunistic manipulation. The goal of democratization, or the mandate of democracy, is, if anything, more resistant than other ideologies, precisely because the concept can do critical work even as it is deployed opportunistically. It remains a fair question to the popular leader who seeks to expand his power whether such a move is really consistent with the democratic ideals he espouses. And lessons about the preparations necessary for a genuinely pro-democracy intervention—and the self-defeating nature of most of those interventions—can temper the enthusiasm of even good-faith proponents while also offering an obstacle to the opportunists.

I now want, however, to focus on another aspect of democracy that can undermine human security more insidiously, because it is grounded in neither political naïveté nor opportunism. This is the way a conception of political legitimacy, as rooted in democratic processes, serves to undermine the values of the rule of law and individual protections by rendering such claims as nondemocratic, matters of elite or foreign opinion.

2.5. LEGITIMACY AND DEMOCRACY

"Legitimacy," in its normative rather than sociological sense, has to do with the justifiability of political authority. It is sometimes conceived in terms of a "right to rule," or the justifiability of the exercise of political power; but both of these conceptions seem to me too restrictive to capture its full sense—or at least the sense that needs to be captured in order to discuss international law. A "right to rule" only makes sense in the domestic context, where "ruling" involves extensive or total control over the lives of subjects. But whatever one might think about the legitimacy of the UN Security Council—which is legitimate if any international institution is—it neither claims nor exercises any general power to rule subject states, but only endeavors to fulfill the limited terms of its charter to keep the international peace. Similarly, defining legitimacy in terms of justifications for the exercise of political power is too narrow. If we understand power as an ability to enforce compliance with an order, then because many international institutions and agreements lack enforcement mechanisms and so lack power, they would not be able to make claims to legitimacy. The Convention against Torture is one such institutional agreement, for its "enforcement" system is limited to a power to demand reports of violations.[12] It prejudges debates about the justifiability of such agreements, especially given their complex effects through domestic incorporation, to look at them solely through the lens of power.

So the working definition of legitimacy I prefer focuses on the justification for an institution to declare an authoritative norm, whether or not it has the power to enforce that norm. Roughly, an institution, institutional process, or institutionally defined agent, enjoys legitimacy when its announcement of a norm gives actors subject to the norm substantial reason to comply with it. (Derivatively, a norm has legitimacy when it is issued by a legitimate institution or by a legitimate institutional process.) The crucial part of this definition is that the announcement *gives* reason, in the sense that it adds substantially to the reasons the actors have to act (or refrain from acting) in compliance with the norm. Consider again the Convention on Torture and assume that an investigating commission, created by Article 20, determines that US practices of mass incarceration, administered nationwide, violate the Convention.[13] If the commission is correct, then presumably the United States would already have independent moral reasons to cease its forms of incarceration, including the reason that it would be in breach of its obligations under the Convention. But if the commission is legitimate to boot, then its declaration gives the United States an additional reason to cease, on grounds of deference to the authority of the commission to define party obligations under the Convention. This is true even though the commission lacks any enforcement power.

Putting aside for the moment what kinds of arguments can support claims of legitimacy, I point now to some facts about the term's usage. "Legitimacy" is a *challenge* term: it gets used in order to contest claims of authority. In the domestic context, the challenge is usually of the form "Who are *you* to do this to me?" And in the international, it is, often "Who are *you* to say this to me?" Legitimacy, in other words, functions contextually as the silent shadow of illegitimacy—as perhaps, as Judith Shklar has famously suggested, justice is defined by the shadow of injustice.[14] My point is not that legitimacy is defined in terms of illegitimacy, however, for the opposite is true. It is just that what we need to take note of are the circumstances in which challenges to legitimacy do *not* arise. The absence of those challenges does not entail legitimacy; their absence just means that there is no practical pressure on the issue.

Consider, as an analogy, how the question of the meaning or point of life arises. While it might arise in a philosophy seminar, or while stretched on one's back and contemplating the stars in the wilderness, it arises poignantly only when something has happened to raise with urgent force the question whether one should go on—the death of a loved one, the defeat of a goal. In those cases, the question demands an answer, not mere speculation, and the demands on the sufficiency of an answer are very great, perhaps insuperable. What one seeks is to return to conditions in life where the question does not arise at all.

When political institutions are functioning well, or circumstances are providing no obstacles, the question of the legitimacy of those institutions simply does not arise. Of course, it might arise on idle reflection, as for example someone might simply wonder about the grounds for the authority of the WTO. A quick reference to the WTO's origins in the Uruguay GATT round of 1986, for example, will suffice, for its legitimacy was not really under challenge, just investigation. But sometimes the question of legitimacy arises with urgency, because a real challenge has been set—for instance, the conflict of the national health regulation with the terms of global free trade. Conflicting claims of democracy and local self-governance press on the claimed legitimacy of the institution, and we must enter the realm of normative argument for the authority of the WTO. And once we move down that path, we must be prepared to acknowledge the failure of the institution to meet norms that properly apply, even if they are rarely applied with their full force. The open question is whether, once the crisis has been put to the past through diplomatic finesse, we can return to reside in the unchallenged, and perhaps unsustainable, normal attitude of legitimacy.

I have thus far simply asserted the dominance of democracy as a legitimation conception. But it might be worth comparing the relevant alternatives. First, and most primitively, is *relational* or *natural* legitimacy: an institution, or person representing an institution, simply claims authority in virtue of its nature, origin, or relation to the subject of the norm. "Because I'm your parent," or "because I come from the House of Stuart" are claims of this sort, and ever since the Enlightenment they have had only marginally better rhetorical success in the household than they have in the nation-state. Second is *procedural* legitimacy, whereby questions of legitimacy are answered by reference to the outcome of some favored procedure—for instance, free and fair balloting, or parliamentary decision making, or entrail divination. Third comes *instrumental* or, as it is sometimes called, *performance* legitimacy.[15] On such accounts, institutions are legitimate if they produce or protect certain goods or interests, relative to some further specified baseline. Hobbes's conception of legitimacy is arguably performance based, for the sovereign's warrant flows from his success in maintaining the civil peace; and so obviously are utilitarian or other welfarist conceptions. On a performance theory, nothing succeeds like success, and success in delivering the goods gives legitimate title. Fourth comes the dominant modern forms of legitimacy arguments: voluntaristic legitimacy. *Subjectively voluntaristic* legitimacy claims are grounded in the actual consent, assent, or acquiescence of norm subjects to the authority, while *objectively voluntaristic* claims are based in what parties would choose or could not reasonably reject, given their prior aims or evaluative commitments.

Clearly, reductions of some of these categories to others are both possible and necessary. Purely relational claims are empty unless they are themselves grounded in other arguments—for instance, an instrumental argument that restricting political authority to a single dynasty reduces political violence. Procedural claims bring up the question of why some procedures are favored over others, for instance, as ways of maximizing subjective welfare or revealing popular will. They turn, ultimately, on the question of what factors they process into the currency of legitimacy. Instrumental theories, meanwhile, are actually only theories of legitimacy in part. If the institutions are delivering goods subjects actually want, then subjects have independent instrumental reason to comply with the institutions in question, so the claim to legitimate authority by the institution is redundant. It adds no significant reason of its own to their compliance. Alternatively, if performance measures are grounded in interests individual subjects do not think they actually have—for instance, an interest in maximizing aggregate welfare—then they raise the question of why some particular goods or interests should be protected or promoted rather than others. That question might be answered intuitionistically; but more frequently in contemporary theory, it itself gets an objectively voluntaristic basis, in terms of what people would want, in the right deliberative circumstances with the right information.[16]

The upshot of this anatomy of legitimacy claims is that democracy starts to loom quickly once we reflect on the basis of legitimacy claims. If the question is what goods are to be promoted, and the initial answer is "the goods people show they need by what they try to do," we must still answer the further question of *which* people can do the showing, and how they can do so. While various forms of elitism are conceptually possible, political pressure pushes towards goods with broad audiences. Similarly, if consent or acquiescence is the basis for legitimacy, then the question of whose consent (real or hypothetical) arises. The question of the legitimacy of an international institution might be answered by reference to state consent in the treaty process. But, since states are artificial persons, this merely moves the question to the relation between state consent and citizen consent and how that relation might be discerned. Again, pressure builds towards a broader conception of the consenting constituency and a method of revealing and actuating that consent.

In the domestic context, where what is to be legitimated is institutions with extensive control over their subjects' lives, the pressures towards democracy are especially intense. The possibility of lethal coercion obviously raises the justificatory stakes in a general way, as does the broad domain of control. If political institutions restricted themselves to indicating salient points for coordination and providing requisite reassurance for cooperators, with perhaps a dash of jawboning thrown in, then few questions of legitimacy would arise. But domestic politics are not so easy: the state must arbitrate between competing claims on the same scarce resource, deter the free rider and punish the malefactor, or restrict the claims of the majority to domesticate the unruly minority. The contexts in which legitimacy challenges arise sprout like daisies, and so the justificatory stakes are raised.

More specifically, the problem of how to justify the subjection of a whole population, each with particular interests, to the control of a central authority, makes some version of Rousseau's solution highly attractive. Provisionally, the forms of control exercised over the population will be illegitimate unless they both capture the assent and secure the common interests of all. Institutions that can credibly claim to represent that assent, such as robustly deliberative popular assemblies governed by consensus or, at worst, by a preference for supermajoritarian decision making, will be the standard form of practical solution to the theoretical problem. (Simple majoritarianism has its defenders as a legitimate system of governance, but not among the dissenting minority crushed underfoot.) Legitimation discourse quickly converges on radical democracy once dogmatic or natural justifications are no longer on the conceptual table.

2.6. LEGITIMACY IN INTERNATIONAL POLITICS

I have hinted that matters might be different on the international front. This is not because the standards of legitimacy are lower or the institutions better, but because the crises are less frequently provoked. First, as I mentioned above, much of international law is toothless, either because the obliging treaties do not provide for sanctions or because the norms are embedded in so-called soft-law voluntary undertakings that don't even rise to the level of obligation.

Second, a great deal of international law, perhaps unlike domestic law, represents forms of non-zero-sum coordination over the long term, generating internal pressures of compliance. Obvious examples are the treaties governing international air travel and currency exchange; more controversially, so might be the law of war, or international humanitarian law, which has long-term substantial benefits in the form of reciprocal treatment of prisoners and easier transitions from war to peace.

Third, the international arena is—relative to the domestic arena—passive. There are many treaties but relatively few formal disputes. Particular subject areas, notably trade, may generate a lot of disputes, but overall the workload of international legal institutions is a fraction that of their domestic analogues. True, much of the business of international law is channeled through diplomatic systems rather than litigation, but precisely to the degree that interstate diplomacy is at stake, the legitimacy of a third-party international institution is not.

Fourth, a lot of international law is treaty-based; there are roughly 50,000 treaties recorded as in current force. These are voluntary obligations and voluntary accessions to jurisdiction, whose force stems (when true) from freely given consent. While it would be a mistake to see state consent as strictly parallel to personal consent in the domestic context—insofar as states can thereby bind nonconsenting individuals—explicit state consent displaces many legitimacy concerns.

Fifth, it is a peculiar feature of international law that for customary international law, its validity depends on its efficacy, by which I mean efficacy at the level of the individual norm, not of the legal system as a whole. On the domestic side, a necessary condition of a legal system's existence is the general efficacy of the system in ensuring popular compliance with its norms.[17] But if the system (or its operators) is generally effective in securing compliance, then the validity (understood as an existence condition) of a given legal norm demands no special compliance. A new statute might be widely ignored or disobeyed, but it would still count as valid law in the jurisdiction so long as it met the relevant formal tests. But efficacy and validity are far more closely connected in the case of customary international law, where the existence tests involve the question of the scope of actual international compliance with the norm, arising out of subjective deference to the norm as a principle of law (the *opinio juris* test). An ignored customary norm is no norm at all; and when formally declared norms (or the canonical interpretations of those norms) come to be ignored, the law itself is seen to have shifted. What was illegal at first may, through force of intransigence in the face of the norm, particularly by great powers, pass through to permissibility. Conversely, when a violation of international law succeeds in delivering clear gains to commonly recognized interests, the very efficacy of that violation redefines the governing norm.

What follows is that international legal institutions are rarely called upon to meet standard criteria of legitimacy—by which they would likely fail if tested. At most, they are generally tested by reference to criteria of performance, which have only an intermediate force in justifying ultimate legitimacy. And yet, on the other hand, it is precisely these international institutions that are asked to do the hard work of furthering human security. Their democratic deficit undercuts the human security agenda and shows the tension between democracy and security. Two examples will show this.

The first example is the *Atkins* decision by the US Supreme Court, which aroused much controversy when it was decided in 2005, when the court drew upon foreign legal practice to declare the juvenile death penalty unconstitutional, on the grounds that the evolving standards of decency invoked by the Eighth Amendment's prohibition on cruel and unusual punishment now condemn the practice.[18] Formally speaking, this was fully a decision of domestic law, governed by the terms of the US Constitution. In fact, however, international law seems to have played a significant part in the decision. Justice Kennedy's majority decision rested on three legs. First, he claimed that a national "consensus" has come to exist on the question—not a real consensus, marked by unanimity, but a consensus by a majority, with indications of a trend in the abolitionist direction. Second, he argued that psychological evidence showed cognitive immaturity among juveniles, which supported a hypothesis of mitigated culpability and poor risk assessment, which undermined both retributive and deterrent rationales for the punishment. And third, he referred to the extraordinarily isolated global position of the US in executing juvenile killers, which was one of but eight countries to permit a practice outlawed by a large number of international treaties.

In fact, the international leg is the only one capable of bearing much of the weight of the opinion. As dissenting Justice O'Connor noted, evidence of any national trend, much less a consensus, is equivocal at best, given that a significant number of states have recently made explicit provision for the juvenile death penalty. And the empirical evidence best supports narrow tailoring of the penalty to the most culpable juvenile offenders, not the bright-line categorical rule. But the force of the international claim was substantial, where a real international consensus exists with such vigor that there is strong support for the claim that juvenile executions are a violation of a non-treaty-based *jus cogens* norm, binding even on those who—like the United States—have exempted themselves from treaty provisions on that point. International law, toothless as it is, presumed to speak with authority to the US case.

Justice Kennedy's invocation of the international community of opinion generated an explosive dissent from Justice Scalia. Scalia called into question the legitimacy of using international public opinion to rebut the deliberate policy choice and decency standards of the citizens of Missouri, as well as the other five states permitting the practice. He wrote, "Though the views of our own citizens are essentially irrelevant to the Court's decision today, the views of other countries and the so-called international community take center stage."[19] Despite the hyberbole, Scalia had a point—if one takes seriously the distinctive legitimating power of democracy. Since the force of the international norm is itself ostensibly established by the universal practice of nations, the court is effectively holding that the muted reflection of democracy in that norm trumps the direct exercise of democracy in Missouri. And it is indeed hard to see how the practice, however universal, of other states restricting their own punitive practices could legitimately be brought to bear on what Missourians should do in their territory, especially given that the national political community has refused, at each opportunity, to join in the international consensus by treaty. While a paean to democracy in support of juvenile executions is less than compelling, Scalia's complaint rings true. We cannot simply presume that the international norm ought to apply to Missouri because of its moral truth, for its moral truth is precisely what is in question among the citizens to whom it has been made to apply. The dignity claims of human rights conflict with the dignity claims of democratic voters.

My second example comes from the domain of trade. As part of the WTO system, the state parties made a number of ancillary agreements governing, among other issues, health and safety. Article 3 of the Sanitary and Phytosanitary Measures (or SPS) Agreement formally permits nations to adopt health measures they deem necessary to protect their domestic constituencies, even exceeding international standards, but only insofar as the measures have an adequate "scientific justification."[20] The point of this test is to screen out ostensibly health-related measures that are, in fact, protectionist measures.

In 1996, the relation of domestic health norms to WTO authority was tested by the United States and Canada, when they brought a complaint against the European Union which had, the previous year, adopted a rule prohibiting the importation of cattle treated with various growth hormones.[21] The EU decision was taken under the guidance of the so-called precautionary principle, which directs risk minimization in the face of scientific uncertainty and high stakes. In the abstract, one might well think that extreme risk aversion concerning hormonal additions to beef would fall within the scope of reasonable judgments about the public health, whether or not one agrees with the merits. In fact, the measure was rejected by the Appellate Body, not on the basis of its content but on the lack of any "reasonable support or warrant" for the measure.[22] This conclusion, which may accurately represent the scientific evidence put before the Appellate Body, also reflects what was at stake: an essentially normative, political judgment about how to manage health risks of unknown magnitude was supplanted by an expert, trade-focused body's essentially technocratic standard.

While the EU standard-setting process is no model of democracy, it is fair to say that resistance to genetically or hormonally modified foodstuffs runs deep in the popular will. On the other side of the books is the mandate of the Appellate Body itself, which flows from the SPS and WTO agreements entered into and ratified by the legislative assemblies of the member states, and applying international standards set through the ostensibly über-democratic norm of consensus. And while one may easily be critical of the actual voluntariness of the decision by less-developed states whether to accept the terms of the WTO, the concern about coerced consent hardly holds for the European and North American players. On this view, the Appellate Body simply enjoys power delegated to it by its members, who all seek the common good of trade harmonization. In principle, the democratic deficit of the Appellate Body doesn't seem different in kind from that enjoyed by US Article III courts or their international equivalents, also mandated by statute and—at least in the United States—thereafter capable of rejecting seemingly reasonable health or environmental regulations on their own judgments of adequate empirical basis.[23]

So much is true and can ground the legitimacy of the WTO institutions in ordinary business, below crisis point. But in the case of a real conflict between local and international standards, these considerations provide little comfort. Delegated powers within a domestic system come with greater powers of popular revision, however balky the process, and greater opportunities for political monitoring, as well as with a sense that a common cultural and political matrix will ensure a fair degree of harmony between regulation and adjudication. These formal and extraformal considerations, which make direct or indirect democratic institutions mainstays of legitimacy, are significantly less present on the international stage, particularly within the WTO's secretive "green room" policy discussions and appellate decisions. When a crisis arises, international institutions fail the comparative test of legitimacy.

2.7. RESERVING OUR ENTHUSIASM FOR DEMOCRACY

The two cases I have described feature conflicts between principles protecting fundamental aspects of human security—freedom from state violence, and access to the benefits of globalization—and basic principles of democratic legitimation. Nor are these conflicts incidental. Norms such as restrictions on execution, or protection of the benefits of a free trade system, are much likelier to arise from nondemocratic institutions than from democratic ones, given the political economies of the relevant policy questions: local interests will almost always defeat global interests in a democratic match. In some cases, we outside observers might side with the international forum; in others, with the local constituency. But the point is such conflicts are endemic, and they will inevitably sap the resources of the institutions the human security agenda depends on. Indeed, an argument from democratic premises is one of the central struts of the recent influential critique of international law in the United States, Eric Posner and Jack Goldsmith's *The Limits of International Law*.[24] Posner and Goldsmith combine a descriptive thesis, that international law only appears to bind nations, who act in conformity with it only when they have separate, self-interested reasons to do so, with a normative thesis, that democratic states should not regard themselves as bound by international law unless and until it is legitimated through local, democratic incorporation.

Put aside the merits of their descriptive thesis. Their normative thesis is essentially tautological, so long as we cede the ground to democracy as a source of legitimate authority. The human security movement risks doing so, by tying its agenda too closely to the agenda of democratization. We should be prepared to recognize and reap the human security gains brought by democratic institutions. But we should resist accepting the tautology that states may be bound only through assertions of their own legislative wills: recognition of values, including basic dignitarian and welfare values, can be a legitimate restraint on state behavior. Democratic institutions are only a part of the set of practices that can support human security. Other practices include frank nods to technocratic or intellectually authoritarian institutions, which look not to electoral but to deliberative or performative success in meeting their goals.

But recognizing the value of technocratic performance does not mean forswearing the attractions of democracy. Rather, it is a matter of recognizing the way in which democratic self-governance, and the forms of collective agency that make such governance possible, distributes responsibilities of moral governance internally and horizontally within a political community. The next chapter, which takes up more fully the democratic way of war, explores the nature of political responsibility among a people.

3

CITIZENS AND SOLDIERS:
THE DIFFERENCE UNIFORMS MAKE

The wars in Iraq and Afghanistan have put front and center the problem of dealing with non-uniformed combatants. They have also made central profound questions of the legitimacy of resorting to martial violence, and responsibility for picking up the pieces thereafter. I argue here that the special problem of non-uniformed combatants and the general problem of justifying war are profoundly linked. War, I shall argue, is but one form of a more general species: collective violence. Collective violence poses a particular set of challenges to the application of moral principles. In this chapter, I identify a conflict between two themes in our response to collective violence. I call these themes of *inculpation* and *exculpation*. I illustrate these themes in section 3.1 with three stories derived from actual events. Section 3.2 elaborates the law of war principles that govern these scenarios. Section 3.3 opens the discussion of whether new norms, appropriate to a democratic age, should be defended; and section 3.4 looks to the historical sources for the combatants' privilege. Section 3.5 introduces the figure of Rousseau more fully to the themes of this book; his conception of a collective will is the anchor of democratic responsibility, while his argument for combatant impunity serves as one of the foundations of the modern law of war. Sections 3.6 takes up the limits of instrumentalist reductions of the principles of the combatant's privilege; while section 3.7 pursues the alternative route, by way of a conception of complicity in political agency.

3.1. THREE STORIES OF COLLECTIVE VIOLENCE

3.1.1. *Crime Story*

Smith and Daniels approach Taylor. Daniels tells Taylor that Jax Liquor would be a good target for a robbery. All they need is a car and a getaway driver. If Taylor will sit outside the liquor store till Smith and Daniels come out, he'll get a third of the haul. Taylor is in.[1]

Smith and Daniels come into the store, Smith waving his gun, both shouting, demanding the money. But the situation fails to unfold as planned. Linda West, the owner's wife, is working in the back of the store when she sees the men. Fearing that Smith is about to shoot, she grabs the gun in her pocket, and shoots and kills Smith, then wounds Daniels as he runs to escape in Taylor's car.

Taylor and Daniels are later arrested. Taylor, although he did nothing more in preparation for the robbery than sit in his car, is charged with both robbery and murder, for Smith's death. Though Ms. West actually shot Smith, the death is treated as causally flowing from Smith's own frightening gun-waving during the robbery, and as a species of murder because it manifests an extreme indifference to human life. By the logic of accomplice liability, according to which any member of a criminal group is liable for any reasonably foreseeable acts done by any other member in furtherance of the group's common design, Taylor is also responsible for Smith's death. The result is that Taylor may be convicted of a murder he did not commit or even cause.

3.1.2. War Story

Imperioland has invaded its small but oil-rich neighbor, Petrostan, in order to seize its oil wells. Sergeant Blue, of Imperioland's volunteer army, is aware that world opinion holds Imperioland's invasion to be a flagrant violation of international law, but he follows the judgment of his political leaders. Blue, however, intends to fight the war in full compliance with the international law of combat, known as *jus in bello* or, more currently, as international humanitarian law (IHL). IHL is independent of the legality of the conflict itself (the rules governing which are known as *jus ad bellum*). Among its principal requirements are that soldiers proportion the violence they deploy to military necessity, discriminate between combatants and noncombatants (a category including civilians and wounded and surrendered soldiers), and respect the life and well-being of anyone not currently deemed a threat, including surrendered or injured enemy combatants.

Blue's squad is ordered to capture an engineering building at one of the refineries. Blue enters the building. He shoots and kills the Petrostan soldiers on guard. His mission appears successful. And because Blue killed only combatants, it was unquestionably consistent with IHL.

Suddenly a company of Petrostan's soldiers arrive and capture Blue. He is sent to a detention camp, called before a military tribunal, and charged under Petrostan's domestic criminal law with murder, for the intentional killing of the sentry, not in defense of himself or others. He is sentenced to death.

Before the sentence is carried out, a member of Petrostan's foreign ministry arrives. Petrostan (like Imperioland) is a Geneva Convention signatory, and the minister is waving a copy of the Third Geneva Convention (often abbreviated as GPW, for Geneva–Prisoners of War), which deals with combatants taken prisoner. According to the GPW, Blue, as a regular, uniformed soldier, must be treated as a "privileged combatant" and can only be held as a prisoner of war. This means he cannot be punished for his killing (assuming it did not breach the laws of combat). He may be held in captivity only until the cessation of hostilities.[2] Though Blue kills without justification, as a soldier he is impunible.

3.1.3. Rebel Story

The tide turns in the invasion, and Imperioland's troops begin to rout Petrostan's army. Remaining members of the Petrostan army doff their uniforms, move to the backcountry, and become a partisan resistance. They are joined in their efforts by Petrostan citizens and foreigners from the region who infiltrate the border and join the resistance.

Gray is a foreigner who wants to join the partisans. She too crosses the border, affiliates with a partisan unit, receives weapons training, and is sent out to fight.[3] The partisans' resistance movement employs classic guerrilla strategy: they hide among the population and seek low-intensity engagements. To paraphrase Raymond Aron, they believe that they will win so long as they do not lose their ability to inflict losses, and that Imperioland will lose so long as it does not wipe them out.[4] Their goal is to protect and restore the political institutions of Petrostan, as well as to defend a religious and cultural tradition they reasonably see as under threat by the occupation. The partisans strike only at military targets and are as scrupulous as Sergeant Blue was about observing the international law of combat. But, unlike Blue, they do not wear uniforms or otherwise reveal their identities as combatants, because it would be certain death or capture. Only when they draw their weapons in battle do they reveal themselves as combatants.

Gray is preparing for an assault when her house is swarmed by Imperioland soldiers. She is armed but not uniformed. Imperioland has ratified the GPW, which accords POW status only to combatants who wear uniforms or otherwise bear "a fixed distinctive sign recognizable at a distance." But it has not ratified the additional Protocol I to the Conventions, which broadens combatant status to non-uniformed, "liberation"-seeking members of the armed forces of a party to the conflict who bear their arms openly while engaging in or preparing for military operations.[5]

Like Blue, Gray is brought before a tribunal and charged with conspiracy to commit murder and sabotage. Her claim that she is a combatant entitled to POW status is dismissed. While she is spared from the death penalty permitted under Imperioland's regulations, she is sentenced to indefinite confinement at an Imperioland prison. (The Imperioland army fears, reasonably enough, that Gray will rejoin the fight when released.)

3.2. TWO THEMES IN THE KEY OF COLLECTIVE VIOLENCE

These stories reflect the differential treatment of collective violence in law and ethics. I put this in terms of two conflicting themes. The first is the theme of complicity, and every jurisdiction in the world plays a variant of it. Ordinarily, moral responsibility and criminal liability attach to an agent only on condition that the agent has performed a wrongful act, perhaps producing a wrongful result. This is a principle of individual culpability, and requirements (in Anglo-American terms) of the existence of a culpably done criminal act and proximate causation of a result undergird and limit the attribution of wrongs to individuals. Complicity doctrine, however, attaches liability through a different route. Even though individuals on their own might have done nothing wrong, they can be held responsible for someone else's wrongful act, if they are members of a group whose other members do wrong in furtherance of a joint criminal plan. To put the point yet more strongly, so long as any member of a group with a criminal project does a foreseeable wrong, each member of that group bears responsibility for the wrong.

Take Taylor, from "Crime Story": driving a car to, and sitting in front of, a liquor store one hopes to rob is not itself wrongful. Those acts, on their own, would probably not support a conviction of attempted robbery in most jurisdictions, as they fall short of a "substantial step" towards the crime's completion.[6] Taylor's liability rests not on what he actually does but on a combination of what he intends to do—participate in an armed robbery—and what he might expect his fellow participants to do—instigate a shooting. His complicity in the group robbery renders him liable for another's killing. This I call the theme of *collective inculpation*.

A contrasting theme, of *collective exculpation*, runs through the law of war. The function of the law regulating the conduct of war (IHL) is to demarcate a zone of impunible violence: killing, maiming, and property destruction. The boundaries of this zone are set chiefly by the rules of proportionality and discrimination mentioned above; but the central presupposition of the zone is the collective, political character of the violence: these acts are only impunible when committed by a member of the armed forces of a state or insurgent party to the conflict (provided they are otherwise in compliance with IHL).

Sergeant Blue kills by his own hand and without justification, and so would be guilty of murder if he were simply trying to rob the refinery. But because he is a member of Imperioland's army, no liability attaches to him personally. Even if Blue fires the only shot in the war, he bears no liability for the killing. Moreover, the injustice of his army's war is irrelevant. Blue's permission to kill depends on the fact that he is part of a certain sort of group collectively intent on violence. This ought to be shocking, but it is all too familiar: participants in normalized mass killing, territorial occupation, and political transformation enjoy permission to do together what would be infamous crimes if done separately.

Non-uniformed fighters like Gray mix both themes. Is the rebel Gray more like Taylor or more like Blue? Should she be inculpated or exculpated? Gray's cause, Petrostan's independence, is presumptively just, unlike Blue's. But, Gray, unlike Blue, may be criminally liable and executed or detained indefinitely. Her legal status depends on a two-step analysis: first, Gray's acts are removed from the context of a collective partisan resistance, and she is treated as an individual with criminal intent. Next, her collective status is reasserted in the complicity or conspiracy charge. As in Taylor's case, she is liable for rebel-caused deaths whether or not she fires a shot.

My subject is the contrast between the themes of collective inculpation and collective exculpation, and the tension that arises when the two themes encounter each other in the treatment of irregular, usually non-uniformed combatants.[7] These are individuals engaged in the ordinary business of war who, if they were part of conventional military units, would enjoy impunity so long as they proportion their violence to military necessity and discriminate between civilians and combatants. The case of non-uniformed, irregular fighters is, of course, an especially current practical challenge for the law of war. It also brings into the open the question of why certain forms of collective action privilege violence, while others serve as the basis for punishing it.

The European partisans who fought Nazi occupation during World War II are exemplars of this category, including the storied Maquis of France. Others include anticolonial rebels of the developing world. The anticolonialist movements were a major motivation for the 1977 Protocols amending the Geneva Convention provisions; Article 44 of Protocol I (hereafter API 44) specifically deals with the question of irregular combatants. API 44 permits violence by insurgents and partisans who conceal their status generally but engage openly in combat. Protocol I was widely ratified, thus binding its signatories, which do not include the United States but do include most other major powers.[8] Modern examples of irregular fighters, to whom the application of API 44 is controversial, include the Taliban and al-Qaeda fighters in Afghanistan, the Fedayeen and Baathist resistants in Iraq, the posses of Afghan and Somali warlords, and some of the Colombian antigovernment rebels, in whose disputes US forces are entangled. More pointedly, so may be US Special Forces soldiers and CIA field operatives, who typically serve out of uniform and without clear insignias of their national affiliation. (Recall the photos during the Afghanistan war of US Special Forces riding their horses in the company of the Northern Alliance.)[9]

The category of irregular combatants is not new but its instantiations have increased (perhaps because of greater US military adventurism). As has been widely discussed, this is a consequence of three principal "developments" in modern violence.[10] First, state military conflict today rarely occurs in the form of major battles between armies but increasingly through the tactics of "asymmetrical" warfare, including guerrilla raids, hiding among either one's own or one's enemies' populations, infiltration of enemy lines, sabotage, and joint operations with collaborating civilians. Second, recent conflicts are increasingly transnational in character, where the transnational element includes collaborations between intelligence units of one nation and military units of another, or involves foreign volunteers linked by ideological or religious affiliations. Again, this is not new—witness the Spanish Civil War—but it is resurgent with militant Islam. Relatedly, some recent conflicts have been neither internal to a state nor transnational, in that they have taken place in political conditions where no state exists because power is too fragmented; Somalia is a prime example. The third development is the renascent phenomenon of war through mercenary proxies, which predated the modern era of war, subsided during the consolidation of state power, emerged again during decolonization, and then subsided once more. It is now on the rise again through the distinctly postmodern phenomenon of the "corporate warriors," who provide outsourced logistical and "tactical" (read lethal) support to everyone from the US Army to the United Nations to Sierra Leone to the petroleum industry.[11] Modern combatants look increasingly unlike the army regulars around whom the Geneva Conventions were drafted.

The results of these developments are troubling. It is, at the least, conceptually anomalous that greater numbers of combatants in modern war fall outside the regime crafted to control war's violence. It poses a practical problem, in that if combatants lack impunity for engaging in violence bounded by the norms of proportionality and discrimination, they have no incentive to observe these bounds. And it is a legal problem, in that we lack criteria to assess the legitimacy of the treatment of the large number of irregulars captured on the battlefield and held indefinitely by occupying powers. As ever more warfare involves stipulatively unprivileged combatants, the normative systems controlling war become more and more strained. If lawlessness is a problem, an even deeper problem is normlessness.

3.3. DESIGNING NORMS FOR NEW WARS

What norms should we adopt? What difference should uniforms make? In this chapter, I look at and reject some traditional answers to the problem, including answers generated by premodern conceptions of sovereignty and by straightforward consequentialist reasoning. Instead, I turn to a modification of a tradition inaugurated by Rousseau, who conceived of political authority as resting in a special relationship among individuals. When individuals' wills are linked together in politics, this affects the normative valence of what they do individually as part of that politics, even to the point of rendering impunible what would otherwise be criminal. The salient Western form of these political relationships is democracy, which I understand here as involving some form of majoritarian decision making coupled with a universal franchise. But by "political," I shall mean any form of social action oriented around state or institutional formation, where power may in some sense be seen to rest at the level of individual voluntary commitment to the shared project. (Thus, I mean to contrast "political" relationships with authoritarian, fear-motivated hierarchical relationships.) A consequence of my conception of political authority is that permission to engage in collective violence turns on combatants' attitudes and relations to one another, not on any external sign of their obedience, including wearing a uniform. Put directly, citizen-soldiers enjoy combat privileges because they enjoy the political status of citizens, not because they wear the uniform of a soldier.

In actual policy terms, this chapter defends a regime like that specified in the First Protocol (API 44), which permits combat by non-uniformed combatants fighting for "liberation" or "self-determination," a paradigmatic political category of collective violence. I depart from that regime in one important respect, however. API 44, as a matter of positive law, is fully consistent with the separation of *jus ad bellum* from *jus in bello*. My argument opens conceptual space for denying the privilege to some otherwise lawful combatants waging clearly unjust wars, a position considered and rejected by the drafters of the First Protocol. For a number of reasons, both practical and conceptual, this logical space may be closed for all likely cases. But principled reflection demands that we understand the deep links between the responsibility for war and the privileges of warfare, rather than simply assert their separateness. The very idea of an ethical regime of war generates paradoxes, which I now consider.[12]

The first paradox is substantive: even if a state is illegally engaged in war (in violation of the UN Charter or, in an earlier day, of just war principles), its forces enjoy a right to wound and kill enemy combatants subject to IHL's norms of proportionality and discrimination.[13] This is puzzling: domestically, no one could defend a murder on the grounds that he had shown special delicacy, à la Hannibal Lecter, in the manner of his killing. Means are normatively inert. Yet it is a commonplace that the rules of IHL are independent of the justice of the war itself.[14] This commonplace obscures a deep puzzle: how can there be permissibly violent means of pursuing impermissible ends? The very premise of the normative independence of IHL brings into question the nature of its justification. This is the paradox of permitting the impermissible.

A variant of this paradox has frequently provoked puzzlement among newcomers to the law of war: how can there be *any* significant distinctions within the field of killing? If a war is unjust, then any killings done in its prosecution are unjust, even if they are permissible. It is therefore hard to see how a normative regime can determine that some of these unjust killings (for instance, killings not using dum-dum bullets, or killings by uniformed combatants) are categorically better than others, such that they are permitted and the others banned. Even in a just war, killing is a terrible thing, permitted out of necessity rather than utility. Once necessity is in play, one might think, distinctions among necessary killings seem somehow beside the point. In domestic criminal law, while we sometimes grade punishment in relation to the manner of killing, reserving the most severe sanctions for the most heinous forms of killing, we do not distinguish among the varieties of justified killings. But international law promulgates precisely such distinctions.

An instrumental answer comes forth immediately: restrictions on methods and targets of killing in war reduce the suffering of combatants, risks to noncombatants, and the costs to states, and hence are justified by their good consequences. The permission to kill within the bounds of these restrictions is the bribe paid to combatants to induce their compliance with them. I mention this justification now to acknowledge it, but, for reasons I elaborate below, I do not believe it accounts for IHL's normative authority, and I think it particularly fails to justify a central feature of them, the categorical quality of the rules.

There is a related historical point. Many of the customary rules of IHL come from the chivalric tradition, particularly rules regarding the treatment of those *hors de combat*. The rules thus have their ground in a conception of warrior virtue, and again an instrumental account seems inadequate to the underlying ethical view on which they draw.[15] This point is hardly decisive, since a revisionary account of our intuitions might in fact provide the best justification of the norms these intuitions support (as, for example, Mill argued of utilitarianism). But it is a prima facie objection that an instrumental justification seems to "argue back" to a conclusion more certain than the path of argument itself.[16] However we assess the force of these considerations, then, we need a framework of principles within which those considerations can be deployed.

Without these broader puzzles in sight, the question of whether to grant battle privileges to the irregular combatant appears easier than it is: just a matter of estimating the marginal costs and benefits of additional suffering that a change in the rule would impose. We need a deeper solution.

3.4. CONCEPTUAL SOURCES OF THE COMBAT PRIVILEGE

We can identify three sources for the conceptual foundation for the privilege of uniformed combatants. The first source is the early modern conception of sovereignty itself, where the concept of the state was wholly identified with its ruler. This notion, theorized most radically by Jean Bodin's 1576 *Six Books of the Commonwealth* [Six livres de la République], was as much a logical and metaphysical claim as a prescription for political unity. According to Bodin, the very idea of political authority requires a distinction between the agent who exercises authority and the subject who receives it.[17] The idea of an agent who was at the same time a subject, or, alternatively, a subject who was bound by laws he himself imposed, was for Bodin a logical impossibility.[18] With a firm distinction in place between the state, embodied in its ruler, and its subjects, the moral qualities of the state cannot flow logically to its inhabitants. Just as the fact that the sovereign might incur a debt does not mean that a given peasant in his realm is also liable for that debt, so the fact that the sovereign was at war with another state would not mean that his subjects were at war with the other state. War could not be, in moral terms, a relation between the soldiers actually doing the fighting. They are merely the technology for resolving the interstate dispute.

The moral and metaphysical separation of state from subjects thus opens up a logical space for a distinct code of ethics for soldiers, an ethics independent of the legitimacy of their sovereigns' dispute. The war is not about *them*, it is about their sovereign. Within the field of combat, there is room for codes of chivalry, especially with regard to the norms of respecting surrender and discriminating between civilians and soldiers. The permission to kill within these limits, under this theory, is not a deep justification of killing, in the sense that it does not justify the killing itself. Rather, the permission reflects the limited moral status of the soldier *qua* soldier, who was not expected to justify his role in the war before God or his conscience, but only his conduct in the war. Responsibility for the war itself belonged solely to the sovereign.

A further norm restricting the privilege to the uniformed makes sense in the context of this conception of sovereignty, although the regular wearing of uniforms postdates Bodin considerably. While uniforms were hardly unknown before the modern period, they did not feature prominently (at least in Europe) as the garb of national militias until the seventeenth century, when Oliver Cromwell dressed his citizen army uniformly; and the trend came to a head with the elaborate uniforms of Frederick the Great.[19] The systematic uniforming of armies in fact tracks the post-Westphalian establishment of a system of internally ordered sovereign states. Disciplining the army and disciplining the nation-state go hand in hand.[20] A norm that war should be between uniformed combatants simply mirrors the claim that war is a relation between states, not citizens. Because the basic relation of sovereign to subject is an external relation, on this conception—a matter of the power of the sovereign to compel obedience[21]—it follows that the relation of privileged combatant to sovereign would also be established through an external mark. The uniform is, in effect, the stamp of ownership the sovereign puts on his army, and this stamp renders the external quality of what they do, namely killing others, attributable to the sovereign rather than to themselves.

The inadequacies of an account of the privilege grounded in Bodin-esque sovereignty need not be belabored: the separation between state and citizens on which it depends is not sustainable under conditions of mass, bottom-up politics. But a second and more resonant conceptual source of the privilege emerges from the rival conception of sovereignty that super-seded Bodin's in modern, post-Enlightenment thought. This is the con-ception we take from Rousseau. Rousseau famously argued in *The Social Contract* that not only can a subject, collective or individual, give itself law, but that giving oneself law is a necessary condition of political freedom and legitimate authority. It follows from this, Rousseau thought, that a people is sovereign when and only when individuals' agency, in the form of their wills, is linked in the structure he calls the "general will." A people whose individual wills are so linked is committed to acting together in the interests of all, on the basis of a distribution of rights and responsibilities that guarantee their equal freedom. When this is so, a people produces

> [a] moral and collective body made up of as many members as the assembly has voices, and which receives by this same act its unity, its common *self* [*moi commun*], its life and its will. The public person thus formed by the union of all the others formerly assumed the name *City* and now assumes that of *Republic* or of *body politic*, which its members call *State* when it is passive, *Sovereign* when active, *Power* when com-paring it to similar bodies.[22]

The sovereign, on this conception, is dependent upon but not reducible to the individual citizens taken together. This is because the sovereign is a relation among wills, not a set of persons. The individual citizens retain their personal wills, notwithstanding their voluntary commitment of their rights to their collective sovereignty. Indeed, this retention of their per-sonal wills is what explains the self-evident strains of committing oneself to even a just polity: the temptations to free-ride for personal benefit do not disappear merely because one acknowledges the force of the public interest. Thus sovereignty reflects an aspect of the citizens of a state, their public face, in a sense. Their relations as members of the sovereign—or, better, as participants in the collective achievement of sovereignty—to themselves as private individuals are what enables Rousseau's response to Bodin as to how a sovereign can bind itself.[23]

So war, conceived as a relation between peoples linked constitutively as sovereigns, can still be distinguished from a relation between individuals per se. What would seem to follow from Rousseau's account is that in war, soldiers relate to one another as citizens rather than as individuals. Thus, an ethics of international relations, not an ethics of interpersonal relations, constrains their conduct.

Interestingly, this is not what Rousseau says. What he says instead is: "War is not then a relationship between one man and another, but a relationship between one State and another, in which individuals are enemies only by accident, not as men, nor even as citizens, but as soldiers; not as members of the fatherland, but as its defenders."[24] On its face, this is puzzling: why should men in war encounter each other only as soldiers and not as citizens? As with much of Rousseau's writing, answering this demands recognizing an imprecision forced by context. Rousseau's concern in the sentences above is to limit the power of victors by defining the scope of the relation of enmity. His specific task is to deny the traditional victor's right to enslave the vanquished. His argument must therefore be that, if war is between states, and if states consist of citizens (appropriately bound), and if soldiers confront each other as citizens (as well as soldiers), then in prosecuting a war against another state it is not sufficient simply to disarm its solders; one must further kill or enslave its citizens. To deny this line of reasoning, Rousseau must show that on the battlefield norms appropriate to the circumscribed role of the soldier, not the more expansive role of citizen, determine the range of permissible acts.

Rousseau has two arguments for doing so. The first argument is at work in his claim that

> [t]he foreigner, whether he be a king, a private individual, or a people, who robs, kills, or detains subjects without declaring war on their prince, is not an enemy, he is a brigand. . . . Since the aim of war is the destruction of the enemy State, one has the right to kill its defenders as long as they bear arms; but as soon as they lay down their arms and surrender, they cease to be enemies or the enemy's instruments, and become simply men once more, and one no longer has a right over their life.[25]

A declaration of war is a special kind of collective act, reflecting the will of one sovereign to engage in hostilities with another. The collective aspect of a citizen's agency in the domestic sphere lies in his participation in forming a general will, constituting sovereignty. But on the battlefield, the collective aspect of his agency consists simply in fighting as part of a unit, that is, as a soldier. In the external relations of state to state in war only the potential for belligerency is significant to the citizen's normative identity. Once a citizen-soldier is disarmed, that external aspect of the citizen's identity is destroyed; he can no longer properly be considered an enemy of his victor. He is simply an individual, and there is no ground for the victor to claim any right to kill or enslave a private individual.

The second argument amplifies the first: "It is sometimes possible to kill the State without killing a single one of its members: and war confers no right that is not necessary."[26] Sovereigns formed by interdependent citizen wills are "killed" when the relation among those wills is broken; and that relation can be broken by isolating an individual citizen-soldier, not just by killing him. Even in authoritarian states, where sovereignty is vested in an individual prince, killing the soldier does not kill the state. More generally, so long as sovereignty is understood as an abstract property of an individual or individuals, killing disarmed soldiers is neither a necessary nor a sufficient means for vanquishing a state. This argument too, then, rests on the special nature of political organizations.

The logic of this position supports both the permissibility of killing and its subordination to a nonpartisan system of rules. While the citizen-soldier is at war with other citizens, he bears no personal relation of enmity to his foes. The general will in which he participates creates in him only an obligation of military service.[27] Since he has an obligation to fight, and since ought implies can, it must be permissible for him to fight. It also follows that since he engages in battle as a soldier, the chivalric ethics suiting the soldier's role are appropriate. Thus, Rousseau's account would seem to deliver an account of the normative autonomy of the battlefield, one derived from the collective aspect of war. That autonomy is a consequence of the fact that wars are relations between collectives, fought through individuals.[28]

Moreover, one can see how Rousseau's argument for the limited right of the victor, grounded in sovereignty as the product of the general will, can support (though not entail) a uniformed condition for the permission. What motivates his argument is the isolation of the citizen's identity in the context of battle, and (as with Bodin) the construction of that identity in external, functional terms. A citizen in uniform has permitted his identity to be reduced to the aspect of soldierhood. His relation to the state is not, as it was with Bodin, a mere tool of the sovereign's will; but it still limited to the functional role of "defender" obliged by the terms of the social contract to fight for the state. By contrast, the irregular, non-uniformed combatant can be taken as asserting an individual rather than a collective identity: he presents himself as an individual force vector, not as part of an armed host. Since reducing their battlefield identity from citizen to soldier is why vanquished soldiers retain rights to life (thus, impunity for normal acts of war), it makes sense to condition that right on individuals' formal acceptance of that identity: by donning a uniform.

I now want to argue that while Rousseau's account suggests a path forward, it will not justify the normative autonomy of the battlefield, much less the restriction of the privilege to the uniformed. If what really links citizens to the state is an internal relation of their wills, garbing in uniform is ultimately window dressing. That a group of soldiers wears uniforms might be external *evidence* of internal collective organization within a larger political community, and requirements of providing such evidence have clear instrumental value. But the evidence of the tie is not itself constitutive of such organization or ties; a squad of undisciplined mercenaries might be uniformly clothed.

Rousseauian sovereignty poses a major problem for the independence of *jus in bello* from *jus ad bellum*. The problem arises because the conceptual isolation of the identity of soldier from that of citizen cannot be maintained. After all, under the victor's sword there is but one person, whose normative identity has different aspects. A father does not cease to be a father when he becomes a soldier; it is simply that his fatherhood is not relevant on the battlefield. But an individual's identity as a citizen *does* seem relevant on the battlefield, as well as his identity as a soldier. Insofar as he has partly authorized a war, why not hold him responsible for that choice? If the collective decision to wage war is unjust, then as a citizen he is responsible for that injustice.

It may be true that as an individual, he is obliged to fight in the service of the collective waging of war. But all that follows is that he should not be punished as an individual for his belligerency, assuming it meets with the norms of proper combat.[29] (Even this point does not hold if fighting is voluntary.) It does not follow that he may not be punished as a member of a collective; that is, he and his fellow soldiers may be held collectively responsible for the war they wage.[30] Think of a criminal sentence passed on a business entity: if the sentence is just, then the costs of that sentence are legitimately borne by the business's members: its partners, for example, or shareholders, or employees. Though they are not being punished as individuals, they are punishable as members of the corporate entity.

3.5. SOURCES OF THE PRIVILEGE: THE INSTRUMENTALIST STRATEGY

Thus a Rousseauian argument fails to account for a blanket privilege to kill in war, a privilege independent of the justice of the war itself. One might well respond, "So much the worse for the privilege of collective, unjustified violence." But in the service of trying to make sense of current norms, we should pursue the matter further. Indeed, a third and now dominant strategy remains for defending the privilege: the consequentialist strategy I mentioned above, which plays a central role in the International Committee of the Red Cross's understanding of the case for IHL. This strategy effectively links a political realist premise—wars happen—with a normative premise demanding the minimization of human suffering in their wake. Since wars will happen whether or not combatants have special international legal status, the question is, What incentives can limit the suffering they impose? Impunity for certain forms of violence, coupled with the special treatment for the captured, is stipulated as necessary to induce restraint among combatants.[31] The further restriction of the privilege to the uniformed is then justified by its role in promoting the distinguishability of combatants from noncombatants.

As is true of most consequentialist arguments, the force of this is difficult to assess. The privilege must be defended not only at the margin but also categorically. For example, if a war might be shortened through relaxing efforts at discrimination, as Allied forces claimed in World War II when they initiated strategic bombing campaigns, a purely instrumental rationale must permit this. Presumably shorter wars cause less net death and suffering than a prolonged and discriminating war, and must be permitted. But the strategic bombing campaigns are now widely regarded as a grotesque moral mistake, whatever their strategic value.[32] For those who consider them a moral mistake, moreover, the mistake clearly does not consist in an aggregate miscalculation, for instance, that relaxing area bombing restrictions will increase suffering in other conflicts. That might be true, but the real mistake lies in the tolerance of the wholesale slaughter of civilians per se. The instrumental account suffers the problems of any two-level form of consequentialism: it is unable to offer categorical support for the categorical rules it defends.

There is an analogous point as well, familiar in ethics: if the rules of IHL are justified instrumentally, then that fact must be kept from combatants. For a combatant who knows that IHL is justified on the basis of wholesale calculations of humanitarian advantage will always have reason to ask himself in a given instance whether playing by the rules makes sense or whether it is a case of what J.J.C. Smart has famously called "rule-worship."[33] What we want to inculcate instead is a combatant's thought that the rules of IHL, and the system of values that sustain them, command categorically. Since soldiers, being human, are reflective creatures, this means that we must provide a noninstrumental argument for those rules.[34] So we must anyway exit the path of instrumental justification.

Furthermore, the empirical assumptions underlying the argument are open to question. First, the realist premise assumes that the amount of combat is fixed independently. But it is hardly clear that the amount is fixed; and indeed it might well be thought that the amount of combat is increased when all participants are guaranteed impunity, especially those fighting criminal wars. It is now widely thought that individual prosecutions for war crimes are necessary or at least useful in reducing the number of war crimes that might occur. Individual prosecutions for unlawful belligerency could also, by the same reasoning, tend to deter individual participation in that belligerency. This is especially true in states with volunteer armies; but even for conscript armies, the prospect of post-capture prosecution might well dampen the ardor of the soldier. A similar argument can be deployed against the familiar claim that the absolute privilege rule reduces suffering by making surrender more attractive. That may be true once the war has begun, but if fewer wars might be initiated in the first place under a privilege restricted to just wars, then killings might be yet further minimized. Without a way to assess the realist claim of the inelasticity of violence, the consequentialist arguments are indeterminate.

Granted, there will be profound disagreements about what constitutes an unjust war, whether in relation to positive international law or in a broader justificatory argument, as with NATO's Kosovo 1998 intervention.[35] Resolving those disagreements would be necessary to justify punishing cases of unlawful belligerency. But those disagreements already need to be resolved for the post-Nuremburg routine practice of prosecuting political and military leaders for wrongful aggression. Convictions of captive line soldiers could simply adhere, as a form of accomplice liability, to the leadership convictions. As well, a prospective soldier's uncertainty about the permissibility of engaging in combat could be a good thing, insofar as it might dampen efforts in dubious wars (and, more generally, might hinder recruiting and deploying combatants). Cases of clear justification—for example, territorial self-defense—would present no problem, as the permission would be clear.[36] Third, it is unclear whether combatant privileges really do function as incentives to comply with IHL. A soldier in combat cannot know in advance whether he will in fact receive the treatment he is due under IHL, and a little knowledge of history should make him dubious. (The Allied Forces' and Germany's treatment of their POWs appear to be historical exceptions.) A rational combatant conditioning his conduct only on the proposed benefit of POW status would have to discount that benefit greatly. On the other hand, a credible threat of greater marginal prosecution for violations of IHL, on top of a prosecution for belligerency itself, would seem more than sufficient to motivate compliance.

The consequentialist argument for a uniform requirement is even weaker. A rule demanding no visible distinctions between combatants and noncombatants *might* result in much higher civilian casualties than a rule requiring that combatants bear a "distinctive mark, visible at a distance." But two further claims are also plausible. First, by the "in for a penny, in for a pound" rationale, nonprivileged irregular combatants have little interest in refraining from indiscriminate violence; their incentive is just the marginal difference in punishment for war crimes over the punishment for belligerency itself, and both may be death.[37] Thus the gain in the ability of the uniformed side to discriminate comes precisely at the cost of a reduced interest on the non-uniformed side of discriminating themselves. Second, and conversely, if it makes sense to provide uniformed combatants killing privileges in order to induce IHL compliance, then it must make sense to offer the same incentive to non-uniformed combatants. The only question is whether costs outweigh benefits, and this cannot be settled from the armchair.

A consequentialist can offer a stronger response: apart from the instrumental value of any particular rule, the existence of some determinate scheme of rules makes a profound welfare contribution. A regime of absolute combat privileges for the uniformed improves decision making in the fog of battle, makes for clearer policy choices at the state level, and provides for stability in international cooperation and treaty formation. Indeed, the even partial regularization of war is one of law's great achievements.[38] Nonetheless, the claim is overstated. First, at the level of fact, the world we live in is, as I said above, increasingly characterized by asymmetrical and nonconventional warfare. Distinguishing innocent civilians from perfidious enemies is already a central, and extremely debilitating, part of modern warfare, at least for occupying armies intent on minimizing the killing of the innocent. No system of rules can really dispel the fog of war, and it seems an exaggeration to think that granting POW status to non-uniformed soldiers otherwise innocent of war crimes will do much to thicken that fog.

Second, a moderate form of rules is clearly available that provides for some, but less, discriminatory effect than a uniform. This is precisely the theory behind PI 44's requirement that when exigencies exist, combatants need only distinguish themselves during combat by carrying their arms openly.[39] Third, and most broadly, whatever humanitarian benefits flow from restricting combatancy generally have to be set off against the real costs of discouraging irregular resistance. In historical retrospect (and in many national narratives), some fights against alien occupation or for national self-determination are worth fighting par excellence. These are fights that can only be waged plausibly by guerrilla techniques. Giving an asymmetric advantage to a uniformed occupier, whatever the justice of its occupation, means resistance struggles will be rarer or harder than, by hypothesis, they ought to be.

So, simply on its own terms, the consequentialist argument for the limited privilege is too indeterminate to serve. The costs and benefits of privileging combatancy are speculative and necessarily involve the kind of gross estimates of long-term consequences that invite contamination by wishful thinking. But this merely confirms a deeper point: if there is an objection to prosecuting combatants for IHL-consistent killings, that objection comes from the domain of right (or fairness), not cost-benefit calculation.

3.6. ANOTHER TACTIC: COMBATANCY AS COMPLICITY

I began by emphasizing the puzzling distinction between the themes of collective inculpation and collective exculpation, between "Crime Story" and "War Story." Why, in the context of war, should doing violence together make right what in the domestic context it makes wrong? But the discord of these two themes might also be taken as an invitation to harmonize them. In fact, as I argue now, the same logic of collective action that underwrites complicity law also underwrites the law of war. With some help from Rousseau—at least some help from what he should have said, rather than what he did say—we now have the materials to explain and justify a limited form of the privilege of combat. The answer is to draw upon the conception of democratic agency (or agentic democracy) that I have been developing throughout this book. The moral judgment of complicity will be our guide.

Take the ethics and law of complicity first, as well as its partner, conspiracy. Complicity functions not as an independent crime in its own right, but as a distinctive form of moral and legal responsibility that links agents to outcomes by way of their participation in a collective effort, largely independently of their individual causal contributions.[40] Recall Taylor, in "Crime Story": if he genuinely has thrown his lot in with the armed robbery, then he bears responsibility for Smith's killing, and punishing him for that killing is just, even if we do not regard him as Smith's literal killer. Or consider the British case of *DPP for Northern Ireland v. Maxwell*.[41]

James Maxwell, a standing member of the Ulster Volunteer Force (UVF), was asked by a fellow member of the UVF to help on a "job." In Maxwell's case, this meant driving his own car to guide a following car to an inn. Maxwell drove past the inn, but knew that the tailing car stopped. In fact, the tailing car had left a pipe bomb at the inn, a bomb that, fortunately, the son of the inn's owner was able to defuse.

Although Maxwell did not know the specifics of the terrorist "job," and though he neither touched nor saw the bomb himself, he was nonetheless convicted of planting of an illegal bomb, on the grounds that Maxwell knew some form of terrorist action was afoot, and that he had played a significant role in guiding the bombers. Maxwell was criminally liable for the foreseeable acts of the group in which he participated, for when we act together, we individually bear responsibility for what we together bring about, within the scope of our common venture.

The logic of complicity is the logic of collective action more generally, and that logic pervades our social, ethical, and legal existence. It explains and justifies, I believe, much of the pride we take in our collective accomplishments, even when our own contributions lie at the insignificant margin. It explains the special importance we attach to the signal act of collective freedom, voting, an act whose individual causal significance is far outweighed by its costs.[42] In addition, it explains and justifies much of the shame and guilt we feel when the groups in which we live do wrong, even when we have been dissenting voices within. In all these cases, we begin with a group act and then derive and distribute the individual responsibilities thereof. Individual pride makes sense because of our participation in a collective accomplishment; the decision to vote makes sense because the collective selection of political authority is a necessary condition of freedom; our shame makes sense because the wrongs we do together are consequences of the collective systems and institutions to which we contribute.

Our individual responsibility for these collective acts is point one. Point two is that individual responsibility is not the same thing as collective responsibility. When I take pride in, say, my orchestra's brilliant performance, I do not regard myself as individually responsible for that brilliant performance. When I feel shame for my nation's prosecution of an unjust war, I do not regard myself as personally responsible for that war. Recognition of responsibility involves recognition that such responsibility is a relation in social space, one that links me in normative terms both horizontally to the other members of the group and vertically to those whom my group affects (or to the outcomes it produces). My response to, and responsibility for, what we together do is essentially mediated by membership in the group and grounded in my individual participation therein.

In considering the case of asymmetric, non-uniformed conflict, the logic of collective action both enables and disables an account of the combatants' privilege. As Rousseau saw, under modern conditions of politics, war is also something we do together, a normative relation we bear as a group to another group.[43] As an individual, I share the responsibility for the decision to go to war. But my responsibility as an individual is not identical to the responsibility of the group. My individual responsibility is, rather, a duty to serve if called and if the war is not clearly criminal, and to protest if it is criminal (and perhaps to refuse service as well). The fact that my nation is at war, not I, does not absolve me of responsibility towards my enemy, but it does create a normatively distinct relation between us, one structured through a set of rules specific to our interrelationship as individual members of warring nations in confrontation with one another. This is the logical space in which *jus in bello* can claim independence from *jus ad bellum*.

Specifically, the logic of collective action can make appropriate a limited scope for an essentially *political* permission to do violence, because when I do violence, I do it as a member of one group towards another. The privilege to kill as part of a collective is not a moral permission attaching to the individual soldier. A soldier who kills as part of an unjust war morally wrongs those he kills, and bears a share of responsibility for their deaths. But it does not follow that an enemy state can legitimately punish him, even if it can kill him in battle. Rousseau was right: the victorious state encounters the individual only accidentally: its essential normative relations are with the soldier's state, not with him. As Rousseau says, enemy soldiers confront each other as *defenders*.

Or as attackers, and there's the rub. The argument I have just given seems to me the best case for making *jus in bello* independent of *jus ad bellum*. But, as with Rousseau's argument, which it parallels, it requires an over-strong distinction between individual and collective responsibility. For it is plausible, particularly on a retributive theory, to say that the soldier who kills while prosecuting an unjust cause is fit for punishment.[44] After all, it is as an individual that he participates in the unjust war. A collective response to the enemy state does not preclude an individual response to the enemy soldier.

Perhaps this is the proper conclusion: collective decisions to go to war confer no individual immunity from punishment (for those participating in the collective).[45] When the injustice of the war is clear, so is the justice of prosecuting the aggressors in that war. There would be, of course, profound questions about the appropriate degrees of punishment given the range of pressures placed on individuals to fight, and difficult issues of post-punishment reintegration. But at the level of principle, there is not only conceptual room but conceptual pressure towards linking *jus ad bellum* to *jus in bello*. Nonetheless, there is another aspect of the collective nature of war that tells against drawing too tight a link between the individual and the state for which he fights. Wars, like many of history's uglier monuments, come to look very different in retrospect than they do in prospect. Many belligerent acts, like many violent revolutions, are easily condemned at the time but become praiseworthy in retrospect. This is because history happens in messy ways, and it involves a kind of normative mistake to apply ex post the same criteria that one applies ex ante.

To take some recent, albeit controversial, examples: Israel's 1981 preemptive destruction of Iraq's Osirak reactors seemed to be an outrageous violation of limits of aggression at the time and are viewed now as a prudent and regionally responsible intervention. NATO's Kosovo intervention, intensely debated at the time, now seems to be one of the alliance's finest moments. And if the US intervention in Iraq, which seems, a decade later, still to be a moral and practical disaster, should somehow nonetheless lead directly to a peaceful and democratic Middle East, then retrospective judgments will surely shift.

This does not just concern the difficulty of establishing uncontroverted criteria for assessing the justice of war. It is, rather, a point about the vulnerability of judgments of a war's justice to an analogue of what Bernard Williams called *moral luck*, and what we might call *political luck*.[46] Williams's example was the painter Paul Gauguin, who (in Williams's version) went to Tahiti to paint and, in so doing, abandoned his wife and children to poverty in Paris. According to Williams, if Gauguin's paintings had been aesthetic failures, then his trip would have been a moral failure. Since they were (at least stipulatively) aesthetic successes, however, his trip cannot be condemned in moral terms.

Williams's argument may not fully convince, for we might well come to a more complicated judgment: "Gauguin may be a louse, but he painted some beautiful pictures." In fact, Williams is fairly nonspecific about the normative consequences of the aesthetic triumph; he does not claim that the trip becomes morally justified, but only that condemning it is beside the point. In political and historical contexts, Williams's claim is amplified. Retrospectively we care less about the properties of actions and more about the possibilities and constraints inhering in the outcomes they produce. The immoralities of acts are swept with the economists' broom into the dustbin of sunk costs. Because politics is fundamentally about the question of what we together should do, its perspective is anchored in the now and moves forward, aggregating over collective interests and values. Conversely, its outcomes can only be assessed in retrospect, and that in the longer term.[47]

Criminal judgment also applies in retrospect, but the gap in time between act and judgment will usually be too short to accommodate vicissitudes in judgments of some wars' justice. The normative autonomy of the battlefield, at least for the great range of conflicts in which judgment might reasonably be thought to vary in time, might then be thought to reflect the gap between the immediately postwar assessment of individual battlefield conduct and the longer-term assessment of the war's justification. A war's justification might emerge *post bellum*, in the epistemological sense that while the warrant for military action might have been deeply controversial in advance—perhaps because facts on the ground were in dispute, as in a developing genocide—facts available after the war might render that initial judgment much less controversial. The Kosovo intervention might be an example of this phenomenon; and so, contrarily, might be the Iraq war. But this justification may only emerge long after the battles ended, and after prosecutions would have begun. More radically, the judgment of whether a war was warranted, made by victors or third-party tribunals, might end up turning on the cost of the war or the success of the postwar peace, with "good" but unjustified wars grounding immunity and costly but perhaps justified wars grounding prosecution. Given the likely vicissitudes of these essentially political and post hoc judgments, it would be unfair to punish line soldiers except in the cases of the most grossly unjust wars, such as extraterritorial genocide (when they would be liable anyway for war crimes or crimes against humanity). By contrast, the norms of proportionality and discrimination can be easily deployed in judging individual conduct, so the regulatory force of IHL is preserved.

In any event, the question of whether to expand combatancy's privilege to the non-uniformed can be resolved quickly and independently of resolving the precise scope of that privilege for the uniformed. On either of the accounts I have offered for the general combat privilege, the privilege is grounded in the relation of individual combatants to a collective decision to go to war. That relation is a matter of individuals' commitments to the collective: their mutual orientation around each other as fellow agents in a collective project. If an essentially intentional relation among individuals grounds the privilege, then the privilege ought logically to be extended to any who together constitute a collective at war, whether or not they are uniformed. Instrumental considerations of the sort canvassed above might tip the decision one way or another; but if those considerations are as indecisive as I argue, then there is no reason not to extend the combat privilege and a good reason to do so. Thus, something like the moderate regime of PI 44, requiring only open carriage of weapons in deployment and combat, can be justified as a matter of principle and defended as a matter of practice.

This conclusion may seem a bit quick, for it cannot be that any group of individuals, merely because they act as a group, can earn for themselves the privilege of combat. That would, obviously, be to erase the line between criminal law and the law of war, in favor of the latter. We do surely want a way to distinguish between the "Crime Story" gang and the "Rebel Story" partisans. What was implicit above needs to become explicit: only political groups engaged in violence in support of political goals, in the sense of aiming at creating (or restoring) a new collective ordering, can rightly claim the privilege.

Whether a group's violent acts count as political or as merely criminal turns principally on three factors: the existence (or not) of an internal ordering, the character of its aims, and its degree of success on the ground. The existence of internal order is necessary, because it is a legitimate condition of extending combat privileges to a group that it be itself capable of regulating its own conduct by the laws of war.[48] Groups on the verge of internal anarchy would thus fail to meet this condition. As to the second factor, the character of its aims, the substantive criteria of recognition created by the First Protocol—that groups be engaged in projects of national liberation or self-determination—mark an understandable starting point, albeit a contentious one. For liberation and self-determination are political aims and are prima facie the sort of causes that can justify violence if anything can; but so might also be disputes over regional autonomy or the flow of resources to particular regions, as with the Zapatistas, or struggles for religious or cultural autonomy, as with the Kurds. This criterion effectively excludes groups like the Columbian narco-trafficking groups that have sought and attained powers of territorial governance (and popular acquiescence), but only for the sake of securing their coca supply, not for the sake of political aims.

The third criterion, degree of success, is more problematic. The point of such a criterion is to recognize the practical need of state authorities to suppress disturbances to the peace that lack the legitimating force of broad popular support and thus to deny the privilege of war to groups

59

whose violence, however symbolically justified, can do nothing but create civil unrest. There is no sharp way to define such a criterion. In principle, popular support (however gauged) or territorial control might be the right guides. Such measures of success indicate that a group may be able to bargain effectively to achieve some of its goals, even if it cannot force concessions of all of them. In practice, only those groups that actually have popular support or territorial control will have the leverage necessary to force recognition, and such recognition might only come with time.

More abstractly, the success criterion recognizes that engaging in politics is not just a matter of positing wishes but one of creating a real, mutual social ordering.[49] This criterion makes the moral permission to fight dependent on nonmoral factors, so that rebels fighting clearly just but hopeless causes are subject to punishment. This is a hard position, for it denies the privilege to groups that might have had popular support but for the success of state terror. But it seems right. Occupations may be real usurpations of self-government, but if and when they bring civil order, any group opposing that order bears a large normative burden in justifying its resort to violence. The game may be worth the candle, but only if it is a winnable game at a tolerable human cost. A group engaged in violence but whose aims are part of no actual or reasonably possible system of social ordering engages not in politics but rather in a deadly solipsistic fantasy.[50]

It is a feature of this account, indeed a virtue, that whether a group of irregulars engaged in combat count as political, and are thus entitled to combat privileges, may change over time. In fact, the status of those captured may turn from criminal to POW as their colleagues find success in the fields and in the towns. (Such transformations of status happen anyway as a matter of negotiations between states and increasingly powerful insurgencies.) In any event, the importance of POW status for groups on the margin of criminality may be oversold. As a matter of practice, states will deny them that status until the groups are sufficiently powerful to demand it, whether or not the groups would be entitled to POW status as a matter of law. Since even lawful combatants may be held until the cessation of hostilities, which in civil or quasi-civil conflicts may be indefinite, and since they may also be interrogated exhaustively (but not punished for refusal to answer), the state loses little security by acknowledging combatant status. Moreover, since violations of the law of war can be punished among lawful and unlawful combatants alike, granting POW status hardly precludes prosecution for terrorist acts. In short, while expanding combat privileges to irregulars brings risks and disputed judgments, it may actually be less disruptive than the resisters fear, as well as more in consonance with the best case to be made for the categorical character of IHL norms.

3.7. THE LIMITS OF DEMOCRATIC RESPONSIBILITY

Where on the traditional view, "War Story" is the easy case and "Rebel Story" is the hard case, on my view, the situation reverses. The rebel Gray, although not a Petrostan army member, is a member of the group seeking Petrostan's liberation, a political goal. She has linked her will with theirs and so inhabits a common normative space, in pursuit of a paradigmatic political goal. That she wears no uniform is irrelevant to the collective aspect of her individual action; and it is the collective aspect that underwrites her privilege. Assuming she has obeyed the laws of war, she ought to be impunible.

Sergeant Blue's case is harder, because the question of his combat privilege now depends on whether the injustice of Imperioland's invasion is so great as to fall outside the scope of reasonable disagreement or reasonable retrospective reassessment of Imperioland's case for war. Given the bare facts I stipulated, this is unclear. An invasion to acquire another nation's resources looks clearly illegal, but the question becomes more complex for resources located near hastily drawn or colonially imposed borders, or when legitimate international disputes exist about access to those resources. So long as some of these factors are relevant to assessing Imperioland's case, it seems appropriate to defend a privilege for Blue as well. He may have acted badly, in moral terms, insofar as he took part in collective violence on grounds he knew or had reason to know were morally dubious, and the deaths he caused should sit uneasily on his conscience. The question of whether it is legitimate for Petrostan (or an international body) to punish him, however, is far more difficult.

Closer to home, my view entails that Taliban fighters and the foreign volunteer "Afghan Auxilliaries," whether or not they were garbed "distinctively," ought to have received lawful combatant status, assuming they displayed their weapons openly in conflict and respected IHL norms. The Taliban regime may have been unjust, but self-defense of even a wicked regime sits squarely within the scope of privilege for uniformed soldiers, and we have dispensed with the reasons for discriminating against the non-uniformed. So too, I think, combatant privileges could belong to members of Iraq's Baathist insurgency, provided again that they obey the rules of war. None of this turns on approving the regime they aim to install or defend, and it is fully consistent with punishing all humanitarian excesses. This is only to recognize that the claim to engage in the form of collective politics known as war belongs prima facie to all and can logically be withdrawn from each, uniformed or not.

Clearly, these cases pose difficult questions of policy, and controversy will inevitably remain for any set of legal rules that might apply to them. Seeing the law of war through the lens of the criminal law of complicity reveals an underlying logic of collective action that can make sense of both bodies of law. Further, seeing that logic in the special collective context of politics can help us understand a deeper rationale for the core of the law of war, the combatant privilege. More importantly, understanding war in terms of collective action forces us to reckon with the real individual responsibilities that come with participation in collective violence: relations of value that go beyond *dulce et decorum est pro patria mori*. (This is the topic of chapters 7 and 10.)

4

A MODEST CASE FOR SYMMETRY:
ARE SOLDIERS MORALLY EQUAL?

4.1. THE UNCOMMON COMMON SENSE OF WAR

The symmetry principle, which we have just examined in the context of irregular warfare, states that the normative permissions and restrictions binding co-combatants in a single conflict are identical. Each side, normatively, mirrors the other in how it may and may not fight, and in its respective postbellum liabilities to blame and punishment (assuming they both observe the restrictions). Historically, the symmetry principle is linked to, though not derived from, an "independence principle," which holds that the justifiability of a nation's engaging in war is independent of the permissions and restrictions binding its troops. Taken together, the symmetry and independence principles make up what might be called the common sense of the normativity of war, the independence of the *jus ad bellum* from the *jus in bello*.

Strange common sense! There is no easy case for symmetry in the laws of war. If death and destruction matter morally, as they do, and if reasons matter morally, as they do, then differences in combatants' reasons for bringing about deaths and destruction must matter morally. Since reasons are rarely symmetrical—indeed, it would take a philosopher's exertions to render them symmetrical in an example—the symmetry thesis would seem to require a fundamentally *arational* connection between reasons and normative permissions and restrictions. (This point holds, *a fortiori*, when there are differences in degrees of death and destruction brought.) To put it another way, the symmetry principle appears to hold that the fact that a combatant's nation has decided to go to war, for whatever reasons, is sufficient (and also necessary, under ancillary principles) to justify the combatant's acts of killing and destruction. Again, since killing and destruction ordinarily require very grave justifications, the symmetry principle seems not just anomalous but in contradiction with any rational aspirations of political morality. More specifically, the symmetry principle seems to flout what I have called the fundamental value of democratic legitimacy—indeed, to be vulnerable to a criticism insofar as it pays no special respect to democratic status.

So how can such a peculiar principle lie at the heart of the modern morality of war? One obvious answer would be to say that it does not. What truth there is in the symmetry principle comes not at the level of principle. At that level, it is surely and unproblematically false. Rather, the truth of the symmetry principle comes at the pragmatic level of institution and application. There are many reasons for thinking, in terms both of consequence and fairness, that the symmetry principle on the whole does more good over the long run than its denial. I will explore these in greater depth in section 4.3, but here is a brief summary. First, denying the symmetry principle risks opening the moral floodgates to any who think themselves justified in exceeding the standard range of permissions and restrictions, in virtue of the righteousness of their cause. Second, put positively, an institutionalized version of the symmetry principle, sustained by concerns of reciprocity, might well be better able to ratchet down war's violence to some significant degree than any attempt to institutionalize a more morally nuanced alternative. Third, the conditions for the fair infliction of punishment on soldiers indoctrinated by their nations, remade by their militaries into killers, and numbed by the general fog of war can simply not be met in anything but the most egregious cases, in which case liability for violation of the symmetrical restrictions on combat is likely to apply anyway.

I believe that the pragmatic case for symmetry is compelling, at the level at which institutions operate, including the institution of international humanitarian law (the law of armed conflict). For purposes of institutional design, critique, and justification, the reasons I explore in section 4.2 are enough to make the case. Yet the pragmatic case for symmetry ought to leave a bad taste in the philosophical mouth, for the reasons I sketched above: it elevates function over reason, means over end, and creates an entrenched normative structure that is fundamentally incoherent with the structures that govern our lives in the realm of private violence.

My object in section 4.4 is, therefore, to defuse the tension between the symmetry principle and the normative structures that govern private life. My strategy is to seek not a form of reconciliation between the two, for I believe that the normative principles governing war are genuinely incompatible with the principles governing private violence. It is, instead, to offer a modest form of skepticism about the role individualized normative principles can play in assessing conduct during wartime. The skepticism is modest, not thoroughgoing, in that I want to deny that anything goes in wartime, morally speaking. The further "common sense" of war—especially the fundamental principle that violence be employed with discrimination and proportionality—captures important moral constraints (even if further constraints might also be justified). But the view I shall try to defend is nonetheless truly skeptical: over a significant range of cases, claims about the permissibility of a combatant's actions have no truth value, hence no direct consequence for ascribing liability in those cases. Symmetry as it pertains to individual culpability is a consequence of this skepticism in the end, not a positive ethical doctrine. It takes its force independently of democratic thought, and needs insulation from its pressures.

4.2. CLARIFYING THE PROPOSALS

The conventional wisdom is that an institution of symmetrical combat privileges and constraints is an important, if not necessary, part of the success of contemporary humanitarian law. This is essentially a pragmatic, and consequentialist case for symmetry: whatever moral deficits symmetrical privileges exhibit, or moral costs they entail (in particular, the absence of punishment for combatants who kill in an unjust cause), they are justified by the net death and destruction they prevent.

In section 4.3, I argue that the conventional wisdom has a point, though enough empirical uncertainties remain that the case for symmetry cannot rest on pragmatic grounds alone. But before weighing into the normative argument about asymmetry, we should establish a more concrete context for discussion, so as to narrow the range of options to be considered. Asymmetry comes in different flavors, as does independence. In the abstract, any form of asymmetry can be alternatively described from one position or the other—for example, we can say that one party has greater privileges than the other, or that one party has fewer privileges. But, helping ourselves to a recent discussion by David Rodin, we can do better, by comparing each party's privileges to a stipulated, symmetrical baseline.[1] With a baseline defined, we can then distinguish forms of asymmetry in which one party's privileges are expanded above the baseline versus asymmetry in which one party's privileges are reduced below the baseline versus a dual asymmetry in which both are true.

What could this mean, more concretely? Assume the baseline represents the fundamental norms of the status quo, the symmetrical Hague-and-Geneva restrictions and privileges. This consists, roughly, of the following: First, combatants may intentionally target other combatants with impunity, while noncombatants may only be killed as a consequence of legitimate targeting and only in proportion to the military value of the target. Second, certain structures and institutions, such as hospitals, may not be targeted. Third, captured or surrendering combatants must not be tortured, killed, or otherwise treated inhumanely (nor, of course, may noncombatants). And fourth, certain weapons judged to cause indiscriminate suffering may not be used, principally dum-dum bullets and chemical and biological weapons; more controversially, nuclear weapons are probably also disproportionate in the suffering they cause to virtually any legitimate target.[2]

This baseline is, to a certain extent, morally arbitrary: it represents merely what nations have agreed to as a regime of normative control, not an ideal system. But its substantive claims need not enjoy a presumption of moral justification in order to serve as a basis for answering the incremental question of whether one, but not both, party to a conflict ought to enjoy greater or lesser privileges. This leaves open the question of ideal theory, whether both parties ought to be permitted substantially fewer (or, less plausibly, greater) privileges.[3] Plausibly expanded privileges would then include permission to use otherwise impermissible weapons or impunity for indiscriminate targeting, for intentional killing of civilians, for targeting protected structures, or for killing, torturing, or interrogating captured combatants. Restricted privileges, by contrast, might plausibly strip combatants of permission to kill at all, or to inflict any but the most narrowly tailored damage on noncombatants or protected structures, or to deny the use of otherwise permissible weapons, such as recourse to air power or incendiary weapons. No doubt other variations are possible, but these would seem the principal ones.

Simply describing the expanded-privilege form of asymmetry, against this baseline, is tantamount to discrediting it as an option. The intrinsic support for the status quo norms comes from a reaction to the special moral badness of violating those norms: the special wrong of deliberately killing noncombatants, or of increasing suffering beyond that necessary to gain a military advantage, or the special horrors of certain kinds of weapons. To paraphrase Thomas Nagel, no elaborate moral theory is needed to explain why each of these acts is wrong; the real demand on theory is to explain why any of the status quo–permitted acts of war are actually permissible.[4] Of course, if the baseline were set considerably lower—for example, forbidding all killing (as in the domestic context), or banning any use of weapons more powerful than swords and slingshots—expanded privileges might well make moral sense.[5] But the baseline is unlikely to shift in any significant way, except perhaps to eliminate certain weapons from the arsenal, such as cluster or fuel-air bombs. So the case for expanded privileges must be made in rougher terrain, against an already broad privilege to kill. Thus it could only be as a product of a highly consequentialist argument that expanded privileges could be defended—for instance (as was argued on behalf of the atomic bombings of Japan), on the grounds that increased privileges might end wars faster. Asymmetry would then be defended as a more efficient means to this end than simply allowing both sides to take the gloves fully off.

By contrast, reduced privileges are morally more attractive, simply in reducing the scope (or impunibility) of acts that, prima facie, are clearly undesirable. Under a policy of reduced privileges, either the reduced party will not engage in some acts of killing or destruction that it might have otherwise or it will engage in those acts, but its leaders or troops will be punished, thus at least producing justice—and possibly deterring some further parties downstream. The burden of argument here consists in showing why privileges should not be reduced symmetrically, since that would further reduce morally undesirable acts. Obvious arguments against symmetrically reduced privileges would rest either on consequentialist grounds (e.g., that the privilege to fight serves as an effective deterrent against aggression) or on deontological ones (that aggressed-against parties enjoy an entitlement to violence as self-defense). As above, symmetrical reduction is probably unrealistic, but its force in this context is to put argumentative pressure on the case for symmetric reduction. In effect, we must rank the three feasible proposals: status quo symmetry, revisionary asymmetric reduction, and revisionary symmetric reduction. If asymmetric reduction is to surmount the others, it will be on some combination of consequentialist arguments, coupled with principled arguments for the asymmetry. And so now I turn to the dimension of independence.

Consider now the dimension of independence, for the justification of the asymmetry might itself vary as well. Asymmetries might depend on the justice of one party's cause, as measured against some common baseline of assessment (e.g., concurrence with the UN Charter), or on the parties' relative military or technical capacity,[6] on their records of compliance in previous conflicts, on their capacity to maintain internal discipline or acceptance of *post bello* international tribunals to prosecute war crimes, or on some combination of all these grounds of dependence.

Some capacity-relative asymmetries are clearly plausible, such as the regime of Article 44 of Protocol I (API 44) to the Geneva Conventions, which permit combat privileges to non-uniformed, irregular forces, thus giving an asymmetric advantage of blending with the civilian population to one party to internal conflicts. While API 44 has been rejected by a number of important participants in the law-formation enterprise, including the United States, it describes a plausible legal regime.[7] Other asymmetries are perhaps less realistic, such as relativizing permissible collateral damage to specific-targeting capacity, thus giving states with "smart bombs" less leeway as a matter of law than states with more indiscriminate technology. While imaginable, the limited stocks of such weapons would be grist for the advanced state's argument that judgments of military necessity governing the rationing of scarce resources must control when it deploys precision weaponry, not humanitarian concerns alone. While a powerful state that chooses less rather than more discriminatory weaponry in a particular attack might be subject to political criticism (and might well vet its targeting decisions with military lawyers, as some states currently do), it is hard to imagine effective control of these choices through an external, international system.

By contrast, the most straightforward form of dependence would be grounded on the legality or extralegal justification of one position to a conflict. While symmetry independent of justice is deeply entrenched under the status quo, pressure towards asymmetry can seem plausible. Imagine, for example, that contemporary France sends a battalion across the border to Germany, in a brazen and unprovoked attempt to seize Saarbrücken by force. While, formally speaking, the French soldiers if captured would be entitled to POW status, such an act by one democratic state with a volunteer army might well, by dint of international outrage, entail punishment for individual French soldiers. (I will discuss this example, as a limit on the argument for symmetry, later in section 4.4.) Since there already exists an international justice system with the capacity to address questions of the justification of a state's acts of war, such a form of dependence would be far easier to administer than capacity-relative bases.

Taking these points in combination, the most plausible form of asymmetry is one in which either the privilege of combat itself or the use of even moderately discriminatory weapons is withdrawn from one party's troops, on the basis of an assessment of the justice of that party's cause. Alternatively, a very modest form of asymmetry on such a basis might leave legal entitlements as they are but release the moral sentiments and underwrite findings of moral culpability on the part of wrongful combatants. But it is asymmetry with institutional consequences that is the focus of contemporary debate. Most concretely, then, the question is whether we would be justified in shifting from the current regime of general impunibility within wide constraints, to a regime of individualized punishment for acts of violence found to be unjustified by the *jus ad bellum*. Ideally, both findings and punishment would be meted out in a neutral, international forum; but there is every reason to expect that countries would help themselves to asymmetrical justice during the course of a conflict, and perhaps even postconflict, in defiance of a neutral arbiter.

4.3. THE PRAGMATIC CASE FOR SYMMETRY

The foregoing fixes the context for discussion. The pragmatic case for symmetry must be made against its likeliest rival, a system of justice-based *in bello* privileges backed up primarily by first-person threats of reprisals. The pragmatic case consists of two parts. First, while asymmetry of the form just defined is institutionally *possible*, it is less likely to form part of a stable set of reciprocal institutions than symmetrical principles. Given the overwhelming pragmatic interest in a stable, violence-reducing institution, the platform of symmetrical rules has a clear advantage over its alternatives. The second pragmatic case is more specific to the question of the punibility of individual line soldiers. Given first-party enforcement, there is no reason to think that the range of mitigating circumstances and potential defenses that ought to be available to soldier "defendants" would play the role necessary to justify the infliction of punishment. Even given an idealized regime of neutral, third-party enforcement (as by an international tribunal), it is highly unlikely that the institutional conditions of justified punishment could be met. These arguments are all pragmatic, insofar as they are consistent with the possibility that, but for these practical considerations, a system of asymmetry would be morally preferable.

As I suggested above, any regime governing combatant privileges will essentially depend on first-person policing by the parties in conflict. Although the International Criminal Court portends the possibility of effective, neutral, third-party enforcement, its role will necessarily be limited at best to the postbellum stage. Instead, for the foreseeable future, during conflicts, restrictions and privileges will be enforced against captive soldiers, vulnerable civilians, and civilian property. This basic fact has important consequences for the structure of combat restrictions. The absence of third-party enforcement means that the combat regime must be sustained, essentially, by reciprocity between two parties in massive conflict, with only a limited degree of overlap in interests. And that reciprocity in turn depends, I will argue, on symmetry.

The pressure for symmetrical rules looms in the background of the laws of war, if their central function is identified first with making some difference in war's savagery, and only secondarily in attuning the evils of war to the wrongs of the parties. Parties at war operate in a context of fear. But this fear comes in different degrees. The first degree is the fear that the enemy will inflict particular losses on one's own soldiers, civilians, and the like. This fear gives specific contours to the tactical environment, for it establishes the conditions under which risking offensive or defensive moves make sense. But there is a second degree of fear as well: the fear that war will go total, that the killing and destruction will overrun even the limited degrees of confinement that the law of war provides. The second fear compounds risk into uncertainty, for in total war, parties may find themselves forced to fight to the point of destruction rather than strategic surrender, and that point is virtually always unpredictable.

The first degree of fear is generally asymmetrical, since parties have different interests in prosecuting their wars and fear their loss differently— for instance, territorial expansion versus dissolution. The *jus ad bellum* is also asymmetrical: an interest in territorial expansion has negative value under the *jus ad bellum*, while an interest in self-defense has great value, and all the greater as the risks rise. Hence a regime of rules keyed to these first-order fears would take asymmetrical shape. But the second, existential degree of fear is shared symmetrically: both sides have reason to fear their destruction, and their destruction matters to them equally, insofar as it matters as much as anything can matter. The rules of war, secured by some plausible system of enforcement, are the response to this essentially Hobbesian situation. The logic of the symmetrical, underlying interest against destruction leads to a uniform set of rules, whose function is to stave off total war. Thus, for example, the basic rules of POW status are aimed at preventing a retaliatory bloodbath of prisoners; the rules of discrimination and proportionality, likewise, protect against the annihilation of an enemy state's citizens.

This point hardly decides the matter, for it principally restates the status quo regime of symmetry. And it is consistent in principle with a more ambitious regime, which aims both to (symmetrically) reduce the prospect of total war while (asymmetrically) tying privileges to justice. But the basic symmetrical function of the law of war is important, because if an asymmetrical regime were to compromise the capacity of the law of war to fend off disaster, then that would be a very grave cost indeed. As I now want to argue, the cost of an asymmetrical set of privileges is, in fact, to threaten the reciprocal foundations of the principal symmetrical goal of catastrophe avoidance. What follows is speculative, but if the risks are high enough, then the case for asymmetry is much weakened.

The success of a first-party-based enforcement system is a matter of the effectiveness of one party's sanction (or threat of sanction) in bringing the other party to heel, resulting in an equilibrium of observance rather than an escalation of mutual defection. First-party sanctions can do this when the sanctions are significant enough to motivate compliance, yet not so significant that they motivate retaliation (or general defection from the regime). And this, in turn, depends on the parties' viewing the sanctions as a stable and roughly proportionate measure of harm in relation to the underlying wrong. At best, parties view the regime as a normatively attractive system of mutual governance, for which enforcement serves primarily to provide assurance. At worst (but still in equilibrium), parties view the regime as a classic modus vivendi, stabilized by fear of the worse consequences of breakout. There is reason to think that the modern regime of *jus in bello* hovers between the two, with some progress, at least in training programs, from modus vivendi to normative acceptance. (The difficult and destabilizing *in bello* questions associated with drone warfare are the subject of chapter 10.)

The question, therefore, is how either a modus vivendi or a normative acceptance might best be sustained. I want to suggest that, whatever the abstract normative attractiveness of asymmetry, purely symmetrical regimes have much greater prospects for stabilizing cooperation. The reason is salience, that is, a subjective sense of fittingness: with symmetrical rules, parties share a common standard both for judging deviation and for exacting penalties. With salience comes both predictability (what sanction will be inflicted in the future, for what infraction) and normative resonance (a sense of the fittingness of the sanction). With asymmetrical rules, by contrast, with parties inflicting either identical or different sanctions for (by hypothesis) different infractions, judgments of inappropriateness are more likely. And if sanctions are judged inapt, then the regime destabilizes, and we reach the worst outcome: constraint by no rules at all.

An example may help. Suppose Franconia and Desmonia are at war, with Franconia deemed the aggressor under the *jus ad bellum*. Under a symmetrical regime, both parties' fighters have limited privileges to kill, cashed out in terms of protected POW status in case of capture; and both parties' noncombatants are immune from deliberate assault. Say Desmonia is considering killing, torturing, or punishing Franconian POWs. If its leaders are rational, they must do so in the awareness that Desmonia's violations will result in a reprisal by Franconia. If Franconia is rational, it will seek to provide a basis for Desmonia's expectation. In particular, Franconia will need to project a willingness to inflict a reprisal calculated to price out any further infractions without eliminating all motivation for future compliance.

This means that Franconia must have a metric for establishing commensurability, and individual POWs will perform this role quite nicely. It can calibrate its reprisal in terms of the number of Desmonia's own violations, plus some "kicker." Since these reprisals are not otherwise permitted by the symmetrical regime, they are salient both in quality—a distinctive sanction, as opposed to an ordinary act of war—and in quantity. Since the metric of individual POWs is common across the two, Desmonia will recognize that this is the standard Franconia will use, and if all goes well, the threat of reprisals will dampen the likelihood of future infractions by the other side. A similar story can be told about noncombatant deaths as well.[8]

Now contrast asymmetry. Under the most radical asymmetric proposal, the combatants of unjust parties would enjoy no combat privileges, and though presumably they would be protected (symmetrically) from torture or extrajudicial execution, they would be fully vulnerable to the capturing party's domestic criminal law (which might include capital punishment). Franconia might still retaliate for Desmonia's lawful acts (unless its leaders are deterred by the slim prospect of postbellum punishment, since this would be a clearly unlawful reprisal), and it might seek to do so in the same measure as Desmonia. This threat might have the effect of deterring Desmonia's acts of (lawful) punishment, but it is at best undesirable normatively, since Desmonia is, by hypothesis, entitled to punish while Franconia is not, and at worst highly destructive, since whether or not Desmonia complies, its motive would be fully independent of the legal regime. Rather than supporting the *in bello* regime, Franconia's threats would be bypassing it. This would dramatically reduce the likelihood that the regime would guide Desmonia's future acts, or the acts of any other states for that matter. On the other side, if Franconia is considering violating the more restrictive rules binding it—for instance, by punishing Desmonian captives—it will realize that Desmonia is normatively unlimited in the comparable retaliation it can exact. Franconia therefore has no reason to think Desmonia will limit its retaliation with an eye to restoring the effectiveness of the legal regime—and at this point, any incentive to comply with the regime evaporates on both sides. Thus, from both perspectives, the lack of a shared set of rules undermines the capacity of the enforcement regime to generate pressure for further compliance.

The problem of enforceability ex post, after derogation, represents one face of the practical limits of asymmetry. If asymmetrical rules cannot be enforced without excessive risks of destabilization, then they cannot be justified. But the problem is not merely ex post; it is also ex ante. Would asymmetrical rules be accepted by parties abstracted from a particular conflict, and from its particular grievances and ambitions? The question implicates the basic fairness of an asymmetric regime as well as my concern here: whether, in actual fact, such a regime could endure. For a regime no one could reasonably endorse in advance would likely not last long even if imposed.

Rodin pursues the ex ante point in an instructive manner. Following John Rawls, he argues that we can effectively replicate genuinely fair-minded discussion of common rules by imagining that the parties to the discussion are bargaining out of self-interest (i.e., without any strongly moralized goal), but in ignorance of their own identity or particular advantages.[9] The rules resulting from this artificial choice situation, called the "Original Position," can be considered justified, insofar as they reflect a free and fair choice situation. Rawls famously argues that parties in the Original Position seeking common rules to govern extensive and long-term social interaction would choose a combination of symmetrical and asymmetrical rules. First, they would seek to guarantee an equal and maximally extensive scheme of liberties and rights. Second (and most controversially), they would ensure that any inequalities of income and basic goods serve to maximize the position of the worst-off in society, such that any more (or less) equal distribution of income and goods would leave the worst-off in society even worse off in absolute terms. Hence, income and wealth distribution would be asymmetric in two respects: in actual holdings (or expected holdings), some are better off than the mean, while the justification for the unequal holdings asymmetrically emphasizes the status of the least well off. This second principle is known as the "Difference Principle."

Rodin, too, suggests that Original Position reasoning in the context of *jus in bello* theory would lead to a mix of symmetric and asymmetric rules. He argues that parties would agree to hold the line on the restrictions extended under the current regime, thus symmetrically protecting noncombatants from direct targeting or disproportionate collateral violence. To put it another way, parties would reject one plausible form of asymmetry: increased privileges, or latitude in combat, for one party to a conflict—presumably the party fighting for a just cause. (In Rodin's terms, mentioned above, they would reject above-the-line asymmetry.) Rodin argues, very plausibly, that parties aware of the evident fact that many (if not most) participants in war are likely to wrongly believe their cause is just, will therefore fear that asymmetrically increased permissions will redound to their detriment, with little offsetting advantage. Among other things, if one party acts on a sense of extraordinary entitlement while the other party also regards its cause as just, each will regard itself as entitled to the increased permissions, thus aggravating the apparent injustice in the eyes of the other. War's violence quickly spirals even higher. Thus, an asymmetrically increased permission regime would tend to increase the risks to both parties, without any compensating advantage.

But Rodin does think parties in the Original Position would choose asymmetry in a different respect: they would opt for an asymmetrically *contracted* permission for unjust combatants. As above, this would leave in place the basic protections humanitarian law gives noncombatants, plus some, but would contract the permission of unjust combatants to kill even other combatants. Rodin's reasoning is simple: if unjust combatants (typically aggressors) might suffer institutionally from an asymmetric regime, then states contemplating aggression may find themselves deterred, or at least have greater difficulty finding forces willing to risk both combat and post-combat trial. Thus, asymmetric restriction will tend to dampen violence, reducing the general ex ante incidence of risk to all parties in the Original Position. Parties contemplating the possibility of themselves as just defenders will take comfort in this, as will parties contemplating themselves as aggressors mistaken about the justice of their cause, who need deterrence from themselves. Only parties contemplating themselves as unjust aggressors would fail to benefit, by this reasoning—and their complaints cannot register in a process of deriving fair principles. Thus, asymmetric restriction would redound to the benefit of those disadvantaged by either attack or ignorance. A similar line of reasoning would follow for Rodin's other suggested form of asymmetry, in access to certain war technologies, which would also reduce the total level of violence.

The parallel to Rawls's argument thus seems firm, and a good case for ex ante asymmetry made. But there is a crucial point of divergence. Rawls argues for the asymmetric Difference Principle not only from the ex ante Original Position but also from its contribution to social stability outside the Original Position.[10] According to Rawls, the Difference Principle minimizes the "strains of commitment": the difficulties, parties might have ex post in living up to the demands of the principles they endorsed ex ante and, more generally, in maintaining a commitment to productive social interaction.[11] The strains of commitment loom large, since principles are being chosen to regulate an enormous breadth of social and political interaction over indefinitely many generations. Rawls argues that the Difference Principle can be shown to be superior to what he regards as its closest competitor, a distribution dictated by average utility. Under the Difference Principle, those at the bottom of the distribution can recognize that any more egalitarian distribution would leave them worse off. While those at the top end could resent the fact that the inequalities are not even greater, they can take comfort in both their absolute and relative positions, in the form of social insurance provided by the Difference Principle, should their fortunes turn, and of course in the fairness from all points of view of the principle itself. By contrast, a utilitarian distribution leaves winners happy, but losers wondering why they should take a hit either for the sake of the abstraction of average utility, or for the sake of those at the top end. On this account, utilitarian policies would breed resentment, ultimately stagnating or unraveling.

Since a chief advantage of Rawls's asymmetric principle is its tendency to stabilize extensive social and economic cooperation over generations, we might already wonder whether the ex ante Original Position argument is an apt method for the quite different situation of occasional "partners" to the enterprise of war. Considerations of intrinsic fairness surely matter less, in reflective equilibrium; and given a presumed general background of social noncooperation, the strains of commitment are likely to be higher in any case. Parties to war, in effect, are already committed to working out their problems without recourse to a common set of rules. If rules regulating interests they do have in common (treatment of POWs, treatment of noncombatants) are to be effective, they must be effective against that background of nonreciprocity. But asymmetric rules would seem much less effective than their symmetric counterparts outside the Original Position, not just for the reasons I mentioned above, namely the difficulty of their implementation, but because they would be seen as fundamentally unfair or unfounded once the veil of ignorance is lifted.

Now, it is an important part of Rodin's case that the asymmetric regime comes equipped with a fair and thorough third-party enforcement scheme, since parties in the Original Position would clearly prefer that to first-party enforcement. Under first-party enforcement, it is quite clear that the regime would collapse, for each side, regarding itself as just, would also regard itself as entitled to punish any prisoners it takes, for violating the laws of war. Since each side can expect this of the other, mutual punishment of the other's combatants will dominate. Conceivably, this prospect would have a dampening effect on the general incidence of war; but in an actual conflict, either the humanitarian protections achieved under symmetrical rules for POW status would be lost or the parties would bargain ex post around their ex ante regime and arrive at symmetry. Thus, with first-party enforcement, asymmetry would not long survive the strains of commitment.

Under Rodin's ideal regime of third-party enforcement, the result is similar. Return to the war between Franconia and Desmonia, and again assume that deterrence has failed. If Desmonia thinks it is at risk of having its position deemed unjust under the *jus ad bellum*, then it will expect that Franconia will hold its Desmonian captives as pretrial prisoners, waiting to hand them over to the tribunal. But what happens to those prisoners will be a matter of uncertainty. If Desmonia wins the war, then it may be able to secure their release directly, as a condition of Franconia's surrender. If it thinks it might lose the war, it might be able to secure better terms by threatening Franconian POWs with complementary punishment. Since Desmonia gains nothing in this conflict from observing the rules of asymmetry, it will, as suggested above, attempt to position itself to bargain back to symmetry. It need not commit grave war crimes to do so, but need only threaten to hold its captives to a symmetrical standard. The basic notion of hostage exchange, which underwrites the current symmetrical regime, is an equilibrium point that operates whatever the nominal legal regime. Even if threatening foreign POWs with trial constitutes a war crime, since Desmonia's leaders are already on the hook for violations of the *jus ad bellum*, there is likely to be little marginal deterrence effect from further prosecutions, and some potential benefit.

Moreover, assuming Desmonia does not torture or kill Franconia's prisoners, it has little reason to fear echoes of its breach in future conflicts. If its position is just in the future, then its combatants will be privileged; and if its position is unjust, then future combatants will be subject to the same risk of punishment, in which case the logic of the current situation will unfold again. And since Franconia realizes all this, it recognizes that the third-party enforcement scheme will count for little. Thus, since both parties fear what will happen now to their soldiers held by the other, and because this fear is more salient (and predictable) than fears of consequences meted out by a postconflict tribunal, both parties have reason to revise whatever rules they might have adopted ex ante. The system may not collapse into anarchy, but the asymmetrical regime is unlikely to survive actual practice. Unlike the asymmetry of distributive justice, the pressures of actual conflict undermine rather than stabilize the regime. Since this ex post speculation is available in the Original Position, there is little prospect that asymmetry would be adopted at all.

4.4. THE SKEPTICAL CASE FOR SYMMETRY

I have argued so far that even if asymmetrical rules were favored in principle, they would fail in practice. Because asymmetrical regimes would probably lack a common basis for measuring both the degree of defection and the appropriate response, parties to the regime would tend to overpunish defections. And since this fact would be common knowledge, the efficacy of the regime would be undermined by the very attempt to enforce it, at least through the self-help methods of enforcement that have dominated the law of war for centuries. But the practical problems go deeper still: because all rational pressure is in the direction of destabilizing asymmetry, no one would adopt such rules ex ante—even if, in the abstract, an asymmetrical regime would be preferred as a matter of justice. Excessive strains of commitment mean that asymmetry would never be adopted in the first place, notwithstanding its independent merits.

I now turn to question the principled case for asymmetry, with which I began this essay. I began with the observation that symmetry in the *jus in bello* seems arational, because the normative considerations that determine the justice of the war are withheld from determining the overall normative status of those actually fighting the war. Here, I want to argue that symmetry is less irrational, as a matter of principle, than it might appear. Or, put positively, a symmetrical regime of privileges reflects the fact that the normative considerations governing the *jus ad bellum* substantially underdetermine the normative status of individuals. Thus, skepticism rather than moral clarity offers the best support for symmetry.

Skepticism matters because the normative context is one of ascribing institutional forms of responsibility to individuals—adding punishment to the already long list of war's evils. The asymmetrical regimes I described above all attempt to limit combat privileges through deterrence, by punishing those who violate the terms of the regime, punishing wrongful killing in unjust wars ex post, or both. For reasons familiar to anyone who has taken a tour through theories of just punishment, serious punishments demand clear criteria of application. On a retributive theory, just punishment demands a clear index of proportionality criteria of fairness, which requires clarity on both the gravity of the wrong that justifies the punishment, as well as the gravity of the punishment itself. On a deterrence theory, there needs to be a well-established behavioral mechanism that translates threats into behaviors, which means in turn that the likelihood of the threat and its severity must be clearly communicated to potential offenders. (Of course, retributivists also require fair notice to potential offenders for intrinsic reasons.) And for anyone committed to some account of fairness in the distribution of punishment, considerations of horizontal equity (who, among the whole class of offenders, actually receives punishment?), and of an overall weighing of the benefits of a punishment system against its human costs, will matter decisively.

In domestic systems of punishment, the requisite clarity is found in the classic, fully voluntary, individually committed *mala in se* offenses: the crimes of violence, basic forms of property destruction or appropriation. Outside this core, the moral justification of institutions of punishment decays quickly. Debates over the appropriate punishment of remote co-conspirators or accomplices fill the law books, as do debates about the thresholds and limits of duress excuses and about the requisite levels of legal knowledge for regulatory offenses. The legitimacy of modern punishment regimes, which extend serious liability far into networks of complicity, and within complex systems of social regulation, comes seriously into doubt under these pressures.

In the law of war, the clear core of liability is occupied by the crimes against humanity. Here, notice is clear, and the severity of the wrongs is a matter of firm and virtually universal moral judgment. But the case of liability for line soldiers is far more like the disputed territory in the domestic context than like liability for crimes against humanity. Other scholars have nicely explored the fraught issues of duress and mistake as they apply to line soldiers.[12] It should also be noted that, given the fog of war and the organizational complexity of the enterprise, most combatants would have to be charged as accomplices in murder rather than as direct perpetrators. (This is not only a question of distinguishing the successful killer from the soldier who fails to get off a shot, but of distinguishing both from the non-weapons-carrying support personnel.) As I have argued at length elsewhere, while a basic judgment of moral responsibility for accomplices is well justified, there are serious problems in defending a particular schedule of punishment.[13]

But it is perhaps the special issue of just punishment for regulatory infraction that presents the most pressing issue. For while the immediate crime at issue is murder (or property destruction), the normative framework in which the killings occur bears many of the marks of a complex regulatory regime subject to constant political renegotiation. The consequence is that combatant liability looks more like the show trial of aggressive accountants during a national change in economic mood than like the dispensation of justice to clear malefactors. To the extent that the background normative framework of aggression is a matter of changing expectations, hence uncertainties, the justification for liability erodes. And that is a very great extent indeed, for at least two additional reasons. First, the abstract justification of state violence is highly dependent upon the identity of the actors and the issues at stake. Institutionalized rules, such as the UN Charter, cannot reduce the context dependence enough to establish warrant for individual liability. And second, particular justifications of state violence, or—better—of the appropriateness of third-party response, display a relativity to the success of the military adventure. Combined with the difficulties of allocating institutionalized forms of liability across and within complex organizations, I conclude that there are simply not enough normative facts to underwrite liability. Hence there is no justifiable form that an institutionalized system of asymmetrically restricted privileges could take.

Let me spell this out in slightly more detail. Idealists in international relations have moved the normative standards regulating war from a fully realistic baseline, according to which warfare is a costly but normal form of interstate politics, to a form of self-help limited to imminent self-defense, as enshrined in Article 51 of the UN Charter, with a possible current exception for third-party interventions to halt genocide or other crimes against humanity. State practice has, however, varied quite dramatically from the Charter's norms. This is in part a function of the political and military capacity of the United States to set its own normative criteria for when it will deploy force, and in part a function of the limited international resources available to police or deter conflicts that fail to meet Charter standards. And it reflects the incapacity of many states, not otherwise tied to each other through relations of cultural or economic interdependence, to find means of dispute resolution that are more beneficial, or less costly, in their own domestic terms, than recourse to war. The UN Charter represents an attractive centering point for diplomacy. Morally speaking, as well, its narrowing of the window of permissible state violence can only be applauded.

I do not wish to gainsay any of the legal or moral critiques made of state resort to violence. But since actual state practice lies so far from the terms of the charter, one can only conclude that states are unwilling to treat the moral and legal considerations contained in the UN Charter, or other customary forms of the *jus ad bellum*, as fully decisive as a political matter. And it is this political judgment, reflected in states' unwillingness to commit political and military capital to the project of fully realizing the Charter's ideals, that matters for the purpose of legitimating individual liability. In narrow terms, the lack of actual consensus on the wrongfulness of many military adventures means that inflicting punishment on one set of soldiers threatens enormous unfairness in the nonpunishment of other combatants.[14] In deeper terms, lack of consensus on the wrongfulness of war in many cases entails lack of consensus on the wrongfulness of individual acts of combat.

Related to this is a second consideration I advanced in chapter 3, that success may, ex post, rewrite the norms of permissible warfare. In part, this is just a corollary to the point above: one of the contextual factors affecting the political assessment of war's costs is the history of the success of certain types of war in achieving desired aims. But I think the point runs somewhat deeper as well. The practice of politics, as well as the ethics of politics, is a matter of withholding certain forms of moral judgment (and sanction) when such judgments would otherwise preclude peaceful coexistence.[15] In domestic terms, this practice, and the related attitude of withheld judgment (or unacted-upon judgment), constitutes the paradigmatically modern institution of toleration; and it also, and relatedly, sustains the public-private distinction central to modern liberalism. Internationally, the practice underwrites the tendency (selective or hypocritical, according to your preference) of third parties with the capacity to intervene but no local interests at stake to turn a blind eye to other states' violations. Retaliatory or warning strikes that are strictly illegal under the Charter are given a bye, so long as they are viewed as not exceptionally destabilizing, or perhaps even stabilizing—Israel's 1981 strike on the Osirak reactor being the case in point.

I do not mean to claim that formal criteria of legality, or informal criteria of morality, themselves change ex post.[16] I only mean to claim that political judgments vary with success, and with a range of other factors. Nor is this (I hope) a simple confusion between the "oughts" of international political morality and the "ises" of international politics. Punishment is itself a political practice, and its legitimacy depends on the legitimacy of the institution inflicting it. Political legitimacy is a matter of more than moral truth. Political legitimacy depends, among other things, on the transparency of the criteria with which power is exercised, and the potential acceptability of the reasons offered by political actors to those against whom power is exercised.[17] If the political criteria for just war are unsettled, or at least unsettled at the time punishment would be inflicted, then the punishment itself is illegitimate.

I also acknowledge that there might be clear enough cases of unjust war—analogues to crimes against humanity—that asymmetrical punishment of combatants can be justified. I adverted earlier to the fanciful example of France now invading Germany to seize Saarbrücken, in the absence of any diplomatic overtures. Given the political relations between the two, the common knowledge among all European citizens of the possibilities of diplomatic resolution, and putting aside the Geneva Conventions, one can imagine the international community punishing France's soldiers without obvious injustice to those soldiers. But such clear cases will be rare—so rare that it is hard to imagine any serious attempt by international actors to amend the third Geneva Convention to exclude such cases from the symmetry regime.

Rather, by removing punishment of combatants from the table, and reserving punishment of national leaders for only the most egregious cases, the current regime obtains legitimacy through the modesty of its efforts. This is not high praise, and there is surely room for political practice to hew more closely to the legal and moral lines that have been drawn. This is, in effect, legitimacy by default, and legitimacy can be weakened by underexertion as well as by overexertion. But overall, symmetry represents a bracketing of certain moral questions about war, and a concession to the worry that overly punitive criteria defined in a particular conflict will come back to bite in future cases. If state actors are unwilling to retire violence as a central technique in their repertoire, there is something untoward about philosophers insisting that line soldiers nonetheless bear the full price of abstract ideals.

4.5. FEARFUL SKEPTICISM, FEARFUL SYMMETRY

I have argued that the law of war generally is grounded in fear: fear of war's violence and fear of the fragility of any regulatory regime attempting to restrain that violence. Total war, whose nightmarish form is not merely a nightmare, lurks in the background. As Judith Shklar famously counseled political theorists to look more to liberalism's promise in limiting cruelty than to its aspirations to complete justice, so international theorists should look—and have done so—to humanitarian law's promise in reducing fear, rather than pressing upon it headier ideals and aspirations.[18]

The argument for asymmetry is an argument from ideals, not from fear. But mutual fear of escalation undermines the prospect of enforcing a regime of asymmetry. Fear's usefulness in moving states to alternative regimes undermines the likelihood of asymmetry's survival as a governing regime. And—perhaps to overstretch the theme—state fear of relinquishing violence as a tool of international politics means that the conditions for justifying individual punishment can rarely be met.

There is room for asymmetry in our moral judgments, and in our aspirations for state practice and international institutions. By definition, nations in the wrong should not be at war; and if they should not, their soldiers should not either. Establishing consensus on the (actually accepted) limits to war's justification would do a great deal more to limit fear, whether or not systems of asymmetric privilege are ever institutionalized. For that matter, philosophical debate about the moral privileges of the individual combatant, detached from institutional questions of punishment, can serve to clarify fundamental questions of the relations of citizens to their states. But symmetry as practice is here to stay, grounded in an effective if uninspiring mix of doubt and fear.

5

LEADERS AND THE GAMBLES OF WAR: AGAINST POLITICAL LUCK

But what awaits us tomorrow? A hundred million of the most diverse contingencies, which will determine on the instant whether they run or we do; whether one man is killed and then another; but all that's being done now is mere child's play.

—PRINCE ANDREI TO TIMOHIN, *War and Peace*[1]

5.1. THE UBIQUITY OF LUCK

The previous two chapters raised the issue of how to make sense of the principle of symmetry at the heart of the war convention, with respect to the *jus in bello*. The symmetry principle seemed paradoxical, because it seems to entail that the justice of killing in war is entirely independent of the justice of being at war. This seems, quite clearly, to let the tail wag the dog of justification. The response I offered is that the strongest reasons for restraint and impunity in how we fight wars must come from a much thinner morality of consequence than from the richer resources of democratic principle.

We may raise a version of the same question about the *jus ad bellum*, the justification of war. Historically, war has served as a dispute mechanism, useful for when both sides claim right in, say, a matter of disputed territory. Hugo Grotius was emphatic that while peaceful resolution is to be preferred in international disputes, in good-faith cases a decision for war can be just on both sides, and therefore the conflict can serve as a means of administering justice.[2] This position, part of the tradition of regular war, allows for outcomes to play an ex post facto role in justification—and that is peculiar. For one might think that justice is a matter of the alignment of facts on the ground with the good and the right. Justice is therefore not, in principle, a matter of luck. Yet war is, as Clausewitz famously said, politics by other means. And politics is permeated by luck. Political action is messy by nature, involving the intersecting lives and acts of many people and institutions. As a consequence, policy initiatives and political gambits succeed or fail not simply on the basis of good intentions and wise planning but because of the myriad contingencies that affect any large-scale endeavor. A strong rain in a swing state can affect the turnout of one set of partisans rather than another at an election. International crises determine the options open to political leaders. Domestic policy reform succeeds or fails because chance alignments of interests and judgments of public sentiment either provide the force to drive past obstacles or make those obstacles impassable. And, more controversially, a general's head cold might cause misjudgments at a crucial battle, leading to the end of an empire rather than its extension.

To say that politics, then, is a domain of luck is to state a triviality. Politics is a branch of life, and like all life it is inhabited by fleeting contingency as much as (or more than) inevitability. But politics is not just impersonal poll results, military successes, and policy changes. Politics is an activity of persons—persons with moral concerns and moral character—and it is impelled and sustained by their concern for their values, goals, and reputations. To speak of political luck in relation to political agency is not just to point in the direction of the contingency of outcome, or *fortuna*, to use Machiavelli's famous term, but in the direction of evaluation, of both the outcomes and the agents who produce them. Politicians who insist, despite the disastrous news of the day, that they shall be vindicated by history, gesture hopefully in this direction, that a lucky outcome will save their legacy; whereas the losers of history seem already to have received luck's judgment. To return to Machiavelli, the question is not just whether a politician's *virtù*, or skill, can dominate *fortuna*, but whether *fortuna*, for its part, can determine *virtù*.

And yet here we seem back to a triviality. Of course, the politician's hopes and fears are well-founded. As a matter of brute fact, we heap rewards on the lucky winners of historical gambles (if only posthumously) and scorn on the losers. Some of these rewards and punishments are as direct as triumphal laurels and ritual humiliations. But they also take subtler form, through a form of cognitive error: the overattribution of success or failure to the inherent qualities and aptitudes of the actor, rather than to the situation. While Napoleon may be no hero to his valet, his heroism in the eyes of the many confounds success with virtue.

These observations about our social practices and biases in awarding political honor and disgrace—in reflecting political luck, in this thin sense—mirror our practices in interpersonal morality. The twin papers by

Bernard Williams and Thomas Nagel that launched the discussion of luck in morality can be seen as trying to extract strong normative conclusions from these sociological commonplaces, moving from the *is* of moral psychology to the *ought* of moral evaluation. In particular, both Williams and Nagel sought to demonstrate, or at least illuminate, a number of related theses (not all clearly laid out, to be sure). These theses include at least the following:

(1) Some acts depend for their justification, or their absence of justification, on facts which only obtain subsequently and in virtue of contingent outcomes. Thus, luck can retrospectively validate or invalidate agent choice.

(2) Among these post-justified acts are those grounded in first-personal practical judgments, whose content involves the basic parameters and motivating ideals of the agents' life. (These two points reflect Williams's particular interests.)

(3) Agents' accountability for acts—the degree of praise or blame they are due—depends in part on the actual, contingent consequences of those acts. Thus, a theory of accountability cannot be exclusively intention based.

(4) Since the normative (the "ethical," in Williams's preferred sense) values relevant to assessing persons is partly a function of external, contingent factors, exhausted neither by good intentions nor ex ante judgments, a moral theory that vests value solely in internal qualities will be inadequate to ethical reality (and may also be incoherent in its own terms).

Taken together, these theses amount to a radical challenge to intention- or reason-based moral theory of a roughly Kantian sort. For if a large class of normative judgments—What should I do? How should I respond to what has happened? How bad is what I have done?—is meant to be products of reason but subject to fortune, then moral theory looks more like the weather forecast than like the Ten Commandments. Morality might instead offer good advice for the future, and retrospective rationalizing descriptions, but the moral value of one's acts, hence one's life, remains fortune's hostage. So, at least, Williams and Nagel suggest, in offering instead a less coherent but descriptively more apt account of the interplay of will and circumstance in ethical judgment and response.

My focus in this chapter will be only obliquely on the merits of these theses in relation to the claims of intention-based moral theories. Instead, I want to pursue the particular relation of democratic politics to luck and, in so doing, to pay particular attention to Williams's excavation of the concept. First, I offer a charitable construction of the concept of moral luck, and while I will not pretend confidence that the conception can withstand all objections, I believe it can be rendered sufficiently coherent and attractive such that its role in our everyday moral practices can be tolerated. (Indeed, as Nagel and Williams both say, purging everyday morality of luck would be far more disruptive, whatever the force of the arguments for the purge.)

I then turn to the more dramatic form that claims of outcome dependence can take in politics. In particular, when politicians absorb the possibility of political luck into their own deliberations, they set the scene for great geopolitical gambits as the predicate for historical grandeur. As such, I want to argue, the concept of political luck is itself deeply pernicious, as it can feed a dangerous monomania all too common in historical tragedy, one that presents a specific risk in populist, democratic politics, where vindication through mass sacrifice is seen as a path to historical greatness. The problem is not with the idea of outcome dependence itself, but with the way in which political leaders game our luck-dependent intuitions in search of immortality, or even just political longevity.

My path to these conclusions is as follows. Sections 5.2 and 3 examine Nagel's and Williams' accounts of moral luck, respectively, with an eye to rendering them plausible as philosophical accounts, and not merely descriptions of our practices. Section 5.4 extends the moral account to political life and makes extended use of a contemporary foreign policy adventure put in terms of a historical gamble: the 2003 invasion of Iraq. Section 5.5 concludes with a caution about the distorting effects of political luck on political agency.

5.2. LUCK AND BLAME: NAGEL

Williams and Nagel support their claim for the radical character of luck more by example than by argument—albeit examples of quite different character. Nagel's central examples of outcome-dependent moral assessment concern either comparisons between equally reckless actors, only one of whom actually causes harm; or well-intentioned political actors whose gambits, like the Decembrists' failed revolt against the czar, simply enable tragedy. According to Nagel, while the *mens rea* (intentions, or levels of awareness of the risk) of the reckless actors might be equivalent, the moral value of what they have done is not equivalent: "If one negligently leaves the bath running with the baby in it, one will realize, as one bounds up the stairs toward the bathroom, that if the baby has drowned one has done something awful, whereas if it has not one has merely been careless."[3] Similarly for the well-intentioned failures: "If the American Revolution had been a bloody failure resulting in greater repression, then Jefferson, Franklin and Washington would still have made a noble attempt, and might not even have had to regret it on their way to the scaffold, but they would also have had to blame themselves for what they had helped bring on their compatriots."[4]

Nagel is not simply making the point that something worse has happened in the unfortunate cases, namely death. Rather, because something worse has happened, the actor has *done* something worse, and that therefore he warrants greater reproach—at least from himself. Intuitions might well vary with this case, and one might wonder whether the difficulty of psychologically separating the badness of the outcome from the wrongness of the conduct had led Nagel to an erroneous metaphysical conclusion. Let us therefore put aside the difficult metaphysical question of whether an act, separated in time from its consequence, can change in normative value as a result of the consequence—say, going from careless to awful. It will certainly be true that reactions to that act—the way it lingers as a shameful memory, or the antipathy it arouses in others—are dramatically inflected by the consequences.

Of course, one can imagine a dialectic seeking to move the two cases together, to the effect that on reflection, one ought to be more horrified by even harmless negligence, or less moved by actual outcomes.[5] On this line of thought, those reckless drivers who actually cause harm give proof positive of the dangerousness of their conduct, while our grounds for judging the potential dangerousness of the harmless driver are usually far weaker. But, as Nagel remarks, the dialectic is likely to leave space between the assessments of the two drivers.[6] If one accepts the controversial point that our reflectively stabilized practices of accountability are, at bottom, the foundation of our norms of accountability, then outcomes will warrant differing responses—that actors' deserts vary with the consequences of their acts. (Below, in section 5.4, I will try to make the case for this thesis.) Put aside the merits of the claim for the moment, however. As a matter of social practice, it will be simply true that we respond to agents partly in terms of the outcomes they produce; and any conception of morality that fails to acknowledge this feature of our practice would be revisionary enough of our entrenched reactive attitudes that it could not be accepted as an interpretation of our practices. To be sure, intent and motive might be as relevant to retrospective moral assessments as they are to legal assessments. The discovery, for example, that a lethally reckless driver was rushing a loved one to the hospital would change one's assessment relative to a nonlethal reckless driver who was simply enjoying the imposition of risk on others. In such a case, it would not be true (much less clearly true, ex ante, as Nagel suggests) that the first driver had done something far worse than the second.

Left like this, then, Nagel's account of moral luck is properly a theory of retrospective accountability rather than a guide to practical reasoning. The philosophical implications of the claim still run deep, for to ground accountability even partly on outcome rather than intent is to deny the sufficiency of the usual mentalistic apparatus of normative assessment. And this, as we have seen, is to deny what many consider a deeply seductive image of morality, as a form of judgment concerning what is up to us rather than what merely happens. As a normative thesis, Nagel's view might also be seen as underwriting a version of victors' justice, legitimating the celebrations of historical triumphs that conveniently excise the harms and wrongs done along the way. But it is also worth noting what it does not revise: the permissions and constraints that feature ex ante, at the point of decision making. For there is nothing in Nagel's account to suggest that, absent extenuating circumstances, the possibility of mitigated blame in the event of success should make an otherwise impermissible act appropriate. While I might feel relief, say, that my failure to check behind the car before backing out led to no tragedy, there is no symmetrical compensation at the advance end, except in the obvious sense that one can permissibly engage in risky behavior (driving) but not in behavior that will certainly produce an identifiable harm. But I cannot say to myself in advance that if no harm happens, then the risk I took was clearly justified.

I will discuss below, in section 5.4, more direct applications to politics. The first application, however, is straightforward: the practice of assessing political leaders, like other actors, is clearly outcome dependent. To the extent political leaders concern themselves with their place in historical memory—which is to say, all of them, all the time—they recognize that success washes clean the reputational dirt earned achieving victory. Whether they should make use of this truth is another matter.

5.3. LUCK AND CHOICE: WILLIAMS

Williams situates his discussion of moral luck very differently, not in terms of norms of reproach or the underlying value of acts, but on the question of how, ex ante, first-person practical judgments can be justified and how they can be unjustified. His famous example is a fictionalized painter Gauguin, who decides that the possibility of realizing "his gifts as a painter" requires him to leave his family to destitution in Paris, while he sails to Tahiti.[7] Gauguin recognizes the cost to his family, and even sees it as a moral cost; but he weighs this cost against the possibility of becoming what he most wants to be. The question for Gauguin, and for Williams, is whether he can justify the choice to himself—that is, justify imposing certain costs on his family, in exchange for uncertain aesthetic and reputational success. (Williams, in a puzzling passage I take up below, says that a justification for Gauguin in terms of these values need not justify him to his family, nor to us.) For Williams stipulates that Gauguin does not know whether he has talent sufficient to justify the act—or even if he can be said, retrospectively, to know that he has the talent, he does not know this before he leaves.

Williams's answer is no less perplexing for its familiarity in the domain of politics: eventual success, and only that, will justify Gauguin's choice. If Gauguin is able to realize the paintings he believes he can produce, then and only then will it have been worthwhile to him to have stranded his family. But without artistic triumph, Gauguin by his own lights will have unjustifiably betrayed those he loves.[8] On the other hand, according to Williams, there are distinctions among the possibilities of failure. While certain "extrinsic" or coincidental failures in the project, such as an accident en route, or illness, will not undermine the justification for the act, an "intrinsic" basis for the failure—namely, a lack of talent—will cause the initial act to become "unjustified."[9]

How can this be so? It is hardly priggish to wonder, first, how aesthetic triumph can outweigh betraying vulnerable members of one's families—whether any sort of comparability between the values is possible. After all, one might think, as we nonrelatives of Gauguin's perhaps do, that he might have been a very bad man and a very good painter.[10] Moralists might go on to wonder in what sense Gauguin's decision could be justified at all if it could not be justified to those most closely affected by it. Put aside for the moment, however, these concerns about the nature of moral value and the relation to practical justification—I will offer below some defenses of these claims. The truly puzzling claim is how a choice can move from being neither justified nor unjustified at the outset to being justified or unjustified in virtue of its outcome. The question is not whether there is, in the abstract, logical space for "neither-justified-nor-unjustified" verdict; ternary logics are well developed to deal with such possibilities. Although the intermediate verdict is usually interpreted as "unknown" in such logics, and thus as a matter of epistemology, not metaphysics, intermediate truth values are defensible. But it is not clear whether intermediate truth values are consistent with the two models of rational decision making at hand: expected-utility maximization and deontological/principle-based.

Take deontological, principle-based decision making first. Assuming that operative principles can be determined, there would seem to be no problem in applying such a perspective ex ante. Either it will be the case that, even in conditions of uncertainty, it is permissible to inflict certain harms and betray trusts for the sake of possible personal achievements or it will not be permissible. It is hard to see, as Williams says, how the permissibility branch could be maintained: how, that is, conditions could be specified that would render inflicting such harms permissible ex ante. For example, if what is at stake, per hypothesis, is the thought that some possible aesthetic gains can offset moral injuries, then the argument for permissibility in a deontological framework, no less than in a utilitarian one, must go by way of assumptions about the probability of producing those gains. Such principles would, presumably, license a range of gambles subject to deontic thresholds: one might inflict such and such a harm (but nothing worse), provided the gains to be expected are of such a character, and there is some sufficient likelihood of their being realized. If the conditions are met, and Gauguin can permissibly inflict these harms, then he is warranted in acting as he does, and his eventual triumph is gravy—a matter of supererogatory value. Apart from the issue of value commensurability, the situation is simply like that of any well-intentioned soul whose attempt to act rightly produces a beneficial outcome.

It may well be true, as Williams says, that no set of plausible principles could be defined for this or any comparable case involving hugely uncertain, ego-driven self-reflexive assessments: can I be a great artist, a hero to my cause, et cetera? Any such principles would fall prey in their subjective variant to problems of moral hazard (namely, how "reasonably" can one assess one's prospects for greatness) or, on their objective variant of "actual" potential greatness, simply be inapplicable.[11] But if, in fact, no plausible set of permitting conditions can be defined, then the conclusion that most readily follows is that a deontological framework would simply forbid Gauguin's choice, not that deontology must instead struggle to integrate the notion of prior permission based on retrospective justification. (Though one might conclude independently, so much the worse for deontology, if one rejects its insistence on the priority of moral claims.) There seems to be no pressure from within deontology for a suspended judgment, that Gauguin's act is neither justified nor unjustified, or that it could be unjustified ex ante and somehow justified ex post. Rather, all pressures in the direction of accommodating Gauguin's choice can be accounted for at the level of reasoning about the operative scope of the relevant principles. There simply is no gap for retrospective justification to fill.

It is also hard to pay mind to a justificatory gap in an expected utility framework. According to expected utility theory, an act is justified when the benefits (utility gains) it could bring, discounted by their improbability, exceed the costs it could impose, discounted by their improbability. The risk of failure ex post is thus calculated into the ex ante judgment. Put aside, again, the problem of commensurating and ranking aesthetic gains against personal betrayals. Assuming, despite the implausibilities mentioned above, that probabilities and values can be assigned to Gauguin's aspirations towards greatness, then either it will be the case, ex ante, that his gamble is rationally justified or it will not. Nothing that happens once the die is cast can subvert the initial judgment, except insofar as it reveals misestimates of the values or probabilities. One might regret the loss taken on a rational financial gamble—say, an expensive raffle ticket whose discounted potential value nonetheless exceeded its cost. And one might rejoice in the winnings from a raffle ticket whose expected value is significantly exceeded by its cost. But it would clearly be an error to think that the outcome, either way, affected the justifiability of taking the gamble in the first place—or, more radically, to think that the rationality of the act could be an open question—until matters are resolved.[12]

Williams's specific complaint about utilitarianism, in this context, is confusing. Apart from the important point that any attempt to fit the relevant values into the utilitarian framework will inevitably be either handwaving or vulgar reductionism, he says that utilitarianism also fails, importantly, to distinguish between different types of failures: namely, the "intrinsic" failures I mentioned above, rooted in the agent's own incapacity (despite his hopes), and "extrinsic," accidental failures.[13] Presumably Williams means that an expected utility framework can at best only price out, and thus accommodate, extrinsic failures, which do not "unjustify" the ex ante gamble but rather treat it as the downside already taken into account. He does not spell out the difference made by intrinsic failures, although the peculiar difficulties in assigning probabilities to such failures, mentioned above, are surely part of the story. To return to the raffle ticket example, one might say that while the failure of a ticket to be drawn is simply the rationally calculated downside of the risk, one's discovery that one has instead bought a counterfeit ticket could be counted as outside the zone of calculated risk undermining the project itself.[14] Or, to take Williams's other example, the doomed love affair of Anna Karenina and Vronsky: while the lovers might have reckoned the risks of separation, poverty, or accidental death, perhaps there was no way for them to estimate the actual hazard of the impossibility of a socially isolated love. The problem, in these cases, is not simply a paucity of data on the relevant risk but the reflexive and even self-fulfilling nature of those risks, all of which go to preconditions of the possibility of success. Gauguin's actual shot at greatness is affected, for better or worse, by his ego; the love affair, by the anxiety it arises in Anna; and perhaps even the prospect of buying a fake ticket, by concerns of being gulled. The nonoccurrence of these risks is, in effect, assumed as part of the baseline, and it is only from this baseline that agents can then rationally project their upsides and downsides. This offers an interpretation of Williams's remark that when a project fails intrinsically, the agent's hopes are "not just negated, but refuted": refuted because the gamble, in hindsight, never made sense at all.[15]

Such a distinction, between inestimable baseline probabilities and estimable outcome probabilities, could if sustained make sense of Williams's rejection of a utilitarian framework. It is, of course, open to question whether the distinction can be maintained, or whether these baseline conditions can be subject to some rational estimation as well. In any event, I think there is something more telling to the distinction Williams has in mind, and which goes further to explain the retrospective effects of the outcome. This is the dimension of reputation. For it is clear that what Gauguin fears is the obverse of what he hopes for: not quite that he will fail to produce great art, but that he will prove himself to be a pompous fool, a *schmuck*. And Anna's place in literary history is as a beautifully limned romantic idiot. What "refutes" the gamble, in these cases, is not the fact that the benefit did not materialize, nor is it even that the direct costs still have to be paid. Rather, it is the further effect on the self-understanding, as well as the public reputation, of the gambler. And this cost, of appearing foolish or, worse, actually being revealed as a fool, might be thought to lie beyond a utilitarian calculation that might otherwise justify the gamble.

These points might all be disputed, of course. A consequentialist might simply say that the cost of looking foolish is one among many risks to be accounted for, and if it is a bad enough risk, then it provides a reason not to engage in an otherwise rationally justified gamble. If it is bad enough, yet also so uncertain that a probability cannot be assigned, then there is a case for adopting a maximin strategy, precluding such a gamble (or, instead and to the same effect, applying the precautionary principle). But the expressive character of the stakes are nonetheless unruly with a utilitarian framework; and whether or not the costs can be balanced against the

anticipated benefits up front, the actual realization of the cost—the reve-
lation of the failure—is such that it cannot be assuaged by pointing back
towards the ex ante justification. Whether this is a consequence of the
psychology of regret and shame or of the nature of justification is unclear.
But Williams's point, and the distinction between intrinsic and extrinsic
failure, clearly has some bite.

If Williams is right, then, that principle-based reasoning is too indeterminate, or otherwise inadequate, to accommodate outcome sensitivity
in cases where, intuitively, the prospect of the outcome matters to its ex
ante permissibility; and if utilitarian reasoning is unable to accommodate
certain kinds of outcomes as well—namely, the intrinsic failures—then
it does look as though, at the least, life is capable of presenting us with
a range of choices that can be regarded only ex post as clearly justified
or unjustified. Of course, even if utilitarianism and deontological frame-
works are unable to provide an ex ante justificatory framework for these
cases—or, rather, even if the conclusions one might reach about justifiability are subject to ex post revision—it does not follow that the strong thesis
is true, that the decision to act, at the time, is neither justified nor unjustified. It could be the case that it is justified (or unjustified) by some further
theory of choice, perhaps a nonreductive, all-in form of consequentialism which can also discount future expectations. As formal possibilities,
such theories are easily described. But an air of handwaving must surely
accompany claims of their meaningfulness, unless and until the ex ante
forms of reasoning are spelled out. At the least, it would seem Williams
has shifted the burden of argument to those who would assert that such
choices have a determinate form of justification.

But even if Williams has shifted the burden from one who would assert
the possibility of an ex ante permission to risk current suffering for future happiness, one might still question whether the freedom of the choice
is fully symmetrical. The notion of a radical, self-defining choice is a familiar one in existential literature, and it appeals to romantic longings of
self-realization. But it has also often represented a desire to flee the ties of
mundane obligation, and the fact that such an escape is fantasized does not
mean it is acceptable. Claims of outcome-based justification might reflect
nothing more than the desire to transcend those obligations, grounded in
a self-absorbed psychology that revels in triumph and ignores the costs.
I have already indicated concern that the notion of ex post unjustifica-
tion has more to do with an agent's focus on his or her reputation than
on the status of norms governing his conduct. The idea of an intrinsic,

choice-justifying success, grounded in the agent's own capacities (for art, for love, for remaking a political landscape) looks a lot like a fantasy of repainting an interpersonal normative landscape in the hues of one's own ego.

All that being said, a weaker and perhaps more accurate version of Williams's claim might still be developed. This would be the claim, not that the original act occurs outside a space of objective justification, but that from the point of view of the actor, it must be treated as such. The indeterminacies of system, or uncertainties of prediction, render the choice up for grabs ex ante and only subject to justification or rejection ex post. Such choices might still be constrained by ex ante principles, prescribing maximin reasoning with regard to the worst extremes, for instance. But there will be a core set of choices for which justification will come subsequently as an epistemic matter, if it comes at all.[16] And it is to this first-personal, epistemically constrained perspective that Williams's claims about moral luck are addressed. Gauguin, at least, cannot settle in advance the question of permissibility. And since his perspective on his decision is, ultimately, the only determinative view on what he should do, there simply will be no practically effective ex ante perspective that can offer justification in advance.

There is another benefit to construing Williams's claim about the subjective availability of justification. For it is only by rendering Williams's claim about moral luck in subjective terms that we can make sense of his further, equally provocative claim about the nature of moral justification: that "even if Gauguin can ultimately be justified, that need not provide him with any way of justifying himself to others, or at least to all others."[17] On Williams's view, then, outcomes can justify ex post, but only relative to certain classes of agents—namely, those who give priority to the values inherent in the outcome.

But this is a puzzling position. Surely, one might think, moral justification is nonrelative, position independent. This, after all, is the distinguishing feature of moral justification. Prudential justification, by contrast, is positional. An act might make sense for me, given my assessment of its costs and benefits, even though its costs weigh too heavily on you for you to find it reasonable. Indeed, the tradition of contractualism in ethics treats the notion of interpersonal acceptability as the basis for moral justification.[18] Questions of justification are pragmatically relevant when the act under question runs counter to some other party's interests or preferences. The prudential justification for the agent's act is presupposed (assuming this is not a case of irrational, perhaps weak-willed, behavior.) In such a case, for the aggrieved party to ask for moral justification simply is to ask for a reason why she too might see the act as one that ought to be performed—or, alternatively, why some related set of considerations entail that, her preferences notwithstanding, the agent is still entitled to perform the act. For example, someone offering justification for their trespass onto private property in pursuit of a stag might offer respect for traditional patterns of land use as a reason for permission or forgiveness, not—or not simply—the hunter's own reason, namely the pleasure of the hunt or the prospect of a meal.

What is puzzling about Williams's remark is that the outcome-relative justification Gauguin offers is not merely prudential, nor does it appear to be moral in any familiar sense of that term. For all the talk I have offered above, of deontological versus consequentialist justifications, Williams himself points to a notion of justification that is distinctly nonmoral when he writes that the Gauguin case illustrates the point that "we have deep and persistent reasons to be grateful that" the world we have is not one in which "morality [is] universally respected."[19] The justification Gauguin comes to have, and which he might not have had, resonates in this broader dimension of nonprudential value, yet it is not a value whose allegiance can be demanded of those hurt by its attainment, or those who otherwise deplore the values it realizes.

So Williams here treads a difficult line: avoiding pure relativism on the one hand, where justification simply reduces to realization of whatever values the agent has, and avoiding the overriding dictate of purely moral values on the other. His position in this essay thereby calls to mind another famous and related claim of his, in "Internal and External Reasons," along with the concomitant difficulties of his claim in that essay.[20] In that essay, Williams argues that we are properly said to have (normative) reason to act in a certain way when and only when one can construct an argument showing that the act in question would realize some value or desire already held by the agent. Lacking such prior motivations, agents lack reason to act in terms of those values or ends. Thus, more generally, the claim that someone has reason to act is relational (or "internal," in Williams's terms), and cannot necessarily be universalized.

The difficulty with Williams's view that reasons are internal, relative to agents' prior motivations, lies not with its logic but with its frankly revisionary aim to remove from our moralistic repertoire the charge that an agent who fails to comply with what he himself might acknowledge are the moral considerations at issue thereby fails to act on the reasons he has.[21] As Williams readily acknowledges, to give up on the universalistic language of morality as a source of external reasons, applicable to all agents in virtue of their capacity to think, feel, or act, is to give up on a great deal of the persuasive force of morality. We are left with the resources of internal reason, and might for all that be able to show that, indeed, most people actually have prior motivations that, properly construed, would support the course of action morality (in our view) demands. But the claim that morality itself is anchored in reason is instead cast adrift—and once that is so, it is not clear that the remainder is recognizably a moral institution at all. Morality, in other words, might not survive Williams's internalist reduction.

So much the worse for morality, one might say—and the lessons of moral luck provide yet more reason to be skeptical of the institution. The problem, however, is that a central part of the claim of moral luck rests on a notion of justification that is clearly broader than a claim of internal rational support. Williams writes, in reference to political decisions that leave losers as well as winners in their wake, that

> [i]t is not reasonable, in such a case, to expect those particular people who have been cheated, used, or injured to approve of the agent's action, nor should they be subjected to the patronising thought that, while their complaints are not justified in terms of the whole picture, they are too closely involved to be able to see that truth. Their complaints are, indeed, justified, and they may quite properly refuse to accept the agent's justification which the rest of us may properly accept.[22]

On pain of triviality, the language of "proper" acceptance of a justification must go beyond the limited question of whether political actors have individual reason to act as they do, or whether victims have reason to voice their objections. Justification is perforce intersubjective and nonindividual. But perhaps Williams's notion of justification can be resurrected on collective grounds: in terms of values *we* share, not just in terms of the agent's own motivations. On such an account, Gauguin is justified to us—properly justified—because his acts realize values we endorse, even in competition with morality. That is a real justification, to us, and stands apart from whatever reasons to act he may have had. It calls upon others—us—to assess his reasons in the dimensions of value he puts forward—here, aesthetic and Romantic values—and to weigh those reasons ex post, in light of their attainment (or his failure to attain those values). The ex post perspective is reasonable in this case, for to value a value like aesthetics is to value principally its instantiations. Until the scale of the realized value is actually in play—is concretized in a body of work—there will simply be no way to judge whether the game is worth the candle.

By contrast, while Gauguin's family doubtless also appreciates the value of the beautiful, they likely weigh it differently against the disvalue of poverty. As a result, Gauguin's justification to himself, perhaps to us, is not a moral justification—it makes no moral claim on all others (as moral claims do, simply as a matter of semantics), nor does it provide a basis for seeing his family's supposed resentment as in any way unjustified.[23] But it does amount to an interesting and significant form of ex post justification.

Such a view is also consistent with the point that justification cannot be simply a matter of *cui bono*, for one can value certain values independent of their personal benefit. For example, an aesthete might regard Gauguin as choosing wisely simply on the hearsay claim that Gauguin had produced great art, unseen by the evaluator. Gauguin would be justified in the eyes of the aesthete, but not in the eyes of those who value hearth and home over gallery success, though neither set of evaluators would either gain or lose in any meaningful sense. Justification may be nonmoral, but it operates in the same space of intersubjective argument as morality. It is nonrelative individually while also nonuniversalistic. The further claim of outcome dependence supports this limited relativity insofar as it illuminates the gap between the outcome values we third parties might prefer, as against the intrinsic, deontic values at stake in the sufferings of intimates. But this connection is exegetical, not logical.

5.4. EX POST JUSTIFICATION AND POLITICAL GAMBLING

I now want to turn to the question motivating this chapter, namely whether and how the notion of ex post justification, which we have derived from reflections on interpersonal, moral cases, applies in the domain of politics. First, however, we should take stock of the conceptual equipment in play. Nagel's account of moral luck provided us with the outcome-dependent nature of accountability; and while he did not provide us with a justification for that dependence, his account of its pervasiveness in moral thought indicates its centrality. Williams, meanwhile, has given us an ex ante perspective on ex post dependence: on the way in which certain decisions to act can be taken in light of potential resultant values, without being able to claim the force of those values in advance. On the ex ante face, this means that a straightforward consequentialist justification will be lacking, and that actions aimed at the values at stake will be gambles of a sort—gambles that must produce both the desired outcomes and the justification for the gamble itself.

We can also see some normative support for Nagel's observations on the nature of accountability. While accountability is a moral notion, to be sure, our social practices of accountability need not only reflect moral values, nor need moral values be dominant. I remarked above on the positional character of accountability: Gauguin owes his family one response for his betrayal and owes the world quite another; reciprocally, those affected differently are differently warranted in the responses they may mete out to him. If the account I have ascribed to Williams is plausible, that non-moral normative justification can be relative to particular assignments and experiences of value, then assignments of accountability might also vary along these dimensions. If aesthetic values have been realized, even at grave human cost, we bystanders might warrantably respond in one register, while family members might respond in another. Furthermore, our responses as bystanders might well be more outcome dependent than the responses of family: the wrong of betrayed promises occurs at the moment of the decision, before its fruits are gathered. (Whether our response as bystanders is actually justified can only be settled from within a moral theory; but it will be perforce a moral assessment of that response, not simply a reflection of whether our local interests were served.)

Taken together, then, we have a coherent account of an outcome-dependent form of normative assessment, with logical space for the normative gamble. But we also have been given notice of a set of hazards inherent in this form of normative assessment. Two of them I have noted already. First, while this account does provide a justification for outcome-dependent accountability, the justification only has force insofar as we can see its values as properly rivaling moral values. When we forgive the bloodied victor his sins, our forgiveness and celebration might reflect nothing more than a temporal myopia or a discounting of the costs of suffering simply because those costs are not known to us. The fact of value pluralism *might* support the claim of justification, but the justification might also be specious, by our own lights, even without acceding exceptionless priority to moral value. Second, Williams's distinction between intrinsic and extrinsic sources of failure, and the concomitant notions of refuted versus negated hopes, reveals a further degree of egoistic distortion in this decision calculus. While Williams is surely right that Gauguin would have rued the discovery of limited talent more than a chance failure to mount his Tahitian expedition, this fact only reveals the degree to which his concern is a discovery about himself—whether or not *he* is a great artist—rather than a discovery about whether great art will, in fact, be produced (by him, as it happens).

This combination is a heady mix. Kant warned long ago of the difficulties in accurately assessing the relation of our wills to the moral law.[24] These difficulties are amplified in the domain of politics. The possibility of retrospective justification, coupled with the unconscious prominence of reputational considerations, invites ego to take on the cloak of political heroism. Needless to say, the invitation has often been accepted in history. Consider Machiavelli's famous endorsement of incaution: "I think it is certainly better to be impetuous than incautious, for fortune is a woman, and it is necessary, if you wish to master her, to conquer her by force; and it can be seen that she lets herself be overcome by the bold, rather than by those who proceed coldly."[25] The confusion of prudence and eros (and, in Platonic terms, *thumos*) is at the surface in Machiavelli's account, and it points to the pernicious hold the concept of political luck has taken on the political imagination (of men). Whatever the possible truth to outcome sensitivity in political evaluation, the temptations it offers have been at the root of grand historical follies.

The modern exemplar of political incaution is the invasion of Iraq. While a full account of the deliberations leading to this epic historical disaster has yet to be given, one reason for the invasion seems to have been a desire among a cadre of like-minded political figures—the "Vulcans" as they called themselves—to establish a new geopolitical mapping of the Middle East. The Vulcans, whose most famous members were Paul Wolfowitz and Douglas Feith, both of the Department of Defense, saw in the wake of the 9/11 attacks a chance to "sweep the table" in the region, displace the Israeli-Palestine conflict from its pivotal role, to cement an American military presence less dependent on the stability of Saudi Arabia, and to encourage the development of stabilizing democratic political and civic institutions.[26] They aimed, in other words, to wage a grand gamble, with war as the means and a US-friendly coalition of new regimes as the end.[27]

Now, I do not mean to insist on the truth of this particular account of the motivations of the Iraq war. First, whatever the declared justifications for the war, the actual motivations of the policymakers might have been far cruder: the sheer macho thrill of war (especially when fought from the policymaker's perch) or the pursuit of material advantage. Or the motivations may have been more cautious: a preference for a worst-case scenario of an unwarranted invasion as against Iraq's use of weapons of mass destruction. On such a calculus, even a high probability of error in threat assessment would be dominated by the risks of a nuclear bomb.[28]

All of these accounts of the decision to go to war enjoy some support. But I wish to concentrate on the argument of the grand gamble, because of its resonance in longstanding ideals of political leadership. While there are purely calculative politicians, to be sure, the narcissistic motivations that often lie at the heart of political ambition go hand in hand with the ideal of the gambler, each politician a potential Napoleon or Churchill, impetuous as to the future and with the wind of war at his back. To the extent—and it is a great extent—that the glorious future revolves around one's own celebrity, it is hard for the would-be gambler to distinguish genuine consequential calculation from adolescent fantasy. The trope of the gamble does not just offer a moralized and romanticized rationalization of cruder motives—for instance, of war as a venue for displays of power—but dresses that rationalization up in heroic garb. Moreover, the cognitive distortions entailed by these layers of fantasy are further evident in the mistaken planning for the postwar period, with its now notoriously inaccurate estimate of direct and indirect costs.[29] If a preferred self-image of the gambler is that of the card counter, the hard-nosed actuary of chance, the Iraq war presented us with a more realistic image of the fantasist looking for a triumphant score.[30]

The second distorting feature of the concept of political luck lies not in the manifest temptations of the gambler-hero image but in the difficulty of comparing costs against gains, where both estimates are done under multiple layers of uncertainty. In discussing Gauguin, I suggested that one reason for thinking in consequentialist terms, that ex ante no determinate assessment could be given, was the substantial uncertainty of the relevant variables, compounded by the reflexive nature of some of the outcomes. This class of political gambles invites a long and familiar list of biases to the table, including optimistic biases in overestimating success (and hence underdiscounting the benefits and overdiscounting costs), and a general discounting of remote or statistical, but nonetheless real, costs—human suffering and death, in the case of war—against more easily visualized symbols of success.[31] The reflexive nature of the estimating problem is fully present as well, for the prospect of success in waging war, fomenting revolution, and so forth, depends on the political actor's own future actions and skills of leadership, not just one's courageous act of taking the gamble in the first place. The failures of Iraq policymaking become highly predictable under this lens.

There is a third distorting aspect as well, and it comes from the relativized sense of justification that one must invoke to make sense of Williams's claim. While the justification is not moral—and cannot be moral—the fact that it is also not purely personal allows it to displace moral demands. Williams does not imagine that Gauguin can defeat the grievances of his family by pointing to the glory of his art, but only that he can convince other onlookers to ignore their complaints. By hypothesis, recall, moral justification is simply unavailable. Were the art capable of redressing the moral costs, then that prospect could have been taken into account, as a basis for reasonable assent by the family, or by consequentialist calculation. Instead, the aesthetic success displaces the moral costs.

Imagine what would have had to be true for a war like Iraq to be justified in moral terms. Assuming some disregard for international law is compatible with moral justification, it would at least have to be the case that the new political and legal ordering that accommodates preemption as an alternative legitimate basis for war is likely to make the world more secure on balance, despite the risks of providing other states with a legal cover for cross-border raids. Second, the direct and indirect human costs of war and national recovery, discounted by their high probability, must be outweighed by the reduction in risks generated by the Hussein regime, and the reduction in the very real costs of that regime's political repression, all discounted by the lower probabilities of reducing the costs in those dimensions.[32] And third, there must be an answer to the deontological challenge whether an external invasion can, even in principle, legitimate a new regime—that is, whether only internal agents of political change have moral standing to engage in these cost-benefit calculations in the first place.

All of these are hard questions in moral and political philosophy, and although I believe history has made clear in Iraq what the right answers were, given an estimated casualty toll of more than 500,000 Iraqis dead, along with nearly 5,000 in coalition forces, I do not pretend that they are easy to answer in real time.[33] Nor do I want to insinuate that political choices can never be made in the face of uncertainty, in light of the likelihood of bias and distortion. The first would be a recipe for dogmatism; and the second, for stagnant conservatism. But there is a continuum between the fearful caution of a Chamberlain, willing to wager nothing, and the rashness of an Alexander, willing to wager everything. Lasting legacies of political leadership fall between the two, with an honest eye directed at the payouts.

If questions about uncertain payoffs were properly directed deliberations about the political future, then the concept of political luck would have no purchase: the invasion could have been either justified or shown unjustified ex ante on the basis of the estimates one could make and the principled reason one could engage in. Actual success or failure would be icing. The most pernicious effect, however, of focusing on the possibility of ex post justification is that it renders these questions moot, because justification will be at hand when, and only when, success obtains. One need not account for the real downside costs, as a moral accounting would demand. The only downside cost that looms large for a political gambler is the risk of looking a fool, and that risk is itself probably overdiscounted by the unattractiveness of its realization.[34] Moreover, a keen awareness of the outcome dependency of social accountability, with the realization that the victory will be celebrated and its costs forgotten, means that there is essentially no pressure for an honest moral accounting of the decision at hand. The irony here is that morality will have little purchase on politics not for its lack of realism, as many charge, but precisely because of its realism.

5.5. REJECTING POLITICAL LUCK

The elaboration of the role of luck in prospective choice, by Williams, and in retrospective accountability, by Nagel, performed a service for contemporary moral philosophy, by revealing the unreality of the picture of moral assessment it offered. Noting luck's role allows us to understand dimensions of moral assessment that integrate better with our life embedded in a world of chance and mutual vulnerability.[35] Williams's discussion further limits the role of a related philosophical ideal, that of the fully rationalized decision. While Williams's explorations of the notion of justification are puzzling, they do not seem simply confused, but instead they genuinely reveal complexities in the nature of agency.

Yet moral luck is, in the end, more modest than political luck. One might accept the coherence of the concept and accommodate oneself to its role in our practices of allocating praise and blame. But political luck presents special dangers, in large part because of the magnifying lenses provided by the imagined audience of history—an audience lacking in the moral realm. Thus, I have sought here to accentuate the negative instead: the dangers that arise when the concept of luck is taken as the lodestar of consequential decision making, and the threat that poses for politicians competing for votes. Williams did not invite these dangers, of course. But his emphasis on the limited role of moral justification provides more support than is needed for one of the deadliest temptations in political thought, ever since Plato visited Sicily: the desire to rework a political landscape in toto, rationalizing a choice that piecemeal analysis would quickly convict of foolhardiness. Actuarial thought in politics may be less stirring than the gamble of a Machiavellian statesman. But a reminder of its virtues can serve to inoculate a democratic politics from the dangers of luck-seeking adventurism. Barack Obama was harshly criticized by neoconservatives for his anti-dramatic approach to foreign relations, and his risk-averse preference for "leading from behind," in a regretted but trenchant phrase by one of his aides.[36] But leading from behind—at least behind the actuary's calculations—is the mark of a politician who knows that *virtù* lies in discipline rather than luck.

6

WAR, DEMOCRACY, AND PUBLICITY:
THE PERSISTENCE OF SECRET LAW

6.1. THE NEED FOR SECRECY

We are used to secrecy in government. Secrecy, in the form of confidentiality, protects privacy; secrecy, in the form of anonymity, can protect the candor and integrity of review processes; and secrecy about enforcement practices, as for taxes, lets us partially relax into the belief that we are not simply suckers, while those who know the rules of the game can avoid taxes at will. But secret laws, or secret amendments, are chilling because they strike at the foundation of law itself and the government's right to rule. Even Draco, author of the infamously punitive laws of Athens, saw fit to publish his laws. King Louis XIV of France, at the height of his absolutist power, also scrupled on this point: for the king's words to be law, they must be written and public.[1]

We received a reminder of the salience of secrecy in the twilight of the G. W. Bush administration, and a foreshadowing of concerns still ramifying throughout the second term of Barack Obama's presidency. In 2007 the *New York Times* revealed that the Office of Legal Counsel (OLC) had issued secret memoranda justifying "enhanced interrogation techniques"— waterboarding, sleep deprivation, and induced hypothermia—all of which would be considered consistent with US prohibitions on both torture and "cruel, inhuman, or degrading" treatment, even when combined. The legal opinion was offered notwithstanding the fact that these techniques have long been considered torture and, as such, serious criminal violations under both international and domestic law when practiced by US or other nationals.[2]

The OLC memos echoed the infamous Yoo-Bybee "Torture Memo" of August 2002, which argued two points: first, that only the infliction of pain tantamount to organ failure or greatly prolonged mental distress would constitute torture and so be prohibited under federal law; and second, even as to torturous techniques, that the president has the inherent constitutional authority as commander in chief to order any interrogation methods.

Some background on the OLC is in order. The OLC's charge is, traditionally, twofold: first, to provide candid evaluations to the executive branch of the legality (including the constitutionality) of proposed policies; and second, to serve as an arbiter of interagency legal disputes. When its opinions are signed by the attorney general, they bind the executive branch as a matter of internal policy and custom, although they are not enforceable against the executive by any third party.[3] In effect, the opinions of the OLC can offer immunity to any executive actor later accused of violating federal law who acts on their reliance, because they can offer an authoritative interpretation of federal law consistent with what the actor has done. Executive-branch actors, including prosecutors, are bound by the opinions, unless and until they are rescinded by the president. Moreover, the process of rescission can itself, by tradition, only go by way of a further determination by the OLC that the earlier opinions were incorrect.[4]

What makes the OLC opinion-writing process a legitimate rather than corrupt exercise of internal discipline is the way in which the OLC has traditionally understood its client, the United States, not the current chief executive; its role, as a purveyor of sound legal analysis untempered by particular policy goals and conducted in delegation of the president's "take care" duty; and its process, entailing careful and judicious legal analysis. This tradition has been effectively dismantled, by many accounts, during the Bush administration.[5]

The legal effect of the OLC opinions means that they serve as functional amendments to the scope of congressionally defined law for purposes of executive enforcement. Put another way, if the OLC decides that a case cannot be prosecuted because an agency's conduct complies with the law, it matters not at all whether a court or any other interpreter would disagree—would assert, for example, that induced hypothermia and simulated drowning clearly meet the semantic criteria of "torture" as laid out in a range of domestic and legal provisions and precedents. Thus, the OLC opinions are more than statements of internal executive policy. As binding limits on prosecution, they define the contours of the criminal law they purport to interpret and so make new law, regardless of congressional intent. Moreover, because the effect of the OLC opinions is to limit, rather than expand, the possibilities of prosecution, there is no prospect of a judicial appeal of these opinions. This is because taking a case to court, in the United States, requires showing that the plaintiff has "standing"—an identifiable and discrete injury caused by the defendant.

But in a non-prosecution, only the public interest is injured. There is no one, save the executive branch itself, to challenge the opinions, and thus they will stand until a new administration's appointees decide begin the process of withdrawing them.[6]

Condemnation of secret laws and legal amendments can seem too easy. Rejection of secret laws is morally and politically overdetermined after two centuries of the rhetoric and developing practice of liberalism and of democratic self-government. The contemporary value of "transparency" in government makes any alternative hard to digest. Indeed, that fount of liberal political theory, Immanuel Kant, declared that a principle of "publicity," meaning a requirement that any law must, hypothetically, be defensible even if rendered public, served as a "transcendental" standard of justice for all legal regimes.[7] Moreover, just as hard cases are said to make bad law, policies implicating a range of values make it hard to single out the destructiveness of a particular one. Nonetheless, it can be worthwhile to tease apart the problems with secret law, not just so we can understand our objections, but because by doing so, we may reveal something about the nature of law and its moral and political qualities.

First, and most obviously, secrecy subverts democratic accountability, raising the possibility that we do not know what our government does in our name, and so cannot demand a change—even if legislators are frequently happily complicit in that subversion, for fear of needing to take difficult stands on principle in public. This aspect of law's secrecy prompted Senate hearings, led by Senator Russell Feingold, titled "Secret Law and the Threat to Democratic and Accountable Government."[8] The democratic case against secret law rests, to be sure, on a particular conception of the province of legislative oversight, but I take this case against secret law to be unproblematic.

Second, law's secrecy hurts us existentially, because it deprives us of the way in which, once we are organized as a polity, law tells us who we are, by constituting our *orientation* in moral and political space—what values and acts we project into the world. This orientation is law's subjective contribution to our moral personality, complementary to the objective contribution it makes in the form of incentives and disincentives to align one's behavior with interpersonal norms. Understanding and probing the nature and threat of secret law is important because it exposes a deeper epistemological dimension of democratic agency: the need for a self-governing people to know its own mind and will. The threat is not just to a democratic people's capacity on particular occasions to police its executive and legislative agents, but to its being a democratic people at all.

In the case of torture, it may be said that foreigners came to know the United States better than Americans know themselves. Any secret law deprives us of this central form of self-knowledge, making us subjects rather than citizens. I take up this argument not just by reference to the extreme case of torture but also to a more complicated case, presented by Israel's sotto voce decriminalization of sodomy. Consequently, secrecy undermines not only our democracy but the legitimacy of the state itself. This is, perhaps, the most repugnant aspect of secret law: it is barely law and, by its very existence, undercuts the authority of the state it claims to serve.

The subject also casts light on an issue within legal philosophy, especially the theory known as "legal positivism," the legal philosophy associated most strongly with Hans Kelsen and H.L.A. Hart, and which has defined orthodoxy in modern legal thought. Legal positivists hold that law's validity rests on social rather than moral facts—that the mark of legality is conferred, at root, by criteria no more morally robust than the decisions and practices of the frequently morally wanting individuals to whom the decisions and practices belong. On a positivist conception of law, a value of *publicity*, which insists on the nonsecrecy of law, could as a contingent matter count—or not—among the validity criteria of a legal system, just as could other democratic or antidemocratic criteria. True, a positivist might hold that publicity may be a necessary condition of a legal system as a whole, on pain of inefficacy.[9] But beyond this wholesale condition, there seems to be no basis for a retail restriction on secrecy: the criteria of validity might well make no mention of publicity. Whatever publicity exists in the system could be merely nonbinding custom or understood as a demand of justice, not law. A particular statute, then, could count fully as law, despite its secrecy. But focusing on secret law in a concrete political environment, rather than a philosophical abstraction, reveals that publicity is both a wholesale and a retail value, connected with the validity of particular laws, in a way that suggests legal positivists must make room, beyond constraints of efficacy, for the fundamental, noncontingent value of publicity.

6.2. SECRET LAW IN HISTORY

Historically, secret law has been seen as a mark of tyranny, inconsistent with the notion of law itself. A ruler who acts without law is a tyrant, whether democratic or monarchic. Tyranny, in its original Greek manifestations, was understood as governance that was lawless in two different ways: a ruler who took power without benefit of law or constitutional principle; and a ruler who ruled without regard to form of law. While, as Jean Bodin noted, usurpation by conquest was not seen as pejorative, the political threats a usurper faced tended to lead in the direction of rule by terror.[10] Hence the modern conception of tyranny as lawless rule was born, as expressed by Bodin: "Tyrannical monarchy is one in which the laws of nature are set at naught, free subjects oppressed as if they were slaves, and their property treated as if it belonged to the tyrant."[11] There is a practical basis for law's centrality, to be sure: how can a leader's dictates be obeyed, much less enforced, if they cannot be known? If a central justification of the state comes from its capacity to coordinate social life, it is hard to see how coordination can be achieved in law's absence. As Plato argued in Book VIII of the *Republic*, a lawless state is incoherent, undisciplined in its passions—like a wanton in its aims and actions. Thus Plato linked (as we would not), tyranny with democracy, seeing democracy as forgoing reason's rule to the chaotic claim of the appetites. Once the appetites are unleashed, free of the rule of logos, there is nothing but power to control the polity—power exercised through a popular dictator, or tyrant. The violence of the tyrant's rule, to put it another way, is not the basis of tyranny but rather the effect of living without law, without a rational, public principle under which the law is known and articulated.[12]

But the problem with tyranny is not just disorder and the terror such disorder brings. Tyrants are despised not just for the chaos of their rule but for its cruelty. And what makes the enforcement of a ruler's will cruel is its application without notice—without the chance for subjects to decide on their own whether to abide by that will or to risk its defiance. The harshness of punishment—delivered or withheld—is another matter entirely. For punishment to be punishment, to be something other than the arbitrary infliction of pain, law must do at least this much: it must mediate between ruler and ruled. By the same coin, a ruler who fails to punish someone otherwise deserving, independent of any principle of forgiveness or excuse, is not merciful but only indulgent. Without law, there is nothing to distinguish sentimentality from principle on the part of the ruler. Moreover, this law must be known to the ruled, not just the ruler, to have this effect. Principles must be public to be seen as principles: rules must be known by the ruled.

This is made clear in the Roman law tradition, beginning with the publication of the Twelve Tables which were, following the Greek precedent, inscribed on ivory tablets and put together in front of the rostra, so that they might be open to public inspection.[13] Written law, publicly displayed, had precedence in this system, whether composed by statute, judgment, or imperial edict (determined in a letter over the emperor's signature). Even the unwritten law of Rome was public in its way, consisting of ancient custom, livened by continuous observance.[14] The annals of Roman history are full of derogations from this principle after the fall of the Republic, where state policy came to consist of the whim of the emperor, promulgated without Senate deliberation, without regard for precedent or public principle. But as a principle, an ideal, the public nature of law went hand in hand with the nature of the Republic itself. Indeed, the very idea of a republic—of *res publicae*—things pertaining to the public—supports the idea of matters of public concern being regulated by public rules. Law is the point of correspondence, and mutual intercourse, between the public and its deliberative body.

The relation between legitimacy and law has been maintained throughout the history of political thought, even among such theorists of absolute sovereignty as Jean Bodin. Bodin, who gave the notion of sovereignty its first rigorous elaboration, needed the concept of publicity to distinguish the private acts of the ruler from his law-making acts, lest the separate political identity of the state be merged with the private opinions of the ruler.[15] Thomas Hobbes, likewise, insisted that even his absolutist sovereign must inform the public about the content and grounds for the law he promulgates: "It belongeth therefore to the Office of a Legislator, (such as in all Commonwealths the Supreme representative, be it one Man, or an Assembly,) to make the reason Perspicuous, why the Law was made; and the body of the Law it selfe, as short, but in as proper, and significant terms, as may be."[16] Hobbes's reason for insisting on law's "perspicuity"— its knowability—lay primarily in the dangers ambiguity presented for the contests over justice he saw as undermining the possibility of the state. But this is simply to underline that the very idea of an unknown or unknowable law stands, in Hobbes's mind, in opposition to the basic project of state authority. Authority, including absolutist authority over the very terms of justice, requires public law.

The relation between law's inherent authority and its public knowability is most strongly manifest in the greatest (successful) attempt to rationalize law's institutions the West has known: the Code Napoléon, of 1804. The first article of the Code provided that "[t]he laws are executed through out the French territory, in virtue of their promulgation by the Emperor. They will have executory force from the moment of their promulgation, when they can be known."[17] Unpublished law, let alone secret law, is nugatory, an oxymoron. On this line of reasoning, the need to know law is a function of the structure of the state and its basic purpose in creating coherent social order, in which ruler and subject can locate themselves. Jeremy Bentham makes this aspiration explicit, linking the conceptual necessity of promulgation to the moral quality of the citizens and state:

> That a law may be obeyed, it is necessary that it should be known: that it may be known, it is necessary that it be promulgated. But to promulgate a law, it is not only necessary that it should be published with the sound of trumpet in the streets; not only that it should be read to the people; not only even that it should be printed: all these means may be good, but they may be all employed without accomplishing the essential object. . . . To promulgate a law, is to present it to the minds of those who are to be governed by it in such manner as that they may have it habitually in their memories, and may possess every facility for consulting it, if they have any doubts respecting what it prescribes.[18]

> To the subject-citizen, again, it will, taken all together, according to the extent occupied by it in the field of morals and legislation, serve as a *code of instruction, moral* and *intellectual* together: applying itself to, and calling into continual exercise, the *intellectual* faculty; and not merely, as in the case of a code of ordinary structure, applying itself to the *will*, and operating upon that faculty, by no other means than the irresistible force of a superior will, employed in the way of *intimidation* or *remuneration*: intimidation of necessity for the most part: intimidation, with only a small admixture of remuneration, in a comparatively small number of cases, and to a comparatively minute extent.[19]

This argument is independent of the moral quality of the law and so is consistent with positivism, reflecting Bentham's break with Blackstone's naturalism. But the connection between law and the moral aspiration of doing justice, law's traditional work, is equally deep, as reflected in the difficulty lawless regimes have in establishing order. Terrorizing regimes can survive long enough precisely through the unforeseen and unforeseeable application of power, in the absence of constraining rule. Internal wars, like external wars, are won through the fear of overwhelming force being applied to the captive population. A captive population will work under siege and will otherwise acquiesce in the theft of its treasure. Jacobin France and Stalinist Russia are the models. But an acquiescent population is not a population living under law, nor does its compliance with the orders of the regime indicate anything about that regime's legitimacy. To be clear, the point is not that secret law entails terroristic rule. The risk of terror, or tyranny, is simply the deepest manifestation of the way that secret law undercuts law and undermines the right of those in power to rule.

6.3. IS LAW INHERENTLY PUBLIC?

Law has been associated with the value of publicity for a couple of millennia. Indeed, Fuller describes nonpromulgation as the first way in which one can "fail to make law," and names publicity as one of law's cardinal virtues, singling it out as a possible constitutional condition that can serve as a clear floor for legality, and not just a murkier aspiration.[20] The positivist critique of Fuller, on the other hand, maintains that whatever might be said on behalf of the inner morality of law, actual legal institutions and particular laws can depart very far from these ideals without a sacrifice of legality. We need not sign on *tout court* to the "separation thesis," which insists that there are *no* necessary connections between law and morality, but these observations suggest a limited form of its truth: even such a great fault as secrecy does not render the category of secret law an oxymoron.

And yet, the history I have described, from Solon and Plato through Hobbes, Louis XIV, and Napoleon, and including even Fuller, must count for something in our understanding of law's relation of value. For since law is, as all acknowledge it to be, a human construction, it is perforce a human construction existing in time. And if those who have elaborated the concept of law over time have come to the conclusion not just that there is something not just undesirable about secrecy in law but fundamentally repugnant, then the charge of conceptual mistake in the understanding of law is better leveled at those who deny the history.

To put it another way, the problem of secrecy reveals something about the way in which publicity functions not just as a condition of law's efficacy, but as an essential normative component, part of what makes law law. This is to go beyond Jules Coleman's attempt to reconcile observations about law's normative value with his positivist commitments. Coleman says,

> Law just is the kind of thing that can realize some attractive ideals. That fact about law is not necessarily part of our concept of it. After all, a hammer is the kind of thing that can be a murder weapon, a paperweight, or a commodity. . . . However, the fact that a thing, by its nature, has certain capacities or can be used for various ends or as a part of various projects does not entail that any or all of those capacities, ends, or projects are part of our concept of that thing.[21]

The largely unbroken historical record of condemnation of secret law reveals that a demand for general publicity is part of our running experience, such that any analysis of law had better build it in from the start. In fact, Fuller does not go far enough in establishing the norms of publicity, restricting himself to general reflections of the inefficacy of secret law. But wholesale publicity, coupled with retail (or marginal) secrecy, is precisely what has motivated concern with tyranny over time. Positivism's new-found sympathy to a value-embedded analysis needs to include publicity.[22]

6.4. FROM SECRET LAW TO META-SECRET LAW

In the modern state, secret law occurs in different forms on a continuum from the directly secret, in which the existence of secrecy is known, to the meta-secret, in which the existence of secrecy is unknown.[23] Sometimes directly secret laws come with a regime of classification and penalties for their disclosure. In other cases, the effective secrecy is maintained by making the law invisible, a matter of very low salience. Caligula, Blackstone tells us, promulgated his laws "in a very small character, and hung them upon high pillars, the more effectively to ensnare the people."[24] Today, a budget item might be disclosed but buried in a mass of other provisions so that only someone who knew about the change in advance could discover that it had been made. Or, as in the Israeli case I discuss, a law could be changed without apprising the most significant constituencies for that law. Clearly there are differences between secrecy and low salience, just as there are differences between lying and other forms of equivocation, including misdirective truth-telling. But, in practice, mere secrecy and low salience are subject to similar moral evaluations, and I treat them as equivalent.

I do not mean to minimize the extent to which "merely" secret operations or guidelines can undermine ideals of principled governance, but I do not want to overstate their threat. Since the fact of their secrecy is known, such laws still operate within the realm of political accountability. I want to identify another form of secrecy, which I call *meta-secrecy*: when the fact that there is a secret is itself secret. Meta-secrecy is interesting, and especially troubling, because it is by nature unbounded. Ordinary secrets are black boxes, identifiable and roughly quantifiable from the outside. But meta-secrets are invisible, and so resist the kind of monitoring that can fix their location in political space. To take a homely example: as a professor I try to keep my political views secret from my students—they know I have views, but their content is undisclosed. By contrast, an undisclosed financial interest, for example in a technology I tout in class, is much more subversive to trust, because the secrecy of that interest opens to question the full range of my activities in the classroom.

What follows is a spectrum of legal secrecy from what I take to be the unproblematic to the highly problematic, roughly tracking the shift from directly secret laws to meta-secret ones. This categorization is not meant to be definitive or uncontroversial. Clearly much depends on the stakes, the possibility of later disclosure, and the extent of the secrecy. Moreover, secrecy of the sort mentioned at the beginning of the spectrum can easily transform into secrecy of the second sort.

(A) *Covert operations*: One of the prime sites of secrecy in government is military and intelligence operations. Such operations are not themselves law, although they are initiated and regulated by legal rules, usually generated by the executive (with the consent of congressional staff), but also sometimes by legislative initiative.[25] The military regularly deploys troops and engages in cross-border operations that are sometimes secret from the country whose border is crossed; but even when the target nation has provided a quiet promise of noninterference, such programs are still kept secret from the public at large, as well as other nations.

Secret operations present evident problems of accountability, as well as international stability. When they go wrong—think Bay of Pigs—the consequences for public diplomacy can be disastrous. Large-scale operations, like the secret bombing of Cambodia and military actions in Laos, or the funding of the Contras in Nicaragua, can rise to the level of constitutional crisis, where the secrecy is an attempt to evade one of the few legislative checks on executive military action. I do not mean to minimize the costs of such adventures. Yet they do not strike at the heart of the notion of law, so much as at questions of stability or separation of powers in a particular constitutional configuration. They are a prime example of "mere secrets," or known unknowns, for it is itself a matter of common knowledge, both domestically and internationally, that there will be a range of operations whose efficacy demands secrecy. Domestically, such operations may require consultation (for example with congressional leadership or the chairs of the intelligence committees) and limited disclosure; and where such disclosure is made, they will be tolerated. Internationally, the continued existence of secret operations is in the general interest of states, and so no third party demands are heard for general transparency. While foreign states may complain about particular actions, there are no serious objections by state actors to the category of secret international efforts.

On the domestic front, there is an analogue to the covert international operation: the undercover police investigation. At the level of principle, undercover operations are uncontroversial, provided they meet ordinary civil liberties requirements, such as judicial approval of search and surveillance, and are attentive to the possibilities of entrapment. Clandestine criminal activity is an obvious social threat; and clandestine penetration of that activity is usually the only possible remedy. But application of the principle depends on two further factors: the scope of criminal law, and the degree of clandestine policing.[26] Combine laws criminalizing large swaths of putatively antisocial behavior with extensive secret policing or informant systems, and the result is Cuba or the DDR. Large-scale infiltration of social networks destroys trust within a society, rendering ordinary relations impossible.

My focus, however, is not on the distinctive evil of state practices of enforcement and popular terrorization, which may be controlled at the level of law (if not discretion) by perfectly public laws. Rather, it is on control of government operations by rules that are themselves secret. Needless to say, the categories overlap, insofar as secret practices may be used to enforce secret law.

(B) *Prosecutorial guidelines*: Given general laws, substantial temptations to disobey, and limited state resources, prosecutors have an obvious and powerful incentive not to disclose their particular strategies, lest citizens try to gain benefit via tactical safe harbors, where they can expect no scrutiny. The same practice is true of tax authorities, who must maintain a general fear of audits even (and especially) when the rate of auditing becomes a matter of poor lottery luck. The consequences for noncompliance would be serious if the audit guidelines were made public. By maintaining discretion about where and when enforcement will be made, all are on potential notice that their behavior might come afoul of the law.

Such secrecy in enforcement is unproblematic in principle, as are speed traps and sting operations. As long as the general norm is legitimate, it is hard to see the objection to a little *in terrorem* strategy in law enforcement. The problems arise from the possibilities for selective prosecution that flow from the secrecy, or other deviations from good-faith efforts. Since the law being enforced and the fact of secrecy are known, and assuming internal controls on the exercise of the policy, there is no apparent objection from the point of view of law (except the windfall unfairness that some malefactors will simply not be punished).[27]

(C) *Black-box budgeting*: More secret yet are the budgets for covert programs, both domestic and international. Intelligence operations and weapons development are subject to special protocols, and an interesting body of regulation has developed around them.[28] Practices vary in the quality of briefing given to legislators who approve the funds. In the United States, typically only congressional leadership and committee members are given access to even outlines of the program, and fewer yet are allowed to read the annex before voting on it. The classified annexes have rested in a disputed middle ground between executive action and law; until 1989, the president had treated the line items in the annex as congressional "suggestions," without force of law, but Congress in 1990 declared that the annex too should enjoy binding legal status. (One might imagine difficulties policing the fidelity of secretive agencies to congressional will on the one hand; while on the other hand, agencies failing to respect congressional preferences might well suffer wrath in the following budget cycle.)

Such secrecy in the budget process, as well as other forms of accounting gimmickry that enable the invisibility or low salience of expenditures, clearly are a source of mischief, even if secrecy may in other cases represent a reasonable balance between democratic accountability and national security. One congressman, Randy Cunningham, was convicted of a host of influence-peddling offenses, which included inserting earmarks into the classified portion of the Defense Appropriations Bill.[29]

(D) *Secret treaties*: With secret treaties, we move into the realm of metasecrecy. Secret agreements have played a significant role in international diplomacy. Many of the famous intrigues among the kings, queens, and popes of Europe occurred through secret emissaries and diplomatic instruments, with covert promises of assassination.[30] More recent examples include agreements on mutual defense, joint administration, and deaccession of territories. The destabilizing effects of secret treaties are clear: they enable coordination among factions, reduce the predictability of response in the international arena, and sow distrust among international actors generally. Hence the first of Woodrow Wilson's Fourteen Points for Peace was: "Open covenants of peace, openly arrived at, after which there shall be no private international understandings of any kind but diplomacy shall proceed always frankly and in the public view."[31]

Since Wilson's efforts, a norm has developed that strongly disfavors secret treaties, although they still play a significant role, especially in making possible bilateral agreements whose content, if otherwise revealed, would be destabilizing for other actors. The agreement ending the Cuban missile crisis, whereby Kennedy agreed to withdraw the Jupiter missiles from Turkey, is a case in point: revealing Turkey's cooperation with the nuclear missile program would have undermined Turkish political actors internally and threatened to align it more closely than it would like with the

United States internationally. Despite the emerging norm against secret treaties, the War on Terror and the particular conflict with ISIS seems to have increased their frequency, simply in virtue of the incentives they provide for cooperation between countries (like the United States and Iran) that are divided diplomatically but nonetheless find coordinate interests.[32] Short of formal treaties, relations with Pakistan, involving a shared interest in suppressing the Taliban forces who retreat from Afghanistan to the Pakistani tribal regions, may also be subject to formal but secret agreements between the executives, with legislative briefings.

(E) *Secret executive legal action*: Many secret executive programs of the sort mentioned above begin with secret legal action by the executive, exercising his regulatory authority. In the United States, this authority is exercised through the "executive order." Most famously, in the United States, the authority of intelligence agencies to assassinate individual civilian political leaders, has been restricted by a series of executive orders.[33] The executive orders represent a form of administrative law, relied upon by our own agencies, and undisclosed changes to the orders reflect a significant shift in law. Many such executive orders are made public, but they need not be, under an exception in the Freedom of Information Act; and in the important class of National Security Directives, they frequently are kept secret, in whole or in part.[34] The National Security Agency's warrantless surveillance was conducted pursuant to a classified directive, and important aspects of the continuity plans for the executive branch in the event of the deaths of both the president and vice president, are governed by a further secret annex to a public executive order.[35]

The OLC memoranda were not formally regulatory instruments but interpretations of already existing law. Nonetheless, the effect of these interpretations, when accepted by the attorney general, is to establish the legal position for the United States on the matter at hand. And when the interpretations are at variance with statutory authority prohibiting the forms of interrogation or domestic surveillance permitted by the opinions, then their effect is to work a change in the underlying law. When the opinions are sharply at variance with conventional understandings of the statutes, have broad scope, and are issued in secret, then they are tantamount to a secret executive revision of the penal law. The opinions thus amount to new, secret law—quasi-legislation—and might just as well be grouped under category (G), below.

Moreover, the opinions fall into the category of meta-secrecy, not just ordinary secrecy. Where the domain of (provisionally) tolerated secrecy are those programs consistent with, but not disclosed by, higher-level rules and programs, the torture and surveillance programs were decidedly at odds with governing law. An ordinary citizen—in fact, a sophisticated legislator or administrative lawyer—would have been shocked to discover the existence of these opinions: the fact of their secrecy was itself shrouded in secrecy. Indeed, the OLC opinions permitting the surveillance, in apparent violation of the governing FISA statute, were so secret that they were kept even from NSA's legal counsel.[36]

There is another striking example I will discuss at odds in some respects with the OLC torture opinions: the decriminalization of consensual homosexual sodomy in Israel reveals a disturbing face of secrecy. Israel maintained on its books, and occasionally enforced, a statute forbidding anal intercourse, defined as "carnal knowledge of any person against the order of nature."[37] The statute was general, and covered consensual as well as nonconsensual sex. But secret prosecutorial guidelines were issued by Israel's attorney general, Haim Cohm, in the 1960s prohibiting prosecutions for violations of the act not involving lack of consent or minor partners, instructions reissued, again secretly, in 1972. As with the OLC opinions, which won a decriminalization of torture for CIA and military personnel, these guidelines accomplished a dramatic narrowing of scope of the governing statute, which was not itself repealed by the Knesset until 1988, again mostly in secrecy. I elaborate this example below.

(F) *Secret trials and secret evidence*: The Court of the Star Chamber earned its infamy through secret processes based on secret evidence. Used to combat political opposition to the Tudor-Stuart political interests, it made use of the King's Privy Council to legitimate the straightforwardly brutal repression of political dissent and threats to executive power. In recent centuries' political history, Star Chamber trials have featured as an oppositional lodestone, an example of what criminal justice is not—and indeed, form much of the backdrop for the provisions of the Fifth Amendment, as well as modern English criminal procedure.

While secret trials have persisted around the world, as a way of administering political repression with minimal backlash, secret trials per se have played little or no role in liberal states, even in the post 9/11 legal regime of the United States.[38] What *has* played a role, continuously but increasingly, is the use of secret evidence and redacted public records of proceedings at nominally public trials. (Secret evidence has been used in a range of military and national security cases, as well as immigration cases, for a long time.)[39] The due process objections to secret evidence, and *a fortiori* to secret trials, are familiar and serious, but they do not raise the special conceptual and political problems posed by secret law as such.

(G) *(Meta-)Secret law*: A law that is secret—that is, legislation that is passed by due process and approved by the executive but whose existence and content are secret from the governed—would seem to be a real institutional possibility under most systems of government. Indeed, Thomas Aquinas argued that since natural law remains in force without any further act of promulgation, promulgation is not part of the essence of law.[40] John Austin comments that a British statute constitutes law even if unwritten, on the basis of the Blackstonian fiction that the people are present at its making, through representation. While Austin subjects Blackstone's rationale to ridicule, he appears to endorse the descriptive jurisprudential point. On such a principle, if the fiction is honestly maintained, then secret law is a conceptual possibility as well, since everyone is, in principle, in on the secret.[41]

Large swaths of Soviet-era law, known as the Sobranie, including criminal, environmental, and agricultural law and regulations, were either formally secret or strictly limited in their promulgation.[42] Nor is secret law unknown in the United States. The eighteenth-century Continental Congress met in secret, and the Senate sat in secret until the Third Congress; both houses continued to meet in secret to hear confidential messages from the president through the War of 1812.[43] Between 1811 and 1813, the Eleventh and Twelfth Congress passed a number of statutes authorizing the president to seize adjoining territories; the statutes were not actually published until 1818 and were omitted from the ordinary volumes for those congresses.[44] The Confederate Congress, between 1861 and 1864, also passed a number of secret resolutions in closed sessions.[45]

The second chapter of Israel's decriminalization of sodomy provides another example. The statute itself was eliminated from Israel's penal code in 1988. But the mode of removal was curious: it was part of a wholesale revision of the sexual offenses law, with this particular change introduced during the legislative conference; and no record was made of the fact that the law had changed so dramatically. That is, homosexual sodomy was decriminalized secretly, first by the attorney general, and then by the legislature. As a number of commentators have suggested, the reason for the secret change was not a pragmatic desire to minimize resistance to a controversial decision. It was, rather, a stratagem by Israeli religious conservatives to preempt a gay rights movement, for anti-sodomy laws had served as a salient point of opposition and coordination for movements around the world. In order to prevent an Israeli Stonewall, and the flourishing of an above-ground homosexual culture, repressive law was altered silently.

Poignantly, law's central role in shaping identity became the reason for denying knowledge of the law to Israelis.

6.5. THE DEFECTS OF SECRECY: (DE)LEGITIMACY AND (DIS)ORIENTATION

I want now to argue that the real problem with secret law is that it undermines two fundamental aspects of law's value, of what makes law function as law. First, secret law deprives the governor of his legitimacy, undermining his right to rule. Second, secret law deprives citizens of their understanding of themselves in relation to the state and, thus, of their identity as legal subjects. This double assault—crippling the governor's right to rule and citizens' ability to position themselves in relation to the state—undermines the state's overall authority, which is what makes meta-secret law so troubling beyond its assault on democratic sensibility.

A governor's claim to rule is a claim founded in law—not as a matter of constitutional pedigree but as a distinctive form of governance, with aspirations beyond mere thuggish control. While one cannot infer from legality to legitimacy, one can infer from legitimacy to legality. The first step of disentangling legality and democracy is recovering an older, pre-democratic conception of legitimacy. Law is the predicate of state legitimacy. Legitimacy, broadly speaking, involves the right to rule.

Historically, a right to rule could be earned through a variety of channels: through success in establishing the basic conditions of civil order, through claimed divine provenance, or through genealogical pathways embedded in convention. Today, in the shadow of democracy, it is hard to conceive of any principle of legitimacy that does not, at base, consist of the exercise of popular will through constitutional channels. Yet, even today, we deploy a concept of legitimacy in our foreign relations that has little to do with democracy and even less to do with constitutionalism. Presidents, generalissimos, and kings, whether they sit on thrones of ballots or bayonets, are deemed the legitimate rulers, in implicit (and sometimes explicit) contrast to the thugs and warlords who aspire to the status. Moreover, their claim to legitimacy—to be treated as the rightful addressees, for example, of international diplomacy—is not merely a descriptive status. Other possible leaders, or other forms of government, might have a better claim to legitimacy in an evaluative sense, but the fact that alternatives would be better does not mean that the current rulers are without right.

As I have described it, legitimacy comes partly from the form of rule, not just its substantive underpinnings. While there are some substantive matters that serve as a floor for claims of legitimacy, such as respect for basic human rights, it is the articulation of rule in a lawful—possibly constitutional—form that underlies its legitimacy. Of course, legal form does not guarantee legitimacy, for a democratic state can act illegitimately even if it has passed an electoral test in a host of ways, ranging from violation of basic rights, to corruption, to acting without due process. The crucial aspect of form is law.

So, law is necessary to legitimacy, essential to a state that can claim authority over its citizens. But to serve this purpose, law must be public. After all, one can imagine a constitutional framework in which legal power could be exercised in secret—indeed, this was the constitutional framework imagined by former Vice President Cheney. Secret law might even be effective, in some instances, if just enough people know the secret. A secret law forbidding certain kinds of communications would provide a basis for arresting and convicting people deemed enemies of the state, and the trap set by the law would be enhanced by its secrecy. In relation to the Torture Memo, a secret legal permission to torture was known by members of the CIA charged with interrogation, and some details of the program were disclosed more broadly within the agency as early as November 2002, when the CIA Inspector General was notified that a special "Terrorist Interrogation" program had been set up.[46] But information even within the agency seems to have been substantially incomplete or incorrect; the 2014 Senate Report on CIA Detention and Interrogation alleges that the Inspector General was misinformed, and its attempts to secure internal oversight were deliberately evaded.[47] The report is equally critical of what it asserts was a policy of deliberately misinforming the OLC and congressional overseers about the way in which interrogation methods would be applied and the value of the results obtained.[48] This suggests that a fully legal but secret program represents a difficult accomplishment: to the extent secrecy of the program was maintained within the agency, it seems to have slipped past the secret boundaries established to govern it. Whatever the conceptual possibility of fully secret law, the two are clearly in practical tension.

Here the practical import of the distinction between ordinary and meta-secrecy has bite, for where the fact of secrecy is known, the governor's private realm is demarcated, hence made public. With meta-publicity and first-order secrecy, the public, and supervising legislators, knows what it does not know, and can evaluate externally the ruler's claim to use the techniques of secrecy as a way of advancing the commonweal (whether or not the pubic can affect that decision directly). Meta-secrecy, by contrast, hides the limits of the ruler's power, and so releases those limits altogether—collapsing the space between public and private will. Thus meta-secret laws are a hallmark of tyranny. And if tyranny is, at root, lawlessness, then secret laws are—paradoxically enough—a form of lawlessness. They are quasi-laws rather than real laws, making use of the legal machinery for creating public laws, thus resting on the legitimacy of a state conceived in law without being themselves actually law.

As to meta-secrecy undermining law's orienting function, we can start by remembering that law mediates between the ruler and the ruled. We are social animals, and this means not just that we run in a pack and share our prey or scavengings, but that—as the particularly linguistic sort of social animals that we are—that we orient ourselves mutually in a normative space.[49] Knowing who we are means knowing our relation to the norms that purport to apply to us—knowing that my loyalty is to this group, while those others are my enemies; knowing that we wear our clothes or hair a certain way, mate in these patterns instead of those, or can extend the terms of cooperation this far with this group and not with that group.[50] Knowing these norms simply is knowing the criteria and implications of the social memberships that provide not just protection but cultural meaning for us.

Now, even if our self-understanding depends on an orientation in normative space, it does not follow that we must orient ourselves with respect to law. Clearly, many people are happy with ethno-racial identities that see law only as a colonizing opposition, not a source of meaning. Moreover, understanding oneself "in terms of the law" suggests a monolithic-like identification belied by the departmentalization of law and the complexity of human identity: the role of family law, for instance, in forming a conception of "normal" love and intimacy, bears little relation to the role of criminal law in forming a conception of social harm or deviancy. But insofar as we do think of ourselves as political—as members of political, not just ethno-racial, communities—we think of ourselves in relation to law. For reflective persons living in conditions of social pluralism and uncertain or transient sub-political memberships, law provides the most stable basis of normative identity.[51]

Secret law undermines the identity-giving character of law, not just its guidance function. It deprives us of our subjecthood, both in its meta-secret form, when we do not know of the secret, and then again, disruptively, when we come to know of its secrets. We discover at that point what was true of us all along: that the group to which we belong has a different normative character than we thought. We are not who we seemed.

The conception of value-tracking that I have in mind is actually quite simple. Many people look to role models or others as value guides: their values are pegged to these leaders. It is easy to see this operationally: I might have a policy of always asking my rabbi when I am in moral doubt. But this process has an identity component as well. I might simply assign to myself the values of my rabbi. For example, seeing my rabbi's kind and respectful dealings with women, I assign to myself his attitudes, treating him as a model. Perhaps I think, based on what I have observed, that he regards women as properly equal in the temple, though he has bided his time in forcing a change of practice. But I then overhear a remark of his, where he says that he regards women as naturally subordinate and not suited to full participation in the rabbinate. In this moment, I may be confused, for his values are my values, and I now must adjust to what he has said. I can, of course, revise my beliefs in one of two directions: I can assimilate his to mine and reject my interpretation of his claims. That way, I too come to see women as naturally subordinate. Peculiar as it sounds at first, this might well be described as a case of discovering that my values are not what I believed.

We can see this clearly in both the OLC opinions and the Israeli antisodomy history. Since the United States signed and ratified the Convention against Torture, we have come to think of ourselves as a state that does not torture—helped by the frequent declarations of our president that "we do not torture." This aspect of our identity was known most acutely by military and FBI interrogators, who were drilled that deviations from the Geneva Conventions meant a stay in Leavenworth. The stomach-churning aspect of the revelations, for many, was the discovery that in fact we are a nation that tortures—indeed, worse yet, we are a nation that tortures and yet claims adherence to the Convention against Torture. Jeremy Waldron has written evocatively of the central, keystone role played by the norm against torture in our concept of the rule of law.[52] To lose a grip on this norm is to have to accept a very different definition of the core norms governing the state.

Moreover, the relevance of these norms is no weaker, just because you might not be subject to them, because you are an unlikely interrogator or interrogee. As a member of the polity, you nonetheless have a stake in the question of torture, a stake independent of whether you can or have cast a vote on the matter, or see the state as speaking in your name. The acts may be done by the executive, without regard to democratic voice. But the executive is nonetheless a part of our embodiment in public space, and we understand ourselves internally at the same time as we understand ourselves externally as well.[53]

And while I, at least, am prone to celebrate Israel's liberalization of its laws of sexuality, one can understand, from the perspective of both the right and the left, what is troubling about the sotto voce decriminalization, then legalization, of sodomy. For religious conservatives not in on the secret deal, such a change in the law would reflect an enormous moral shift in Israel's politics, a repudiation of an important part of its foundation in the Torah, for all that document's illiberalism. To be wrenched away from religious sources, towards contemporary liberalism, represents a kind of abduction of the moral identity of the state—one, again, that goes beyond questions of consent. Similarly, for the left, secret removal of the provision eliminated the possibility for gays to insist on their subjection and marginality, not to wallow in victimhood, but to force a more public accounting that could restore them to full subjecthood, not a tolerated deviancy.[54] While the secret change in the law did not threaten them with a loss of control over their particular futures (hence did not raise the ordinary concerns about legality and notice), it disrupted their sense of their oppositional relation to Israeli life, without marking an acceptance within that life.

Clearly, not all parts of a state's law perform this general orienting function, especially in the legal environment of the modern administrative state. Changes to obscure regulatory provisions might have grave economic consequences but would not necessarily bear on subjects' sense of self or nomic identities. But it is more than laws touching on state violence, or basic categories of sexual morality, that can have this function. Broad swaths of family and property law, for example, forge an understanding of one's relation to both time and place. Foreign relations, within a system of strong nationalist identification, can wrench identity as well—for which the revelations of the Hitler-Stalin pact serve as evidence. And environmental law and regulation has increasingly come to serve as an important repository of social values, such that secret changes to those policies could have comparable effects.

This reveals an interesting aspect of the repugnance of secret law: its secrecy is distressing even when the secret is one whose truth we could happily acknowledge—as is perhaps the case for many with the OLC opinions, given public opinion polling about the permissibility of torture.[55] The distressing point about secrecy is not just that the state is acting in discord with my values but that the secrecy of its acts denies my capacity to understand my values in relation to the state. I cannot thereby understand myself *either* as in harmony or in dissonance with my polity. Practically speaking, this may make no difference if I have no effective voice in the policy matter. But politically speaking, it severs me from membership in my state.

6.6. CONCLUSION

What might have been thought a merely academic question, whether secret law can be law, is anything but academic. If law is the way a state is governed, then a legal self-understanding is how a people governs itself. The *democratic* problem of war and counterterrorism is not just whether an open society can keep necessary secrets, but what parts of its rules, practices, and norms must remain public so that war, among other forms of controversial politics, can be a form of genuinely collective agency. Paradoxically, it is the strong democratic default of openness that drives the push for deep secrecy. But that drive must be resisted. A state apparatus that allows meta-secrecy to fester has inflicted a form of schizophrenia on itself, hiving off its agency between an insubstantial democratic form and an effective non-democratic set of techniques. The choice to self-govern secretly is one of the ways a democracy wounds itself. The next chapter, which pursues the subject of torture as a matter of substance and fundamental value, and not just a problem of public governance, further examines the ways a democracy can lose its soul.

7

MUST A DEMOCRACY BE RUTHLESS? TORTURE, NECESSITY, AND EXISTENTIAL POLITICS

[I]f there is something worse than accepting slavery,
it consists in defending it.[1]

—BERNARD WILLIAMS, *Shame and Necessity*

7.1. INTRODUCTION: THE COSTS OF RIGHTS

Rights have costs—that is their point. The cost of rights is in the coin of forgone welfare gains. No one minds a claim to a particular right when honoring that right simultaneously enhances welfare. For example, the distinctively modern achievements for speech and conscience have been to demonstrate the consilience of rights protecting those domains with the promotion of a flourishing public and private life. As a result, claims of rights to free speech and conscience are among the most easily accepted in US public life. The test of a claim of right, however, comes not when its exercise serves the public good, directly or indirectly, but when it represents a direct cost to welfare. At the level of institutional and philosophical discourse, the United States used to honor the right of individuals to be free of torture in this way. The US government viewed it as justified independently of the costs or gains that might accrue from respecting it.[2] In the early days after 9/11, the US government decided no longer to bear those costs. Instead, it chose to use coercive interrogation techniques that would conventionally be thought of as straightforwardly torturous, most notoriously including waterboarding, false burial, "Palestinian hanging" (where the prisoner is suspended by his arms, manacled behind his back), leaving the prisoner naked in a cold cell and dousing him with cold water, sleep deprivation, forced standing, confinement in tiny spaces, and a form of anal rape called "rectal feeding and hydration."[3] The override of detainees' rights against torture was justified on grounds of "necessity," that is, that the general welfare cost of observing the right would be too great for the nation rationally to bear.

Legitimacy also has costs. As I elaborated in chapter 2, legitimacy, normatively understood, refers to the complex conditions under which exercises of institutional power can be justified. While democratic approbation is a central and necessary condition of legitimacy, it is hardly sufficient; populist approval of racist or terroristic policies may provide political protection, but it does not make such exercises normatively justified exercises of power. Nor, for that matter, is direct promotion of social welfare sufficient for legitimacy. If maximizing welfare were enough for legitimacy, then any sufficiently effective and benevolent despot could claim legitimacy, substituting reports on the GDP for elections. According to any theory of constitutional democracy—which is to say, under any political theory plausibly relevant to the practices and institutions of the United States—state power has legitimacy only when it is exercised on the basis of popular will, through representative institutions, and as constrained by principles of equality, fairness, and humanity. Principled constraint, that is, is a centerpiece of democratic legitimacy.

Justifying the actual conditions of political legitimacy constitutes a time-honored debate of political theory. But while there is substantial disagreement about the best foundation for these conditions, there is no disagreement that the conditions are institutionally complex and significantly restrictive.[4] A series of legal memoranda from 2002 created a backdrop of argument for the executive's "plenary authority" over foreign affairs and "complete discretion" over military manners, free from legislative intrusion into the arena of national security.[5]

Though the interrogation program ended by 2004, and many of the issues related to the "legal black hole" at the Guantanamo detention facility were resolved, against the executive branch, in subsequent Supreme Court decisions, the heat of the debates rose again with the release of the Senate Report on Detention and Interrogation in December 2014.[6] The criticism by CIA officials and former members of the Bush administration, notably former Vice President Cheney, of the (Democratic) Senate investigation of detention practices, which included a broad defense even of waterboarding, has shown how a shrewd opposition can attempt to pay the costs of legitimacy in two of the three coins of legitimacy, populism and welfare, while putting aside principled constraint.[7]

As is evident in this chapter, my own feelings still run hot as well. But my intent here lies less in focusing attention on questions of culpability but instead on the relations between rights, on the one hand, and democratic law, on the other hand. The idea that rights, by way of law, constrain democratic politics, is a chestnut of political thought. But the torture program, enacted under a conception of political necessity, raises a deeper issue: whether the ideas of democratic lawmaking, and democratic power, are themselves constrained by an idea of pre-political rights. The work of the twentieth-century German constitutional theorist Carl Schmitt posed this question starkly in the dying days of the Weimar Republic, arguing that an excessively rights-conscious constitutional order would betray the interests of the people it was meant to serve, by becoming the instrument of domestic enemies eager to destroy the state. The Office of Legal Counsel (OLC) Torture Memo of August 2002, introduced in the last chapter, essentially made the same argument in relation to the conflict with foreign enemies.[8] Even though the formal legal positions of the Torture Memo have been repudiated, the *political* arguments within still resonate, providing a frame to examine an essentially philosophical question: what is the force of principle *in extremis*? If rights have bite only when they impose costs, how can we think about their nature in relation to those costs without simply adding them to the social welfare sum? Here I hope to clarify these considerations, so to set limits to necessity's conceptual force.

First, I argue that attention to the concept of necessity as a justification for torture, and especially to the limits of that justification, reveals that we make use in legal and political thought of two very different normative concepts of rights. The first concept serves to impose limits on institutional considerations, while the second is far more sensitive to such considerations. Instances of the former are core human rights protections; instances of the latter are rights of disposition over property. Legal and philosophical arguments purporting to justify torture by reference to necessity betray a failure to grasp these distinctions.

Second, I argue that the Bush administration's theory of executive power displays striking parallels to the political theory of the Weimar and Nazi era scholar and jurist, Carl Schmitt, who developed an argument about the need for extraconstitutional executive power in times of existential crisis for the republic.[9] Schmitt was uncompromising in his rejection of the modern, post-Hobbesian ideal of the law-governed state, whose fallacy he saw as revealed in times of national emergency. By comparing the administration's subordination of ordinary law to emergency with Schmitt's argument for unlimited executive power, I mean to show how deeply radical the Bush administration's theory of political legitimacy was, and how subversive it was in undermining a basic precept of liberal political thought and institutional design: that there must be no source of unlimited political authority. As with Schmitt's theory, the administration's theory ostensibly gains executive effectiveness at the cost of grave dangers of abuse and error. But I also want to argue that both the justification offered by the administration for using torture in specific cases and the justification offered for broad executive authority commonly misconstrue the force of claims of necessity in these instances. Necessity cannot serve as a justification for overriding rights against torture or congressional authority to dictate constraints on warfare. Taking the points above together, the administration's policy can be seen as rejecting two of the deepest legacies of the Enlightenment: the inviolability of the individual and the priority of right to power.

Section 7.2 sets out the administration's justification of torture under claims of necessity and situates these within positive law. Section 7.3, the heart of my argument, takes up the claim of necessity in ethics, first in relation to the infamous "ticking bomb" example so often put forward to establish a principle of permissibility. The ticking bomb is a particular example of a general problem for principle-based (deontological, in philosophers' jargon), rather than welfare-based (or utilitarian), ethics—namely, making sense of limits to rights claims without giving up the core of deontological theory. I distinguish here between two different familiar and ubiquitous conceptions of rights: rights that are inherently sensitive to necessity claims, and rights that are insensitive—of which, I argue, rights against torture are the primary example. Section 7.4 provides a synopsis of Schmitt's existential model of political authority and develops the parallel to the administration's theory of executive power. It then argues that both suffer from a similar, devastating weakness, in that both permit the prospect of necessity to defeat the claim of constitutional limits. Questions of executive power in times of national necessity, like questions of necessity at the individual level, must recognize the force of the two different forms of right. Section 7.5 concludes with observations about the role of necessity in political thought.

7.2. MICRO- AND MACRO-NECESSITY AS A CRIMINAL DEFENSE TO TORTURE

To summarize the story of the US path to authorized torture: in the spring of 2004, the leak of government memoranda creating a legal basis for US personnel to use torture in interrogations was a shock to many outside the administration. The shock lay less in the acknowledgment that the United States was deploying torture than in the lawyerly *justification* of torture, particularly because, despite the erratic and frequently cruel course of actual state practice, the eradication of the moral and legal basis for torture has been one of the defining features of post-Enlightenment liberal politics. This moral and legal evolution began with the early polemics of Voltaire and Beccaria and continued with the now twenty-year-old UN Convention against Torture and Other Cruel, Inhuman, or Degrading Treatment or Punishment, which has been ratified by sixty-five countries, including all of the OECD nations save South Korea.[10] Against growing international consensus, the US administration made clear in the days immediately following the terrorist attacks of September 11 that, in Vice President Dick Cheney's words, "we have to work, though, sort of the dark side."[11] With a political go-ahead, the CIA decided to use a number of formerly proscribed interrogation techniques on "high-value" interrogees, notably including water-boarding, which consists of repeated submersion in cold water to create the impression of drowning.[12] At some point, before or after the interrogations had actually begun, the CIA apparently became worried that its personnel might be subject to the harsh penalties dictated by US Code Title 18, Sections 2340–2340A, the implementing legislation for the Convention against Torture. Section 2340A authorizes up to twenty years imprisonment for anyone who outside the United States "commits or attempts to commit torture," with capital punishment authorized if death results.[13] Insofar as the statutory definition of torture includes acts "specifically intended to inflict severe physical or mental pain or suffering," which pain or suffering can result from "the threat of imminent death," orders to deploy waterboarding (which by design arouses a sensation of imminent death by drowning) would clearly have focused the minds of US personnel on the consequences of the torture statute.[14]

Prompted by the CIA's request, the OLC, under the signature of Jay Bybee but principally authored by John Yoo, provided a memorandum to the White House on August 1, 2002, which became known as the "Torture Memo."[15] The Torture Memo made a number of arguments towards several aims. First, it sought to reduce the potential scope of Section 2340 to include only the most heinous forms of torture. Second, it sought to suggest a range of complete criminal defenses US personnel could deploy if charged under the statute. Finally, it sought to establish as a principle of constitutional law that Section 2340A could not constitutionally be interpreted to bind the president while he was exercising his war powers as commander in chief.[16]

I am chiefly concerned with the second and third arguments in the Torture Memo, which I take up in reverse order. After giving its restrictive definition of torture, the memo contemplates the case in which US personnel may be found to have engaged in acts within the scope of the statutory prohibition, namely to have inflicted with specific intent or attempted to inflict severe physical or mental pain or suffering.[17] It then argues for the claim that "[s]tandard criminal law defenses of necessity and self-defense could justify interrogation methods needed to elicit information to prevent a direct and imminent threat to the United States and its citizens."[18] As the memo describes the Model Penal Code (MPC), necessity will justify a defendant in violation of a law when he or she engages in conduct that the actor "believes to be necessary to avoid a harm or evil to himself or to another," provided that violating the norm is necessary to avoid a "harm or evil" that is "greater than that sought to be prevented by the law defining the offense charged," but only so long as there is no specific legislation or "legislative purpose" to exclude the justification.[19] Necessity justifies otherwise criminal acts against subjects who do not directly pose a threat to the actor. In its paradigm applications, for example, necessity justifies sailors jettisoning cargo to save their ship or a hiker breaking into a cabin to escape a sudden storm.[20] Necessity is, therefore, a potential justification for the situation under consideration in the memo: the decision whether to torture a subdued detainee who may have information that may help avert a threat that may arise.

Specifically, the claim would have to be used to justify an interrogation technique believed to be the sole effective means of avoiding yet worse harms. On its face, then, necessity might provide a good fit for the interrogation practices in question. However, and somewhat peculiarly, the memo explores a much less suitable defense as well: other-defense.[21] The claim is peculiar because other-defense justifies the use of force against an adversary who is himself deploying unlawful force against the defender.[22] As the Torture Memo itself acknowledges, a confined and subdued interrogee is not, by hypothesis, actually deploying unlawful deadly force against the interrogator or another, even if the interrogee might reasonably be believed to be planning to do so, or to have already set such force in motion. By its very terms then, the common-law defense of other-defense would seem inapplicable. Indeed, the only doctrinal support mustered by the Torture Memo for the use of "defensive" force against a nonthreatening actor is a single law review article—an article that, in fact, asserts that while "the literal law of self-defense is not available to justify" torturing a "terrorist" who, while not presently attacking, has "culpably caused" the conditions that threaten the torturer, a *moral principle* may be derived analogically from the situation countenanced by the law.[23] Even this moral principle offers little actual support, insofar as it is premised on the claim that the interrogee has "culpably caused" the threatening condition. Putting aside the case where the interrogee might simply know about such conditions but not want to disclose them (whether out of fear or enmity), the status as culpable causer is frequently what the interrogation must discover, not its premise. The nonmetaphorical case of defense against an actual attacker doesn't lend itself to such doubts, except in the limiting (and here inapplicable) case where a gesture might be ambiguous between threat and innocence. Thus, the conditions that might make other-defense even metaphorically appropriate would be very unlikely to obtain.

Given the lack of doctrinal support for the position, one can charitably read the Torture Memo's invocation of other-defense as resting on two reasons. First, the case law of self-defense, unlike the case law of necessity, provides authority for the use of force against others. Second, self- and other-defense claims can be seen as specific cases of the broader necessity defense. As the memo correctly states, the core of self- or other-defense lies in the defender's belief that such force is "immediately necessary" to avoid the harm posed by someone presenting a direct and imminent threat of serious bodily harm to oneself or another.[24] Necessity grounds the permission to use otherwise impermissible force.

So the argument for the justifiability of torture as a matter of criminal law must stand or fall with the force of the general necessity defense and its limitations. Let us return, then, to the general justificatory element of necessity, specifically, the "necessity" of deploying force in order to prevent a more serious harm. Taken literally, the defense is limited to cases in which the use of force is the only possible response to the threat and is sure to be an effective response to the threat. Only when the defendant's act is a necessary element of a set of conditions sufficient to avert harm can it be said that the defendant acted as he had to, in order to minimize evil. It cannot, in other words, be necessary to act when one's act will be ineffective, even if, were other conditions in place, it might have been part of a set of conditions sufficient to avert the harm.[25]

In fact, the criminal defense of "necessity" presents much softer constraints than true, logical "necessity" would indicate, in large part because it is applied relative to the actor's beliefs about the threat and its projected alternatives. Under the MPC, actors can assert the defense so long as they believe in the necessity of their acts, both regarding the likelihood of the threat and the effectiveness of the alternatives, even if in fact there is no threat or if the means chosen could not be effective. Thus, the MPC defense protects actors who believe, however unreasonably, in the necessity of their acts. However, the necessity provision also provides for liability for defendants who are reckless or negligent in either bringing about the conditions demanding their response or in assessing the necessity of the response.[26] The net result, under both common law and the MPC, is that full justification is provided only to actors who reasonably appraise the situation as calling for their violation of the law.[27] But it should be understood that the subjective extension of the defense, to the reasonable but mistaken defendant, clearly gets its justificatory force from the objective situation where, under the circumstances, the defendant performed an act necessary in fact to avert the greater evil.[28] Put otherwise, an actor's *judgment* of necessity can only be exculpatory if, when the factual premises of that judgment are true, the actor really would be justified. If necessity were instead conceived as an excuse, then any belief, however unreasonable, would be sufficient to exculpate. Since common law and the MPC are clear that only reasonable mistake fully exculpates, the underlying principle must be one of objective justification.[29]

Note the slippage in the theory of necessity—a slippage that, as we shall see, plays a role in evaluating the special case of the ticking-bomb hypothetical. The objective situation is posed timelessly, where the antecedent threat can be weighed against the future consequence of the law-breaking response. But in reality, of course, the defense must apply to conduct undertaken before the threat materializes. It is nearly always impossible to know whether the threat really would have been realized—perhaps the attacker would have suddenly run rather than shot, or a rescue ship might have appeared on the horizon, had defendants waited a few more days.[30] Furthermore, it is almost always impossible for anyone, let alone a defendant, to know in advance whether the use of force will be effective in meeting the threat. Defendants cannot act timelessly, but must instead calculate the expected value of their response, in relation to the expected disvalue of the threatened harm. This is an elementary point, but when understood, it means that in practice actual "necessity" almost never exists. The defense must instead be read to justify the rather oxymoronic category of "probabilistic necessity": the defense justifies extralegal acts when and only when they are highly likely to avert a virtually certain threat, and it is also highly likely that there are no other options. The normative force of necessity resides in the epistemic requirement of high certainty—a requirement necessary to foreclose the possibility of defendants taking extremely low-probability gambles on high-payoff results.[31] In sum, it is a form of cost-benefit analysis that justifies criminal acts when, given only two options, good consequences outweigh the bad, restricted to some indeterminate extent by a requirement of substantial certainty as to the relevant gambles.[32]

In principle, then, the Torture Memo looks as though it staked out a defensible legal position: if the expected value of information extracted through torture is high enough to outweigh the expected disvalue of the materialized threat about which intelligence is sought, then torture could be justified. This is a much broader justification than that offered by self- or other-defense, for necessity would seem, in principle, to justify the use of torture against any person whose suffering might thereby motivate another to talk or otherwise impede the growing threat. And while an official government document asserting the applicability of the necessity defense to torture is remarkable in modern criminal law, it is not unprecedented, as the Israeli Supreme Court has famously mooted application of the defense.[33] But the most remarkable feature of the Torture Memo is the way it embedded the discussion of act-specific necessity, as a criminal law doctrine, within an effectively wholesale conception of necessity. For the most striking claim in the Torture Memo arises even before canvassing the criminal law defenses. According to the memo, "We have also demonstrated that Section 2340A, as applied to interrogations of enemy combatants ordered by the President pursuant to his Commander-in-Chief power would be unconstitutional."[34] Thus, in addition to the *micro-necessity* claim of the criminal law defense, the Torture Memo also invoked what I will call a *macro-necessity* claim in its constitutional argument. According to the memo,

> [T]he Department of Justice could not enforce Section 2340A against federal officials acting pursuant to the President's constitutional authority to wage a military campaign. . . . Within the limits that the Constitution itself imposes, the scope and distribution of the powers to protect national security must be construed to authorize the most efficacious defense of the nation and its interests in accordance "with the realistic purposes of the entire instrument."[35]

The memo argues that "intelligence operations, such as the detention and interrogation of enemy combatants and leaders, are both necessary and proper for the effective conduct of a military campaign," and that the Constitution grants the power to wage such campaigns exclusively to the executive.[36] In other words, the president can authorize his agents to use any ordinarily extralegal means when he judges such means appropriate (the real sense of "necessary and proper") to meet a military objective.

On its face, this is an extraordinarily generous amount of power, which does not even require a state of war, but only the context of a "national security" concern. The position can be read as a broad form of necessity justification. According to the Torture Memo, the governmental structure under the Constitution is itself conceived functionally, an instrument for preserving the "security of the United States," and the president's role within that scheme is defined derivatively, as necessary to effect the goal of security.[37] Thus, extralegal policies are justified immediately as exercises of instrumentally justified discretion.

The Torture Memo came in for severe attack as an interpretation of criminal law, as well as its interpretation of constitutional law. According to critics, its legal reasoning ranges from unconvincing to ludicrous.[38] As David Luban elaborates, the memo derives its definition of torture from a health statute.[39] It fails to acknowledge the total absence of federal or state case law supporting its assertion that the necessity defense might apply to intentional acts of violence under color of law beyond the narrow contexts of self-defense or restraint of a fugitive (as well as the fact that the necessity defense has only been recognized in federal criminal law in order to be rejected in each case). In order to avoid the contravention of legislative purpose (one of the limiting conditions of the defense), the Torture Memo interpreted Section 2340A's absolute prohibition of torture as, by negative implication, creating statutory space for exceptions governed by necessity.[40] And finally, as mentioned above, the memo invokes self- and other-defense justifications outside their ordinary context of force used against an active threat, grounding the claim not in doctrine at all, but in a single instance of philosophical argument.[41]

So much for micro-necessity doctrine. The constitutional, macro-necessity analysis is similarly thinly sourced. While making the extraordinary claim that statutes cannot be construed, as a matter of constitutional law, to restrain the commander-in-chief's war powers, the Torture Memo failed to cite the principal modern case on legislative-executive relations in time of war: *Youngstown Sheet & Tube*, which held that President Truman must rely on explicit legislation or a constitutional provision even when acting during wartime on grounds of military necessity.[42] Nor does the memo mention the contrary constitutional text empowering Congress to "make Rules for the government and regulation of the land and naval forces" and to "discipline" the militias.[43] In its excursion into original intent, it further relies on extremely exiguous material. For example, the memo quotes Alexander Hamilton's vision for broad national power to "provide for the defense and protection of the community." However, this implies nothing about the specific authority of the president in relation to Congress.[44] But even if original intent were controlling—the consequence, obviously, of a complex argument in political theory—it is highly implausible that the Framers, who were students of Montesquieu's separation of powers and the English debates on the limits of royal power, would have endorsed such a sweeping view of the executive's authority.[45] As Jack Rakove, one of the leading historians of the founding era, wrote, "[O]n balance there is little evidence that the ratifiers expected either that the president would have the dominant voice in the making of foreign policy or that the Senate would be reduced to acting as a mere check on the executive."[46]

Thus, whatever might be said on behalf of the Yoo-Bybee analysis, a great deal more clearly needs to be said before it could be deemed independently convincing, let alone serve as a foundation stone for an enormously controversial change in the United States' legal conception of its duties to detainees. Yet the memo was influential, serving as the basis for the subsequent and widely disseminated Department of Defense Working Group Report, which set policy for interrogations involving military personnel around the world.[47] Considering the high professional reputations of the OLC lawyers, the thin legal arguments, and the number of hands the memo passed through, it is hard not to conclude that the Torture Memo was meant more to frame and justify a policy position in ethical and political terms than to provide a legal analysis. Indeed, its legal analysis is now a matter of historical record. After the Torture Memo leaked and before the confirmation hearings of Alberto Gonzales as attorney general, the OLC withdrew the memo as an authoritative legal statement and repudiated its arguments as to the scope of "torture."[48] The repudiating memorandum, under the signature of Acting Assistant Attorney General Daniel Levin, displays far higher standards of legal reasoning. It also replaces the pain threshold for torture, previously defined as pain tantamount to that experienced in organ failure, by a requirement of pain or suffering that is "severe" in a concededly undefined but still quite serious way.[49] As a formal matter, at least, this would appear to leave open the question improperly foreclosed by the Torture Memo: whether significant suffering (arising, for instance, from stress positions or waterboarding) could amount to torture. But the Levin memo specifically does not address the Torture

Memo's analysis of the micro-necessity criminal defenses, nor does it take up the Torture Memo's claim that legislation may not constrain the president from acting on military necessity during times of war.[50]

The Levin memo's basis for declining to address the claims of executive authority was itself peculiar: the president's "unequivocal directive" that US military personnel not engage in torture or other forms of inhumane treatment.[51] In other words, the broad limits on executive power insisted upon by the Torture Memo need not be addressed because of an exercise of executive discretion. Between the issuance of the Torture Memo and the superseding Levin memo, the OLC apparently took action to ensure that US interrogation policy did not henceforth rely on the controversial executive-power analysis (with the possible implication that the analysis had been relied upon to justify practices in the interim).[52] But the reasoning behind the memo has still not been repudiated, at least to the knowledge of anyone outside the government. To the contrary, the Torture Memo's broad assertions of executive power have reappeared publicly in two forms: (1) in the analysis provided by a Justice Department white paper supporting its claim that the president acted with inherent constitutional authority in authorizing the National Security Agency to engage in warrantless wiretapping of suspected al-Qaeda interlocutors, in apparent violation of the Foreign Intelligence Surveillance Act;[53] and (2) in the "signing statement" issued by President Bush when he signed into law the Detainee Treatment Act of 2005, which on its face prohibited US personnel from engaging in "cruel, inhuman, or degrading practices" (CID practices) with any detainees.[54] The signing statement, which followed an unsuccessful administration attempt to lobby against the prohibition of CID practices,[55] declared:

> The executive branch shall construe Title X in Division A of the Act, relating to detainees, in a manner consistent with the constitutional authority of the President to supervise the unitary executive branch and as Commander in Chief and consistent with the constitutional limitations on the judicial power, which will assist in achieving the shared objective of the Congress and the President, evidenced in Title X, of protecting the American people from further terrorist attacks.[56]

In short, the Bush administration offered two distinct propositions about the justifiability of torture and has supported those propositions with its actions even as it has backed away from its legal claims. Those propositions were:

(i)   Micro-necessity: A governmental actor may use torture in interrogation at least when torture is the only available and a highly likely means of avoiding a near certain threat of harm graver than that incurred by the act of torture.

(ii) Macro-necessity: The president, pursuing national security or other military objectives, may authorize torture as a necessary response to a threat to national security, irrespective of statutory restrictions.

I turn now to considering these propositions as matters of ethical and political theory.

7.3. NECESSITY, THRESHOLDS, AND TICKING BOMBS

As I remarked at the beginning of this chapter, the core philosophical notion of rights is that they provide us with reasons to act (or not act), even when considerations about overall welfare raise morally powerful concerns about the consequences of those acts.[57] There are always illegitimate reasons not to honor a rights claim—my selfish desires give me (illegitimate) reason to take your property or to make you an instrument of my desire. Rights claims do rule out such obviously inappropriate claims, but were their force maintained only in such cases, they would have no distinctive content. Long-run welfare-based considerations ("consequentialist" considerations, in philosophers' jargon) about the general misery of a world lived amid theft and abuse would rule those claims out of bounds as well. For claims of right to have distinctive content, for them to be more than a rule of thumb for maximizing welfare, they must apply even in the face of putatively good reasons, particularly if violating the rule would maximize social welfare.

This is a point about the philosophical concept of a right, for that concept to have distinctive content. It is not a general justification of rights, or even a specification of what rights we humans may be said to have. It is simply a point about what the concept must mean, given the role it is meant to play in arguments about morals, politics, and law. But this descriptive, conceptual point has a consequence: it makes clear why a general ethical defense of micro-necessity and a deontological conception of right are incompatible. The necessity justification proposes precisely what the rights claim denies: that action may be taken when the good pays for the bad, as measured by the "cost" of the rights violation. An unconstrained micro-necessity justification consists, effectively, in the forcible conversion of a deontological ethical framework into utilitarian one. Necessity justifications ignore the concept of right.

7.3.1. The Necessity Defense in Criminal Law: Beyond the Torture Memo

Criminal law protects individual rights of bodily integrity and security of possession as much as it protects aggregate social interests such as the maintenance of public order or the rendering of just deserts. Given the disparate goals of criminal law, you might think that theoretical discussions of the necessity defense would recognize the inherent limits of any basically utilitarian mode of argument applied to individual rights. On the contrary, Anglo-American criminal law theorists and treatise writers, including the authors of the Model Penal Code, are typically critical of the courts for giving the necessity defense so little force beyond its formal recognition. Theorists complain about the failure of common law courts to extend the justification beyond its well-recognized instances (where it typically justifies regulatory violations, such as speeding en route to the hospital or very local property violations).[58] And on "economic" theories of criminal law, where the point of the criminal norm is to block transactions that could, were they Pareto-improving, go through with mutual consent, the necessity defense would, indeed, exemplify the logic of the criminal law in general—a form of "efficient breach" theory.[59]

To some extent, legal theorists' quick assumption that necessity can be assimilated into the criminal law generally reflects the contingent fact that many of these writers have, independently, utilitarian sympathies. But the lack of attention to the evident incompatibility of right and necessity reflects more than ideological blinders. There are several additional factors at work. To begin with, the basic comparative-value conditions of the necessity defense are virtually never satisfied in practice. Criminal conduct is paradigmatically conduct that causes far more harm to the victim and society than it gains the perpetrator, whether or not the criminal norms are themselves justified in deontological or consequentialist terms. Were society rife with wanton Benthamites rather than egoists, the question of necessity's scope would be ever present. As it is not, the illusion of consonance is more easily maintained.

The relatively few decisions on the necessity defense meet this pattern: necessity claims usually lose, and when they win, it is for easy cases, which fall far short of the infliction of violence, let alone homicide (excluding self-defense). This statement from a recent California case, *People v. Coffman*, is typical: "It is not acceptable for a defendant to decide that it is necessary to kill an innocent person in order that he [or she] may live."[60] To the extent that there is any Anglo-American authority for granting the defense in cases of homicide, it is typically in cases (or, more often, hypotheticals) involving a choice between certainly killing some and probably letting all die, as with shooting down a possibly hijacked jet plane, or pulling a fear-frozen shipwreck victim from a ladder so that others might pass, or throwing some passengers into the sea lest all drown in the overcrowded lifeboats.[61] Commentators have sought to extend this line of cases into true trade-offs, such as the MPC hypothetical in which an inhabited family farm is deliberately flooded in order to save a town.[62] But this highly revisionary aspect of the MPC defense has not been incorporated into law, and the fact remains that there are no decisions in Anglo-American law, or any documented decisions not to prosecute, in which innocents not otherwise in harm's way are assaulted or killed in order to avert harm from others.[63]

The same appears also to be true in European jurisdictions. France's Penal Code exculpates a defendant who, "facing an immediate or imminent danger to himself, another, or his property, performs an act necessary to save the person or property, provided the means used are proportionate to the seriousness of the threat." In principle, the defense covers all crimes, including assault or homicide, but I have found no recorded decisions showing even rejection of the defense in such cases.[64] Germany's Penal Code has a virtually identical provision, called the "state of emergency" (*Notwehr*) defense, but it adds a requirement that the means be "appropriate" to the harm averted. This is read by some commentators, including criminal law theorist George Fletcher, categorically to exclude at least homicide from the scope of the defense.[65] Again, I have found no cases justifying assault or killing someone not already in harm's way. Fletcher cites one case rejecting the defense, in which a German officer was found guilty of battery for beating Soviet prisoners in order to interrogate them regarding whether they had been stealing food and thereby, the officer maintained, threatening the well-being of all.[66] In an especially relevant precedent, in 2004 a German court rejected a necessity defense for a police detective who ordered subordinates to threaten a kidnapping suspect with torture in order to find the victim, unaware that the victim was already dead.[67] The standard Continental examples of successful necessity defenses are, in essence, gleaning cases: squatters found justified in taking over abandoned housing, breaking and entering to shelter poor children, and in principle the theft of food (though it is generally impossible to show that theft was the only option).[68]

7.3.2. Necessity in Moral Philosophy

This leads to the two positive, deeper, reasons why legal commentators and moral philosophers continue to discuss micro-necessity as though it were easily compatible with systems of rights. First is the deontologist's embarrassment at the stance's apparent absolutism, its rejection of any concessions to catastrophic considerations in the name of right. *Fiat justitia, pereat mundus*—Let there be justice, though the world may perish— ought to be disproof of a moral theory, not its motto. How can one both accept principled exclusion of the gains to be made through the commission of wrongs in some cases, while insisting that the gains be forgone even if that means the end of the morally upright existence? While belief in an afterlife would do the trick, that is not an available option for a secular ethic.[69]

The problem is real, but solutions have not been apparent. To reckon with the embarrassment, rights enthusiasts therefore declare themselves deontologists up to a "threshold" of "disaster," after which point welfare considerations are taken to dominate rights claims.[70] For example, Michael Moore uses the metaphor of a dam to explain the finite scope of deontological restrictions: welfare-based considerations build up on one side of the deontological dam until finally they spill over, justifying whatever policies were foreclosed by the "dam" of principle.[71] But, according to Moore, the dam remains and re-emerges once the welfarist waters recede.

The image of a threshold, a dam, or some other discontinuously permeable barrier of principle is tempting, for it captures the form of popular intuitions that (a) it must be wrong, and not merely a poor choice in cost-benefit terms, to inflict some serious evil in exchange for a local benefit; while (b) it seems like an indulgent and even insane concern with one's own moral purity to insist on principle in the face of really catastrophic costs. In the famous line of the moral philosopher William Frankena, "Morality is made for man, not man for morality."[72] The trouble is that although the threshold image is apt, it merely describes rather than explains how deontological principles could function in this way. To be unbearably literal, principles have no underlying physical anchor, as does a literal dam; to be slightly less literal, nor do they have a determinate and finite jurisdiction, like the laws of a polity. They are, rather and simply, expressions of value: that some acts are wrong, or that others are permitted, or that they are required.[73] One might defend complex principles that state, for example, that an act is forbidden unless a certain condition is met. But given what is supposed to be (and appears intuitively as) a primitive, basic concept of being forbidden, period, such principles look simply incoherent. More to the point, such principles raise the classic problem of establishing the marginal trade-off once the values are no longer absolute. Put crudely, once principles have a price, all that is left is the bargaining. This is, of course, the intellectual force of the ticking-bomb hypothetical, which I turn to below. Threshold deontology doesn't avoid this embarrassment but merely pretends it does not exist.

The apparent incoherence of threshold deontology explains why the most prominent foundational account of deontological ethics (Kant's) is commonly criticized for its absolutism. The underlying value of rational dignity is, in Kant's literal term, priceless—incomparable to any other range of goods.[74] The pricelessness of principle is, in fact, its deepest feature and gives rise to the deepest and most notorious puzzle about deontological conceptions: the so-called paradox of rights. This paradox inheres in the fact that rights claims bar consideration of consequences even when these consequences include identical (and larger-scale) rights violations. Thus, one person's right not to be killed (or murdered) will not be outweighed by the benefit of saving two, or more, others from being killed (or murdered). How can the considerations that support honoring the right on one side of the relation not simultaneously demand honoring it on the other side? Again, philosophers have mainly *described* rather than argued for stances and commitments consistent with tolerating the paradox: that the value of the person protected by the right is not aggregable across persons but instead simply demands respect, or that the reasons supporting rights claims are in the form of principled demands, not invitations to maximize.[75]

These formulations are appealing, but they are not justifications. Each might be seen as expressing a conception of individuals as free and equal beings, with lives of individual and distinct value. This was Kant's view, and whether or not one accepts his argument for it on the basis of rational necessity, it remains a deeply entrenched and fundamentally attractive feature of modern political and ethical thought. Robert Nozick has put the point poignantly: "[Using] a person [for another's gain] does not sufficiently respect and take account of the fact that he is a separate person, that his is the only life he has."[76] But the paradox remains, especially in the face of catastrophe, when the actor is faced with a choice between honoring the value in one instance and countenancing its destruction many times over.

Let us look now at the infamous ticking bomb, which can seem to present that puzzle in a particularly troubling way. In the standard story, an interrogator is faced with a terrorist who has planted a bomb that will kill many innocent citizens. Torturing the terrorist is the last, best hope for saving them. The first thing to be said, and the first thing that was said, in Henry Shue's seminal article twenty-five years ago, is that at best the ticking-bomb hypothetical is of virtually no practical significance, and at worst it is utterly corrupt in the illicit conclusions it invites.[77] The example gains its force from its stipulated perfect satisfaction of all the traditional criteria of necessity: the interrogator is certain of the threat and its attendant costs, knows that the person to be tortured is responsible for the bomb, and is reasonably certain that torturing him is the sole means of avoiding catastrophe and is likely to be effective. While under these conditions, there might be widespread consensus that torture would be justifiable, relax any of the dimensions of justification—maybe it's a hoax, maybe it's the wrong guy, maybe the interrogator has chosen to torture the terrorist's child instead, maybe the suspect will lie—and dissensus emerges immediately.

In the real world, it is most likely that some or all of the traditional criteria will be unsatisfied. Moreover, institutions and institutional actors tend to abuse the limits of their discretion, and coerced confessions are demonstrably of inferior intelligence quality to detective work.[78] For all these reasons, attempts to institutionalize any principle of morally permissible torture invariably either (1) define the circumstances under which torture is permissible so *narrowly* that the requisite criteria are virtually never met or (2) define the circumstances under which torture is permissible so *broadly* that the torture is allowed even when it is not morally justified.[79] To the extent that the Torture Memo goes beyond the hypothetical exploration of an ex post defense to a charge of torture and actually lays out ex ante an institutional space for torture (grounded in the qualified immunity of officials relying on its legal advice), I believe it is tantamount to criminal complicity.[80]

With all these considerations against it, the persistence of the ticking-bomb hypothetical might seem hard to explain. Since the conditions under which its conclusion results never actually obtain, it might be best to treat it as a kind of ethical "singularity," a black hole that swallows up intuition and lets nothing emerge. But, in fact, the ticking-bomb example is no harmless anomaly. It persists because of a series of related mistakes in thinking about rights under pressure from welfare, and how to conceive the role of necessity in these cases. Necessity really does justify overriding some kinds of rights claims in many instances, but these are rights of a fundamentally different nature from the ones involved in the ticking-bomb

example. Criminal theorists have overgeneralized the appropriate normative scope of the necessity defense by confusing those rights whose abrogation the defense can legitimately justify with all rights.

7.3.3. Institutional versus Pre-institutional Rights

Let us put aside, for a moment, the cases of torture and ticking bombs
and shift to the law of torts and property. As controversial as a legal decision authorizing homicide or torture would be, so decisions in tort cases
are uncontroversial, like *Vincent v. Lake Erie Transportation Co.* or *Ploof
v. Putnam*,[81] which involved intentional trespasses upon property clearly
justified as necessary under the choices of evils at hand. So clear is the force
of the necessity defense in such cases that no prosecutor would consider
them, and the question of justice is simply who should pay the costs. As
I discussed above, criminal necessity defenses are generally found to lie
in affronts to property rights as well as in violations of regulations that
impair no rights.[82] The difference might be thought simply a matter of the
relatively weaker interests at play, property versus life, but I think it goes
deeper than that, to the kind of right the law of property protects, versus
the kind of right protected by homicide law—or, in the instant case, by
Section 2340 and the body of international treaty and customary law that
stands behind it.[83] This is the difference between what I will call *institutional* and *pre-institutional* rights.[84]

Institutional rights are the rights consequentialists defend: individual
claims secured by a general promise that their respect will promote welfare. Pre-institutional rights, by contrast, are claims that institutions must
honor, and the institutions' basic justice or legitimacy is assessed by reference to these claims. At least since David Hume, property rights have been
broadly (if not universally) understood to be of the institutional sort, both
philosophically and positively. They constitute a conventional system of
assigning ownership whose specific forms are grounded instrumentally,
not in claims of natural right. As a matter of positive law, informal social
institutions, and economic arrangement, this point is clearly true. There is
simply no way to understand our complex system of divided interests and
fractionated claims, much less to justify the economic systems that depend
on them, except on an instrumental, conventionalist basis.[85]

Within contemporary philosophical thought, to the extent that views
of property rights as natural have any lingering force, it is largely to defend claims that the *capacity* to own property must be conceived pre-
institutionally, or that individuals must have some minimum of personal

property in order to be recognizable as equal subjects under law.[86] Even if one accepts the most prominent version of a stronger, Lockean theory of pre-institutional property rights, that of Nozick, this theory does nothing to vindicate current patterns of holdings or the legal doctrines that prevent disturbances to those patterns. Current patterns of holdings, on any realistic view, are built on histories of force and fraud and cannot be consistent with any understanding of what pre-institutional rights to acquisition and transfer would demand. As an account of the way in which property is normatively conceived today, we are deeply committed to both conventionalism and instrumentalism.[87]

The problem with instrumentalist conceptions of rights is that they only work well in the easy cases, when honoring them also promotes welfare. For this reason, they might best be regarded as pseudo-rights. Given some natural assumptions about the value of stable institutional expectations, many cases will turn out to be easy, and markets transferring those rights can function efficiently. But sometimes the instrumental calculus points the other way, even taking into account indefinite future costs and benefits. And when defenders of an instrumentally justified right are faced with the clear choice—respect the right or promote welfare—they must opt for welfare, on pain of being accused of deontological "rule-worship."[88] The consequence is that instrumentally justified rights must go hand in hand with an unrestricted limit of necessity: the right will be respected so long, and only so long, as that respect pays out in the long-term aggregation of welfare.

We know what an explicit version of such a scheme looks like because we live with it every day. Takings doctrine, according to which property rights are secure so long, and only so long, as the state has not determined that the public would not further benefit from an alternative use of the property.[89] The *Kelo*[90] development decision perfectly represents the instability of an instrumental approach to property. As Thomas Merrill has observed, what was chiefly remarkable about *Kelo* was the public furor it evoked, notwithstanding its unremarkableness as a piece of doctrine.[91] *Kelo* simply followed doctrinally in a long line of cases permitting takings that the state could justify by reference to some aggregative benefit, independent of any formalistic requirement of "public use." Translate "public use" into "public necessity," in Blackstone's phrase, and it is clear that takings law embodies the concept of micro-necessity.[92] Whatever substantive criteria of judicial review remain in takings doctrine can best be seen as forcing the assessments of competing values in the direction of the certainty of a welfare gain. When the contingent, instrumentalist foundations of property rights were suddenly laid bare for all to see in the ensuing media coverage, public uproar was entirely to be expected, at least by those who feared their property might become subject to public use or necessity.

7.3.4. Limits to Necessity in War

There is another scenario where rights become uniformly subject to necessity, which ought to disrupt more than bourgeois complacency. This is the scenario of civilians caught in war, where rights to life are balanced against aggregative concerns. Under the principles and agreements of international humanitarian law and the Law of Armed Conflict, while civilians or their property may not be directly targeted, they may be killed incidentally or their property destroyed, subject to military necessity.[93] Their rights to life and property are to be respected, so far and only so far as that respect is not overly costly to the tactical goals of the military commanders. This form of utilitarianism is more restrictive, insofar as potentially optimal strategies of targeting civilians are categorically ruled out, and insofar as the requirements of "necessity" and "proportionality" are supposed to have more bite than simple weighing of costs versus benefits. But the consequences of this regime for civilians caught in war are enormous. The invading and subsequently occupying US military in Iraq was probably as disciplined and effective as any force in history at attempting to keep civilian casualties within the guidelines of international law. The effect is that rights generally honored in near-absolute terms become subject to a highly institutionalized and conventionalized calculus, whereby target planners route their proposals through military lawyers to ensure conformity with law. Even so, estimates of civilian casualties directly traceable to US (or coalition) actions are in the range of 14,000 dead, with estimates of total civilian excess deaths in the range of 400,000.[94] Still, the rate of civilian deaths in the current conflict is considerably lower than in other wars. Estimates of civilian/combatant casualty ratios for the twentieth century as a whole range from 2:1 to 10:1.

My point is not that war is terrible for civilians. It is rather to suggest what a regime of rights limited by necessity looks like. Importantly, the regime of legal rights against torture does not look like this, any more than the right against homicide in domestic law looks like the right to property under the discipline of the takings clause. That the right against torture is not like this, not subject to instrumental calculation, is—ironically—perhaps most evident at war, where the torture of even a captured combatant with tactical knowledge is absolutely proscribed.[95] This point had become so deeply embedded in the law and training of the modern military before the Iraq and Afghanistan invasions and occupations that no one was angrier about the attempt by the civilian leadership of the Bush administration to relax the rules on interrogation than the professional military, especially its lawyers and officers. In particular, the officers expressed concern over the decision, in Bush's terms, to subordinate detainee rights against inhumane treatment to "military necessity."[96] What disturbed the officers, apart from concerns about reciprocity inflicted upon our own soldiers, was that a right specifically excluded from the instrumental calculus was now included. For the right against torture, along with the other rights whose violation constitutes grave breach of the Geneva framework,[97] is the background set of principles against which the particular institutions, permissions, and conventions of war are justified. To put it positively, they are the pre-institutional backdrop against which the institution itself can legitimately be maintained. If there were not restrictions on the killing of civilians or the mistreatment of any persons during the war, the specific set of combat privileges that constitute the Law of Armed Conflict would simply make no sense. If nothing is restricted, then everything would be permitted.

A full account of the force of the right against torture would focus on the peculiar horror of torture, the combination of suffering with the deliberate subordination of the victim's consciousness to the will of the interrogator.[98] But it would share with the peacetime right against homicide a commitment to the value of the individual life, a value that cannot be aggregated, or so our legal and moral theories have generally presumed. The scene of torture, in the imagination of those who reject it, makes the nature of this value especially clear: the interrogee is not confronted as a part of an armed host, but as an individual, already disarmed and vulnerable.[99] This is the field of basic, pre-institutional human rights. There is something unfortunate about Dworkin's oft-invoked metaphor of "rights as trumps." The metaphor suggests that rights are moves in a game, and that the game is separable from the players. This might be an appropriate picture of rights in a court of law introduced as part of a debate about what ought to be done. But there is no argument in the torture chamber; there is merely one person preparing to do violence to another. In such a context, rights are simply constraints on how one person may treat another. They might not be observed, but they exist as moral claims whether or not the justificatory game is played.

7.3.5. Summary: The Anatomy of Necessity

In criminal law, the defense of necessity runs out when it confronts pre-institutional rights, whose value is not the product of an instrumental calculus.[100] My point is not that we could not conceive it in these terms, nor even that we do not, since obviously some people do. My point is that the tradition of criminal law, across the civilian and Anglo-American spectrum, is remarkably fallow ground for justifying acts of violence against individuals, outside either the peculiar space of warfare, or the narrow context of immediate self-defense. While torture and other forms of intentional violence against persons occur on the battlefield as well as in the station house, such acts have received no official legal authorization beyond the awkward discussion in the Israeli Supreme Court and the Torture Memo in the United States. Criminal law theorists have commonly remarked that the absolute value of life shows that the law is "not utilitarian after all."[101] It would be more precise to say that the law responds in a utilitarian fashion to institutional rights and in a nonutilitarian fashion to pre-institutional rights.

7.4. NECESSITIES AT WAR: FACT VERSUS JUSTIFICATION

I have so far argued that we operate across ethics, politics, and law with two distinct concepts of rights. Institutional, instrumentally justified rights, of which property rights are exemplary, are subject to override by what I have called a micro-necessity justification. But pre-institutional rights, which reflect a conception of the distinct value of individuals, are as a conceptual matter immune to micro-necessity overrides. Assertion of a necessity justification in their face simply denies their deontological status. Rights against torture are core examples of pre-institutional rights, and so it follows logically that they are immune from violation justified by necessity.

While recognizing this distinction helps to make clear why necessity justifications have the limits they do, this does nothing to solve the puzzle posed by the ticking-bomb case or, more generally, by the paradox of rights. Pernicious as the example is, it still demands a rational account, for it puts great pressure on the essential element of deontological reasoning, namely, its categorical, exceptionless character. If justified departure is not the response, what is?

At this point, it is worth paying even closer attention to the way the standard necessity justification is not really about necessity but about the conditions under which actors may exercise judgment to depart from conventionally secured rules. As I explained above, real, existential necessity does not play a role in the necessity defense: in the real world, there can never be absolute certainty that the threatened harms will materialize, or that there are no other options, or that the strategy in question will be effective. Functionally, the necessity justification is an ex post application of an ex ante (and unconfirmable) probabilistic weighing of various courses of action. But in the hypothetical, idealized case, the ticking-bomb example does confront us with real necessity, if only in our imaginations. Confronted by real, existential necessity, we find that our principles yield. But we must be precise about what this means. The image of ourselves torturing, or authorizing torture, is not a *deduction* from ethical principles. It is, rather, a *recognition* that our principles could imaginably be unable to withstand the pressure from concrete, opposing values.

It may seem peculiar, even unintelligible, to claim that we can respond to necessity in a way that neither excuses (for we are responsible for our choices) nor justifies. Nonetheless, it is a familiar stance, one whose invisibility is itself a product of its familiarity. Bernard Williams's magnificent account of ancient Greek ethical thought, *Shame and Necessity*, provides a possible model in its discussion of slavery. Chattel slavery was an ordinary and deeply rooted part of ancient Greek life, and the economies of the city-states pervasively depended on it. It was a kind of chance that made people—mostly non-Greek-speaking peoples, to be sure—into slaves: the chance of being captured at war, or by slave hunters. What is essential to Williams's account is that this chance-like feature of slavery was widely recognized by the Greeks. They saw it, he says, as "arbitrary and cruel," as "a paradigm of disaster, of which any rational person would complain." All the same, it was a part of their world, and they lacked the imagination, or the will, to put anything else in its place. As a consequence, Williams says, they saw the slavery system as "not just but necessary." They treated slavery as necessary in fact but derived no lesson of justification from this necessity.[102]

Aristotle, however, departed from this stance. He did not merely accept slavery, but actively defended it. In the *Politics*, he set himself to the task of showing why the slave system was not only necessary but also just.[103] Prefiguring later racist ideology, Aristotle argued that slaves were essentially animals rather than humans, suited by nature to being coerced by their masters, who in turn were suited by nature to ruling.[104] Regarding this step from necessity in fact to justification, Williams remarks, "if there is something worse than accepting slavery, it consists in defending it."[105]

Why should this be so? Why not think that the attempt to offer a justification for a disputed practice at least credits the power of reason, as mute acceptance does not—the tribute vice pays to virtue, in the words of La Rochefoucauld? In cases of genuine normative dispute, the practice of seeking justification in terms of broader principles is part of the underlying practice of ethics itself. But when the acts or institutions to be justified present, on their face, such a disruption to ordinary principles of ethical thought—in slavery's case, concerning the lives people hope to lead—the practice of justification looks more like rationalization than genuinely ethical deliberation.

Let me be precise about the point of invoking necessity against principle here. It is not to claim, fatuously, that we are on occasion faced with "necessary evils," and that we must make the best of the choices we have. The Greeks, on Williams's account, did not see themselves as making the best of a range of difficult choices. Rather, they simply confronted the fact, as they saw it, that their values condemned an institution they could not avoid. Still less do I mean to downplay the danger, on the other side, of mistaking mutable human institutions or natural circumstances as insuperable necessities. The Greeks clearly did so, seeing false necessity in the institutions they knew. If the stance of accepting necessity as fact makes sense, it does so only at the moment of crisis, when the appearance of necessity is challenged at the forefront, both intellectually and practically, and when a return to ordinary principles comes quickly. The sedimentation of necessity into routine practice is the obverse of justification's transformation into rationalization.

Thus, my point is not that the Greeks were right to accept slavery as inevitable, nor that blind acceptance of an injustice is better than a fallaciously justified acceptance. My point (and Williams's) is that it would be better for those who see slavery (or, closer to home, an injustice like mass incarceration) as necessary at least to see it as a brute and inevitable affront to their principles, not as something their principles can domesticate and make safe to perpetuate.[106] Let these hypothetical people indeed marshal their principles—as the Greeks did not—in a struggle *against* the perceived necessary evil, and *not* work to accommodate it on the level of principle, lest they fall—as Aristotle did—into outright justification. The demand of principle is that we honor it even when we cannot obey it, rather than simply view it as receding under the pressure of other values.

7.5. MACRO-NECESSITY AND THE POLITICS OF EXISTENCE

As a matter of constitutional principle, the Torture Memo claims, the existential demands of war limit the force of statute.[107] As I argued in section 7.2, the Torture Memo puts forward an argument that ordinary, constitutionally limited politics, understood as congressional regulation of the armed forces, become unconstitutional transgressions of the president's commander-in-chief powers—powers that click into place when a state of war exists.[108] This I called macro-necessity. I want to argue now for two claims. First, there is a parallel to the Torture Memo's political theory of macro-necessity in the political theory of Carl Schmitt, and this parallel is instructive because the two theories share the same weaknesses and dangers. Second, I argue that the theory of macro-necessity repeats the mistake of micro-necessity: confusing necessity as fact with necessity as justification. By removing politics from formal legal restraints that legitimate it, the theory of extralegal authority transforms necessity into a device for overriding all rights in the name of the security of a nation whose political identity has perforce been lost.

The OLC lawyers, of course, are not the first to argue for a doctrine of emergency powers, motivated by political necessity. Extraordinary legal powers have been part of the constitutional imagination since at least the ancient Roman Constitution, under which the senate could direct the appointment of a dictator, who would then rule Italy by decree until the danger had passed.[109] Although celebrated by Machiavelli and Rousseau, this personal model of emergency rule has generally given way in modern thought to a legalistic model, in which an ordinary office such as the presidency, rather than an individual, is temporarily vested with extraordinary powers, usually by reference to explicit constitutional provisions.[110] European constitutions, including the French Constitution of 1958 and Italy's Republican Constitution, formalized provisions for states of emergency, while the Anglo-American constitutional tradition has preferred to leave them informal (although traces of such thinking can be seen in the US Constitution's provision for legislative suspension of habeas corpus).[111] This exception has frequently been noted, and during the Cold War, when a post-nuclear state of emergency was envisioned, conservative political theorist Clinton Rossiter argued for legislation to provide for a Roman-style commissarial dictatorship during times of emergency.[112]

As part of a general theory of broad executive power, the Bush administration did not seek to make sense of national necessity by changing formal law. As I mentioned above, the chief argument underlying the assertion of the president's supra-statutory authority in times of national emergency is frankly functional: the Constitution is, at bottom, a plan for state survival, and it must be construed to provide the means adequate to survival.[113] Since, by hypothesis, only supra-statutory executive authority is sufficient to ensure survival, the Constitution must be read to legitimate this authority. The Constitution, on this view, demands that its own framework of separated and balanced powers be recalibrated during war, to effect a quite different balance, one of "complete" executive discretion on the battlefield, checked if at all by congressional power over the purse.[114] Law, which as a conceptual matter aims to provide reasonably determinate criteria demarcating the legitimate from the illegitimate, becomes instead a general imperative that the executive do what needs to be done. The job of nonconstitutional law is essentially to get out of the way of the president's strategic and tactical decision making.

Certainly many presidents in US history have argued for, and acted upon, a presumption of extra-statutory authority.[115] The most famous include Jefferson's purchase of the Louisiana territories, and Lincoln's expansion of the army and suspension of habeas corpus. Both presidents justified their acts by reference to public necessity. But, as Jules Lobel and Daniel Farber have argued, both also accepted the authority of the law they broke, making possible post-hoc congressional ratification and opening themselves to the legal consequences should that ratification not be forthcoming.[116] In one sense, both presidents justified their use of extrajudicial authority post hoc by returning to the scene of their crimes, as it were, and looking for ratification. We must therefore be careful to distinguish claims regarding what must be done from what can actually be done under principles of justified authority.

In the Torture Memo (and, arguably, in the white paper concerning NSA surveillance), the Bush administration took a different tack. Rather than concede the extralegality of its positions, the OLC put forward a striking constitutional theory of presidential authority that rendered even very general congressional limitations on intelligence gathering themselves illegal infringements of executive prerogative. That the Yoo-Bybee position was phrased in the lawyerly terms of avoiding statutory constructions that raise "constitutional difficulties" should not obscure the "extravagant" (in Richard Posner's word), even radical, wholesale nature of the claim.[117] Put aside historiographic claims whether this is a plausible interpretation of the Framers' or ratifiers' views of executive power.[118] The roots of the position are theoretical and are illustrated by the early work of the German constitutional theorist Carl Schmitt, who was prompted, in response to threats of both right and left radical politics to Weimar's democracy, to undertake an investigation into the relation between states of emergency and political authority.[119] In a debate with the leading lights of German liberalism (notably Hans Kelsen), Schmitt argued for an expansive understanding of the president's emergency authority as including but not restricted to the particular powers mentioned.[120]

During the 1920s and early 1930s, when Schmitt produced a wide-ranging theory of politics, law, and legitimacy, the Weimar government functioned substantially under the authority given to the Reich president (then Hindenburg) by Article 48 of the Constitution of 1919.[121] Article 48 permitted the president to "take the measures necessary to reestablish law and order, if necessary using armed force," and "[i]n the pursuit of this aim," to suspend specified civil rights, notably rights of privacy, free expression, assembly, and security of home.[122] Thus, according to Schmitt, Article 48 specified the particular civil rights that could be suspended, while enabling all other manner of extralegal authority.[123] While Schmitt was mindful of the danger that a dictator charged with returning the state to normal politics might simply perpetuate his own extraordinary rule, he thought the attempt to restrict a dictator through legal forms was both practically mistaken and intellectually dishonest. As a practical matter, a restrictive understanding of the Reich president's emergency powers might prevent him from defeating internal political threats to the republic—threats generated by those who, like the Nazis and the Communists, used the forms of legal process to subvert the constitutional order. As Schmitt colorfully put it, "In the exception the power of real life breaks through the crust of a mechanism that has become torpid by repetition."[124]

As a theoretical matter, Schmitt argued that the classically liberal emphasis on the rule of law mistook the real nature of sovereignty, conflating genuine legitimacy, which resides in an executive's protection of the will and real interests of a people, with formal legality. According to Schmitt, law is a system of governance designed to cope with specific circumstances—not, fundamentally, a system of normative authority, as in Hans Kelsen's view.[125] Necessarily, law will encounter legally ungovernable situations, and those situations will demand action by someone in a position to act. The key claim for Schmitt is that this practical demand for decision and action itself imparts authority, as shown by the popular acceptance of emergency rule. Put another way, actual political authority shows that authority is logically prior to law. Thus Schmitt's most famous pronouncement: "Sovereign is he who decides on the exception."[126] Real political authority lies with him who can suspend the law, not with him who is bound to it. Or, using the tag of Hobbes that Schmitt takes as his leitmotif: *auctoritas, non veritas facit legem*. Authority, not truth, makes law.[127]

For Schmitt, the claim that sovereignty consists essentially in the power to rule beyond law captures the core of a broader theory that can be called *existential politics*. Existential politics means making central the concepts of order and national identity and making peripheral the formal processes of legislation and administration. This model of politics is seen in Schmitt's other famous aphorism, that "The specific political distinction to which political actions and motives can be reduced is that between friend and enemy."[128] According to Schmitt, just as aesthetics can be summarized in terms of developing criteria for distinguishing the beautiful from the ugly, or economics in distinguishing the profitable from the unprofitable, so politics consists in making and deploying a distinction between "friends," or co-members of the unified state, and its "enemies," or those with whom the state is in actual or potential conflict.[129] But unlike aesthetics or economics, whose distinctions follow on independent characteristics of the objects in their domain, political action itself contributes the characterizations as friend or enemy.[130] Schmitt writes that the friend-enemy distinction is independent of any other distinctions, moral or factual. Prior to governance, friendship and enmity (or peace and war) are fluid, depending on mutable affinities and coalitions. Politics gives sharp borders to those concepts. Politics is "existential," both in that it serves as the basic logical principle of identity—and therefore of conflict—in the world and in that it serves as the very real condition of physical survival or death.

Existential politics is Hobbesian politics, seeing everything through the lens of conflict. In the absence of politics, there is only individualized conflict; politics renders conflict collective by monopolizing force within the collective (thus making "friends") and holding the potential enemies of the collective at sword's point. Maintaining order by policing the friend-enemy line is therefore the central task of political authorities, the condition of all "ordinary" political processes. Since law is a product of ordinary politics, order is also the condition of law. And since the executive's task is to create order, his sovereign authority must thereby transcend law, deciding when ordinary politics can take place and when instead it must be accepted. Legitimacy resides in a people's acquiescence, understood as nonresistance, to the concrete problem-solving capacities of "administrative" political authority, and while Schmitt maintained that executive authority in contexts of emergency was "democratic," this amounts largely to plebiscitary basis in popular acclamation.[131] In principle, executive decision making is meant to be constrained by respect for what Schmitt termed the "concrete orders" of society—the organic, deep social structure provided principally by religious and civil institutions.[132] On this view, legitimacy is partly functional, or "decisional," and partly organic. But since structural separation of powers is a key instance of the misguided emphasis on legalism that both obscures real political agency and prevents state responses to genuine existential threats, only the executive determines what these concrete orders demand.

In our current context, however, Schmitt's eventual embrace of fascism,[133] through the vehicle of a myth of a legitimating popular spirit, is less interesting than the basic move of relocating legitimacy to the space before law. For in their common emphasis on the existential demands of order and the need for swift response, there are clear connections between Schmitt's theory of existential politics and the Torture Memo's macro-necessity justifications for executive overrides of legislative authority.[134] Like Schmitt, the Bush administration sees national security in time of attack as providing a sufficient justification for expanded, extrastatutory executive authority, governed by the broad mandate of a constitutional charge to respond swiftly and flexibly to enemies of the state, unconstrained in tactics by the legalistic regulation of the legislature. The Torture Memo's broad reading of the commander-in-chief power and its reluctance to seek specific legal authority for its acts are precisely Schmittian in their view of legal forms as inimical to national needs. Most importantly, the administration's theory of wartime executive power echoes the errors of Schmitt's argument. Indeed, it deepens those errors by extending the argument from national survival to national security.

Hobbes, like Schmitt, saw an evident truth: without order there can be no politics. As a logical matter, the first question about political authority is whether it is effective in securing order. At the limit, when total disorder or other forms of political extinction become real possibilities, then the only task for political authorities is to preserve or reconstitute order. The question, however, is what follows from this point. For Schmitt, what followed was a claim about the essence of politics, not about the conditions of its possibility. Politics, viewed clearly enough, is nothing other than the work of order; and the identity of a given state is just a reflection of that order. But this is surely a mistake. In ordinary times, when order persists, the essence of politics is familiar: allocating scarce resources, administering projects and personnel, securing justice. Schmitt's radicalism lies in seeing that ordinary political activity as basically epiphenomenal, whereas real politics involves the existential decisions of the executive, or the cultural work of social institutions. Ordinary politics, the bread and butter of legislative supremacy, becomes degraded in Schmitt's view as a deracinated technocracy and, in the modern view, as a market for legislative favors.[135]

Displacing politics so is a mistake. Under conditions of cultural and ideological pluralism, ordinary politics is the vehicle through which a political community determines and expresses its identity and its commitments, its conception of social justice and collective ambition. Just because that identity can be threatened by war does not mean that it does not have content independent of the conditions of existence. Today, any executive claim to legitimacy in organic cultural order would smack of fascism. Of course, in a post-9/11 world, claims of national security cannot be dismissed airily. But to collapse the notion of legitimacy in times of war, or perceived emergency, into pure functionalism, is to fall prey to the pure decisionism that Schmitt himself tried to avoid. It creates a category of "nation" without content, simply as a placeholder for whatever the executive seeks to keep in power. The existential conception of politics, in other words, fails to see the essence of ordinary life outside the friend-enemy struggle, to see that the relations of friends themselves have a discernible character and a history that matters, and to see that diplomatic détente with one's enemies can define a long-term relation as much as can open war.

The Torture Memo's parallel mistake is to conceive of "national security" in vacuous terms, as the target of executive action, without respect for the content of the political identity whose safety must be assured. When hijacked jets strike our towers and kill our citizens, or when roadside bombs and ambushes kill our soldiers, there is of course real suffering and real death. But, as genuinely terrible as these things are, it would be an exaggeration to say that the security of the nation is threatened when even some thousands of its members are killed. The vulnerability of the people cannot be equated with the vulnerability of the nation itself. Instead, the *nation* is rendered insecure only when its identity and existence comes under siege. The Civil War posed a threat of literal dissolution of the state. Many other nations have also faced (and succumbed to) genuine existential threats, sometimes for the better for their people, sometimes for the worse. Thus, the assessment of Lincoln's unilateral suspension of habeas corpus comes far closer (if not passes) the bar of real constitutional necessity.[136] Were al-Qaeda to get hold of a dirty bomb, it might render a city uninhabitable and wreak huge economic devastation. That said, I know of no one who actually believes the existence of the nation itself is under siege. Our hard-won principles concerning humane treatment of our enemies have confronted graver threats in the past, in the global wars we have faced, not to mention the threat of nuclear annihilation that hung over the nation for more than three decades. Al-Qaeda may be a new adversary, presenting a distinct threat and calling for adjustments at the margin in our scheme of civil liberties. But the case is not yet made that we face real, existential necessity, forcing us to put aside for the duration the principles embedded in our domestic and international law.

Perhaps it is not too excitable to worry instead that the real existential threat comes from the evisceration of our principles in the name of security. This is the second error: Schmitt's failure to distinguish between recognizing the limits of constitutionalism and subordinating it to exigency. Legal and political theorists of very different political stripes have recognized that constitutions are made for normal times and that the ordinary processes and balances they require may make impossible a rapid response to acute threats to the existence of a state.[137] In situations of genuine crisis, as Rousseau wrote, it would be wrong "to consolidate political institutions to the point of depriving oneself of the power to suspend their effect."[138] The question is what to do about this point. One possibility is to treat constitutional structure as a heuristic, a rough-and-ready guide to ordinary political effectiveness, to be suspended when circumstances indicate that the guidance of the rule is unlikely to be optimal.[139] This is, in effect, what constitutionalism became in Weimar, as continuous states of emergency led to governance almost entirely under the aegis of Article 48. This is constitutionalism as nonconstitutionalism, whereby Schmitt's aphorism about sovereignty can become a self-fulfilling prophecy, the exception swallowing law. The weakness of the heuristic model precisely mirrors the weaknesses of utilitarianism in moral thought: all distinctive values—for example, political rights against tyrannical domination, or moral rights against torture—are subsumed by a general value of welfare. The rules that ordinarily serve as vehicles for those values may become so riddled by exception that the values themselves are lost.

It is not hard to come by alternatives to heuristic constitutionalism, though there is much debate concerning the optimal choice for emergency measures: whether formal or informal provision for emergency, in what ways the temporary character of the provision should be ensured, and so forth. Bruce Ackerman's proposal for a constitutional "escalator," requiring ever-greater majorities for ever longer incursions into ordinary rights, is one possibility.[140] What is beyond controversy is Rousseau's next point, that "only the greatest dangers can counterbalance the danger of disturbing the public order, and one should never suspend the sacred power of the laws except when the salvation of the fatherland is at stake."[141] What therefore is most important, as a matter of institutional design, is creating institutions to repel claims of constitutional necessity, not to accommodate them. It does no dishonor to a principled commitment against torture to recognize its limits in the hypothetical of the ticking bomb. Nor do we dishonor a general commitment to life's value by insisting that the hypothetical is imaginary, that we remain outside the state of emergency until we can no longer resist its existential claim. Similarly, we do not dishonor our constitutional system, our structured system of sovereign legitimacy, to recognize its limits *in extremis*. We would only dishonor it by entering too quickly into the feverishly imagined state of national emergency and accepting too easily the claims of necessity and the exigencies of national security.[142] The Hobbesian moment, when order must be beaten out of chaos, must be confronted only as necessity as fact, not as a rolling justification for executive supremacy.

7.6. CONCLUSION

Justifying both torture and extralegal authority by reference to necessity fails. It rests upon a conflation of necessity as fact with necessity as justification and upon a broad and deep misunderstanding of the nature of pre-institutional rights.

It fails at the level of principle and international law, whatever the nature of the political regime, because these rights bound the realm of the political. But the failure is all the more profound for a self-governing people at war. The bedrock principles we have, concerning the dignity of humanity and the limits of legitimate power, are hard-won achievements of the last several centuries. Pieced together out of convention, claimed in the shadow of authoritarian power, they have become the marks by which we know our moral identities as both persons and nations. Threats and emergencies demand response, but that response must be grounded in a confidence in our principles' ability to meet the demands of the world on our own terms. This confidence is equally a form of judgment: the determination that threats to our interests not be confused with threats to our existence. Far more dangerous to us, to who we are, is the threat of finding necessity in every conflict with evil and emergency in every war.

At the level of philosophical reflection, the ticking-bomb example does show something. It shows that we can *imagine* limits to even our most deeply held moral principles. But we should use this realization to strengthen our principles and their application in the world, not to abridge them. Here is how the realization of imagined limits can *strengthen* principles such as the right against torture. By their very divergence from real situations (existential necessity can exist only in a hypothetical world), imagined scenarios like the ticking-bomb example can continually remind us that we have not reached the imagined limits in reality, that we need to push our principles further and ever further, that if we relinquish our deepest precepts in an ideal world of imagined scenarios, there will surely be no hope for them in the real world we all inhabit.

I turn now from the darkness that may befall a democratic state to a seemingly opposite concern: that in trying to live up to its aspirations abroad, it may impose its values through coercion and violence. Both tendencies, I believe, stem from the same source: mistaking the force of necessity that flows from democratic value, confusing the value for us, in our own democratic agency, with an abstract value of democratic institutions. This leads, in the case of torture, to a perversion of principle to save an ostensibly liberal democratic order; and in the case of humanitarian intervention, to an excess of principle that can undermine another people's interest in self-government.

8

HUMANITARIAN INTERVENTION AND THE NEW DEMOCRATIC HOLY WARS

8.1. GOODBYE TO WESTPHALIA AND ALL THAT

It is a principle universally acknowledged that an international system in want of a structure of mutual respect and forbearance is a system on the edge of anarchy. It is a further commonplace that the tradition of Westphalian sovereignty is buried under the legacy of Cold War politics and increasingly potent international human rights. A doctrine of legitimacy in international affairs that before rested mainly on territorial control now reflects a messy normative calculus of comity, individual rights, and balance-of-power politics—a calculus that provides few assurances in practice, and none in theory. The problem of self-defense, targeted by this volume, emerges from the lack of a theory of sovereignty. If a state is conceived as an integrated moral personality, as in the traditional (Vattelian) model of sovereignty, then the justification of self-defense is neither more nor less problematic than in the individual case. Within such a framework, a generally commonsense philosophical position would hold that states (and their members) are entitled to exercise lethal force in self-defense when such force is reasonably necessary to repel invasion, occupation, or other forms of armed attack—roughly, the interstate analogues of rape, kidnapping, assault, and murder. Nice philosophical questions abound in the individual case about the limits of this right, but it is not seriously questioned, so long as the individual is not himself a threat to others (responsibly or not).[1] Where there is a self to defend, the right of "innocent" self-defense is, roughly speaking, axiomatic.

The problem arises when the integrity of the national self is put into question. Since the Enlightenment, state authority is seen as legitimate only when grounded in a people's capacity to rule itself by law—when it emanates from the exercise of democratic agency. A state not so integrated—lacking either or both the horizontal solidarity of democratic will formation or the vertical solidarity between people and appointed state leaders—might be thought to lack the moral personality grounding the right of self-defense. No doubt, some manner of a right of national defense can still be built up out of the residual individual interests in bodily integrity and political agency, but the state as such would seem to have no moral standing to assert a collective right. The point is important because the strategy of cobbling together a collective right through a variety of two-level arguments of principle and pragmatics will still leave normative gaps. In particular, a state may not have a right to self-defend if an invasion can be shown to be consistent with the underlying interests of its individual members—for example, if an invading state's acts will likely leave the targeted state's citizens in as good or better a position, taken overall, after its invasion.

Here enters the possibility for mischief, both political and intellectual. If a lack of democratic legitimacy opens the conceptual space for a weakened or gappy right of national self-defense, it also opens the political window for a variety of forms of intervention. While states (or state leaders) will "army up" to self-defend from external threat regardless of what philosophers or lawyers say about the contours of their underlying defensive rights, the international *perception* that those states (or leaders) lack a right of self-defense will form a component of the argument that such states are "invadable"—too tarnished by their political histories and imperfections to maintain the presumption of sovereign self-defense.[2]

Neoconservatives, sometimes joined by liberal scholars, have treated the absence of domestic democratic institutions as an argument for military and political intervention. Even for proponents of broader permissions of humanitarian intervention, the political uncertainty is disturbing, insofar as it provides ready pretexts for international interventions only loosely tied to humanitarian aims. While pro-democratic, humanitarian interventions are hardly the norm in international affairs, the momentum behind the movement—spurred by the failure of the developed world to act in Rwanda in 1994—should give pause, lest the collapse of traditional sovereignty become, not a force for humanity, but a broad license for military interventions. The difficult cases for modern doctrine and theory lie in a middle ground, between flourishing democracies and genocidal tragedies.

Most polities, indeed, are caught in the middle, undemocratic and culturally plural. As such, they lack a principled presumption against international intervention, instead protected only by the contingent calculus of success. Even taking for granted the rights and duties of international society to intervene in cases of genocidal massacre, the middle ground is one that needs to be made more secure, conceptually and politically. This is the middle ground of, for lack of a better term, what one might call run-of-the-mill authoritarian violence, not enough (or ethno-nationality targeted enough) to trigger the Genocide Convention, but enough to stir international outrage. It is the middle ground now of Syria, Bahrain, and Libya—and it has been the ground of much of Latin America.

In this chapter, I try to fill the middle ground with an account of the moral standing of political communities lacking full democratic pedigrees—an account that entails both (qualified) rights of self-defense and (qualified) duties of other states to forbear from intervention. My strategy is to examine the external permission of intervention in order to map the contours of the right of self-defense. By looking to the moral core of what I call 'active political community'—a core that can, but need not, be realized through democratic procedures—we can recover some of the moral ground of sovereignty without retreating to Westphalian statism.

The salient characteristic of a defensible community, I argue, is the way in which its collective agency is manifest—an agency that depends on, but is not constituted by, the ties of identity, culture, and sympathy. This activity, which can broadly and vaguely be called *politics*, has a distinctive intrinsic value, and it is indeed this value that forms the core of what we admire in democratic states. But it is in the nature of the value of collective political agency that it is best respected by being admired from afar, rather than managed directly. It is at the base of the "hard doctrine" of nonintervention urged by John Stuart Mill and, latterly, by Michael Walzer—a doctrine that requires standing back as peoples stumble and fall, rather than following the instincts of the cosmopolitan heart and rushing in with aid.

8.2. PROTECTING LIVES VERSUS PROMOTING DEMOCRACY

Few people today directly advocate an armed intervention simply to promote democracy—though such arguments were famously made by the Bush administration about Iraq, and by the Clinton administration about Haiti. Rather, the argument for democracy promotion tends to ride in the saddle of a better-established principle of massacre prevention—a principle institutionalized now as the "responsibility to protect," or R2P.[3] The R2P doctrine, as embedded in Security Council Resolution 1674, permits armed interventions in cases of genocide, war crimes, ethnic cleansing, and crimes against humanity. The basis is simple: a state that fails to protect its citizens can make no claim to external legitimacy—specifically no claim to a monopoly on the right to govern and control its subjects; it is hence open to other states to provide the missing protection, through their intervention.

The R2P policy limits itself to crimes of extreme state violence, but the logic is not so limited: if a state is depriving its citizens of other forms of basic justice, then it lacks standing in political morality to object to intervention. Access to democratic institutions is a demand of basic justice. A state, therefore, depriving its citizens of that access has no standing to object to an intervention by others to provide justice to them. Moreover, other states, to the extent they recognize a global duty to create the conditions of justice, find themselves with a duty to intervene, when it seems they can do more harm than good.

The argument from and for democracy is so potent because democracy incorporates such a rich range of values, including values of self-realization, collective deliberation, and the construction of institutions of social justice. As a result, its prescription for action, its global writ, is correspondingly broad, limited only by the values internal to democracy itself. If abiding in a democratic polity represents the greatest hope for a humanity intent on living autonomously and in conditions of justice, then democracy is what people deserve, everywhere, and it should be brought to them unless there are some positive reasons to abjure. Pragmatic arguments about blowback and unintended consequences reflect constraints on the view. But the general form of the argument to limit intervention must come from an interpretation of democracy itself, for if democracy represents the highest form of politics, its value will trump any considerations not themselves resting on democratic footings.

Let us start the inquiry by looking back to Libya, as of early spring 2011. NATO and much of the West (and the Arab League) struggled with these questions in initiating what—as of now—has been a mostly successful intervention in Libya, though its long-term prospects remain troublingly unclear, and its repercussions are clearly haunting international cooperation in the ongoing humanitarian disaster that is Syria.[4] The intervention was immediately justified in terms of Gaddafi's threat to hunt down and exterminate "in their closets" all of his opponents, but within days it became (at the behest of France and the United States) a quest to rid Libya of Gaddafi, period, and to try to keep alive the spirit of the Arab Spring of democratic protest. As a first genuine instance of UN-sanctioned intervention grounded in the R2P principle, it should have been limited to massacre prevention. But once the materiel is in place and the sorties are being flown, once the possible Security Council vetoes have been overcome in favor of abstentions, there is no natural limit to the mission, only potential differences in tactics: a combination of bombings and diplomacy to remove Gaddafi, plus further interventions to install civil democracy.

Indeed, the more poorly organized the rebel force of Libya came to appear, the greater the necessary role for intervening parties. The legitimacy of all of this, of course, was predicated on the democratic aims and character of the interveners, satisfying a new, highly moralized, *jus ad bellum* of democracy, such that war is justified when fought for democratic aims by democratic principalities.

The worry, of course, is that this is not a stable recipe for a system of peace and international relations—it is a recipe for a system, instead, of superpowers and dominated subaltern states, the latter always vulnerable to the judgments of the former, whose standing to assert self-defense depends on the moral assessments of the powerful. Perhaps this is more or less the world we live in, in which some powers exercise a benign surveillance over others. But it falls short of an ideal of public, interstate life that is also appealing, one grounded in the analogy to the life of citizens we expect, of toleration for patterns of life that may not please, even if they do not violate more stringent norms. What we seek, in other words, for democracies and for the world, is an ethic of foreign policy that recognizes the independent standing of even (by democratic eyes) imperfect states, with limits to the gains from promoting democratic values. We need, in other words, an ethic for states taken as they are, not as we would like them to be.

Before I move to the conceptual issues, I will address a potent potential objection quickly: that it is all just a matter of costs and benefits. On the one hand, we know from painful experience that armed interventions frequently make things worse for the state targeted for intervention, by releasing civil and ethnic conflict with no authority to channel and manage that conflict. We know the further risk that interventions will create suspicions, frequently justified, in the targeted state of whatever group comes to power in its wake, entailing the perverse loss of legitimacy for the secular democratic states interveners are mostly likely to support.

On the other hand, we know—or have some reason to think—that certain interventions can be helpful. Kosovo is probably the closest example to a success story, after a multiyear occupation. With enormous expenditures of time, money, and trust in imperfect local institutions, a reasonably stable and legitimate multiethnic state is emerging.[5] The mixed historical record suggests that the right policy is simply a pragmatic and cautious one: with the R2P policy as a basic gatekeeper, democratic states should intervene, or should deepen their interventions, when and only when the intervention is likely to make things net better.[6] What we need, in other words, is not more political philosophy but better political intelligence and policy wisdom: better ways to evaluate ex ante the success of these adventures. Let us call this the pragmatic view. Of course, the pragmatic view is consistent with a highly conservative conclusion: that interventions are almost never likely to leave targeted states net better, and that the knock-on effects of destabilizing international relations tip the balance yet further. But, ultimately, it is all a question of costs and benefits.

The empirical aspect of the question cannot be avoided, and of course in real politics, ad hoc and contextual decision making will always be necessary. But the short response to the pragmatic view is that we are simply deluding ourselves if we think that our predictive powers are sufficient to generate reliable answers to these questions. There are far too many variables in play, with dynamic relations between internal parties and external state interests too complicated for the basic decision whether to intervene to be rationally guided. The empirical fog is what demands the searchlight of principle, here as elsewhere.

So let us begin the philosophical inquiry with a somewhat silly example. Imagine Canadians gazing across their southern border and assessing the problems of the US health care system. They might conclude (reasonably) that an important dimension of justice would be better served if the United States were to adopt a fully national and universal single-payer health care program. They might also conclude (reasonably) that there is little political prospect of this change and much reason to think that even the marginal improvements of recent years will be overturned by subsequent elections. The poor coverage of the US health care system has a serious human toll, estimated recently as at least 45,000 preventable deaths per year. Canadians, however, have determined that a relatively bloodless incursion into the US, would cost no more than 5,000 lives, mostly military, giving a 9:1 ratio of lives saved to those lost, and thus the costs of the invasion would be reasonably proportional to the benefits, with those costs deemed necessary to the goal of bringing about basic justice.

Perhaps some would defend the trade-off of lives for lives, with new (and better) democratic institutions replacing worse ones. But I assume that in a more reflective moment, both Americans and Canadians would agree that whatever the proportionality calculus says, such an invasion would be impermissible—and that Americans would be entitled to defend against it, both soldiers and citizens in a *levée en masse*. Moreover, such a defense would be justified, I think—and certainly international law agrees—even if it would result in many more than 45,000 lives lost. Now some philosophers do believe that a so-called bloodless invasion of this sort would not justify self-defense.[7] Such a position is, to say the least, radically counterintuitive. My point here, however, is not to refute it so much as to excavate the source of intuitive resistance. Put crudely, what grounds the intuition that it is permissible for Americans to kill to defend their right to inadequate health care?

An obvious answer is provided by democratic values. An American might well say that, deplorable as our policy of radically unequal access to medical care is, it is all the same *our* policy, grounded in our democratic politics, and that policy choice deserves respect and noninterference, just because it is a the product of a just decision-making process. Perhaps. But now let us complicate the example slightly. Canadians look a little more closely at the United States, and they note that not only is our system of health care access deeply unjust but our institutions are far from democratic. They note the extraordinary role played by private money in US elections and interstitial politics, and the fact that campaign donations from those who profit from the private insurance-driven health care system have an effective veto over more radical policy innovations. (They might also note, a little more contentiously, that corporate-funded advertising vitiates the legitimating value of American public opinion as well.) And so Canada concludes that not only does respect for democracy not stand in the way of invasion, but it can even accomplish two goals of justice: instituting comprehensive, transparent, publicly funded campaigning as well as single-payer health care.

I suggest that even such improvements in American democracy would not render American self-defense impermissible. Even if justice could be furthered and democratic institutions enhanced at a modest cost in lives, the invasion would be wrong. Of course, there are a range of pragmatic reasons to think it would be wrong (even if we think it would be successful in these cases)—not least, the destabilizing effects of the invasion policy for the entire international system, in providing excuses for less benevolently intended acts of war. The use by the Bush administration's lawyers of the Kosovo precedent of non-UN-sanctioned intervention to justify the Iraq War provides a cautionary tale. But such costs themselves might be worth bearing. First, the precedent might not in fact increase the number of wrongful invasions—arguably such invasions will happen anyway, and it is only the window dressing that changes. Second, with more invasions, more justice might be realized around the world, and so the long-term effects could be net positive. Given the handwaving quality to arguments about practical effects, I think such calculations do not lie at the core of the concern.

Before I lay out that concern, I address one other possibility: that we should distinguish between the permissibility of intervention and a right of self-defense. While we naturally think of the first as negating the second, it could be the case that we are entitled to intervene even though the targeted state is also entitled to resist. In the extreme R2P case, the answer is clearly no—a state that assaults its own people has no legitimate basis for self-defense. But in cases short of imperfect institutions, the question is more difficult. The chestnut of the two men wrestling for a plank is another example of the right to struggle. (The ethical permissibility of mutual assured destruction doctrine—an open question, to be sure—is predicated as well on such rights.) The right of intervention might be, in some instances, something like a right to struggle or to compete for a share of limited resources. There is no logical inconsistency in the coexistence of the liberty rights of two parties to vie for a single path to life.

Even outside the context of existential threats, we might think that permissions to intervene and defend are consistent. Take an analogy from individual life and imagine someone who is suffering from a drug addiction, but not so impaired in other respects that he imposes an immediate threat to himself or others. Friends or family might plausibly claim justification in hiring a kidnapper to take him to a treatment center, even as the individual retains the right to struggle against the confinement and to leave the treatment center if an opportunity arises. In effect, this reflects a conflict between the different interests promoted by paternalism, on the one hand—including the interests of those who love the addict—and the interests protected by concern for autonomy on the other hand. Both sets of interests are real, and neither is fully reducible to the other: our interest in autonomy is not just a matter of belief that autonomous choice serves other interests best. Balancing the two is a matter of understanding the addict as both a continuing person with a stake in his future (a future that will be better without addiction), and as someone with a stake in his present. There is no general formula for how the interests will balance against one another. But the point I wish to make here is simply that we can recognize, simultaneously, the argument for intervention and the argument for self-defense.

8.3. INTERVENTION AND AUTONOMY

Return to the international plane, and to US-Canadian relations, with the United States cast in the role of the addict. Now states are not individuals, and there are serious limits to the force of any argument by analogy. But the ways in which the analogy does not hold emphasize the force of the argument for self-defense and weaken the argument for intervention. In

the individual case, the unspoken frame of the example includes the following: an understanding of addiction as an objective impairment of some
normal rational and physical capacities of self-direction, a perspective that
assumes that the intervening actors have accurately characterized the condition of the addict, and an assumption that the addiction, once resolved,
will leave the addict with ordinary capacities of self-governance. But democratic incapacity in a nation—by which I mean the failure of processes
to meet democratic standards of weighing interests equally in resolving
collective policy—is even arguably not like physical addiction. In a state or
polity with a prolonged period of imperfectly democratic or authoritarian
politics, there is no healthy inner self struggling against a political incapacitation—no self to be healed or restored by an intervention. There is only
a hope for a future, a hope that such a self can be constituted through the
intervention. And we have, to say the least, no reason to think that outside
political interventions are capable of building such a self, of creating a
democratically self-governing entity.

Let me put the point now positively, instead of negatively, and connect
it to the broader philosophical theme. If a Canadian invasion would be
wrong, it is because there is a value in Americans making their politics on
their own, independently of how well those politics meet the standards of
democracy. This is the proper analogy to the individual case, recognizing
the value of another nation's autonomy, with little or no regard for how
imperfectly that autonomy is realized. Such autonomy is, in short, to be respected rather than managed, through a policy of forbearance rather than
intervention. Intervention is a *negation*, not a promotion, of autonomy.

A commitment to autonomy is fundamental to the liberal tradition, to
be sure, but the demand for authenticity and self-command is not only a
liberal value, even if it is quintessentially modern—indeed, it has many
nonliberal forms when it is regarded as a collective rather than individual form of self-realization, as in nondemocratic revolutions. The value
is that of a made rather than found existence, the value, named by Ralph
Waldo Emerson, of taking oneself as one's portion. We respect that value
domestically through building the institutions of republican and democratic governance; we respect it internationally not principally by building
international versions of those same institutions but by restraining our actions out of respect for that value in other places.

Let me now go a step deeper. I think the temptation towards denying
the standing of nondemocratic states arises not just from a misprision of
the value of autonomy but from a misunderstanding of the value of democracy itself, or from a mistaken perspective of its value, if you prefer.

The trouble comes from a perspective on democracy that focuses too intently on democracy as a set of institutions for distributing political decision making on the basis of a universal franchise. Such a conception of democracy, while naturally rooted in the self-understanding (and perhaps self-misunderstandings) of developed Western states provides too strong a justification for intervention and makes it too hard to miss the considerations on the other side. I call the offending conception a *telic conception* of democracy: democracy as a set of political institutions. It is telic because the institutional arrangements represent a goal, or end state, one that can be designed and implemented from within or without.

I want to contrast this institutional conception with what I call an *agentic conception*. The agentic (or active) conception of democracy looks to the form of collective agency exercised in a democracy, not to the particular institutional form of its exercise. On the agentic conception of democracy, democratic agency can be honored, perhaps fostered, but it cannot be designed or imported. It is a flower that must grow from its own soil.

To be more specific: the telic conception of democracy, at its core, reflects an instinct for two principles, one substantive and the other procedural. The substantive principle is a commitment to the moral equality of all persons, to the idea that any right to exercise power over another must be earned in a currency that speaks to the interest of the person being ruled. (Democracy shares this commitment with its close cousin, liberalism.) The procedural principle insists that the substantive commitment to equality be realized through forms of interaction and mutual justification: that equality be supported by, and mirrored in, the ways in which basic decisions of the political community are framed. These principles can be given further specification in relation to the kinds of community and decision they are meant to define. A small community whose interests center on common questions of resource use and planning (such as the use of grazing fields, tithes, and taxes to support public or religious functions; how much grain to store against a long winter or bad harvest) will—if it lives democratically—accord all households a voice in common discussion; it may adopt a decision rule of consensus, supermajority, or majority, any of which can claim to give equal weighting to individual citizens' views, respectively in terms of their objections or their preferences. A larger community, by contrast, might try to realize its principles through representative councils, formalized discussions (such as public notice and comment rules), duties of justification and rights of appeal, and perhaps a broader franchise (if broader interests and power are being exercised). In the international arena, the democratic perspective is more a matter of metaphor: an insistence that decisions reflect welfare interests more than balances of power, that decisions affecting the international community be made in public forums rather than through secret channels.

It is when we add what is now called the cosmopolitan perspective to the democratic one that we arrive at the potent formula for intervention. The cosmopolitan perspective rejects the normative significance of national boundaries, or at least their significance in the first instance, as opposed to their utility in, essentially, dividing administrative zones.[8] The cosmopolitan debate, in its initial Stoic form, focused on the rights and privileges of the subjects of the Roman Empire, specifically the rights of the inhabitants of Asia Minor. Cicero, who deserves credit as the first cosmopolitan, argued that moral standing is independent of the accident of geography, that it is instead a heritage of one's humanity and inherent dignity. He wrote, "Those, too, who say that account is to be taken of citizens, but not of foreigners, destroy the common sodality of the human race, which abrogated, beneficence, liberality, kindness, justice, are removed from their very foundations."[9] All morality flows from an understanding of common human needs, and any politics that insists on intrinsic differences among people based on nationality undermines these moral foundations.

Link the substantive value of universal and equal moral worth to a focus on democratic institutions and you have the recipe for what may be called "muscular cosmopolitanism." The perversity of the position is that while it is grounded in respect for all, it presupposes an essentially clinical and diagnostic perspective on the part of the intervening state, analogous to the perspective of the addict's family. It is the perspective of one who looks across a sea of suffering humanity, burdened by nondemocratic structures, and asks: What can we do to free these selves from their shackles?

My tone is perhaps too mocking. The telic democrat honors real values, and the cosmopolitan commitment to universal justice is, in most of its instances, anything but condescending. It valuably insists, rather, on treating birthplace luck as morally arbitrary, or worse, the state of affairs in which resources and development opportunities are distributed so unequally across the globe. Unlike the position I am advocating, it does not treat the status quo as the moral baseline against which deviations must be justified. Nor do I wish to deny the capacities of any political community to live in democratic institutions. Anything to the contrary is bigotry. But the question is how we should regard those peoples and states living undemocratically—what value to see in their arrangements. Or, more particularly, whether we should see their democracy deficits as conditions that we might remedy.

John Stuart Mill provides a guide to how we might otherwise understand democracy. Democracy, on Mill's view, is the way individuals join with others to pursue common projects, most notably the common project of creating political institutions. In his famous essay defending England's sometimes-honored policy of nonintervention, Mill says, "The only test possessing any real value, of a people's having become fit for popular institutions, is that they, or a sufficient portion of them to prevail in the contest, are willing to brave labour and danger for their liberation."[10] Mill's point is partly epistemic—that the social capital necessary to sustain democratic institutions has to be in place, already realized by a population, before those institutions can succeed, and that the best test of its existence is whether a people is already engaged in a struggle of democratic liberation. On this account, motivations sufficient to sustain a popular struggle are necessary (if not sufficient) to sustain redistributive institutions as well, since both involve the emergence of a collective "me," a view of the self as wrapped up in its collective projects with others. The point is strong but not, I think, extreme: while it would be an exaggeration to say that the established democracies have come about exclusively through mass movements, given the role of incremental change, revolutionary mobilization still has played a role in almost all cases, at least in creating a sometimes latent tradition of democratic practice, later restored.

Now, we must be careful with the limits of Mill's position, which would seem to exclude aid or intervention to any group who have not already proven their capacity to govern themselves successfully—an extreme version of the so-called Matthew principle ("to whom much is given . . ."). Where, in fact, to set the epistemic bar is a matter of political judgment. At its base, Mill's point is merely that there must be evidence of internal political organization, and not just wishful thinking, before a policy of intervention makes sense.[11] I recognize the potential perversity of Mill's position, which denies aid to the weakest and most vulnerable of democratic oppositions, precisely on the ground of their weakness. If we were considering political intervention as a question of distributive justice, namely how to allocate international military assistance, its absurdity would be evident. But the international use of force (covert or overt) and the interruption of domestic political trajectories is not a subject of distributive justice. It is instead a deep and characteristic flaw of the telic view of democracy to see democratic aid as a good to be distributed from on high.

Mill's high threshold for permissible intervention has as its obverse a low threshold for assuming the right of a people to self-defend. If democratic potential is necessary for intervention, then its absence is necessary for the denial of the right of self-defense. Put positively, we should presume a right of self-defense on the part of the state so long as there is some integration in political agency, albeit nondemocratic, between state leaders and the state. Evidence of such integration takes a range of forms, from estimates of the depth and breadth of voluntary participation in political assemblies, to rates of defections from the military, to more fine-grained intelligence about the character of civil society. To be sure, these assessments are complex and will often involve intelligence about states torn between civil and ethnic divisions, with some groups integrated into the political structure and others marginalized, whether through formal or informal mechanisms of discrimination. But it would be a mistake to take the fact of ethno-sectarian division as itself a basis for denying the existence of the relevant form of collective political agency. Whether the outcome of such divisions is internal secession or divorce, as in the Czech-Slovak or Yugoslav meioses, an arc of integration (as in South Africa), or sustained minority repression (for now, the Gulf States), all represent distinctive and morally substantive trajectories for those states.[12]

In this way, democratic agency can be as much a limiting notion for political action as an enabling one, for it calls up the success of the democratic project of forming the general will, not merely the values that explain why the general will is the appropriate resolution to the problem of diverse but equally valuable individual interests. Democracy, from this perspective, is an achievement, one always on the brink of unraveling, to be sure, and thus one to be defended where it exists. We need not grant the existence of a nondemocratic value of sovereignty to see that the mission of democratic states in the world is limited, as a matter of permission and duty, to the rectification of a grave set of human wrongs.

From the perspective of active democracy, what matters about democracy is not just the equal weighting of interests or (more ambitiously) the equal weighting of chances to affect common decisions. To be sure, both of these factors are important and explain the centrality of the majoritarian vote within democratic theory as the most perspicuous way of representing the commitment to a principle of equal effect. But those aspects of democracy represent its passive aspect, the way in which it functions as a managerial mechanism for reconciling different interests.

8.4. WALZER AND THE IMPORTANCE OF CULTURE VERSUS POLITICS

The argument I put forward here bears much in common with the interpretation put forward by Michael Walzer, in his essay "The Moral Standing of States."[13] Walzer was concerned to defend a mildly anti-interventionist position from such cosmopolitan writers as Charles Beitz and David Luban, who argued that a state's lack of democratic legitimacy, or its failure to ensure the protection of liberal rights, opens that state to the permissible intervention by any other state if that intervention would improve the protection of the rights of the targeted state's citizens.[14] Walzer, by contrast, argued that even when a state fails an objective standard of democratic legitimacy, or is less than liberal in its institutions, intervention is only justifiable in cases of gross abuse. Like Mill's, Walzer's argument rests on an epistemic and a moral base. The primary, moral base is Walzer's notion that a state can nonetheless reflect a people's culture and values—its political accomplishments, as I have called it—even if the state is undemocratic.[15] Instead, the acceptance and continuing cultural life of the community provides its own form of value. In turn, this value of authenticity makes it likely, ex ante, that a people will defend even nondemocratic states from intervention.[16] More precisely, Walzer emphasizes an epistemic point, that the presence or lack in a region of a state of normative integration is a matter for the members of the community to judge, not for outsiders, with one exception: no outside state is in a position to determine that a people must be liberated from the state, and so instead outside powers must behave "as if" the state has (something like) democratic legitimacy. The exception is, as with Mill, an internal revolution or movement of self-determination that provides the necessary evidence and so justifies outside intervention in support.

My argument parallels Walzer's but locates value in agency rather than culture. In particular, I think Walzer's prescription is correct, although his diagnosis is mistaken. I do not want to dispute whether cultures as such have intrinsic value—such a question seems hopelessly crude, given the difficulties in individuating and characterizing anything that might be called a unified culture in anything but a caricature of national complexity. More to the point, I think that if cultures have some common value, it is because they are expressions of collective activity—of the messy web of micro-bargains, social, economic, and political, through which we as individuals navigate a dangerous world on the rafts we make together. Like the joke about the dog playing the piano, the wonder is that we can do the thing at all, not that we do it especially well. We need not be Hobbesians to regard relatively peaceable collective life as a thing of wonder. A state's political agency is manifest in its overall structure of organization, in the complexity of its systems of political, moral, labor, and military authority through which life within its territory is ordered. The process includes, fundamentally, the way in which authority is dispersed and collected within the group: which decisions are allocated to which individuals or subgroups, and which remain at the level of family, tribe, or individual. The negotiation of authority is the way in which all the members of the community come to have a place, and hence a mutual orientation, within a common structure (or structures). The key notion of politics is the constitution of this system of hierarchical authority.

Such authority, as in most extant states, may involve force, exploitation of its citizens, and a lack of what Rawls called a "decent consultative hierarchy."[17] The constitution of the polity may be subject to internal and external criticism. But the polity does not thereby lack moral standing, in the limiting sense, of an entitlement to defend its own existence. To hold the contrary is not just to make the analytical mistake of confusing the terms of ideal theory with non-ideal reality. More radically, it is to fail to appreciate the distinctive character of human politics itself, and to see its achievement even when its execution is flawed. To take a case in point, Iranian politics involves a complex blend of local political agency, theocratic (and fear-driven) authority, accommodation, complicity, and repression of movements for radical change. Doubtless many Iranians would prefer political options and institutions not now on the table. But a denial, on all but pragmatic grounds, of the state's authority to resist an invasion, simply on the grounds of a lack of democratic institutions, removes from the Iranian people themselves the right to exercise their own agency in pursuit of that transformation.

One qualification may make the position I sketch more palatable. I have argued that denial of a nondemocratic state's right of self-defense is inconsistent with respect for its people's political agency. But the impermissibility of invasion does not entail the impermissibility of other means of democratic support. While political agency demands resources to be exercised, it cannot simply be maximized by any effective means. Rather, it can only be promoted through means that respect its nature. Support through force (say suppressing hostile state actors) or secret aid may enhance political effectiveness but not agency, where agency is understood as involving the public working out of shared values, in a process of dialogue and accommodation. Clausewitz's dictum about war as extension of politics applies only, if at all, to the sphere of diplomatic politics. Within a state, a military intervention does not do politics but instead replaces it. By contrast, overt help with democratization—providing resources or an international environment hospitable to pro-democratic reformers—is consistent with respecting the agency of the people itself.

8.5. RESPECTING DEMOCRATIC AGENCY

Thus, once we understand value as residing in agency, we can see why the emergence of a democracy is something that, structurally, must be developed from the inside out, not the outside in—why the fantasy of importing governance in a box, as the arguments for the American surge in Afghanistan had it, are not only pragmatic but also normative delusions. The development of a community towards democratic institutions is a project of self-constitution. It is an unending process of transforming the micro-level balances of power and privilege, authority and obedience, that characterize social life, into something approximating the telic ideal. Of course, the pace and ease of that transformation depends on the circumstances in which it occurs, and such transformations and negotiations are always easier in circumstances of relative wealth rather than scarcity. Various forms of international aid, to ease the conditions of scarcity and to enable the conditions of politics, can be an entirely permissible and legitimate way of honoring collective democratic agency. But the transformation itself, the constitution of an ever more universal "we," is a matter of a process through which individuals realize how to find in themselves a collective voice and perspective, to act through what Rousseau called the *moi commun*.[18] It cannot be managed from without.

I do not mean to sentimentalize the process of democratic self-constitution. Violence, whether of interveners or of a demotic people, will often be part of this process But the understanding of this violence, and its legitimacy, is different. On the telic perspective, violence is justified, wherever and whenever it leads to better consequences, measured by a democratic metric. If human welfare is what ultimately matters (at least within a secular political theory), then violence will be justified whenever it maximizes welfare.

On the agentic view of democracy, by contrast, violence is justified when it is essential to the formation of a collective democratic agent—a people defining a politics in its own name. Its value is not absolute but rather extends only so far as the value of democratic agency itself, and of the forms of well-being that such agency can produce. This is a significant value, and can justify a broader range of self-defensive rights than a purely moralized theory of war can do. Moralized theories of war rest on theories of individual interests, as well (in their deontological forms) as individual measures of culpability and liability. By contrast, the agentic view locates value at the level of the active community as well as at the level of individuals. The political community formed by that agency has moral standing in its own right—a standing that generates the right of communal, and not individual, self-defense. Such a value is not absolute, even in cases of genuine threat to the community's continued political existence. But, as with proto-democratic revolutions, the value of political community can justify a use of force going beyond individual, nonpolitical interests.

The truly difficult cases for the agentic view lie in cases at the R2P borderlines: exercises of violence by authoritarian states that are serious, and constitute genuine crimes against humanity, but do not rise to the level of mass genocide. This was arguably the case in Libya, and is now arguably the case as the world watches the Syrian president shell civilians in Homs. Imagine a group of people in the state engaged in some form of rebellion, seeking a democratic state, in the minimal sense of demanding a leader whose authority stems from mass consent. The demand itself for democracy has standing in the international system, for it represents a value that many nations themselves realize and accordingly respect. But if the rebels have not yet put in place anything that reflects this ideal, the claim is weak. It is weak partly on epistemic grounds, for we are not in a position to know whether social conditions are sufficiently developed to sustain democratic institutions over the authoritarian competitors that will, with great ruthlessness, be pursued. And it is weak on metaphysical grounds, because the animating value remains hollow until actually practiced, and so offers little counterbalance against the values that genuinely oppose it, including the values of life, stability, and the benign traditions that even troubled nations and peoples have—traditions that may suffer or disappear in the wake of foreign influence.

In the case of Libya, the case for pro-democratic intervention was weak. The aspiration towards democracy surely existed, and the Libyan opposition included expatriates with experience in functioning democracies. But the militia itself showed no democratic character beyond its haphazard organization, nor were there anything like democratic institutions in place from which the rebellion could gather force. I do not wish to make the NATO decision to intervene seem easier than it was, but it was reasonably evident at the time, and all the more so now, that any intervention that went beyond the R2P mandate would be built mainly on the sands of wishful thinking by Western partners. The problem of wishful thinking by interveners, including—most charitably—the ease with which intervening nations are prey to local hustlers who know how to talk the talk of democracy, correspondingly represents one of the gravest threats to national interests.

Taking this risk seriously, in a case like Libya, means acknowledging an awkward logical space: Gaddafi and his military had forfeited any claim of self-defense through their commission of crimes against humanity, but

Western intervention beyond the R2P boundaries was also illegitimate and would have been subject to legitimate self-defense by Libyans not part of Gaddafi's army.[19] Perhaps no group in Libya, save Gaddafi and his apparatus, was even willing to defend the state against the extension of the R2P effort into the area of regime change—itself a consequence of Gaddafi's destruction of a civic sphere. It still does not follow, I think, that the intervention was right, but only that it faced no one with appropriate standing to resist.

Consider now the case of Syria. At the time of this writing, the Syrian government is engaged in a bloody repression of insurgent movements. So far, the international community has refused military intervention. I offer the following discussion principally for heuristic purposes; I do not know enough about the actual situation to offer firm views. But on the argument I have sketched here, I think the threshold for armed intervention (or for arming the insurrectionaries) has not been made. Apart from the calculus of practical interests, which counsels caution in any event, respect for the process of democratic transformation means letting the process of internal civil conflict work its way. Now, there is much the international community can do, of the naming and shaming variety. And—though this is something we might take up in discussion—economic sanctions targeted at the regime seem to me permissible as well, a matter of outside states deciding how to conduct their own relations. But crossing the threshold of war, by blockade, no-fly zone, or troops on the ground, would represent too direct an attempt to remake a polity from within. That is Mill's (and my) hard line.

So, to the extent that democracy invites participation, it does so in a limited way, as a relation between democratic peoples—or, rather, between peoples already active in democratic politics. I recognize the apparent paradox of this view, that the democracies most worth supporting are the ones least in need of support (a specific form of the general rule that nothing succeeds like success). The arming of an incipient pro-democratic rebellion is, correspondingly, among the most troubling forms of intervention, because it involves the expansion of violent conflict to a people who has not, through collective politics, unified itself in the only way that can legitimate that violence.

8.6. CONCLUSION

I have thus far been discussing how the agentic democratic perspective shapes the principled question of when nondemocratic self-defense is justified, or when, conversely, pro-democratic intervention is permissible. I want to conclude by noting that respecting democracy raises issues not just about whether intervention is permissible in relation to the targeted state but about whether it is permissible for the intervener as well. The democratic state must justify the intervention to its own citizenry, and to the institutions of global governance to which it is, in principle, committed. This can raise an acute problem, for genuinely democratic processes are inherently slow, while humanitarian emergencies quickly erupt. As with Libya, fluid events and stalemated political systems combine poorly, giving a motivation for highly nondemocratic action by executives—and setting a precedent for a permanent extension of war-making powers.

Tension between the needs for action and for deliberation might be thought reduced for R2P interventions, since such interventions might be thought to have a smaller scope. In practice, of course, even limited humanitarian interventions can give rise to enduring commitments. Thus, even if there has been formal legitimation of the intervention, the democratic state can find itself subject to fading public interest. The fading of interest, or replacement by other popular causes, makes it correspondingly hard for democratic commanders to plan operations that extend into the indefinite future, for if popular sentiment changes quickly, the initial investment in the humanitarian effort may well turn out to be wasted lives and treasure.

There is a related problem of exit. States launching attacks may be brought in by the best of motives, of preventing imminent loss of life to civilians. But the conditions that make, for example, the risk of massacre acute are precisely the circumstances that make it a chronic risk as well—the circumstances of governmental failure. This means that local institutions will almost never be in place after the imminent massacre is averted. Unless and until the institutions of the target state meet a rough standard of democratic legitimacy, the intervention will be deemed incomplete; a modus vivendi is not enough.

Thus democratic states may find themselves whipsawed between popular pressure to cut short interventions and opposing normative pressure towards providing better and more robust outcomes for the citizens of the targeted state. The crucial question of "What then?"—What policies or engagements follow the initial military adventure?—resonates in political morality as much as in political tactics. Battle fatigue may lead a democracy to declare an intervention finished so long as a civil war is not boiling hot, as in Iraq or Afghanistan (albeit wars not considered humanitarian interventions, though fought with democracy-exporting ambitions), but it may not consider that an acceptable outcome, unless some proto-democratic institutions are also put into place.

We are too early in the modern history of softened sovereignty to know where these pressures will stabilize. I do not doubt that political choices of whether or not to use violence are driven more by prior outcomes than by philosophical reflection and change. But even if changes in concepts are shaped by rather than shapers of the arc of history, they play an undeniable role in our self-understanding and in the forms of justification we have to offer. I have argued that the telic conception of democracy has lowered the threshold of justification too sharply, replacing the sovereign presumption of noninterference with a pragmatic calculus of beneficence. Liberating democracy from this conception, and instead making central the value of political agency, may help to move patterns of thought and decision back towards the (often abused) presumption of egalitarian relations in the international sphere.

9

DEMOCRATIC STATES IN
VICTORY: *VAE VICTIS?*

A conference took place between Q. Sulpicius, the consular
tribune, and Brennus, the Gaulish chieftain, and an agreement
was arrived at by which 1000 lbs. of gold was fixed as the
ransom of a people destined ere long to rule the world. This
humiliation was great enough as it was, but it was aggravated
by the despicable meanness of the Gauls, who produced unjust
weights, and when the tribune protested, the insolent Gaul
threw his sword into the scale, with an exclamation intolerable
to Roman ears, "Woe to the vanquished!"

—LIVY, *The History of Rome*[1]

9.1. THE WINNER'S RIGHTS

"Vae victis"—the exclamation Livy attributes to Brennus, "the insolent
Gaul"—resounds in our time. The aftermath of war brings more than ar-
mistices and ruined landscapes. It brings also the imposition of new rights
and responsibilities for the vanquished. Among the common incidents of
life post bellum have been and often still are the redrawing of territorial
boundaries; relocations of populations; seizure, conversion, and redistribution of enemy property; taking of captives, for ransom or slavery; imposition of reparative payments; and retributive punishment for leaders of
the conquered state.

We may now take these practices for granted, but it is worth pausing to
ask about the basis of the rights of victors, and whether democratic states
have a special entitlement to remake the targets of their interventions.
Like many questions one might ask about the philosophy and morality
of war, the question springs from an opposition between real practice and
normative ideals. War, understood as a violent confrontation between two
states, routinely results in a conqueror gaining power over a conquered

people. With victory comes the power to institute a conception of justice, as a matter of fact. Yet matters of justice ought to turn on questions of right. And questions of right should not turn on the not only accidental (in the metaphysical sense) but deeply repellent grounds of which state was better able to leverage its engines of war to bend the enemy to its will.

I must be careful not to overstate the premise. Of course, the modern law of armed conflict recognizes strict duties for the victor, including duties to preserve private property not needed for the support of the occupying force, to release and repatriate prisoners of war, and to move from occupation to sovereignty for the conquered state; as well as a general prohibition on transfer of individuals and populations. True, these regulations,[2] like many of the protections of the laws of war, come packaged with the broad exception of "military advantage" or "necessity" and are subject to override.[3] But notwithstanding the soft constraint of necessity, it remains true that the field of victory is a field of privilege for the victor, with substantial rights to remake the social and political world of the vanquished. I ask here how this is morally intelligible, if it is at all.

My aim in this chapter is to see whether democratic states should view themselves as specially constrained in the transformations they can exercise as victorious powers. I echo here the work of Gary Bass, whose treatment of the *jus post bellum* has focused philosophical attention on a range of related questions.[4] Bass's premise is that the traditional criteria of the *jus ad bellum* (or what the just war tradition calls the *jus victoria*) are inadequate, in the sense that a war prosecuted for a just cause, with proper intention and by proper authority and using only just means, might be rendered unjust by a peace that is sufficiently oppressive or vindictive. To take an obvious example, a nation exercising a proper right of self-defense against a border incursion would not (or not necessarily) have the right, upon victory, to strip the aggressor of all its political institutions. Put simply, if norms of proportionality are not built as much into the peace as into the waging of the war, the war itself cannot be considered a proportionate response to the aggression and hence will be rendered unjust. Bass's project therefore was to sketch the criteria of proportionality that a peace must meet in order to meet the overall criteria of just war.

It is clearly true that a wicked peace can vitiate an otherwise just war. An inadequate peace can as well. A war waged against an aggressor must justify its human and material costs in terms of the future security it provides, not just in its rollback of a border incursion or dismantling of a particular threat of weapons. A peace that does not include enough reshaping of political institutions, or of the incentives facing an aggressor's political institutions, to deter future aggression will not justify its costs. But these two points both rest on a hidden normative premise: that the victorious nation occupies a space of right, in which it can do this reshaping. Even as we discard older images of sovereignty, there is still a burden for any outside party to bear in justifying such interference—and presumably the burden is greater than can be met simply by pointing to the fact that victory has made such interference possible.

9.2. INTUITIONS: COLLECTIVE AND INDIVIDUAL

The question I am pursuing, of the rights of victors, will seem odd to anyone thinking in individualistic terms. In ordinary life, we rarely have clear victors and losers, except in the artificial environment of a contest or competition; and in such cases, the rights of winners or losers (say, to get first choice of a prize) are well-defined and grounded in the presumed consent of both parties. In such cases, there is no interesting philosophical question about the rights of victors, even if details in particular cases need to be worked out at the margin. Where more major disputes take place, they are brought to the law courts, where the rights of winners and losers are prescribed by the court, and whose legitimacy is grounded in the general authority of the legal system in resolving such disputes. Disputes that do not go to court but are resolved through social pressure or threat, or merely the weariness of one party (I am thinking, for instance, of disputes between neighbors), may result in an allocation of permissions, but no one is under an illusion that the outcomes of these disputes have anything to do with justice or rights—they are simply compromises. That one party gets more than another is a function of threat or advantage.

If we begin from thoughts about interpersonal morality, then, we will be puzzled. Either the rights of victors will simply be whatever rights they had at the outset or they will be mere compromises, reflecting relative power. But I am hesitant to let matters rest there, with a choice between power and right. My hesitancy comes from three main sources. The first is a general skepticism about the usefulness of arguments about war that rest too much on the analogy to individual interpersonal morality. In the social context, our intuitions about interpersonal morality, including even the morality of violent self-defense, take place against a social backdrop in which, for the most part, social cooperation is the norm and political authority is well established. By contrast, in the international arena, conflict is endemic and political authority is ill-constituted. While we need not adopt a fully Hobbesian conception of our international situation, the relevance of horizontal structures and relations of raw power and threat makes an enormous difference to how conflict expands or is repressed in international life. Intuitions about the range of permissible aggression (challenges to borders, physical or normative) in the domestic setting will not sit well in international politics.

The second reason for skepticism comes from a more general working premise: that we relate to each other differently in political and personal spaces. In particular, our relations to one another in politics (especially in international politics) have an irreducibly collective aspect, in which we naturally take up a perspective of what *we* should or should not do, not what *I* may or may not do. The imaginary scene from which intuitions of self-defense derive is me (or my family) attacked in my home, or a dark alley. The scene of victory is me holding a smoking revolver, having defended myself or my family. (And then the state steps in to clean up the mess.) But relations between states are not like this—the enmities are (usually) not personal, between individuals, but involve contests over access to resources. The proper mode, both psychologically and normatively, for thinking about political conflict is to think about what we should do, with the vastly greater range of possibilities for action that social cooperation provides, as well as with the vastly greater time span over which events unfold. I do not deny that individual-centered judgments move our views about politics. Certainly political leaders may come to personalize international conflicts, usually in ways that are debilitating to proper calculations of national interest. And particular scenarios of national vulnerability, especially those involving attack by WMDs, provoke the same kinds of personal fears as the fantasy of the dark alley assault. My point is not that these forms of intuition and thought occur, in life or in philosophy, but just that we must be wary of them and not be too trusting of their implications. I will have more to say on the substantive implications of this premise, that thinking collectively has a different normative shape than thinking individually, as the argument progresses.

The third reason for skepticism—or, better, wariness—about using individually drawn intuitions stems from a particular "power" that political institutions have, as a sociological and psychological matter: the power to suppress the salience of violence. This is a product of many factors, including the ways in which nations rewrite their origin myths to forget the blood spilled in their beginnings; the desensitization of an audience of citizens to mass violence, so that deaths become merely statistical; the mechanisms through which states train young soldiers to kill and to live with themselves afterwards; and—perhaps—the inherent brutality of those individuals who rise to success in politics, and whose refusal to countenance subsequent moral doubts contributes to the numbing effects of the foregoing. A consequence of these phenomena is that our moral judgments, especially retrospective ones, will systematically differ from our judgments in individual cases, which are so much more attuned to the salience of individual violence.

Of course, these psychological and sociological effects might be thought to constitute a *reason* for working up an argument from an individual baseline, precisely in order to counter the distortion. And, indeed, I think individual case judgments can play a valuable role. But I retain a suspicion, argued in different places, that there may be a normative effect of these distortions as well: that we really should think of collective violence, at least in philosophical reflection, differently from individual violence. Or, to put the idea another way: it is, I think, reasonable, to evaluate individual conduct against a baseline that permits no interpersonal violence, except in self- or other-defense (thus including some police actions). But it may not be reasonable, in the sense of meshing with any real sense of the possibilities of politics, to hold political change and conflict to the same standard. We acknowledge the baseline of violence as a matter of practice, in the willingness to balance immediate possible military advantage against certain civilian death and in the reluctance by most writers on war to dwell too deeply on questions of responsibility for any but the most egregious cases.

This may seem to be an appallingly cynical statement. But it has some plausible analogues. Chapter 12 discusses how revolutions operate to reset baseline principles of entitlement, so that we evaluate a revolutionary "taking" differently from an in-regime taking.[5] This is not to say that no standards govern cross-regime redistributions; clearly there are standards. But there is room, I believe, for position between that of a natural-rights-toting Lockean, who believes that transcendent standards of entitlement govern all takings, and an anything-goes Trotskyist, who believes any conception of individual justice is an oppressive ideology. The intermediate position would be one that attempted to define a limit to the scope of overturned expectations, displacements, and the like, but nonetheless recognizes the right of a nascent people re-establishing its government to make a future not fully encumbered by a past. In the case of war (or political violence more generally), it is harder yet to think about the issue. The standard just short of pacifism, that only violence genuinely necessary to self-defense/liberation can be justified, is impossible to implement and never has been implemented. Indeed, the blanket moral and juridical policy of treating line soldiers as absolved of personal responsibility shows that we consider their violence to occur in a different register. There is much more to be said about the issue of individual responsibility for collective violence, and our policy of a blanket permission can perhaps be justified by considerations, ranging from what we can fairly expect of young people subject to both economic and political pressure to—fundamentally, on my view—the logic of reciprocity.[6]

To treat this issue seriously is perforce not to embrace the brutality of war. It is instead to say that if political philosophy wishes to speak to politics, it must represent a realistic space for collective policy deliberation, one anchored in a history of what we actually tolerate as much as in a set of ideals we preach but never observe. The theory of war is, at risk of triviality, a species of non-ideal moral theory, and how one engages in non-ideal theory (or, alternatively, a theory of the second-best) remains a difficult topic within political philosophy. I do not hope to resolve that topic here, but only to offer as method that we pay attention to history and context as we develop more arguments and ask moral questions.

9.3. THE RIGHT TO IMPOSE; THE DUTY TO REBUILD

To return to the question: what right does victory confer upon the victors? Under what title may they exercise power over the defeated, reshaping its political institutions and punishing its members? And what grounds the duties the conqueror owes the conquered?

We may initially frame the answer as falling between two extremes.

No difference: Victors have no rights that they did not have before the war or did not acquire during the war, because of the wrongful acts of the losing state, which has disrupted an otherwise just pattern of entitlements (e.g., to land or other resources). Thus, victors have a right to reparations only if the reparations are for wrongs or takings by the loser; and they have a right to force these reparations only if (and because) there is no superior political authority who can otherwise force payment of the reparations. On this model, victory makes no normative difference, and the underlying prerogative is an effect of historical entitlement.

We can call this the no-difference (ND) model, because it entails that victory makes no normative difference. It is, I think, the way we conceive the scene of individual conflict. Once, for example, one has succeeded in self-defense, one enjoys no other special privilege in relation to the defeated. It may well be the correct view of collective conflict as well. I put it aside for the moment simply because it does not accord with practice, according to which victors acquire governance rights.

We may contrast this no-difference model with the other extreme, the *vae victis* (VV) model.

Vae victis: Victors have a complete right to rule the vanquished, as an effect of the power they wield (through victory they become sovereign over the territory of the vanquished). On the stronger view, there are no standards to govern what victors may do to the vanquished, including taking prisoners as slaves and seizing property as prize; any gesture at justice is a matter of grace, not right. This is the tradition recognized by Grotius as a matter of the law of nations (though he argues that theological considerations should temper the exercise of these rights): "Moreover, by the Law of Nations, not only he that makes War for a just Cause, but every Man in a solemn War acquires the Property of what he takes from the Enemy, and that without Rule or Measure."[7] Less radically, as new sovereigns, victors are subject to the ordinary constraints of justice in their rule and may not, for example, act towards the vanquished in a way that they could not justifiably act towards their own subjects—thus pillage and enslavement of the captive population would be an excess.

Needless to say, the more rather than less radical version of this position characterized military victory, from Brennus at least through the modern period, and even—for the Soviet army, for example, which treated rape and pillage as a right of conquest—through World War II, before the adoption of the Fourth Geneva Convention in 1949. Of course, even in modern practice, respect for the Convention may be unobvious.

It does not take an elaborate moral or political theory to reject the radical form of VV, which entails the denial of any rights held by the vanquished people as humans, independent of any prerogative that they have to manage their affairs collectively. Put another way, radical VV is the denial of any moral or political standard as well. It is the view put forward, most famously, by Thrasymachus, in the *Republic*: justice is "nothing else than the interest of the stronger."[8] As a social analyst, Thrasymachus has a point. The rules structuring societies, like the rules structuring conflict, may seem like bare masks of the privileges of power. But Socrates has a point as well, even if we depart from his argument partway on: to call the rule of power "justice" is to enmesh oneself in contradiction, for one cannot consistently make use of a vocabulary of right or justice while denying, in effect, any independent normative content to those terms. "Might makes right" is closer to an oxymoron rather than an identity, even if relations of power are deeply relevant to the content of any conception of right (and even if claims of right turn out, on reflection, to be assertions of power).

Socrates, of course, takes the whole of the *Republic* to refute Thrasymachus, on the grounds that real justice involves the structuring of both soul and city in accordance with reason; anything else is mere illusion. Wherever we depart from Socrates' or Plato's specific conception of justice, we are likely to agree that the idea of justice has a content independent of the appetites of the ruler. In the case at hand, whatever the bounds of a victor's right to rule, if the victor wants the mantle of legitimacy, there must be some claim to grounding it in a principle of right. And similarly, if our aim is to construct a political theory to evaluate these contexts, then we too must insist upon some set of principles of justice.

Between ND and the less radical form of VV lie a much more interesting range of positions, any of which will ground some right of victors, and perhaps some duties as well. These positions cleave along a line I will represent as "epistemic versus substantive."

9.4. EPISTEMIC FOUNDATIONS OF THE RIGHT TO RULE

While, as many writers have noted, we moderns are perhaps more distant culturally from the medieval Christian writers than we are from the Greeks, the medieval and early modern tradition of Just War Theory has much to offer, because it can reveal the origins of now well-settled, if differently articulated, doctrines. One of the most important contributions of the medieval tradition is the idea of the "doubtful war"—a war in which the merits of the positions taken by the belligerents are unclear. The tradition recognized that wars, like most human actions, are taken in light of a judgment that the action is justified and for the best. The judgment may often be mistaken, even self-deluding, but the propensity for such mistakes is a universal human characteristic, and it structures the conflicts that arise. Contemporary writing in Just War Theory is plagued by unrealistic clarity about the moral positions of the parties. This is no doubt an effect of the literature being both too immersed in the examples of the fight against Nazism or *génocidaires* and of the particular sources in political critique that move many writers to adopt the subject in the first place. But the older writers treat the topic with a view that is less moralized, more readily cognizant of the possibility that each party to the conflict will claim the mantle of right. (It is no doubt also true that state leaders were responding to histories of dense and bilateral conflict, so each could easily find injury to protest.)

One of the most interesting of the late medieval/early Renaissance theorists is the Italian Raphael Fulgosius, who aimed in turn to resurrect an older Roman tradition of the war seen as just on both sides. Here he is in extended quotation:

> [H]ow is it that one who wages an unjust war acquires the ownership of the things he captures through his unjust actions? I respond that, as it was uncertain which side waged war rightfully, and as there was no common judge above the parties by whom this could be ascertained in terms of civil law, the nations with the best of reasons decided that war would be the judge in this matter; i.e. that whatever would be captured in war or through war should become the property of the capturing party, as if it had been adjudicated by a judge; see *Institutes* [4.17.7]. . . . For victory in war comes about as it were by the judgment of God, because God is a righteous and just judge of all, as Lucan likewise testifies: "The victorious cause pleased the gods," just after having said: "Who more rightly raised arms? It is impious to decide; each one appeals to a great judge" [Pharsalia, 1.127–8].[9]

Fulgosius's idea of a war being just on both sides is grounded in the following premises:

(i)   War properly carries a right to captives (and ransom) as well as pillage.
(ii) Both sides of a conflict will present a claim of injury.
(iii) In the absence of a central political authority, there is no human source to adjudicate the claim objectively.
(iv) Nonetheless, the victor will claim the rights noted in (i).
(v)   An adequate theory of politics must explain why this claim is legitimate.

Finally, and most oddly for modern eyes:

(vi) God uses war as a way of showing who, in fact, is in the right.

The problem for Fulgosius might be restated as the following: given that war carries prerogatives of capture, given that the history of state holdings reflects these claims of right, and given that we humans are not in a position to judge the correctness of the claims, how might they nonetheless be legitimated, so that we do not throw all current holdings up for grabs? Fulgosius recognized a defect of the more heavily moralized just war tradition, that the insistence on the rectitude of one and only one party to a conflict would tend to undermine the capacity of war to settle an issue—and therefore would limit the likelihood of conflicts to settle at all. Terrible as war may be, endless war is worse than sudden conflict. A conception of bilateral *ad bellum* justice, coupled with the epistemic appeal to God, by way of victory, provided a way to close the books.

Now, as Peter Haggenmacher argues, Fulgosius's idea of the appeal to heaven has a very significant effect on the development of another key feature of Just War Theory: the decoupling of the *jus in bello* from the *jus ad bellum* that emerges most clearly in the symmetry principle, discussed in chapters 5 and 6.[10] This is the idea of "regular" war, and it depends for its institutional force on a bracketing of the question of *ad bellum* rightness. But the relevance Fulgosius himself finds for the idea lies in the *jus victoriae*, for it provides a foundation for the claims that result.

We can distinguish, in fact, a number of positions within the epistemic, Fulgosian, camp:

(1) Victory reveals who was (antecedently) right. God's rule is to orchestrate the course of the war to reveal an underlying truth: which party was the unjust belligerent. The unjust belligerent deserves to lose some portion of its citizenry and resources, as either punishment or reparation.

(2) Victory coincides with right, because victory on the battlefield is pleasing to God, and he whom God lets or observes to win is thereby entitled to the prizes that flow from victory. (Fulgosius seems to come close to this point, in quoting Lucan as saying that the "The victorious cause pleased the gods.")

(3) Alternatively, in more secular terms, martial virtue runs together with moral wisdom and confidence, so that the party properly confident of the rightness of his cause is likely to fight more effectively and fiercely.

(4) War is a decision procedure, rather like a lottery, to determine who is right. The legitimacy of the resulting claim of right flows both from the intrinsic moral claim of winners to prizes, and from the institutional needs for such a procedure.

Perhaps there is more that might be said on behalf of some of these conceptions than meets the eye—especially if we grapple with the assumption of a fundamentally contested grounds for war. While position 2 depends on strong theological assumptions, position 3 is more plausible. The genuinely aggrieved party may be able to instill greater determination to win, or may have better-functioning institutions than a predatory state, and its strength may emerge on the battlefield. Of course, the opposite may be true, too, as Vattel noted.[11] More plausibly, the victor may have the power to excavate evidence about the antecedent rights claims—for example, to show a search for a pretext for an attack. War, then, would play an incidental epistemic role.

Position 4, by contrast, might well be defended in the genuine absence of an international court or any better decision procedure. It marks a hard application of the saw that it is often more important simply to decide, than to decide rightly—if endemic conflict about who is (actually) right will have further negative consequences. Within the domain of prizes, we accept a limited version of the claim, recognizing the contingency of any particular victory yet recognizing the strong claims of desert that thereby flow.[12] Certainly, the dueling, or chivalric, aspect of the professional warrior ethic is a major force in stabilizing the *jus in bello*. And if there was ever a time that wars were fought with few collateral casualties, the prize conception could have some weight. But—to speak the obvious—the costs of war are so great, and the need to move states towards other decision procedures so profound, that the prize conception can no longer have much sway for us.

That said, the epistemic conception brings with it an insight that we should retain: that we must be modest in assessing our capacity to determine the justice of the cause and to mete out responsibility to individual leaders for its prosecution. A consequence of this is that we should not be confident that we can derive the rights of the victor from the antecedent rights of the parties. Victors' rights will need different foundations altogether. It is also worth noting an additional point, to which I will return: the need for an account of the rightness of the victor is a function of the extent of the victor's prerogatives. The more extensive or far-reaching we understand the rights to reshape another's territory, the stronger the claim needs to be. Conversely, if we regard the underlying claims of right as weakly founded, we should retract to the extent possible the rights of the victor to the narrowest range possible.

9.5. SUBSTANTIVE FOUNDATIONS

The epistemic foundations of victory being insufficiently robust, I turn now to substantive conceptions. These move us closer to the no-difference position but retain a moral argument:

(5) A victor's rights extend beyond the right to reparations for a wrong, to the right either to deter future conflict or to punish for

wrongdoing, consistent with respect for the nonpolitical rights of the conquered.

(6) A victor has a right to act upon the vanquished when, and only when, the victor enjoys a superior mode of political life and seeks to inculcate that mode in the vanquished. (The superior mode of political life does not provide a sufficient basis for the just cause requirement, but it satisfies the legitimacy condition for the just peace.)

(7) A victor only has whatever rights flow from the need to implement duties of natural justice—for example, to install a governing authority in a now ungoverned territory, or to repair damages and displacements.

Take position 5 first. The right to defend, triggered by an aggressive act, is as entrenched a ground for war as the tradition has. The right to deter, certainly once aggression has taken place, follows closely on its heels. On the principle that fewer wars are better than more, a system in which aggression receives an additional sanction would be to the advantage of all states not themselves seeking to be aggressors. A victorious state that extracts extra pain from the vanquished sends a signal to all potential aggressors, against itself or others, that the costs of attempted aggression far outstrip its benefits. On such an instrumental conception, a victor's rights would include the right to degrade the military capability of the vanquished, to put its leaders on trial, and to alter its political constitution such that it is less likely to aggress in the future. The deterrence argument would thus cover a lot of the ground of the victor's privilege.

What might be said against it? Like any instrumental reason in ethics or political philosophy, deterrence arguments can crowd out other values. We recognize their limits in the individual context of criminal punishment in the insistence that the deterring threat be proportionate to the wrong, and that even additional marginal gains in deterring power overcome a threshold of respect for the rights of individuals to make their own choices about how to conduct themselves. An unlimited right of deterrence is a right to terrorize any potential aggressor, inconsistent with the respect owed to all. An unbounded right of deterrence effectively arrogates all value to the side of the deterrer, whose interest in security trumps all other values. In the international context, the right of deterrence must be balanced against the correlative principle of dignity: the right of national self-determination. We might follow Walzer in recognizing simultaneously the value and limits of self-determination, in particular in recognizing the cases when we might think a vanquished state's political institutions are so toxic that its people can make no claim to value them as a means of self-determination.[13] But we must be wary of a tendency to excess in these judgments, to treat any risk of future threat as sufficiently dire to entail wholesale political transformation and the installation of puppet regimes. If we instead limit the force of the deterrence argument to the exaction of the smallest penalty large enough to make aggression not worth attempting, we will bring the risks within bounds—and will be far short of the actual space of the victor's prerogative. On the other hand, the international system needs to have effective deterrence against individual acts of aggression, given the risks of a cascade of further conflict. Nor can anyone pretend to be able to define with precision what quantum of pain is necessary in the national felicific calculus, especially given that the costs can usually be hived far off from the decision makers. But the conjunction of these two points leaves an impasse—and with the conclusion that here, as elsewhere with consequentialist arguments, ultimately a lot of hand-waving is taking place.

The more moralized, retributive version of the victor's privilege fares yet worse, notwithstanding the long history in Just War Theory of punishment as a ground of just war, from Augustine onward.[14] Let us put aside criminal punishments of the leaders of the state for crimes of aggression and *jus in bello* violations. Such punishments can be justified, even if the process of imposing them is likely to stir charges of inconsistency and dirty hands. The question is whether further acts within the territory of the defeated state can be defended by reference to punishment, and here I am dubious. The state itself is not punished in any meaningful collective sense by the imposition of the victor's power. Rather, individuals have their powers of self-government degraded, regardless of their levels of individual complicity. This amounts to a theory of punishment independent of any theory of the responsibility of those punished. It is, in short, a model of vengeance rather than punishment, and cannot serve as a basis of right.

Position 6 is a version of the *mission civilisatrice*, for which John Stuart Mill, among others, comes under scorn by both Walzer and Bass. The claim is not that, for example, exporting democracy is a sufficient cause for war, but that once (a) the conquered state has forfeited its ordinary presumption against interference through aggression and (b) the conquering state is in a position to impose an alternative, not only a right but perhaps even a duty follows to reshape the conquered state, consuming whatever domestic resources are necessary in the process.

Obviously, the strength of this argument rests on one's confidence in the virtues of the exportable political system, as well as in the likelihood of a successful transplantation. The reconstruction of Germany and Japan point in one powerful direction, while more recent histories point sharply in another. (And, quite obviously, constitutional democracy was not an alien institution to Germany.) It could gain strength by being yoked to arguments for deterrence and punishment. Yet it also clearly carries risks: by expanding the potential benefit of wars, it risks extending them by providing a reason for all-but-victorious states to insist upon unconditional surrender, the better to impose a new regime. The evident geographical parochialism of the claimed superiority of, for example, liberal, market-oriented, democratic institutions is also likely to foster resentment and resistance.

Position 7 presents a somewhat weaker version of the same claim: it treats war as a fact, along with the resulting power vacuum. A people left without functioning political institutions is a people left to civil war, without access to the most fundamental technology for social improvement we know: effective collective governance. Following Kant's claim of a duty to live under government, we might see victors as obliged to install whatever form of governance will accomplish this goal (consistent with the other claims of right of the vanquished subjects). This principle, then, reflects one of the peculiar family of can-implies-oughts in politics, according to which any party with the capacity to effect a rescue ought to do so, grounded in a background, agent-neutral demand of helping all to ensure a possibility of a decent social life. This principle has the virtue of—at least in principle—serving the interests of the vanquished as much as those of the victor, and thus of respecting the fundamental principle of moral equality. It also binds the victor's privilege with the shorter leash of duty, permitting only so much imposition on the conquered as duty demands.

On the other hand, we might wonder if this represents too exigent a view of the morality of war. We might think that an aggressed-against state that successfully defends itself has no such duty to the aggressor. Whatever interest it has in political reconstruction flows from the pragmatic and instrumental concerns of position 5, to prevent having a failed state in its neighborhood. More troubling is the point that position 7 is too independent of the *jus ad bellum*, for it holds of both aggressor and defender states, whoever emerges victorious. We might, for example, think that a clean-hands principle obtains in international politics: that an aggressor nation has ipso facto forgone any right to act upon its victim, whatever its capacities. If help is to come, it must come from an untarnished (and nowadays multilateral) institution.

I am inclined to think this view is too morally scrupulous. For instance, putting aside the *ad bellum* error of the Second Iraq War, once the United States had destroyed Iraq's institutions of governance, it had a duty to rebuild them, as well as an interest in doing so. Of course, its efforts were tainted by the war, and its efforts in building a new regime inevitably brought in specific forms of national interest. Moreover, the good effects (if any materialize and stabilize) of reconstructed Iraqi political institutions will tend to whitewash the history of the war. Nonetheless, the absence of effort by the United States would have principally compounded the damage of the war. To the extent position 7 presents a ground for reconstruction, it is one that cannot serve as a broad basis of legitimation of a war, but only as a peculiar kind of humanitarian duty.

9.6. CONCLUSION

The principal lesson we can extract from examining the epistemic foundations of the *jus victoriae* is one of appropriate doubt at thinking a victor's rights can be grounded in antecedent claims. One response to such skepticism is to see war as a decision-procedure itself. The other response, more appropriate for our times, is to see the force of justification as necessarily limited by the knowledge we can have of the justice of the cause. I see no reason to think that the current set of international institutions are better able to deliver incontestable verdicts on the justice of war than our own philosophical reflections. We should say with Fulgosius (and, later, Grotius) that the question of real justice may not be one we can discern.

This doubt then opens up a basic choice, between a victor's prerogatives as occupying an open normative space and as being entirely a product of the duties of aid and effective governance above. On the first prong, while we see the space as limited by fundamental human rights claims, it nonetheless is one that gives the space for political action that, as I suggested at the outset, is a feature of our considered evaluation of political life. Reversing Clausewitz, it recognizes that politics is the continuation of war by other means. The ending of war is a political fact, and the unspooling of politics afterwards is something to be accepted, not justified.

Among other virtues of this view, it seems the best way to explain the latitude we give to instrumental arguments, especially our reluctance to scrutinize their predictive claims. But it receives a strong challenge from the view that says a victor has no privileges at all, beyond securing its ex ante entitlements. The latter view does not make room for the *mission civilisatrice* of telic democracy, does not treat war as anything other than a sorrow, and so denies the kind of link between a just war and a just peace that might otherwise be seen to license war as a means of peace. *Vae victis*, on this view, is not a battle cry but a danger, one that democratic nations especially must avoid, given the temptations to take their internal values as external license. Not only can one not sit on a throne made of bayonets, one cannot write a law book on it either.

10

DRONES, DEMOCRACY, AND
THE FUTURE OF WAR

10.1. INTRODUCTION

In 2008, presidential candidate Barack Obama campaigned to end "dumb wars." He was clear that this meant not just a withdrawal of troops from Iraq, but also a turn towards a new form of warfare: the extensive use of targeted killing, by squads of special forces or remote killing platforms, inside and outside the ordinary theaters of war:

> When I am President, we will wage the war that has to be won, with a comprehensive strategy with five elements: getting out of Iraq and on to the right battlefield in Afghanistan and Pakistan; developing the capabilities and partnerships we need to take out the terrorists and the world's most deadly weapons; engaging the world to dry up support for terror and extremism; restoring our values; and securing a more resilient homeland.[1]

President Obama has kept his campaign promise to a remarkable degree. While the specific contours of the killing program have been little acknowledged by the White House, even in the jubilation following the killing of Osama bin Laden, outside observers have put the numbers killed by the Obama administration through such techniques at several thousand. In Pakistan, it is estimated that drone strikes have killed between 2,500 and 4,000, of whom 500 to 1,000 were probably civilians. Afghanistan has seen more than 35,000 drone sorties since 2008, but there are no reliable casualty counts. In Yemen, there have been an estimated 430 to 650 total deaths, with 60 to 100 civilians, and smaller numbers in Somalia, the Sudan, Algeria, and Mali.[2]

By 2012, the White House began to lift the outer veils from the targeted killing program. The current strategic guidance statement acknowledges the drone-centered targeted killing strategy only slightly obliquely, listing as the top item in the primary missions of US armed forces:

As U.S. forces draw down in Afghanistan, our global counter terrorism efforts will become more widely distributed and will be characterized by a mix of direct action and security force assistance. Reflecting lessons learned of the past decade, we will continue to build and sustain tailored capabilities appropriate for counter terrorism and irregular warfare.[3]

And more informatively, if less directly, the Obama administration, before the 2012 election, clearly began permitting access to the program to reporters of the *New York Times* and other agencies.[4] The *Times* report, and a later book by journalist Daniel Klaidman, detail the process by which individuals suspected of terrorist activity are "nominated" for targeted killing, with discussion of their individual culpability and the value in their deaths vis-à-vis the family members and other civilians likely to be killed collaterally in a bombing. The article also discusses the process for approving so-called signature raids, which target unknown individuals based on a risk profile: whether they are males of "military age," grouped together, in the vicinity of known militant action, et cetera. (The Obama administration said, in 2013, that it does not use signature criteria, but does not deny having done so.[5]) According to these disclosures, the process for deciding whom to kill is highly personal and vested in the president, who makes the final determinations himself. While there appear to be lively committee discussions of the prospective targets, with dissent encouraged, it is a process strictly and secretly governed by the White House itself. A number of groups have been seeking the official Office of Legal Counsel memorandum that purports to govern the program, at least in relation to the targeting of US citizens, but thus far the public (and most lawmakers) has only seen a brief white paper describing the general outlines of the legal theory justifying both the use of drone systems outside the battle theater and the nonjudicial "process" evaluation of the drone targets.[6]

The immediate advantages to the United States of such a program are clear: it has apparently been successful at killing a significant number of active al-Qaeda terrorists, at disrupting Taliban insurgents in Afghanistan and Pakistan, and at doing both at extraordinarily low cost in American lives, while at the same time relying on levels of technological sophistication that, for the time being, ensure that the capacity is one restricted to the US and few others. It also appears that the success of the drone campaign, from the perspective of the defense and intelligence establishment, has reduced the internal and external pressure to resort to torture and near-torture as central tools in counterterrorism.[7] The shifting tides of interstate politics will affect the number and location of drone attacks over time, with Pakistani objections in 2010 securing a reduction in their incidence, and objections in Yemen likely to do the same. But the capacities being built by the US and other states, and the concurrent dismantling of other military capacities, ensures that the future of war will look very much like this.

On its face, there could be much to celebrate: wars could be fought without the trauma and damage on all sides from the presence of occupying armies, with layers of legal and forensic analysis before orders to kill are executed. The US government's claim that such tactics result in net fewer deaths of soldiers and civilians, compared to alternatives, is credible, even if the manner of counting civilian deaths is highly contentious.[8] Even the White House–centered decision making might be thought to have virtues, by shifting the essential moral decisions of war away from a professional class of warriors, who may have undesirable institutional biases, and towards an accountable democratic leader. So should democrats fear or celebrate the prospect of a riskless war? A war waged, let us stipulate, for permissible and just cause, but without risking our own citizens, should find it easier to pass any moral screen that we impose, if the risks are fewer. But, as the debate over the air-based Kosovo intervention showed, even democracies shy from riskless war. The shift to wars of the future, which will involve (on the US side) much smaller human footprints (special forces) and a much larger component for drones, increase the space of nonreciprocated risk.

I recognize that one may also ask whether drone warfare represents a genuinely distinctive phase or form of state violence. No doubt the shift from sword to longbow, the introduction of the recoilless rifle and hot-air balloon, and especially the cruise missile of the 1990s, occasioned similar forms of soul-searching, only to be assimilated as essentially changes on the margin of war. I want to argue here, however, that drone war is morally distinctive, in part because it accentuates concerns that certainly can and do arise with other technologies, but chiefly because it transforms how government can deploy international violence and thus how we conceive of responsibility for that violence, because it alters the norms and values that make war an intelligible (and thus regulable) political phenomenon, and because it has specific effects on targeted populations. All three of these features implicate the means available to a democratic state to pursue its political interests. My goal in this chapter is to pursue the ethics of drone strikes from the perspective of democracy—asking, in effect, how should a democratic citizen or policymaker think about, and act politically, in relation to this future?

We start with the premise that the radical reduction in risk presented by drone warfare raises novel and troubling questions. But why is war's justice usually measured in reciprocal terms? Part of the answer comes, in traditional terms, from both the specific logic of self-defense and from a tradition of war as glory seeking. Such norms are important to war but have little to do with democracy. My underlying hypothesis is that democratic citizens, and democratic states, face particular constraints, beyond those imposed by international human rights law. Those constraints are sharpest in relation to the procedural concerns involved in a form of war that is as centralized and isolated within the executive branch as drone warfare. But I think the special constraints are perhaps most meaningful in relation to two quite different concerns: first, that a form of war without sacrifice etiolates the evaluative context—the meaningfulness—that does and should serve to make the decision to go to war as radical as it is. And second, the specific effects of a drone-based surveillance and targeting strategy on the citizens of the targeted region present an acute moral challenge. According to credible reports, these effects amount to a terrorization of civil society, rendering a region incapable of even simple forms of self-government and collective organization. If this is so, the systematic deployment of drones itself targets democratic life—and this is a target that a democracy must avoid.

10.2. DEMOCRATIC ACCOUNTABILITY

If war is moving towards disembodied combat, what does that mean for democracy? The most obvious concern is that disembodied warfare minimizes the risk to the democracy and makes the choice of war too easy. But before proceeding to that conclusion (which requires an independent understanding of the "optimal" level of war), we must ask what the "right" connection is between democracy and war. This is not an easy question, since there are at least three important connections between democracy and war: relations of support, end, and means. The support relation asks whether the choice to fight a war is grounded in democratic activity. The ends relation asks whether the goal of the war is coherent with democratic practice—for instance, the defense of a democratic system, or the defense of interests that are consistent with democratic values. And the means relation asks whether the tools used by a democracy at war are consistent with its democratic ideals. Democracies can and have failed on all three fronts: by waging wars hidden from the public or accountable legislators, for the sake of protecting colonial interests or strengthening antidemocratic allies, and using techniques of propaganda or indiscriminate attacks on civilians that fail to respect the core rights central to democratic ideals.

The weakest and most obvious condition is the support condition: a war must be waged on the basis of authorization of the polity, or its representatives. Recent history puts even this condition on tenuous grounds, at least in the United States, where the executive has been disinclined to seek democratic approval of military actions, except when absolutely necessary.

So the question of whether drone attacks are consistent with democracy goes beyond their bona fides as policies directed by democratically elected executives. It is surely true that as war becomes smaller and more secretive, resting on executive branch will and judgment, some aspect of its connection to the people is lost. The issue is not just one of democratic control, however—of the potential for shifting military policy. Realistically, in a modern democracy, mass publics have little effect on decisions to go to war, except in the shadow of their potential future approval and disapproval. Wars are rarely initiated on the basis of a poll, even if electoral success can figure consciously or unconsciously among the conditions of war. Rather, the public serves as a spectatorial audience, expected to provide downstream approbation (or punishment).[9] Perhaps one can say that the shadow of popular approbation is a necessary condition of war's legitimacy, but given the plasticity of public opinion, its dependence on both state propaganda and the contingencies of war's success, it is by no means clear that it serves as an independent criterion of legitimacy. What democratic legitimacy there is to be found in war comes, instead, from the typical channels of representative authority.

Let us be clearer about the sources of democratic authority. Democratic authority typically rests on two possible bases: a coincidence between majority preferences and political action or majority electoral authority delegated to a decision maker. Of course, these bases often overlap, as when a democratically elected politician or legislature makes policy that polls show a majority of citizens support. The process itself can also meet with greater and lesser degrees of refinement, encompassing an ideal of large-scale diffusion of information and mass discussion, coupled with debate and dialogue by elected representatives, among themselves and between them and their constituents. At the other end lies little or no perfunctory debate among elected representatives and little diffusion of public information, such that any public support for policy is indistinguishable from brute moral and political prior beliefs and preferences. The existence of this spectrum, and the correspondingly low value placed on democratic authority with low information and debate, shows that even a procedural conception of democracy involves a presupposition of epistemic agency on the part of the public and its representatives. Or, to put the matter more directly, democratic communication implies both a perspicuous speaker and an engaged audience. Without an effective connection between speaker and audience, speech and endorsement in a democracy carry little weight. The veiled signals and secrecy of the drone campaign thus gut the program of the legitimacy it would have under robust conditions of democratic engagement.

So is the appropriate support relation a matter of projective imagination, of citizens being able to envision themselves at war, thus (vicariously) taking responsibility for not just the choice to go to war but the agency itself? It does seem that if there is something to the alchemy of political violence, it resides in the facts of agency, in the way in which we enter into the agency of each other, if only imaginatively. This form of cross-identification, cross-authorization, or collective agency, is, on my view, the key to a proper understanding of moral and political responsibility. The special feature of collective violence, that known as war, is not its collective aspect as such—after all, collective violence is typically a form of criminality. It is, rather, the connection of collective violence to the specific form of collective creativity that I have loosely labeled "politics." It is because we have a separate (justified or not) ethics and politics that war and revolutionary violence can be justified. But that justification depends on the necessity of the violence in connection to the politics.

Yet, a procedural focus on democracy is surely misleading. For it does not follow that a democracy's use of force itself counts as an expression of democracy. It is a truism that democracies pursue nondemocratic projects, sometimes with no awareness of the contradiction. The great hero of France's domestic project of democratization was Jules Ferry, who established the system of universal, compulsory, and free public education, and who helped to root out lingering monarchism in the Third Republic. Ferry was also the architect of France's vast project of colonialism, rooted in the idea of the *"mission civilisatrice."*[10] While the United States now portrays itself as pursuing democratic aims and protecting its homeland, in its engagements in the Far and Middle East, it too has a history of frankly territorial wars, especially with Spain—a matter of expanding its sphere of influence. We need not debate any particular military engagement to recognize that democracies fight for many reasons, not only to export or protect democracy. For purposes of this chapter, I will assume that a democracy can permissibly try to provide direct protection against, or preemption of, direct threats to the lives of its citizens.

More interesting is the question of whether there are special limits, from within democratic thought, about the *means* of warfare. I will take for granted that the case for many conventional limits on weapons and tactics—such as the protection of those *hors de combat*, and limits on biological and chemical weapons—are morally and politically overdetermined: their underlying humanitarian values, though not exclusive to democratic thought, are integral to it. The case against indiscriminate aerial bombing, though practiced by the democracies in World War II, also rests on democratic ideals that reject widespread suffering and death.[11]

But this point might be thought to apply poorly to drones, assuming *arguendo* that they are no worse, and perhaps better, with respect to principles of discrimination and proportionality.[12] A different explanation of the concern about drones lies, perhaps, in the remoteness of their lethality. This is in part a concern, shared with air wars, both about the unseemliness of killing without risk (predicated on a model of war as a fair fight) and about a potential desensitization to the loss of life, whether or not justified. It is these concerns I aim chiefly to explore in what follows.

10.3. THE BASIC CASE FOR DRONES

There are three trends driving conflict forward: increasing secrecy (and civilian intermingling with military tactical decision making), increased distance from the battlefield (long-range force projection), and the increasing relevance of counterinsurgency warfare. What are the risks of these trends?

The three conditions obviously overlap to provide a great deal of further confusion. Distant and low-personnel attacks (even relative to sea- or air-launched cruise missile attacks) have the effect of (deliberately) obscuring legal accountability, with respect to both domestic and international legal regimes; of expanding the use of force far beyond the bounds of domestic political accountability; and of (perhaps) a dehumanized and fundamentally amoral relation to war.

Let me first address the chief justifications for the expanded role of drones: that they represent a fundamentally more humane (because they are more discriminating and subject to greater control) system of delivering lethal force in a conflict. It is plausible that, on average, a precision-targeted drone strike, with at least some information delivered by focused video feed, will result in a much higher ratio of targeted deaths to collateral death, injury, and damage than the likely alternatives, either kill-or-capture raids, or long-distance bombing. If the primary consideration in warfare is the protection of noncombatants from harm, then this is a major point in favor of drones.

By the description of the targeted killing program, its parameters may extend beyond the targeting of high-level continuous combatants engaged in armed conflict with the United States, especially under the perhaps defunct "signature strike" protocol, since some of those deliberately killed (and counted as combatants, not as collateral civilian casualties) have apparently manifested nothing more than presence in the company of the target.[13] Morally, the questions are less complicated: whether or not the law permits their being targeted as continuously functioning combatants, there is something indecent about their being targeted for death on the basis of, in most cases, a suspicion that they are engaged in activities aimed at causing harm in the United States—the only thing that could generate a complete moral justification in the domain of self-defense. (A claim of other-defense is yet less plausible, since it is unclear whether the targeted state has the right itself to kill its residents without greater due process.) Given that at least some of the targets are drug traffickers who pay bribes to the Taliban in Afghanistan, the lines of self-defense under international law (as well as the authorization under the US domestic legislative authority) is in serious doubt.[14]

The net result of current US policy, then, is a situation equally murky in law, politics, and morals: an unaccountable executive branch declaring its authority to order extrajudicial executions throughout the Middle East; an asserted basis for such killings that includes opium poppy production and being a "military-age male" in the wrong place, with the wrong people; a legal authorization that shows no borders in time or place, given that many of the targets bore no connection to the 9/11 attacks; and an expansion of legally permissible killings begun in the White House offices, run through a staging area in Nevada, and aimed at human targets identified by bounty-hunting local informants residing in countries with which the United States is at peace. At worst, the drone program is deliberately, if sometimes mistakenly, executing individuals whose acts do not conceivably place them within the bounds of permissible targets; this is a grave war crime. At best, the program appears to rely exclusively on assassination and profile-based killing of non-uniformed combatants.[15] Under human rights law, killing is only permissible, even assuming an imminent threat, if less lethal means are infeasible.[16] In practice, however, it would be virtually impossible to show that capture was a feasible alternative, given the balance of risks.

In its targeted killing policy, the Obama administration has left itself open to the ironic critique from the right that its haste to kill its perceived adversaries shows its cowardice in refusing to capture and interrogate them. There is some reported evidence that suggests drone killing as a path of least resistance, combining advantages of safety for American soldiers with "solving" the problem of detention and trial for the executive branch.[17] There is what can callously be called a "policy" question about the effectiveness, all told, of killing versus capturing suspects, including the risks of innocent targets.[18] Such a question would include the diplomatic costs of subverting sovereignty (which include radicalized populations even in tacitly acquiescing states) and the loss of moral standing to object to others' similar deployments.

Policy considerations fall on both sides of the ledger. The first, and least philosophical, is the point that such an argument wholly ignores an expanded base rate in attacks. The ease of ordering, coordinating, and officially, if not fully plausibly, denying a drone attack—along with its rapidly declining marginal cost as its infrastructure is expanded—means that many more such attacks will take place. There is already evidence that drone attacks target not just al-Qaeda and Taliban leadership but foot soldiers.[19] The length and breadth of the list is a function of the drones' capacities. Given that any given attack, however precise, has a risk of collateral death and injury, and given that such attacks do not necessarily substitute for less precise means, drones are surely increasing the collateral deaths of innocents. Equally important, given the risks of error in targeting, the number of wrongly chosen targets is surely increasing as well. Last, on this crude point, there is substantial political reason to think that increased drone strikes, and in general decreased ability of states to shield their citizens from direct attacks by US forces, contribute to an environment of increased deaths overall. There is certainly no reason to think that US foreign policy has accurately judged the long-term utility of its acts.

These points are crucial to an overall understanding of the significance of drones and should play a part in any international discussion of limits to their deployment. Such a discussion, for a variety of reasons, is unlikely to take legal form. The weapons themselves are neither intrinsically horrifying nor indiscriminate, and so are not naturally included within the category of prohibited weapons under the Hague Convention standards of causing unnecessary suffering or superfluous injury. It is thus hard to imagine any form of political pressure brought by nongovernmental organizations or weaker states that could lead to a treaty-based ban (and such a ban, if put in absolute terms, would be counterproductive for the humanitarian reasons listed above, since it would eliminate from the repertoire a weapon that could, in principle, substitute for less discriminatory alternatives).

If significant restrictions are imposed, it will be on the basis of the legal norms that already exist, prohibiting assaults on state sovereignty or extrajudicial execution, whether through direct acts of violence or surveillance of nonconsenting states—that is to say, political pressure will be the source of limits of their use, enforcing the norms of sovereignty in the absence of UN Security Council authorization. In practical terms, this means that states like Pakistan and Yemen must cease playing a double game of covert acquiescence and overt condemnation, either reckoning with the political costs of allowing the United States unfettered access to their residents' and citizens' lives or actually coming to treat such incursions as the acts of war that they are. Such political pressure may apparently be effective, as the dramatic reduction in numbers of drone attacks in Pakistan suggests, which has followed increasingly sincere and vocal complaints by the Pakistani government.

Such a political position, insisting that Article 51 of the UN Charter be given a strict reading to limit cases of self-defense extraterritorial violence to truly exceptional cases, may come to find renewed support. To the extent that Article 51's regulation of interstate violence mediates between traditional concepts of sovereignty and modern restrictions on violence, it represents a hard-fought balance (and is partly constitutive of a remarkable global progress away from war).[20] The expanded interpretation of Article 51, apparently pursued by the United States, threatens the general regime of international restraint and offsets the otherwise laudable return to multilateralism of the Obama administration.[21] Of course, the Obama administration's use of public condemnation by allies to mask private agreement is nothing new on the diplomatic front.

An alternative form of political pressure could come from application of human rights laws and norms prohibiting extrajudicial killing— although there is no clear forum of accountability, given the International Criminal Court's lack of jurisdiction over the main drone operators, the United States and Israel (and China to come). But pressure from internal and external human rights groups may have some effect on slowing the growth of drone-based targeted killing strategies, leaving them reserved for a much smaller and much surer category of targets. It is notable that when Israel began its open practice of targeted killing in 2000, the US position was highly critical, raising concerns about the practice's legality, not to mention its destabilizing effects.[22] The US practice shifted overtly in 2002, with the drone killing of Al-Haraethi, a suspect in the *USS Cole* bombing, and accelerated dramatically with the election of Barack Obama in 2008, with drone- and hunter-killer-team-based approaches to counter-terrorism surging. While the number of attacks, as noted above, has abated in the last year, the policy as deployed by the United States goes far beyond even the Israeli model, and apparently with many fewer evidentiary and procedural safeguards. Given the mounting political pressure, it is reasonable to expect the policy to retreat from public view and to be reserved for more extreme cases. Nonetheless, as the US and global military investment in drone technology indicates, this is the future of warfare, particularly in its (now dominant) counterinsurgency or irregular form.[23]

10.4. FROM LAW TO ETHICS, POLITICS TO MORALITY

It is difficult to know how to begin the ethical assessment of drone warfare, not least because little information is revealed by states, except insofar as it furthers their interests. This makes discussion seem to turn either relatively uncritically on the claimed-success versus collateral-damage rates of states or, perhaps equally uncritically, on locally compiled counts of civilian casualties. We know from recent disclosures that the US rule for designating targetable combatants is highly questionable: any military-age male in the vicinity of a specifically identified target counts as a targetable death.[24] And there is every reason to think that civilian death counts in particular episodes may be skewed upwards by opponents of the US drone war in Pakistan and Afghanistan.

While concerns about discrimination and proportionality are certainly central to an overall evaluation of the trend towards drone warfare, and I will discuss those questions below, I want to begin with a different tack: by considering what even the best real case of a drone attack might show about the ethical problems inherent in the strategy. Critics of waterboarding have accused its apologists of building their case on unexamined assumptions, assumptions typically packed into what has become known as the "ticking-bomb" story. That story assumes that the person being tortured is in fact a terrorist; that the terrorist indeed holds information that, if revealed, would save a number of lives; that no other means exist for getting that information; and that the costs of the consequences of instituting a system of torture, whether in terms of recruitment efforts by terrorists or the impossibility of limiting the practice in the torturing state, will be tolerable.

In practice, of course, nearly all these assumptions are false. We should not make the same mistakes in questions of targeted killing. To assume the targetability of the terrorist for a drone strike is, legally, to assume that the person either is actively engaged in hostilities against the targeting state or otherwise maintains a "continuous combat function"—that is, a position of full-time strategic leadership of a terrorist organization. Many real cases of targeted killings raise difficult questions of international law, mostly concerning the targetability of part-time or peripheral guerilla combatants killed in their home compounds.[25] But, I want now to begin with a case of uncontroversial targetability, at least in respect to international norms: the case of Anwar al-Awlaki, the American-born and -educated Yemeni cleric killed by a drone in Yemen in September 2011. According to news reports derived from governmental sources, al-Awlaki not only played an operational role but was the driving force in a large range of attacks against American civilians, including the so-called Christmas bomber who, in December 2009, tried to ignite a bomb in his underwear while en route to Detroit; the shooting rampage of Nidal Hasan at Fort Hood; plans to poison American water supplies, implant undetectable bombs in suicide bombers' bodies, and ship bombs contained in printer cartridges on international flights.[26] While none of his attempts seem to have borne direct fruit, the evidence provided to journalists by the US government suggests that al-Anlawki was indeed a premeditated and committed attempted murderer, someone whose conduct would entail a life in prison without parole were he to be captured. He was killed without evident non-combatant casualties, assuming his four companions were equally conspirators. And he was killed with zero risk of life to American troops or forces, after deliberations that included the highest levels of accountable American politicians, including the president, the secretary of state, and the State Department's legal counsel.

Put aside for the moment a number of peripheral issues, to concentrate on the underlying ethical question: whether a remote targeted killing like this is an acceptable tactic in counterterrorism. First, put aside constitutional questions about the process required before the United States can kill one of its own citizens who is not, at the moment of execution, posing an imminent danger to vital interests. Second, put aside the epistemic assumptions surrounding the case: that the information about Awlaki's past acts was true (or could be believed to be true to a suitably high degree), that information about the future threats he posed was reliably believable, and that the four others killed with him were, credibly, part of an ongoing conspiracy to attack US civilians. Third, put aside questions of whether capture was a feasible alternative to execution. Fourth, assume that the sovereign state of Yemen acquiesced in the US action. Under these assumptions, what is the moral assessment of his killing?

Moral and legal casuistry would seem to coincide: an extra-territorial killing, if proportionate in its effects, targeting an imminent threat to life interests, done with the consent of the state in which the killing takes place, and performed without feasible less-lethal alternatives available, is permissible.[27] Kant-inspired deontologists generally hold self- or other-defense in such circumstances to be permissible on one or another refinement of the theory that the target has made himself liable, by his own choice, to be countered with lethal force. A right of nonaggression being part of a system of equal external freedom for all, an individual right of protection through self-defense is a permissible substitute for a missing system of impersonal enforcement.[28] Absolute discrimination, targeting only those generating the threat, would be necessary, as would proportionality in force, in order to give life to the injunction to honor the value of the life even of him who attacks.

Utilitarians should, all other things equal, regard a rule permitting limited and proportionate self-defense as welfare-maximizing in deterring wanton attacks on life interests. Putting aside the complications of a rule-based versus an act-based utilitarianism (essentially, between a short-term and a long-term horizon for assessing effects), a highly constrained right of individual and international reprisal has the right sort of ripple effects. As a form of immediate deterrence or incapacitation, it constrains the behavior of actors who have no right (or utilitarian justification) to do as they did. Self-defense, on such an account, may have a number of welfare-benefiting features, including instilling a sense of security (well founded or not) among the defending state's population, and greater long-term international respect for borders and rules against aggression. One can, of course, imagine a utilitarian case made in the opposite direction, towards the overall long-term benefits of denying state rights of reprisal, on the entirely plausible grounds that reprisals increase net violence and delay restoration of the peace. And indeed, one of the principal problems with utilitarian analyses is their motivated quality—the tendency of such analyses to confirm the prejudice of the writer. In any event, the central point is that a plausible case can be made for the permissibility of violent self-defense by a state when what is being defended is the lives and bodies of its citizens (or, indeed, the lives and bodies of any persons) threatened by unjustified aggression.[29]

What of the other features of drone-based self-defense? If the two criteria of just defense are discrimination and proportionality, then drones perform extremely well. Their sensor systems are frequently more sensitive than human eyes and ears in the midst of combat, and the possibility of sustained surveillance can mean greater time and capacity for intelligence analysis, thus permitting targeters to establish more clearly whom, exactly, they have in their sights. And the improved analysis will also mean better detection of vulnerable noncombatants, resulting in a more accurate proportionality evaluation. While the statistics on noncombatant deaths vary with the reporting source, even the high-end estimates of civilian deaths in Pakistan, for example, indicate a learning curve of sharply reducing deaths, and a rate that compares well with ground-based military forces.[30]

There is, however, a central and largely neglected way in which democratic thought might be seen as imposing a constraint on drone warfare, from the perspective of the targets. I have so far accepted the stipulation that drone attacks are more precise and hence better justified under the calculus of military necessity and proportionality than the conventional attacks they may replace. I do not mean to dispute that there have been many well-reported drone strikes that would seem to be poorly explained by these criteria, given the number of (credibly counted) nonmilitants killed.[31] That said, and even apart from the direct effects of drone attacks on those killed, deliberately or indeliberately, the drone program exacts a terrible toll on both local democratic activity and the broader activities of civil society. To take a powerful but not anomalous example, consider the March 17, 2011, strike in North Waziristan, Pakistan—a strike extensively investigated by researchers from Columbia and Stanford Law Schools.[32] Whatever the target was imagined to be in Langley or Washington, it appears to have been a morning gathering of a regional political council, a *jirga*, meeting to settle a dispute over mineral resources and mining rights. A series of missiles hit the seated circles of men. The result was more than forty dead, of whom only four have been viewed by independent sources as likely militants.

Put aside the obvious issue of proportionality and consider what the reality of such strikes means to daily life in drone-prowling territory. Not only is there the psychically debilitating sense of constant aerial surveillance, but there is the reality of a serious risk of violent death—moreover, a risk magnified whenever one engages in any form of social relations involving more than two adults. The concern is amplified if one accepts what has also been reported: that the drone program routinely engages in "double-taps," or secondary, mop-up strikes, which have the effect of killing (or deterring) professionals and volunteers coming to the aid of victims; that funerals and other crucial cultural events have been common targets of strikes; and that the practice of effectively buying target names and sites from local informants has sown rampant mistrust and score-settling in the drone territories.[33] I don't think it is exaggerating to say that Stalinist terror could hardly have been more crippling to Soviet civic life than the drone program is to Waziristan and Afghanistan.

This, again, may be a case of overdetermined wrongs, since what is at stake is the human and civil rights of the people of these territories. But I think there is a case to be made here for a special democratic constraint, in the sense that a democracy must not be in the business of making democracy impossible in the territories it affects. Of course, some degree of hypocrisy, or value slippage, in international affairs is both necessary and excusable. And as I argue in chapter 8, there are serious and obvious dangers in the other direction—namely, the idea that democracies have a special duty of democracy promotion. There is no evident logical objection to a democracy defending its democratic interests by suppressing democracy elsewhere, any more than there is a contradiction in killing to save one's own life. But the suppression of democracy abroad, deliberately or collaterally, exacts a toll on democratic integrity and the general coherence of a democratic state's policies and ideals. And so democrats might well have a special reason to forswear a drone program, just in terms of the effects of that program on democracy abroad.

10.5. DEMOCRATS AND THE IMPORTANCE OF RISK AND BOUNDARY

I want to turn from these important but perhaps more familiar concerns about the morality of drones from the perspective of their targets to consider the issue from the perspective of the targeter. There are two principal distinguishing features of drone attacks with respect to their operators: their risklessness (or, more precisely, the remoteness of the vulnerable human operator), and their unboundedness. I begin with risk. On its face, reducing the risk to a justified self-defender must be counted as a benefit. The principles of justifiable defense do not require the defender to be in danger, either as a basis for violent defense or in the act of defending, because—on any moral view—defending another person under threat is as justifiable as defending oneself. Immediate presence would be prized if it meant a defender would be more likely to make correct risk assessments, but it is equally plausible that a remote defender would have some analytical and informational advantages. Indeed, in law, the chief difference in the privileges of self- and other-defense is that self-defenders typically enjoy more leeway to make mistakes about the specific threats they face, in light of the special emotional pressures they face.

This said, there is no reason to think that the passion of the defender somehow enhances the legitimacy of the defense. Perhaps an abnormally detached attitude on the part of a remote defender might be evidence of lack of empathy, or abnormal insensitivity to the emotional turmoil of killing.[34] This would, to be sure, be a sign of poor character. Such character might also lead to excessive or disproportionate violence. But in the single instance of legitimate other-defense, these concerns are irrelevant. Similarly, while absence of risk might make it harder to celebrate the heroism of the defender, or to recognize him as a "warrior," these are not objections to drone killing per se.[35] So while we may be chilled by the mental image of a remote defender, killing from a desktop in the morning, then taking in his child's soccer game in the afternoon, the aura of such killings is not a well-rooted objection. And if the poetics of war's imagery suffers, that may only strengthen a critical spirit otherwise muted by the felt need to honor warrior virtues independently from the justice of the war.

What then of the vulnerability of the attacker itself legitimating the conditions of self-defense? This is the ideal of *democratic sacrifice*. The ideal is that democratic states should be prepared to offer their own blood and treasure as a condition of legitimate war—that remote war, without sacrifice, is a form of aggression, whatever the underlying cause.

The ideal of democratic sacrifice draws from a number of ideas, both instrumental and constitutive, without being fully supported by any. The first is the proposition first put forward by Immanuel Kant in his *Perpetual Peace*: that democratic states (i.e., states under republican constitutions) are less likely to go to war because, "if the consent of the citizens is required in order to decide that war should be declared (and in this constitution it cannot but be the case), nothing is more natural than that they would be very cautious in commencing such a poor game, decreeing for themselves all the calamities of war."[36] Kant's hypothesis in modern form rests on an empirical link as much as a conceptual one: that under conditions of democracy, politicians will act in the shadow of potential punishment by voters, who can reasonably anticipate paying the costs, both human and financial, of any wars. The physical risk of war is, in this sense, an information- or deliberation-forcing mechanism: forcing decision makers (and possibly citizens) to confront the risks and costs of their decisions, and thus to deliberate seriously. The objection to riskless remote warfare, on this understanding, is similar to the objection to mercenary armies: mercenaries allow the state to hide the costs of its war, giving it a cloak of secrecy that the engagement of citizen soldiers would never permit.

So, put crudely, the Kantian idea is the analogue of Dr. Johnson's quip that the prospect of a hanging concentrates the mind wonderfully: only the visceral threat of war makes deliberation about the use of force rich enough to provide legitimacy. Does it have force? While it is a tautology to say that awareness of the risk of war makes it easier to contemplate the risks of war, there is nothing in Kant's (or Johnson's) thought to support the idea that risk to oneself is necessary for appreciating risk to others. Indeed, awareness of risk to oneself might lead one to understate the risk to others—for example, the risk of collateral killings of people no more liable to be killed than you yourself. The drone case presents the problem of deliberating properly about risks to others in the absence of a known risk to oneself. Clearly, the secrecy of the program makes it harder for citizens to contemplate the financial costs and benefits of the killing program. But it is not clear that citizens would, if exposed to risk as soldiers (or as people who care about the lives of particular others who serve as soldiers), take better account of the risks imposed on others. Thus, unless the Kantian idea is just meant to be a general damper on leaders' plans for war, whatever the justification, its bite in the drone case is unclear.

A second version of the ideal of democratic sacrifice was put forward in a prescient 2002 discussion of NATO's then-recent high-altitude Kosovo intervention by law professor Paul Kahn, who argued that the traditional logic of the *jus in bello* is one of reciprocal risk imposition in self-defense.[37] Kahn contrasts this logic of reciprocal risk with a model of asymmetric risk, which he treats as characteristic of a form of internationalized "police action." In the war context, the special feature of the battlefield is the permission given by combatants to kill one another with impunity, regardless of the justice of their cause. This mutually accepted moral symmetry between (relative to each side's perspective) just and unjust fighters is one of the fundamental puzzles of the ethics of war, as we have seen in chapters 2 and 3. A democratic state accepts the governing liberal precept that the right to life, whether of a fellow citizen or foreigner, may only be abridged when the other's life (or activity) presents a threat to one's own. In war, we are permitted to kill or disable when, and only when, such acts are necessary to our own preservation. A democracy that wages a remote war at no risk to itself thereby fails to fulfill the precondition of the specific form of justifiable homicide constituted by war: whether or not the killings represent a form of collective (or other-) defense, its soldiers, on this theory, are personally entitled to the privilege to kill only on condition of their own vulnerability.

A third version of the democratic sacrifice ideal is one that says that a state can redeem the deaths of the enemy—that is to say, redeems the evil of war—through the consecrating act of the death of one's own citizens. A democracy must see war as evil, as a failure of the possibilities of politics. But such an evil can be redeemed by the hallowing of the battlefield, or so said Lincoln at Gettysburg, in what is effectively the gospel of the United States, post-slavery, and the first consecration, since the Battle of Marathon, to use a site of battle as a temple for the state.[38] Within revolutionary politics, such an ideal is essential to the legitimation of what would otherwise be great crimes: the citizens' sacrifice shows their commitment to a new politics. It is essential to distinguish a genuinely democratic revolution from the revolt of the masses feared by Plato and thereafter.

There is a related point about democratic concerns about mercenaries—fighting forces not linked by commitment to the community. Mercenaries have, of course, been part of war since the ancient Egyptians hired Greek soldiers, but a troubled part. Within the history of democracies, even Periclean Athens deployed them to fortify its defenses and eventually to wage its failed campaign in the Peloponnese. But not without concern: as Thucydides voices through the Corinthians, "The Athenian power consists of mercenaries, and not of their own citizens; but our soldiers are not mercenaries, and therefore cannot so be bought, for we are strong in men if poor in money."[39] Over time, democracies came to disdain the use of mercenaries, in part owing to their capacity to raise mass armies through conscription. While private military contractors have assumed a greater role in America's war in Iraq, this reliance marks a controversial departure.[40] The distrust of mercenaries—indeed, even concerns about a volunteer, professional military are sometimes voiced—are rooted in a concern about impure motives, not just fears of betrayal to a higher bidder. In the specific case of democracies, mercenaries lack precisely the sanctifying virtue of sacrifice for an idea.

But is reciprocal risk the key to the modern tradition? Or is it simply a component of a warrior ethic that is, in turn, a component of a larger ethic of war, one that mixes virtue concerns with deontic limitations on targeting with utilitarian calculations of collateral damage? And how does the imposition of reciprocal risk fit into the theory of regular war? The symmetrical privileges of regular war flow not from the reciprocity of risk but from an epistemic reciprocity, that neither side typically has a privileged perspective on the question whether its side case has merit, legal or moral.

This, I think, is the best interpretation of Kahn's point, that war requires reciprocity of risk, because it provides a justification more solid than the casus belli usually provides. Even in humanitarian intervention cases, as in the NATO Kosovo intervention, the lack of reciprocal risk also denies the state the quasi-justification offered by the basically aesthetic values of war, notably the display of physical courage by the warrior.[41] As Kahn suggests, as states engage in riskless violence, they lose the moral "buffer" of the logic of war and need to look deeper, and in a more individualized fashion, to criteria of individual guilt and dangerousness of the targeting order to justify the imposition force. Risk is, on this view, a sufficient but not necessary condition of the right to use force. This is clearly correct descriptively, insofar as the development of drone warfare has been accompanied by (reports of) a quasi-juridical model of guilt and threat evaluation—hence the policy anxiety over whether actual judicial involvement is also required. Moreover, as Kahn also notes, the general context of massively asymmetric conflict puts the stronger state in the impossible position of justifying its use of force to a world (and especially the population of its targets) for whom the very asymmetry itself makes any justification suspicious.[42]

But the clear separation of state-imposed force, between war and non-war, is a distinction always hard to sustain, both descriptively and normatively. Drone force is incommensurate with the norms governing anything we can meaningfully call "policing." Furthermore, the highly individualized norms of policing are functions of a system of force and control resident in the territory being policed. We should be deeply suspicious of an analogy between the state's exercise of its domestic monopoly on violence and an act whose material reality is a hundred-pound high-explosive missile, targeted and triggered from thousands of miles away, from an entirely independent state. Add in the specific concerns of a democratic people about the regulation of its police force, and the case for analogy fails further.[43] The reach for a policing analogy should make us more troubled, not less, by the disappearance of risk.

Here, perhaps, is another way to get at the significance of vulnerability: a conception of equivalence, related to the notion not of a sanctifying sacrifice but merely of a compensating one. This is the idea, essentially, of *Blutgeld*—money traditionally offered to pay for a death caused by one's clan. Offering one's own soldiers' lives marks the value of the lives we take, not because it makes it a fair fight, not because the life of our soldier makes the death holy, or because it makes taking life morally permissible, but simply because the seriousness of war—of taking life for life—is made manifest through the sharing of risk. This is a different form of seriousness than the standard claim, that risk makes deliberation more serious, and forces a real confrontation with the longer-term costs of war. Here, seriousness functions poetically, not epistemically: it displays the weight borne by the attacker, rather than creating that weight. The value of the life is equally a part of an older ethic of death, one still resonant in cinema, literature, and folklore.

We have, then, a group of reasons for rendering one's soldiers vulnerable: as a reciprocal contract, as a permissive gate, as an element of a warrior aesthetic, as a consecrating gift, and as a mark of seriousness. It would be a mistake, I think, to press too carefully on any of them, or even all of them together. Within the terms of a modern moral logic, whether deontic or utilitarian, none of these reasons has decisive force. Indeed, it is not clear that they are fully coherent. I have already suggested that no logic of personal risk is required by the morality of other-defense. Similar quick work can be done about the (ir)relevance of fairness in a particular individual confrontation representing massively unequal collectives. The modern, reductive conception of war, in terms of harm to individual interests and reciprocal rights of self-defense, runs independently of all these concerns. These concerns instead speak to an older tradition of collective agency and violence.

My point is not that offering sacrifice can legitimate what is otherwise illegitimate. My point is that war without sacrifice represents a symbolic shift of our conception of war, and we have no idea of the behavioral consequences of that shift. It may be that the antiseptic conception of war, run by the powers able to deploy drones and kill teams, will—for its flaws in the realm of transparency—mark a net improvement in human welfare. The analogue might be the shift from informal, mob justice to police justice. The invention of the police station meant that state violence could be easily hidden and abused—but also controlled. And control clearly dominates abuse. With war, executive control of lethal violence may, notwithstanding its abuses, lead to less war—fewer Iraqs, smaller Afghanistans. In such a case, the loss of sacrifice, of direct engagement with violence, may simply be of a piece with other forms of questionable nostalgia for more honest and rougher times.

10.6. DEMANDING BOUNDARIES

The unboundedness of drone operations is harder to defend, both because of the disruption it causes to the settled categories of warfare, which monopolizes a definite "hot battlefield" (whether or not filled with noncombatants) for its operations, and because typical drone operations have tended to occur in ambiguous diplomatic circumstances, where it was unclear whether the state hosting the target had in fact given consent for the attack. Of course, all of these features of drone operations are continuous extensions of cruise missile attacks, airplane sorties, and human-faced covert infiltrations (as with the bin Laden raid). More to the point, the open battlefield of drone warfare echoes the earlier disruption to settled ideas of war and borders arising from the armed navies of the seventeenth century.[44] In the particular case at issue here, the killing of al-Awlaki, the extraterritorial aspect of the killing can be justified. As al-Awlaki was in a part of Yemen that the Yemeni government, by its own account, could not control, it does not appear that there were nonmilitary options available to the United States, assuming it wished to incapacitate him. And while the Yemeni government has not publicly declared its consent to the operation, the combination of Wikileaks accounts and other journalism strongly suggests the consent of its government, thus obviating any concerns of sovereignty. While one can debate the merits of attacking him with a missile versus attempting to capture him, the choice of the missile seems, on its face, reasonable. And since the decision, moreover, was taken after full consultation of military, intelligence, and political staff, by the president himself, and was preceded by vague but definite public statements and indirect acknowledgments of the drone strategy, it would seem to have as good a measure of republican legitimacy, deliberative and representative, as one can hope for in military matters.

Thus, taken as a best case, the al-Awlaki killing makes a strong case for drone use, along traditional moral and legal lines: it meets criteria of internal political legitimacy, respect for noncombatant interests, conformity with use-of-force rules, and external political respect for international borders. It is thus unlike a ticking-bomb example, generated to justify incidents of torture. Whatever one concludes about torture as policy, in isolated or general instances, even its defenders would acknowledge it as a terrible exception to the ordinary principles of humanitarian law and ethics. But a single drone attack does not run contrary to those principles, as a utilitarian exception to deontology's bright lines. Rather, it seems to embody those principles, albeit in an unfamiliar way. Doubtless, much of the point of the public and quasi-public disclosures thus made about the drone program is precisely to make this point: that drones are the ethical future of warfare for a democratic people committed to humanitarian norms and the preservation of its own citizens' lives.

So why the widespread concern over drones? Are we merely in a historical moment of transition, between models of war, a transition accentuated by the borderless war with al-Qaeda? Clearly, a great many of the concerns have to do with the problems of a general strategy of drone warfare, as opposed to their limited deployment for tactical ends. The reduced risk to the defender, the greater freedom of action, the promise of greater precision and discrimination—all of these amount to a temptation to turn to the lethal violence of the drone as a ready alternative to policing and diplomacy. Put the other way, the relative costs—political, moral, and financial—of traditional acts of war make it a less desirable policy than nonlethal alternatives. Reduce those costs while holding other moral constraints constant and nations with drone capacity will increase their reliance on war as policy choice.

A facile response to this point is simply to repeat the stipulation that the drone attack is justified in the first place: that the target is morally and legally liable to be killed, given constraints on alternative, discriminative, and proportional collateral harms. In the deontic logic of morality, one might think that if one targeted death and seven collateral deaths are permissible, then so should be ten targeted deaths and seventy collateral harms.[45] But there are a number of reasons that make this response unsatisfying. First, the stipulation becomes less plausible as a device for justifying the policy when it is generalized, because we know that any increase in the frequency of attacks will increase the number of mistaken targetings, mistakes in proportionality, and will dull the impetus to look for less lethal alternatives. An increase in the number of attacks has political and moral consequences, to be sure.

This is part, but only part, of the uneasiness of many people, including many military, with the remote operation. The lack of exposure to danger, when generalized, also seems to change the moral calculus, even if the logic of that change is not obvious. The underlying moral theory of other-defense, as I said, does not require the defender to be exposed to risk. But the tolerance for preemption is likewise decreased once we subtract the panic inherent in facing danger to oneself. If the threatened danger is remote (even if real), and posed to abstract individuals, then the warrant for taking immediate, concrete lethal action is diminished.[46] This is simply a function of the underlying logic of "necessity," even construed loosely. An individual confronted with a gunman need not test all nonlethal possibilities. But a state, looking to preempt attacks perhaps weeks or months from fruition, must make a fair showing that alternative means are unavailable, even in the threatened time.

This point is reinforced by the systemic nature of a drone *program*. The state is, perforce, no longer confronting an emergent risk but rather managing a generic set of threats to its interests. Traditionally, the resort to lethal violence to manage external systemic risk is called "war," and the decision to wage war incorporates a full calculus of risk—both the risk if the state does not defend its interests and the risk that will result from the resort to war. But a drone program, deployed as a systemic approach to asymmetric war, involves principally the risk of inaction. While the risk of a blowback reaction is real, it does not approach the magnitude of the risks faced by traditional resort to war.

10.7. THE DEMANDS OF DEMOCRATIC ACCOUNTABILITY

Whether the global system will slow the spread of cross-border stealth attacks is a function of complex international political dynamics. But we may well ask whether there are other constraints relevant to a liberal democracy—constraints it does not share with all states interested in preserving their ostensible monopolies over the use of lethal force in their territories. These are constraints (or, perhaps, incentives) that are internal to the norms of democratic states, and they include at least the following, in roughly ascending levels of constraint:

Transparency and publicity: In a weak form, the norm of transparency requires public disclosure of state uses of force and their underlying rationales. Transparency norms are made effective through combinations of (voluntary) official disclosure and through the operations of a vigorous press and civil society organizations (such as the ACLU in the United States).

Public accountability: Decisions about the use of force must be made by officials who exercise authority on the basis of public standards, and whose power rests on a direct democratic basis or who are hierarchically accountable to officials whose power rests on a democratic basis. This is to say that the relations of accountability must be external to the decision-making process, and not merely internal; public criticism or sanction (such as withdrawal of support) must be possible as well, with real political consequences.

Public deliberation: While particular policy choices must be made within agencies charged with their effective execution, the principle of public deliberation requires that broad policy choices be made through a public process of deliberation and debate. "Public" in this context has two senses: both openly displayed and occurring within a civil society sphere, not just within the halls of government. Even if the decision whether to authorize force rests with a legislature rather than with a plebiscite, and hence may be counter-majoritarian, broad public engagement is a necessary condition of the legitimacy of the decision.

Public traceability: It is not enough that a policy question be settled openly and accountably, through popularly elected representatives. The policy itself must be followed through, either in direct public view or with some alternative form of scrutiny (legislative panels or an independent judiciary, for example). It is important to be careful what kind of scrutiny is meant, however. Many of the most controversial policies of the United States have been flirtatiously aired in the public. Obama's drone policy, like the Bush administration's torture and extradition policies, were put before the public in direct terms: as a matter of fighting a "smart war," violating sovereignty if need be; and as a matter of "taking the gloves off," in the words of Dick Cheney. The selective disclosures from the programs, of "intelligence gains" obtained from black-site torture operations and the high-profile killings by drones, have also kept the programs in the public eye. There is little doubt in my mind that American public support for these programs has been consistently strong, even if international opinion has been horrified. Lack of publicity (in both the philosophical and the popular senses of the word) was not the problem. What was lacking, instead, was factually and legally informed scrutiny of the programs, by voices with access to policy decisions: well-informed legislative sessions, closed-chambered or not; some form of judicial or quasi-judicial evaluation of individuals chosen for killing; et cetera. Perhaps some legislative evaluation happened (though briefing congressional leaders on secret programs often involve such confidentiality constraints that little reaction is possible). But the dynamics of aggressive military programs, and the incentives among participants to maximize opportunities for policy or political victories and minimize costs, mean that monitoring is necessary. Such monitoring is partly called for by a general interest in the controlled deployment of any dangerous program or protocol. It has also a specific justification amid concerns of democratic legitimacy, which is keeping the program within the parameters endorsed by the public.

So what would deep publicity be? This, of course, depends on the motivation for the publicity condition and on an explanation of why the legitimacy it has accrued through the public conversation is not enough. If the objection is to targeted killing per se, then review is only a proxy for a ban—and the conversation of review mechanisms does not really have any content. If the concern is factually false positive errors—that is, mistaken targeting of innocent (or insufficiently culpable) people, then what we need is a system of either competitive intelligence gathering or competitive analysis, so that decision makers are not relying on a single feed of information. The decision makers themselves need enough experience in the area to know when to trust and when to be skeptical of threat-assessment intelligence.

If the concern is with the general problem of program creep—the chance that the program will come to encompass targets who don't meet initially more restrictive criteria—then the proper solution is periodic review by an inspector general. As I discussed above, the little we know about the current drone program includes real risks in this area, especially in Afghanistan, as US military commanders and advisers have come to see the program as an effective tool for the variety of security interests before them, such as reducing drug trafficking, as well as the risk that those commanders may be unwittingly manipulated by local political interests.

Finally, if the question is whether the targets are *morally* deserving of death, as Harold Koh, quoted by Klaidman, seems to suggest—whether they are "evil" enough to be placed on the kill list—then there are two things to be said.[47] The first is that it is precisely this kind of evaluation, which smacks of comic-book vigilantism, that lies at the root of much concern, sometimes poorly put as a concern that the president is "playing God." We are comfortable enough with a rhetoric of evil and a discourse that allows us to label, poetically or otherwise, wrongdoers as evil and deserving the torments of hell or earth. But something masked by the easy Weberian formula of the state's monopoly on violence is that the monopoly is itself normatively regulated. Democrats trust the state's monopoly precisely on the grounds that the state's use of violence is based on clearly identified criteria for the deployment of violence.

Granted, in contemporary terms, those criteria have been deeply schizophrenic: within the borders of the state, the legitimacy of police or judicial violence depends on showing not just that the person is a criminal, but that he is an active and immediate threat to the safety of the community. Outside the community, in times of war, it has involved showing that the person is a member of another state in a relation of war with our own. But even those schizophrenic criteria are challenged by what amounts to evidence, in at least some cases, of a non-imminent threat to relatively distant interests of the state (or direct interests of the state, in the lives of its soldiers, deployed remotely). The idea of seeking judicial review of the decision to kill outside these bounds—to identify for permissible people who are not clearly self-identified members of a collectivity at war with the state, who are also not posing an immediate threat to the state—is to go far beyond the ordinary practice of judicial decision making. It is not asking our judges to play God, but asking them to play general, in wars whose borders confuse even the actual generals. It is, in other words, a significant distortion of the judicial role, seeking to leverage the independence of judges into a validation of a practice by states that has always met with extreme suspicion.

We can refer to these conditions jointly as the *norms of democratic political violence*. I have rendered them as what I take to be uncontroversial ideals, reflected to varying degrees in the United States and other democratic states in practices and laws. In the United States, the overarching legal framework is the Constitution's allocation to Congress, in Article I, Section 8, of the right to declare war, but balanced with the president's inherent commander-in-chief power and thus his right to deploy military force swiftly without congressional approval. The post-Vietnam War Powers Act, US Code Title 50, Section 1541, provides further limits on the president's constitutional authority, including a requirement of a report within forty-eight hours to Congress, and a vote of approval within sixty days for continuing the use of force. The European democracies offer a wide range of parliamentary privileges regarding war making, At one extreme is England, where the Prime Minister has inherited the Crown's prerogative over the use of force, not required even ex post to put its deployments to a vote. Nonetheless, the British commitment to democratic legitimacy is shown by the government's willingness to offer its decisions for debate and a (nonbinding) vote, as with Prime Minister Tony Blair's decision to put the Iraq intervention to a vote. At the opposite extreme sit Italy and Germany, which require parliamentary ex ante approval over deployments and funding, even for treaty-based commitments. France, one of the most militarily aggressive states (especially in Africa), lies closer to the American model, giving initial control largely to its president while requiring reporting and later approval by the Assemblée Nationale for extended deployments.[48]

These ideals reflect a common commitment to *proceduralism*, to the idea that the justification of a democratic state's wars rests partly on the quality of the legitimating process, at deliberative and voting stages. They do not, of course, replace the general substantive conditions of just war, namely the contemporary conditions that war be a resort only for self- or other-defense, including the defense of urgent human rights. In practice, one can wonder whether a democratic process has sometimes seemed to supply the deficits in the substantive justification, as with the United

States' reliance on a congressional vote, after rejection by the UN Security Council, to justify its invasion of Iraq. The realities of democratic control are more complex, and although there does seem to be a relation between the degree of parliamentary (versus executive) control of military affairs and a state's displayed willingness to send troops abroad, the level of actual democratic control is relatively weak, as witnessed by the willingness of so many states to commit troops to Iraq, despite (in virtually every country save the United States) large public majorities opposed to the war. How could it be otherwise? The decision to go to war, to call upon the bodies of young (and older) citizens to serve as collateral for the foreign policy interests and commitments of the state as a whole, is the most symbolically freighted, if not the most important, decision a state can make. While decisions over funding, say, public health measures may involve more actual lives saved or unsaved, the decision for war requires, in effect, that the government be able to face each potential soldier in the eye and explain why the mission is worthy of a potential loss of life.

These procedural demands are very high, and they occasion significant resistance, especially in states now far more open to a range of alternative sources of opinion and analysis than in the past. The confrontation with the public becomes harder in the face of skepticism wrought by recent failure (in the United States, the pre-Iraq skepticism flowing from the failure of the Somalia mission, and the long post-Iraq shadow)—a dynamic that may in turn drive executives into retreat from their publics and to avoid even pro forma consultation with their parliaments. In the case of the Libyan intervention of spring 2011, President Obama declined to put the intervention before Congress despite the War Powers Resolution, relying instead on an indicative but (to most observers) unpersuasive argument that the absence of ground combat for US troops meant that the intervention did not constitute "hostilities" for purposes of the statute, thus obviating the reporting and congressional agreement requirements.[49] By any standard of democratic legitimacy, the failure to allow—indeed force—the president to put the armed intervention in Libya before a democratically elected legislature—is more than troubling. It is disqualifying.

If, in fact, what we want is an independent, skeptical, and adversarial voice, we can construct credible alternatives to the constitutional independence of Article III. The United States should establish, with an eye to fixing an international model, a process of adversarial testing of terrorism targets, using advocates from institutions with distinct institutional incentives and perspectives. The current US model, which appears to be organized around loose consensus, with a final presidential decision, has the merits of focusing the attention of those (in the executive branch) most likely to bear accountability for better and worse decisions, as well as assembling the competence of those most likely to make correct informational judgments. But the essential moral questions will inevitably be lost by those immersed in a collective political project. Indeed, what moral scrutiny would seem to demand here is a certain distance from the collective project. This, indeed, is the great irony of drone-based killing: precisely because the moral (and political) questions are so difficult, and so difficult to answer one by one, without being drawn into a collective strategy or project, they demand an alienation or distance that public war does not.

11

DEMOCRACY AND THE
DEATH OF NORMS

Previous chapters have argued for the strict constraints that democratic values place on the decision to use war and the means of war as a tool of international relations. Notably, I have made most of the arguments in the context of decisions taken by the United States to violate those constraints. While the United States is, to be sure, an imperfect democracy, it is nonetheless very self-consciously democratic—indeed, despite its imperfections, if the United States does not count as a core viable instance of actual democratic governance, then the category is unusable for political thought. Moreover, a large and impressive literature has arisen over the past fifteen years concerning the emergence, transfer, and sustenance of political norms in international life.[1] The presumption of this literature has been, for the most part, that the winds of normative change blow in a progressive direction, towards greater or more stringent normative control of individual or state behavior. Constructivist accounts detail a spiral of reinforcing emergence, as actors and institutions discover the advantages of normative self-evaluation and evaluation of others have become common. And there is now much interesting research focused on the question of how to predict the emergence of future norms.[2]

This makes two lines of thought plausible. First, I could simply be wrong in suggesting that democratic principles and values count against, for example, the deployment of high-altitude surveillance and killing devices, or the use of interrogatory torture, or (more controversially) extensive military involvement in pro-democratic institution building. Alternatively, there could be a kind of "democratic paradox": the political structure of democratic states could make it difficult for them to live and act within their own defining values. Such paradoxes are, in fact, familiar from everyday life: someone who vows a life of stoic calm may find that the difficulty of repressing emotional outbursts makes him more, rather than less, troubled.

My aim in this chapter is to suggest that democracies do suffer from inherent challenges to their ability to live consistently with their values—but these challenges can be managed with attention to the character of the deliberative institutions involved in the decision to go to war. While democracies surely do better than authoritarian regimes in adopting and internalizing certain kinds of constraints, in part because of a greater sensitivity to public mobilization around normative questions, that same sensitivity makes their long-term survival precarious. In particular, I suggest that force-constraining norms are most effectively internalized by coherent and relatively insulated professional cadres who see themselves as needing to act consistently over time. But in a democracy, the values and arguments of those cadres are susceptible to undermining by a combination of public panic and policymakers' invocation of a public interest that overrides the claims of restraint. Democracy's soil, hence, can be both fertile and toxic for humanitarian norms at the same time.

The model I will describe may be of predictive use, in helping us to see the special vulnerability of normative orders in democracies. But my hope is that it is also constructive, in showing us how states and institutions committed to maintaining a certain normative order, especially democratic states, might best try to entrench those norms. While my argument is conceptual and philosophical, it draws on this recent history.

I also add two qualifications to this essay's title. First, I am not addressing all norms, but of specific norms concerning the state use of force in national security policy. I therefore do not make claims about the generalizability of the conflict I describe to other norms, such as norms of racial, sexual, or religious orthodoxy or hierarchy, or norms of reciprocal interaction.[3] Second, reports of a norm's death are frequently exaggerated, since norms can be latent, then resurrected. Arguably, the anti-torture norm was resuscitated by President Obama in 2009, when as one of his first official acts, he moved to prohibit cruel, inhuman, and degrading treatment of detainees.[4] I write here about the path of decay, whether or not that path is one-way, and why previously salient norms no longer seem to govern policy choice among political decision makers.

II.2. TALKING ABOUT NORMS

Discussions of norms are now well-entrenched in multiple literatures, and I do not mean to disturb, so much as make use of, some existing distinctions, drawn mainly from the philosophical literature. Nonetheless, because usage varies somewhat, I preface my discussion with some conceptual housekeeping.

I understand norms, at first approximation, as logical (*propositional*, in philosophers' jargon) reconstructions of actual social practice and judgment regarding behavior. Norm statements, when applied to individual or collective choices, actions, expressions, or feelings, yield a verdict in the register of the good or the right.[5] They differ from mere statements of regular behavior in that they implicitly or explicitly contain an evaluation of that behavior from some point of view. "People make eye contact when talking" states both a behavior and a norm, while "People blink every two seconds while talking" states a behavior only. We must be clear that the verbal statement of the norm is not necessarily the equivalent of the behavioral norm itself. For example, every human culture has norms concerning how close to stand to other speakers, depending on relative social status, age, gender, and many other social variables. These norms are very well understood and regularly applied, both in positive behavior and as a basis for reaction and criticism. Yet these norms are very hard to articulate, except in a conclusory way: "Don't stand too close to your interlocutor." As a more general matter, actual normative behavior will be consistent with different possible logical articulations. Thus, psychological norms are not identical to their verbal formulations.

Norms are the basis of accountability, both formal and informal, for actions. To say someone has done wrong or acted badly is to say that his behavior violates a norm. His social reality is grounded in the fact that these rules have intersubjective support, in the sense that multiple members of the social group in question agree that such norms exist, and share a practice of applying these norms to specific choices/acts/et cetera, including a shared practice of arguing about whether the norm applies in a given instance. It is important to bear in mind that norms attach not only to behaviors but also to decisional processes (in terms of both considerations that should apply and procedures for deliberation), feelings (e.g., one ought, or ought not, feel ashamed in particular contexts), and expressions (how and what one can and cannot say is tightly regulated). Nonetheless, for simplicity I will usually refer to norms as governing acts.

Finally, the application of the norm typically includes a labeling of the act as, roughly, good or bad, right or wrong, as well as emotionally laden expressions of praise or criticism, and the possibility of particular sanctions whose legitimacy is grounded, again in the first instance, in the validity of the norm. This is abstract but not impossibly so, I hope. My point is that we want a conception of a norm broad enough to encompass not just the binary logic of permission and prohibition but the weighted valuing of a wide range of the things people do. For example, norms exist in most (American) institutional cultures against the public display of strong emotion. Someone who acts on the basis of or expresses a strong emotion will be subject to criticism for this (in the dimension of good-bad, usually, rather than right-wrong). The norm violation may, despite the criticism, still be quite effective, either intrinsically or because of the additional shock effect of being a norm violation. Many managers yell and curse on occasion, precisely to profit from the ripples of norm violation. This symbolic dimension of norm violation is important, and I will return to it later.

The social reality of norms thus has two faces: an individual behavioral component and a social component, with the latter part constituted by the formal or informal institutions of labeling, (dis)approbation, and punishment. If the norm exists socially, and is understood to have wide (or universal) "jurisdiction"—that is, it is not a norm that applies only to a certain group, like a dress or speech code—then individual behavior will always be in the shadow of the norm, in the sense that behavior to which the norm could arguably apply can always be described as in or out of compliance with the norm. Compliance is thus a weak notion: I may be in compliance with a norm just because I have no opportunity to violate it (if, for example, I would gladly drink and drive, but my host happens to have run out of alcohol). The stronger notion is that of norm-*guidance*, a concept that itself comes in stronger and weaker flavors. In the stronger flavor, an individual is norm-guided when the existence of the norm provides a reason for or against the act in question, the agent takes that reason into consideration, and assigns that reason significant, though not necessarily conclusive, weight. As an example, you are at a dinner party when the host makes a racist remark in passing. Norms of politeness might counsel (indeed require) you not to embarrass your host, while ethical norms might counsel, and indeed require, you to call him out. As you weigh the conflict of norms and social roles, you are guided by them, but only at most one of the norms can be decisive.

In the weaker version, the norm has a psychological but not necessarily occurrent reality: it functions as what the philosopher Michael Bratman has called a "filter," screening certain deliberative possibilities from arising in the first place and thus preserving the coherence of our more complex plans.[6] Faced, for example, with a sensation of hunger, I do not typically weigh and then reject the possibility of simply grabbing food from a sidewalk market; instead I calculate whether my hunger is worth the extra cost of buying food on the run rather than waiting until I get home. While the norm against stealing food is not present to mind in my deliberations, it has a counterfactual reality: if I had not internalized the norm, I would presumably survey the possibility of simply grabbing food from an open container, irrespective of my legal entitlement. Whether or not a norm is deliberatively occurrent depends on a great range of factors, both individual and institutional: how deeply (and by what process) it has been internalized.

The psychological dimension of norm-guidance requires some additional elaboration as well, given the variety of ways in which norms can enter into deliberative space. While I have said that one can be norm-guided even if the norm is not decisive, mere presence at mind cannot be sufficient to constitute guidance. As Bernard Williams remarked, a business person who discusses the assassination of a competitor, only to add immediately "but we can't do that; that would be wrong," is not actually exhibiting norm-guidance.[7] The chief problem lies in distinguishing between being guided by the consequences of norm violation (wanting to avoid a sanction) and being guided directly by the normative consideration. There is a further distinction, as well, between endorsing a norm, to oneself or in discussion, and actually following it. Indeed, one can find oneself guided by a norm while believing it to be irrational, as some find with family religious customs; or paying lip service to a norm that one finds ways to avoid. While it may be impossible for an outside observer to distinguish these cases,[8] I will say that behavior is *minimally guided* by a norm when the thought of violation occurs, and the benefits and costs of violation are weighed. Such weighing includes the reasons or values intrinsic to the norm itself (for instance, that it protects a right), and not merely an external sanction. Finally, a norm is *weakly present* in individual or collective deliberation when it is merely expressed as a possibly relevant consideration to the case at hand, even if only nominally.

To return to the example above, if I am very hungry and very broke, I may be disinhibited enough to now consider theft as a solution to hunger. I will be weakly guided by the property norm if I weigh the putative wrongness of theft against the benefits to me (and perhaps an assessment of the actual harm I do the shopkeeper). And the norm will be weakly present just so long as I realize that I will be engaging in theft, but that fact has no intrinsic deliberative significance.

Behavior can thus be norm-guided without being norm-compliant, as when I weigh the norm but violate it. And it can be norm-compliant without being norm-guided, as above, when norm violation is not practical for independent reasons. Though it is a vexed semantic question whether behavior can be "guided" by a norm when one is only concerned with avoiding a related sanction, I will treat such cases of threat-based compliance as cases of compliance without guidance. [9]

The metaphor of norm death, as I refer to it, suggests a reversal of the entrepreneurial process: a process of waning, from fully decisive filtering and guidance to weighing to weak presence—potentially to total irrelevance and invisibility.[10] In the domain of policy, norm death will be associated with certain distinctive transitions: (1) the emergence in discussion of policy options that were physically possible but were previously excluded from deliberation; (2) a shift from a discussion of norms couched in categorical terms to one couched in weighing terms; (3) the emergence of discussions in which the norm and its enforcement mechanisms figure centrally as obstacles to be minimized or avoided; and (4), ultimately death, the disappearance of even rhetorical evidence of the existence of a norm. To take an example with contemporary sting, in 1929 US Secretary of State Henry Stimson closed the US Cryptographic Office, charged (among other things) with the task of deciphering foreign embassies' communications, with the famous pronouncement, "Gentlemen do not read each other's mail." But Stimson's concern quickly became quaint, as the new institutional norm of respect for diplomatic cables decayed into a practice of simply not getting caught reading them.[11]

I do not mean to suggest that the path to norm death is always uniform, or that each step along the path is always taken or always visible. But it can nonetheless provide a model for plotting institutional change over time. I now discuss two examples of decay and (possibly) death.

11.3. THE EMERGENCE OF VIOLENCE-RESTRAINING NORMS

When we speak of the institutionalization of a norm, we generally have in mind a point on the spectrum, ranging from the weak presence of the norm as a nominal deliberative consideration to intermediate internalization as a significant decisional factor to its deep internalization as beyond the pale of countervailing considerations. The aim of norm entrepreneurs, to paraphrase recent, if still speculative, work on norm dynamics, is to introduce norms into both decisional space and public discussion along this sequence: from potential relevance to a guiding factor to strong internalization. The process of moving individuals towards partial or full internalization usually relies on institutional authorities developing a system of external sanctions and rewards, which function both to mark the importance of the new norm and to provide assurance that one's own compliance will not be unilateral. Norm entrepreneurs can also be relevant at this stage, both in providing a pressure point for state agents who may be less than enthusiastic about enforcing the norm and in publicizing the success of the norm among the broader population, or in other communities.[12]

Much of the literature on norms and international relations has concerned the efforts of norm entrepreneurs to propagate new norms, under pressure from other nations and from NGOs, and focuses on the dynamics mentioned briefly above. Such norms might guide domestic conduct, establishing a new mode of behavior. For example, entrepreneurs have had significant success in helping to propagate norms condemning violence against women inside territories and cultures in which such violence is commonplace.[13] While the direct influence of these antiviolence norms on the behavior of potentially violent actors is still hard to discern, these norms have had an emerging influence on political and governmental actors in places that had heretofore tolerated violence, increasing internal and external pressure to prevent and prosecute attacks on women. The well-publicized 2013 gang rape of a woman riding a bus in India shows the signs of this effort.[14] While the criminals who assaulted the victim appear to have acted with thoughts of their impunity, domestic and international norm entrepreneurs were able to seize upon and highlight the episode, demanding both an immediate prosecution and greater cultural awareness within India of the problem of violence against women.

There are, of course, stronger examples of norm change at the individual level, driven usually in coordination by state and private actors: the standard examples include the emergence of norms against public smoking, littering, drunk driving, and public urination. It is striking that these norms all have a reasonably common content—namely, the treatment of public space, or the exposure of the body in public—and fit into a general neoliberal narrative of increasing personal responsibility. It is also unsurprising that such norms have grown fastest in the soils most fertile to neoliberal conceptions of individual relations to the public sphere, namely the United States and Western Europe. These success stories, heavily relied upon by legal scholars who study norms, are less a matter of transnational export as parallel (though obviously mutually self-aware) transnational developments.

We might usefully contrast these success cases with the deliberately transnational attempts by Western states (especially the United States) and economic actors to propagate norms concerning intellectual property protection in China. The example shows the difficulty of these efforts, if one compares the significant success of content providers in establishing property norms and licensing systems in the United States with the failure of these efforts in China.[15] Indeed, the difficulty of shifting norms supported by powerful economic or security interests points to the limits of a top-down model of normative change: policy dialogue between states, even if done in good faith, can only result in behavioral changes at the individual level when individuals can come to see their choices as congruent or clashing with an ethical environment supported by their perceptions of actors around them. The norm propagation efforts will be stymied unless and until there is active Chinese state support, and this requires propagating the norms first to Chinese political elites, who may then implement both communicative and enforcement measures to introduce the norms to individual consumers—for instance, by allocating resources to prevent illegal production and sale of protected material.[16]

By contrast, there is a better story to be told about the propagation of norms that constrain state conduct directly and do not need to be mediated through low-level communicative and enforcement practices. The period post–World War II, and especially post-Nuremberg, can be described as a period of sustained norm internalization among states of violence-restrictive norms. While the process has been halting, with occasional backslides, through the Geneva Conventions a norm of targeting discrimination in aerial bombing has come to be deeply routinized in modern (predominantly NATO) militaries, technological developments enabling targeting success while reducing collateral casualties, implementation of highly legalistic target review processes, and inculcation in officer training. Norms against desecration of dead enemy combatants have also become deeply internalized, in individual psychology as well as institutional practice.[17]

11.3.1. Torture

Until recently, one of the most impressive successes of the postwar period might have been thought to be the norm against interrogatory torture. (The norm against terroristic torture has been in place for much longer.) In the United States, at least since the 1980s, formal prohibitions of torture in both law enforcement and intelligence contexts have become fully embodied and internalized norms affecting the behavior itself. Police station-house (third-degree) torture in the United States (and, I suspect in many European states as well) went from being a relatively routine practice until the 1940s and '50s to being a source of massive scandal and liability.[18] In New York, the 1997 Abner Louima case of police torture, involving the broomstick rape of a Haitian immigrant arrested on mistaken suspicion of having punched a police officer, represented an important inflection point, where older practices met a new normative environment. While the "blue wall" that keeps police from testifying against each other held in this horrifying case, the thirty-year prison sentence meted out to the main torturer had a transformative effect on incentives within the department. Similarly, while the CIA's activities in advising South American military and intelligence in physical interrogation methods continued at the notorious School of the Americas until as late, perhaps, as the mid-1990s, the curriculum appears to have changed permanently in that decade.

Torture has, of course, been prohibited under the Geneva Conventions, the Universal Declaration of Human Rights, and the International Convention on Civil and Political Rights and has arguably existed longer as a *jus cogens* customary norm.[19] And the practices constituting torture were already proscribed, as forms of battery, in both domestic criminal law and the military code of justice. Torture was therefore normatively marked—but, especially in the state context, usually not subject to criminal enforcement.

As Darius Rejali has argued, most democracies, including the United States, largely eliminated the traditional torture techniques, of severe beatings, burns, and electrocutions, after the 1960s, though the United States was a willing supervisor in many traditional forms of torture in Vietnam, substituting less messy, and hence more concealable, forms of torture.[20] What I am describing as torture includes forms of extreme physical pressure through, for example, "Palestinian hanging" by handcuffed arms, prolonged or intense subjection to cold, long-term sleep deprivation, shaking, false executions, and waterboarding. While the occasional judicial opinion has distinguished some of these techniques as merely cruel and inhumane (and therefore forbidden) but not, semantically, torture, others on this list clearly are torturous—and their infliction in combination, in American, British, and Israeli cases, further makes clear that they constitute state-inflicted torture.[21]

The major change in the normative environment surrounding the practice therefore was the passage in 1984 of the UN Convention against Torture and Other Inhuman, Cruel and Degrading Practices, which required signatory states to agree to prosecute their citizens' violations of the treaty. Even the Reagan Administration, which was generally acutely hostile to international restrictions, became a signatory, albeit with a rider restricting de-internationalizing the definition of torture by holding it to the terms established in American Eighth Amendment jurisprudence. The Convention was ratified by the United States during the Clinton Administration in 1994, which it implemented in part through adopting domestic criminal legislation, US Code Title 18, Section 2340A, prohibiting torture.[22] It is true that the Clinton Administration extensively "rendered" captives with potentially valuable intelligence to allies that were willing to use torture methods. But the "extraordinary rendition" practice is itself evidence that the domestic anti-torture norm had stuck, and the desire by a series of presidential administrations to put deniable distance, through the fig leaf for diplomatic assurances that the ally would respect the dignity of captives.

More generally, direct torture was expunged from intelligence operations, both military and CIA, on the basis of four considerations: the threat of criminal prosecution seems to have been very effective; the military institutionalized its anti-torture rules through explicit training of interrogators, convincing them that criminal sanctions awaited if they acted coercively with prisoners; interrogators were led to take professional pride in eliciting information without torture; and both lawyers and staff believed that US engagement in torture would put American POWs directly at risk.[23] The result was a stable military anti-torture culture, and a comparable culture in the FBI and in police departments: a normative conviction that torture was wrong, that violating the norm bore penal consequences for the torturer, and that the norm was supported by a culture of general international adherence, at least to the extent that US deviation would impel defection from the norm by other actors. The anti-torture norm thus held in the United States for at least fifteen and probably more years, across different administrations. As of September 10, 2001, the safe prediction would have been increasing international pressure by the United States on its allies, in Latin America, Africa, and the Middle East, to substitute noncoercive interrogation for these techniques. It was hard to imagine that the United States would shortly be opening torture sites in Afghanistan, Iraq, Poland, and Thailand.

11.3.2. Assassination

The emergence of an anti-assassination norm is a longer process, with ebbs and flows. According to Ward Thomas, who has provided the best historical and analytical account of the practice, assassination—understood in its broad sense as the intentional killing, on or off the battlefield, of specific enemy political and military leaders—was proscribed by the Romans, then widely adopted as a technique of realpolitik in the Middle Ages and Renaissance.[24] (Even then, Thomas notes, the knightly code of chivalry disdained subtle forms of killing.) Thomas quotes Hans Morgenthau on the practice in Venice: "The republic of Venice, from 1415–1525, planned or attempted about two hundred assassinations for purposes of its foreign policy."[25] Indeed, throughout the sixteenth century, in England, Spain, and France, assassination of heads of state was the "great game" of its day, vouchsafed by the Vatican. But the practice shifted dramatically in the seventeenth century, and as Thomas plausibly argues, it shifts in synchrony with the emergence of Westphalian sovereignty.

By the early modern period, writers have begun to remark on the distinction between treacherous assassination (i.e., making use of trusted particulars to deliver a poison or dagger), and stealthy targeted killing. Alberico Gentili had already laid the groundwork, at the end of the sixteenth century, in his *De Jure Belli*, where he argued that not only was the practice of political assassination "shameful," but it also threatened the international system with instability, because it was a practice that would inevitably reciprocate.[26] Grotius likewise distinguishes between deceitful killings, which typically rely upon a particular subject's betrayal of his ruler, and what today we might call targeted killing: "For to kill an Enemy anywhere is allowed, both by the Law of Nature and of Nations (as I have said already), neither is it of any Concern, how many or how few they be who kill or are killed."[27]

Nonetheless, Grotius recognized strong reasons to prohibit even nontreacherous targeted killings of individuals, namely the reciprocity concern that would render each ruler more vulnerable if the practice was unconstrained.[28] As Thomas further notes, the Westphalian system of mass armies offered an equilibrium in favor of strong states, who could take and hold territory through direct military force; assassination, as a weapon of the weak, played against their strengths. Since these were the states that could mint new international law norms, it is little wonder that the norm would reflect the balance of their strategic interests.

This is the moment to introduce a contested point of terminology. Grotius's distinction is the one followed today, usually by defenders of targeted killing tactics, between impermissible assassination and permissible targeted killing. Even among those who do not simply beg the question by defining assassination as a form of treacherous murder, the term is reserved (by stipulation) for acts of killing with specifically political rather than military objectives.[29] Targeted killing, the newly preferred term, is then contrasted both with untargeted killing (illegal because it is nondiscriminative) and killings that are not immediately based on a rationale of necessary and proportionate defense against an imminent attack. Understood as a focused killing in response to a specific threat, "targeted killing" is virtually by definition defensible.

Although I will now generally use the language of targeted killing, the distinction is more of a piece of moral argument than a characterization of the ways assassination has always been understood. In fact, the broad term "assassination" has, especially in US practice, been used by policymakers as a rubric for both politically motivated killings and military killings, such as the targeting of Admiral Yamamoto.[30] Moreover, as I will discuss below, there is substantial reason to think that the targeted killing program of the Obama Administration relies on such a broad conception of threat and imminence that the usefulness of the pure self-defense paradigm is limited.

By the nineteenth-century drafting of military codes, notably the 1863 Lieber Code's Article 148, the norm is fully crystallized and universalized, with few actual exceptions noted:

> The law of war does not allow proclaiming either an individual belonging to the hostile army, or a citizen, or a subject of the hostile government, an outlaw, who may be slain without trial by any captor, any more than the modern law of peace allows such intentional outlawry; on the contrary, it abhors such outrage. The sternest retaliation should follow the murder committed in consequence of such proclamation, made by whatever authority. Civilized nations look with horror upon offers of rewards for the assassination of enemies as relapses into barbarism.[31]

It is worth emphasizing that Article 148, titled "Assassination," does not distinguish either among means of killing, treacherous or otherwise, or among targets, whether general or private, ruler or subject. It is a blanket prohibition on individualized killing.[32] The Lieber Code reflected American military and intelligence practice until the Vietnam War, with the notable exception of the Yamamoto assassination. The 1960s through 1970 were exceptional, led largely by the CIA, and involving not only the nearly comic assassination attempts on Castro and participation in other killings of political leaders but also the much more lethal CIA-directed Phoenix program of targeted killing in Vietnam. But following the Church Commission congressional investigations into CIA practices, and Gerald Ford's 1976 signing of Executive Order 11905[33] banning political assassination, the norm was restored to legal force in the United States. Indeed, it seems that the norm was internalized to such an extent that the Reagan administration wrestled with the question how to present the targeting (by bomber) of Muammar Gaddafi in 1986, and similarly for the Bush I administration's targeting of Saddam Hussein in 1990. These targeted killings were very plausibly legitimate attacks on commanders-in-chief under UN Charter Article 51 powers of self- and other-defense, and yet the White House clearly regarded the depictions of the attacks as needing to be massaged to avoid the bite of its own anti-assassination norms.

Perhaps the most dramatic evidence, however, of the force of the anti-assassination norm in the United States comes in the form of its response to the Israeli practice of targeted killing. By contrast to the US policy (and in line with the older European practice), assassination has been a relatively overt tool of Israeli policy since before the founding of the state.[34] It has been, moreover, an occasional practice making use of both deceptive and overt targeted killing techniques. Among other incidents, Israeli intelligence used mail bombs to kill Egyptian military leaders and German scientists in the 1950s; the 1970s saw the retaliatory killings ("Operation Wrath of God") for the Black September PLO attack at the Munich Olympic games; and the 1980s and 1990s brought assassination attempts (with bombs and poison) against various PLO leaders. While these assassinations were robustly criticized outside Israel, they met with general acceptance (when they were successful) within. But with the emergence of the Second Intifada in 2000, the scale of Israel's targeted killing program, and public discussion thereof, dramatically increased, and gradually changed from a system of stealthy assassination (or "liquidation") to a more militarily overt selection of individual targets, with a different proposed nomenclature: "preventive killings."[35] The catalytic event was the killing by sniper of Dr. Thabet Thabet in December 2000. An overt act, roundly criticized globally and by the left in Israel (who saw in Thabet someone willing to discuss peace), it prompted the Israeli military and civilian leadership to create approval structures and to litigate the program in the public eye. The resulting program, through which targets are identified, discussed, and then killed, became a mainstay of Israeli defense policy. According to the estimates of the Israeli peace group B'tselem, Israel killed 232 intended Palestinian targets between 2000 and 2008, which marked the Gaza incursion, and another thirty between 2008 and 2012.[36]

Israeli support for the targeted killing policy has been strikingly high, among both the public and the policy elites, and there are no reports of significant change over time.[37] Indeed, the generally pro–civil liberty Israeli

Supreme Court interpreted legal sources to arrive at a relatively permissive standard for the targeted killing program.[38]

By contrast, US official and public attitudes towards the Israeli practice were highly critical, consistent with a broad norm against assassination. Following the acceleration of Israel's program in July 2001, "American Ambassador to Israel, Martin Indyk provided a harsh criticism of targeted killing on Israeli television saying, 'The United States government is very clearly on the record as against targeted assassinations. They are extrajudicial killings, and we do not support that.'"[39] An August 2001 poll showed American public disapproval of Israel's policy at 68 percent.[40] In 2002, State Department spokesman Richard Boucher repeated the US rejection of Israel's targeted killing policy of Palestinian militants—in the course of distinguishing away the United States' drone-based targeted killing in Yemen of al-Harethi.[41] Most notably, the US State Department's human rights reports on Israel and the occupied territories included targeted killings by Israel under the rubric of "serious human rights abuses by Israel" until its 2004 report, when targeted killings were included gingerly under a longer list of Israeli and Palestinian cases of "Excessive Force and Violations of Humanitarian Law."

To be sure, the anti-assassination killing norm was much less securely embedded than the torture norm within international law, where applying it requires making sense of the particular prohibitions on perfidy and treachery and, in the context of nonstate armed conflict, resolving the question of the status of those playing important logistical or planning, but not kinetic, roles in combat. As in Israel, US military law writers have long argued for a sharp distinction between "political assassinations," understood as killings for political purposes, and prohibited by executive order; and permissible individualized killings of military leaders who held simultaneous political office.[42]

Moreover under the self-defense rubric of Article 51, participants in hostilities can generally be targeted and killed, and the state leaders who were or might have been targeted could arguably count as such, given their control roles in military operations. While the ICCPR and other elements of human rights law and the Law of Armed Conflict generally prohibit extrajudicial killings, they permit such killings where they are necessary to avert a deadly threat posed by a combatant (or civil threat in the law enforcement context) and are proportionate to that threat in the level of force used and collateral damages anticipated.[43] Second, as a matter governed by executive order in the United States rather than criminal law (unlike torture), assassination is not generally subject to criminal prosecution.

11.4. WHEN EVERYTHING CHANGED

On September 11, 2001, the Twin Towers fell. In very short order, the CIA was told, presumably by Vice President Cheney, to "take the gloves off," and to "work the dark side" to prevent further attacks by al-Qaeda.[44] The CIA and the Department of Defense quickly began to engineer a torture program, euphemistically called "enhanced interrogation," by charging the contract psychologists, James Mitchell and Bruce Jessen, to reverse-engineer the "SERE" program they had designed to teach American soldiers how to *resist* torture. Jessen and Mitchell developed the program of techniques mentioned above, of physical pressure and isolation, including waterboarding. The techniques both were used by the CIA against so-called high-value prisoners in prisons in Afghanistan and Poland, and were propagated by the Department of Defense to Guantánamo, where they then found their way (through the transfer of military intelligence officers) to Iraq and Abu Ghraib prison.

Of course, developing the physical techniques was only one part of the revolution in norms. Because the anti-torture norm was embedded in criminal law, both the Code of Military Justice and federal criminal law, legal teams were put to work to develop a legal space in which torture could flourish. Led by John Yoo, and under the direction of vice presidential chief of staff David Addington, Justice Department lawyers created a set of memoranda that, however implausible their reasoning, could serve as a good-faith legal defense to CIA or military personnel who relied upon them to determine that their acts of waterboarding, et cetera, were legal.[45] (Since torture is a crime of specific intent, a good-faith defense would exonerate.) The torture program continued in force until the Bush Administration shut it down in 2007, and it was formally closed by President Obama immediately after his inauguration.[46] During the period from 2002 to 2007, hundreds of detainees were subjected to a variety of these forms of abuse, although only a handful were water-boarded. With the exception of a few low-level soldiers at Abu Ghraib prison, no one in the CIA or the military has faced criminal punishment for any acts of torture or other forms of illegal, cruel, inhuman or degrading treatment of prisoners.

The anti-assassination norm has shifted more slowly, probably in large part because of the rapidly and recently evolving Predator drone technology. Initial targeted killing efforts were done through Special Forces military squads and were a continuous part of counterinsurgency efforts in Iraq. The first reported drone attack on an al-Qaeda suspect was in Yemen in 2002.[47] But the pace of drone strikes began to rise quickly under President

Bush in 2008, and has become the antiterrorism technique of choice for President Obama. Again with figures from the Bureau of Investigative Journalism, as of spring 2015 a reasonable estimate is roughly 400 total US strikes in Pakistan, more than 1,000 in Afghanistan, and another 90 to 110 in Yemen. Targets include identified putative militants, drug lords intertwined with Taliban or al-Qaeda activities, and targets identified by their "signatures" alone—presumably groups of military-age males meeting in remote locations.[48]

While the details of operations are rarely disclosed directly, and only the vague outlines of the legal controls on these attacks have been publicly discussed (as opposed to leaked), it is more than fair to say that from the perspective of the Obama administration, the new targeted killing policy represents, in the minds of policymakers, a fully legitimate form of counterterrorist security policy. John Brennan, the current CIA Director and principal architect of the drone program, gave a speech in 2012 in which he argued for the ethical value of drone strikes, as grounded in the international humanitarian law's constraints of necessity (used only against imminent threats), proportionality (ensuring that collateral damage is not excessive in relation to the military advantage), and humanity (avoiding unnecessary suffering).[49] One can, of course, dispute any of these characteristics of the drone program, considered as a policy and subject to the usual forms of policy creep. Brennan's account also fails to mention the collateral harms to psyche and liberty suffered by people living under drone surveillance and in dread of being in the vicinity of a drone attack.[50] But the principal point is that, from the perspective of the policy elite, the norm of broad prohibition has disappeared and become a norm of broad permission. The American public stands firmly behind the permission: recent polling puts US support of drone strikes abroad at 66 percent of all voters.[51]

Are there commonalities in the two stories of the disintegration of these norms? There are certainly very different atmospheres. As Jane Mayer documents, the anti-torture norm was demolished in a mood of real panic by political elites, who not only feared the political costs should a new terror attack succeed but personally feared being targeted by terrorists. By contrast, the assassination policy seems to have been crafted more coolly, as a way of using technology to serve security interests at substantially lower American political and human risk.[52]

Second, while implementing the torture policy involved direct conflict with members of the military and counterterrorist officials who saw both personal and reciprocal value in the anti-torture regime, there have been few direct signs of military resistance to the drone policy (though there have presumably been territorial disputes between the CIA and the Pentagon over control and budget). Third, the legal environment, both domestic and international, is considerably more plastic with regard to assassination, although international opinion on the matter appears to be nearly as harsh on the drone policy as on torture. Finally, there appear to be more clearly demonstrable gross benefits to security policy from the drone strikes than from the torture policy, where indeed it is still disputed whether there was any significant intelligence benefit. (In both cases, any gross benefits may well be swamped in net terms by blowback considerations.)

Nonetheless, I believe we can identify a number of common factors than enabled the swift collapse of these stringent norms. One of these is conceptual, and the other is organizational.[53]

The conceptual point is this: stringent norms rest on a moral psychology of right and wrong, not of weighing good and bad. The anti-torture norm is grounded in the first instance in a categorical inhibition that gets its motivational force from a conception of the dignity of the person being tortured, and in the second instance by the integrity of those complicit in his torture. The wrongness of torture is captured by the image of the total control by the torturer of the psyche of the tortured. Torture, under this image, degrades not only the person being tortured, by annihilating rather than restricting his autonomy, but also the torturer, by enabling libidinal impulses of dominance to surface and override the civilizing restraints of moral codes.[54] The anti-chivalric aspect of torture is one piece of this: torture is no way for a warrior to fight. When the anti-torture norm has psychological bite, it is because it connects to a deep and shared conception of dignity for both agent and patient. The pragmatic arguments founded in considerations of reciprocity add force, but they are parasitic on the basic conception: if we did not think torture was particularly degrading, we would be less concerned about its being revisited. (We accept reciprocity of the infliction of severe suffering in war.)

What defeated this torture norm was thus not fear itself, since fear is a constant in war. Instead, I want to suggest, the norm was defeated by the *utilitarianism* of fear. By this I mean that policymakers' deliberations shifted from choosing best among a principle-restricted set of options, to considering a full set of options, where each was weighed in the balance of probable US lives saved versus lost.[55] I call it a utilitarianism of *fear* because the choice to reintroduce torture to the intelligence armory reflects the reductionism of a panic reaction, in which non-survival values are seen as irrelevant to the decision at hand.[56] The extensive effort by the Office of

Legal Counsel to create a broad legal permission for torture reveals that what had been a stringent intrinsic constraint against torture became a morally irrelevant institutional obstacle to a policy objective of maximal information gathering. Attempts to cash out the normative constraint in the pragmatic coin of reciprocity concerns were doomed to failure, given that there was no reason to think al-Qaeda members taking US hostages would respect an anti-torture norm in the first place.

In the particular context of post-9/11, where the threat of WMDs was taken very seriously, utilitarian reasoning led to a kind of singularity: if the threat is catastrophic, no matter how improbable, then anything is permitted on the utilitarian calculus. That torture can be made to represent an ethical, and not simply ruthless, policy choice is essential to its psychological success. It has also come to be well supported by the American public: with some ebbs and flows, public support for the occasional or routine torture of *suspected* terrorists lies now at 53 percent. Since 2004 (the revelations of Abu Ghraib), no more than 32 percent of Americans have said they always oppose torture of suspects. By contrast, even in November 2001, 66 percent of those polled said they could not envision a scenario in which they would support the torture of terrorism suspects.[57] The American public came along as well on the path from inhibition to acceptance of torture.

The emergent drone policy represents the same conceptual dynamic. While Brennan's defense of drone policy appears to rest on the ethical considerations he names, we should recognize that these are constraining norms rather than legitimating norms. That is, the norms of IHL do not themselves justify the infliction of violence, except in terms of the underlying utilitarian norm of necessity, whose content is, effectively, that a given act is necessary in the sense that its performance is the only route to a net reduction in the relevant costs (here, US strategic interests).[58] Indeed, the IHL norms are fully consistent with a utilitarian view that accords some weight to the utility of the third parties at risk—it merely operationalizes the weighing of the costs to those third parties. The anti-assassination norm, by contrast, was rooted in at least some values that are difficult to defend in utilitarian terms, namely the values associated with openness and a fair fight, and the rejection of perfidy—values of an emergent sense of military honor.

As with torture, these honor and dignity values are fragile when put into play in a context of policymaker fear. But the anti-assassination norm is even weaker yet. I said above that the real ground of the reciprocity argument against torture lies in the perceived indignity of torture itself, and the special fear it arouses in potential subjects. By contrast, the reciprocity argument against targeted killing is, outside the context of perfidy, purely one of international stability. Such concerns have little force in the conflicts in Afghanistan and with al-Qaeda, both because stability is already gone, and because there is little real vulnerability of US-side figures in the conflict. Thus, under even very light conceptual pressure, the anti-assassination norm will fold easily. The chief problem, as I see it, is that with the collapse of the anti-assassination norm, so goes a broader norm that restricts interstate violence to a case of extraordinary remedies to gross threats or wrongs. A drone-based killing policy especially normalizes interstate violence as a response to relatively low-grade threats, and so it has the effect, typical of a utilitarian policy, of smoothing what had been a discontinuous decision curve of when state interests justify war. The collapse of the anti-assassination norm thus rests on the collapse of a broader structure of anti-consequentialist thinking as well.

The organizational point parallels the conceptual point in the two cases. As I have mentioned, resistance to the collapse of the anti-torture norm lay primarily in the cadres of professional interrogators, military and paramilitary, as well as with (many) military lawyers. These were the individuals with whom the considerations of honor had deep traction, and who saw themselves as subject to a pervasive sense of normative discipline. The moral and political transformation of the torture policy was created by civilian leaders, both policymakers and lawyers, who lacked any evident ethical mooring in a dignitarian or honor-centered conception of national security values. Civilian policymakers are, furthermore, directly or indirectly electorally responsible, and the electorate also does not share the deontological sentiments of the professional cadres. It was, therefore, retrospectively likely, if not inevitable, that a system of civilian control, in a context of directly perceived risk, would lead to the sidelining of the professional ethical concerns in favor of pragmatic, publicly visible values. While the values of inclusion and equal respect that lie at the heart of a democratic ethos make democracies natural promoters and adopters of violence-restraining norms, the process and dynamics of democratic politics itself makes those values very hard to sustain institutionally. Democracy's hospitality to these norms is of a piece with its susceptibility to their violation.[59]

Similarly, the trend we are witnessing in drone warfare, of the reliance on drones for a wide range of policy interests outside the hot battle zone, is a direct function of a novel capacity of civilian leaders to control lethal military technology, rather than having to deploy that technology through the broader administration of a military general staff. The drone policy can accelerate much more quickly, and at much lower political cost or electoral threat, than a war mobilization into Waziristan, Libya, Mali, or Yemen, precisely because the decision making can be easily centered in the executive branch, and the operations relatively easily controlled (either via CIA or Air Force command centers). The ordinary military inhibitions concerning the expansion of interstate violence can, again, be easily sidelined. It is noteworthy that, as of this writing, despite suggestions made by President Obama that he would be transferring even covert drone operations from the CIA to the Defense Department in order to increase "transparency," there is no evidence of an actual shift in process.[60]

Now, I recognize that this interpretation of the death of the torture and assassination norms is contentious in (at least) two ways. First, it is hardly the only possible interpretation of the change in policies. One could argue instead, not that a categorical norm prohibiting the conduct had decayed, but that the original norms at issue had submerged conditional exceptions—in particular, that they only prohibited torture and assassination if the stakes were sufficiently low. The attacks of 9/11 changed the stakes and so triggered the exceptions—but the same norms are still in play today. Second, I have interpreted the counterposition to the restrictive norms as essentially utilitarian, a matter of reducing prohibitions to negative weights. But one might instead interpret the counterargument as one of coming to treat the nonutilitarian mandatory norm of a duty to protect one's citizens as trumping the normative constraints in force. I will address these two points together.

On the first point, the historical evidence here, as always, underdetermines the appropriate interpretation, and it is possible to see this history as continued application of discontinuous (exception-sensitive) norms. It is, however, important to see that this is not a challenge to the best ontological account of the norms at issue. Ontologically, there may be no reason to prefer an account of an exceptionless norm that is suspended exceptionally over an exception-containing norm that is applied.[61] But what is at issue is the psychological reality of these norms, in the minds of decision makers: whether they understood the prohibitory norms as merely presumptive rather than categorical. And here there is evidence to suggest that we have witnessed a discontinuous process of decay. First, the legal renderings of the torture and assassination norms were clear and categorical, providing for no exceptions or affirmative defenses. While the actual deliberative norms need not be identical to the formal legal statements, there is no evidence that these norms were understood as having silent exceptions during the time of their full-strength guidance. Military and FBI training, for example, emphasized the exceptionless nature of the anti-torture norm. While there were doubtless policymakers who understood the norms to be suspensible in times of emergency, these views were not articulated publicly until after 9/11. In the case of assassination, it is true that the post-Church Commission norm appears to have been suspended for purposes of (unsuccessfully) targeting Gaddafi and Hussein—but serious efforts were made to show that these were exceptional cases, justified as such, and not part of a general policy of permitting such killings whenever certain conditions were met. Post-2002, the CIA and US military are clearly operating under a very different, exception-based regime, wherein the possibility of targeted attacks on state leaders are openly discussed (e.g., Gaddafi in 2010, Assad in 2013). I think there is no plausible way to understand post-2002 developments as anything other than the emergence of a new deliberative paradigm concerning targeted killing. For both norms, then, the journalistic evidence suggests a deliberate policy shift from general prohibition to managed permission—albeit with a further shift in the torture norm regime after 2009.

As to the second point, my claim that honor- and dignity-based norms have been superseded by a utilitarian logic: again, my point is about deliberation, not ontology. It is true that a norm insisting on the priority of citizen defense can mimic a utilitarianism that places no weight on the interests of noncitizens. Such a self-defense norm will require the state to do whatever furthers the interests of its subjects in continued life, and this will presumptively include using all manners of interrogation or interdiction that will reduce the probability of an attack on those citizens or on other national interests. Put another way, the logic of nationalism (a sort of collective ethical egoism) coincides with the logic of realism. Operationally, a self-defense norm coincides with a utilitarian norm of maximizing US lives saved (or of minimizing the risk of US lives lost). And the political economy of democracy, according to which officials fear voters' reactions to lives lost, is consistent with reinforcing both logics. Both are hostile to the ways in which dignity- and honor-based norms exclude otherwise productive options from the scene of deliberation. Under the instrumental pressure of either self-defense or utilitarian values, the values of dignity and honor will come to seem quaint or fetishistic.

11.5. PROTECTING NORMS?

What we have is a roadmap, under conditions of civilian defense control and technology, for the collapse of norms whose institutionalization was hard-fought. The unthinkable became thinkable, thought, and then done. The irony of this story is that democratic politics, while generally friendly to human rights norms and treaties, are less hospitable to those norms when put to the test. While values of equality, fairness, and due process obviously do well in democratic regimes, counterutilitarian and honor-based norms may do poorly in periods of stress.

The story here is illustrative of a general tension within democratic polities, between the values of a nonaccountable group of policymakers and public accountability—a tension that often plays out in the arena of technocratic decision making, in the design of institutions to protect certain forms of decision making (notably central banking) from direct political pressure. What is striking about the examples of torture and assassination is that the select policymakers—the military and FBI in particular—protected values rather than expertise. The task of institutional design, therefore, might be seen as one of ensuring the continuing salience of those values, ensuring that the deliberative institutions in which they retain a grip continue to play a prominent role in security policy, so that their views are not easily sidelined through bureaucratic maneuvering. A piece of this history that I have not explored is the apparent significant difference between the interrogation cultures of the CIA and the military and FBI. While there was reported concern within the CIA about the use of the new interrogation measures, not only grounded in a fear of legal consequences, CIA officers appear to have had few qualms in moving quickly to import these methods from the SERE training context. Thus, while the excision of torture from the armory of the military and FBI extended beyond the mere prohibition of techniques, the CIA's no-torture period appears to have been merely technical, without underlying value change. Given the unwillingness of President Obama to pursue legal investigations against the CIA officers who destroyed much of the record of the torture program, and his reluctance to permit declassification of the Senate report on that program, it is hard to know how deeply the reinstated anti-torture norm bites within the agency, or whether it is being treated as a temporary order to stand-down.

There is an important further question of whether the newly thinkable can become again unthought, at the public level. Public opinion polling on torture reveals a mercurial public. Immediately following the revelations of the Abu Ghraib abuses, in 2004, 32 percent of Americans polled said they thought torture is never justified, against 43 percent saying it could often or sometimes (as opposed to rarely) be justified. Ten years later, by 2015, and following repeated and emphatic defenses of torture by former Vice President Cheney, the number saying torture was never justified had dropped to 27 percent, with 51 percent saying that it could often or sometimes be justified.[62] While these are not enormous shifts in public opinion, they are significant, and it is striking that public opinion seems to have moved in a direction opposite to official action, post-2009. While the anti-torture norm never rested on a bedrock of public support, the polling suggests that anti-torture values will not find a secure home there either. A full rebirth, then, will need to involve primarily institutional efforts at re-culturation.

I should also acknowledge a different normative lesson that may be gleaned from this history. If, like former Vice President Cheney, you regard the norms against torture and/or targeted killing as obstacles to a rational policy of national security, then the protection of nonaggregative honor and dignity values is itself the problem to be overcome. Indeed, one can justify the substitution of relatively precise drone-based strikes for ground or less-precise air strikes as a serious advance for humanitarian values, as precisely a matter of bringing properly democratic (as opposed to populist) values to bear in national security. Such advocates would be well advised to treat this discussion as a recipe for targeted norm destruction, of reducing the influence in security policy of institutionally discrete and normatively homogeneous actors, like the military, and expanding that of politically accountable decision makers. But I suspect that even such advocates would recognize that democratic accountability comes with its own set of evaluative costs, costs that can build up to the point of destroying values central to democracy itself.

12

LOOKING BACKWARD:
DEMOCRATIC TRANSITIONS AND
THE CHOICE OF JUSTICE

12.1. DEMOCRATIC FUTURES AND UNDEMOCRATIC PASTS

Most of this discussion has concerned political violence in the form of war and occupation (or liberation). I want now to consider the other guise of violence at the heart of many democracies: revolution. Victory in both revolution and war presents democracies with a basic choice: how to manage the inevitable conflict between the claims to repair the past and to construct the future. Indeed, concerns about post-victory score settling are even more acute with the legitimating mandate of a successful revolution behind them.

We are still too early in the story of the Arab revolutions and counter-revolutions of 2011 to know the complete arc of transformation (though the portents are not promising). But the questions presented by post-communist Central and Eastern Europe can serve as important guides. Communism's failure brought with it an important set of lessons; and in the former Soviet Union since 1989, the failure of unbounded capitalism has confirmed some important truths about healthy polities—for example, the crucial role played by social trust in civil society, and the importance of a functioning tax and regulatory system. One important set of lessons, however, is yet to be fully distilled. These lessons arise from Central Europe's recent attempts to undo the expropriations and deprivations that occurred during the forcible transformation of peasants and bourgeoisie, institutions and individuals, from freeholders in land into unlanded participants in socialism.

Many others, of course, were losers under state socialism: those denied a choice of career, freedom to travel, possibilities of political agency. But losing land has had a special salience, partly because of the special role land ownership plays in social memory, and partly because the formerly landed often have other assets, and are able to mobilize political forces effectively. Thus, the restoration of expropriated property in kind or in value has been a legislative priority in the new states. The programs themselves have varied greatly in pace, ambition, efficiency, and scope. Any complete assessment of the success or failure of these programs must be highly local and contextual. Taken together, however, they pose a common problem: what should a state do when deprivation and injustice are systemic, their correction necessarily piecemeal, and other projects of social repair are pressing? How much public attention and how many public resources are the victims of expropriation entitled to claim?

In this chapter I take up the issue of land reparations in transitional democracies because of its intrinsic interest, and because it raises a number of deep issues in political, moral, and legal theory. These include the limits of legitimate political transformation, the relation of corrective to distributive justice, the value of purely symbolic political action, and the significance of place to identity among the goods promoted by a liberal state. Although these questions have force outside the transitional context, they have a special urgency and clarity within it.[1] I will assume that reparations programs are generally permissible, assuming they are put into place by reasonably democratic processes that take account of, even if they do not accede to, the wishes of those who bear the cost of these programs. My focus in this chapter is on whether victims of expropriation can claim reparations as a matter of right—in particular, whether a just state can nonetheless decline those claims in light of other demands on its resources.

I argue the following: First, while injustice has a long life, remedy has a short one; and the general case for complete repair, through monetized reparations, diminishes quickly over time and across generations, especially when the injurers have departed the scene and given that reparations are in competition with the other claimants on scarce social resources. Second, some reparations claims for return of particular lands, such as transgenerational homesteads and cultural properties tied to collective ways of life, do rest on powerful moral and political grounds, chiefly the importance of tradition to the conditions of meaningful individual and collective life. The main argument for repair in these cases comes from distributive justice, not from corrective justice. But even this stronger class of claims will fail or be severely limited under a number of plausible conditions. Thus I do not think the claims for repair typical of the European context are in fact sufficient to generate duties of repair by the post-communist regimes.

12.2. THE SYMBOLIC WORTH OF REPARATIONS

In philosophical and political theory, the functions of national claims and gestures of repair are varied and not wholly consistent. Claims of repair sound in two registers, individual and collective, and are best treated separately. At the individual level, and in the most literal sense, a claim of repair is a claim to be made whole, to have a harm healed or corrected. This is obviously most easily accomplished for those who have lost money or things clearly monetizable, or for those seeking restitution of items or parcels of property, be it homesteads, commercial property, sacred lands, or pieces of art. The claim of repair is, in this strict sense, a claim to reverse the clock to the status quo ante. For those whose harms are physical or psychic, the problem of finding an adequate reparative equivalent looms large. No sum can compensate for stolen time in prison, or for the loss of a loved one's life, or for the degradation of torture. But money may help to rebuild a life, or to pay off debts incurred as a result of expatriation.[2]

Mainly, however, when the damage is nonmonetary, a demand for monetary repair functions symbolically. We are accustomed to thinking of cash as alienating, the antithesis of expressions of genuine humanity and compassion.[3] But the very fungibility of money means that giving it up hurts, for there are always alternative uses to which it could be put by its donors. It is the infliction of that hurt upon the donors that grounds the symbolic value of cash payment, the acceptance of pain for oneself in order to mark the pain in another. This is not a cynical point; the claim of victims is not that others must suffer as they have. Their claim is, instead, that only when their suffering is put in the terms of a common language can the wrong done to them be recognized. (Likewise, the unpleasantness of guilt is a part of its function.) Seen in its best light, then, the claim for money is, in part, a claim of dignity, a belated demand by victims that their equality and humanity be recognized by their injurers.

This point underlies much of our legal system in tort and criminal law; indeed, it is at the heart of both retributive justice, manifest in the criminal law's institution of punishment, and corrective justice, manifest in tort and contract law and their institutions of compensation and disgorgement. If we understand forms of justice by reference to their function rather than their forms or specific subject matters, both retributive and corrective justice can be understood as working a kind of repair, and in that respect as forms of reparative justice, although they have other functions as well, principally deterrence. Neither money nor prison time can heal wounds or unwind the clock, but the very fact of their forced expenditure can reorient individuals in moral space, creating a kind of co-erced respect—and the possibility of a resulting genuine respect. In many cases, the absence of respect was precisely the problem in the first place. The petty thief and the reckless driver fail to appreciate the humanity of their possible victims; neither understands that the suffering they in-flict is real. Corrective and reparative justice force the issue by rendering common both suffering and its predicate, humanity. The thief and driver, when forced to reckon with the losses they inflicted, come to see them as losses to persons like themselves. Punishment and restitution become forms of confrontation, and through confrontation the proper relation-ship between injurer and victim is restored.[4] Compelled empathy is the goal; and for certain offenders in certain social settings, it appears to be achievable through some of the institutions of reparative justice.[5]

The possibility of reparative justice for crimes of passion, or any crime motivated by power or pleasure rather than economic gain, is dimmer. Rape is the central example. While rapists' motivations of course vary, part of the motivation in some core instances is a desire to humiliate and de-grade the victim.[6] Such a motivation obviously presupposes a recognition of her humanity. Similarly for passionate assaults or murders: the injurer not only recognizes the victim's suffering but actively seeks to cause that suf-fering. In these cases, the point of reparative justice cannot be an acknowl-edgment of the victim's humanity, for it has already been acknowledged. If the criminal has funds, of course those can be used to compensate vic-tims for medical bills, time away from work, and other financial costs. A decent society, however, helps victims with those costs whether or not the wrongdoers can foot the bill; victim aid programs are part of reparative justice broadly construed, but not in the specific sense I am exploring here, which aims to reconstruct the relation between wrongdoer and victim. If reparative justice in the second sense has a role to play in violent crimes, it is principally as a form of education for the offender; any further gain accrues to society not the victim.

The great historical crimes of the last two centuries—slavery, geno-cide, mass internment, strategic bombing of civilian centers, Stalinist po-litical repression, Maoist political "re-education"—mix elements of both these categories. On the one hand, these crimes exemplify the denial of their victims' humanity. Indeed, political leaders brought about many of these crimes precisely by getting the direct actors (soldiers, commissars, police, pilots) to see their victims as nonhuman. Either the victims' suf-fering simply failed to register or the suffering was not seen as suffering at all but as a form of healthy discipline for the victims. This suggests that the mechanisms of reparative justice, namely confrontation and compensation, could be an important part of the moral reconstruction of the nation. This is part of the justification for the creation of international criminal tribunals to prosecute human rights violations and war crimes, for example, in the former Yugoslavia and Rwanda. And it occupies a central role in the contemporary US movement for slavery reparations. Slavery's individual victims and perpetrators are long departed, but its institutional legacy lives on in many forms: materially, in white-black wealth, educational, and income disparities; and socially, in white-black differences in social status and vulnerability to official power. The point of reparations in this context is not, by and large, individual book-balancing, but rather mustering a national will to confront and take collective responsibility for slavery's long-term legacy.[7]

On the other hand, often the very possibility of efforts at reparative justice only arises with a change of regimes, when many of the political leaders and direct offenders have disappeared from the scene (as well as their victims in the more lethal instances).[8] Confrontation in these cases will often be impossible, as will compensation for the victims themselves.[9] Moreover, even if the perpetrators are accessible to justice, the only legitimate sentence in cases of genocide or human rights violations will be life imprisonment. Repair of the personal relationship between victims and perpetrators is beside the point. When the relationship between perpetrators and victims is irrecoverable, the aim of reparative justice is not, strictly speaking, repair at all. It is, rather, the creation of a new political community, one less likely to create classes of victims, with a future lived in the shadow of its past. Postwar Germany's undertaking of massive reparations was aimed at restoring the lives of Holocaust survivors, and at protecting international Jewry through support of Israel, but another significant desired effect was that the German public would be forced, in paying the reparations, to accept a long-term burden of atonement.

In short, gestures of repair help constitute the identity of a transforming nation. Despite the truth in Ernest Renan's famous aphorism, that forgetting lies at the heart of the nation, collective memory is also essential to the construction of a national identity.[10] A chief function of reparations movements is to create and hallow a particular set of memories, to restore to collective consciousness events otherwise obscured by official histories and "common sense" as defined by dominant groups. More ambitiously, a reparations movement oriented around recovery from an entire regime, as in Eastern Europe or South Africa, aims at the birth of an entirely new national consciousness. It is with such movements that the truth of

Renan's observation re-emerges. He referred to the wars and conquests among bitterly divided peoples that become, in national myths, stories of ancient racial or religious unity. Reparations movements also aim, paradoxically, at instilling a forgetting, erasing an injustice and the festering resentments that resulted. The ideal of equal citizenship at the heart of democratic culture is one that can only be sustained through a forgetting of the differences in status and power that run through any nation. (In this sense, the ideal of democracy itself is a forgetting of facts of dominance and inequality, replaced by a dream of equality and the common good.)

A different form of forgetting accompanies collective demands voiced by cultural or ethnic minorities who seek the return of traditional and sacred lands and buildings. Their wish is to restore a way of life made unlivable by prior regimes. Even if the land is unreturnable—for example, because it has been profaned—groups may seek money reparations to pay for rebuilding and relocation, or to try to reverse a diasporic trend by attracting former and would-be members of the group. The wish here is not for political inclusion but, to use Charles Taylor's term, for *recognition* of the group's distinct identity and history.[11] As Taylor argues, demands for recognition are claims of dignity, claims that the distinctive cultural formation of a group is not merely a curiosity but a splendor of the nation. Claims of recognition are, in effect, demands that members of the dominant group learn to *see* in a certain way, that they bring into focus the distinct normative contours of individuals or groups otherwise obscured in a nation's history of expansion, colonization, or cultural homogenization. This is a democratic appeal as much as an aesthetic pitch, for the claim is not (just) that a culture matters because it has produced something of beauty. Rather, a culture's beauty consists centrally in its being a presentation of its creators' humanity. *Contra* Joseph de Maistre, such claimants demand to be seen as members both of a nation and of (hu)mankind.[12] It follows that a dying culture's appeals are not simply calls for a new truthtelling in history, for they are invariably acts of creative nostalgia, and so are also acts of Renanian forgetting. As with the construction of national identity, so the reconstruction of a tribal identity involves an imagined past, a consolidation of tradition and ritual. Indeed, a reparative movement, whether or not successful, may be one of the only ways for a cultural group to create unity out of fragmentation. (As I will argue below, the claim of necessity gives cultural groups priority over other claimants to reparative justice in the European context.).

Across all these contexts, the demand for reparations shares a common function: to demonstrate the legal and moral subjectivity of the victims.

The demand for repair makes clear not just that suffering occurred but that it was felt by a person, someone with interests akin to those of the injurer. In the political analogue to this moral point, victims seek re-inclusion in the community as moral and political agents, subjects of a universal kingdom of ends. To skeptics of moralism, the demand for repair represents a form of magical thinking according to which an actual history of subordination of the dominated to raw power can be replaced and reversed through subordination of the dominant to justice. Part of the appeal of the reparations movement is the power it gives to the claimants to determine the state of the national conscience. We need not agree with Nietzsche that morality's triumph represents the victory of subterfuge over strength to see that morality does represent a form of power for the weak—indeed, to see that as its virtue. That power should breed fantasies of revenge, cloaked as demands of repair, is simply to acknowledge its attractions.

12.3. IS SOCIALIST EXPROPRIATION A CRIME DEMANDING REPAIR?

The political acts for which property reparations have been implemented do not count as crimes in the same way that other forms of political tyranny associated with Eastern European communism do; and this, in turn, affects the character of their justification. Expropriation on its own is not a categorical wrong like murder or political repression; it does not by its very nature vault to the head of the line for repair.[13] While some individuals—such as the Soviet kulaks—were subjected to great state brutality—many others, including many of the residents of Central Europe, are better classified as the cost bearers of a failed social revolution whose ideals, at one time, were widely supported. To be sure, the political transformation of postwar Eastern Europe was far more a product of Red Army power than of any indigenous political support for socialism.[14] Even assuming that the majority of the citizens of Eastern Europe might have supported both socialism in free elections and the expropriations socialism entailed, this does not make the transformation legitimate, any more than the fact that I might have given away my wallet makes its theft less disturbing. The anguish and frustration were raw and real for those stripped of family businesses and farms, or who suddenly found families of strangers living in their apartments, running their enterprises into the ground.

Yet, to say that the expropriations that were part of socialist transformation involved wrongs, that they are prima facie candidates for rectification, is not to condemn them as theft, despite all the inadequacies of the process. For one thing, these inadequacies do not fully account for the retrospective sense of wrongs committed. Few social revolutions have happened at the polls, and even the revolutions that do happen at the polls produce losers—people un- or inadequately compensated by the beneficiaries of the changed regime.[15] It is hard to imagine that the call for reparations today would be weaker if electoral majorities had stood behind the original acts. The expropriations would seem just as unfair to their victims.[16]

Understanding this point is a matter of getting right the starting point of the inquiry: moreover, getting it right as much in emotional tone as in normative premises. What we need is a theory of retrospective moral assessment. For such great historical wrongs as slavery and genocide, the normative premises are clear—these acts were profound violations of the dignity of persons—and the appropriate response a generation later, just like the appropriate response at the time of the acts, must include a dose of moral horror.[17] The same is true for some particular expropriations, those punishing the exercise of basic rights that any legitimate regime must respect. But responding to the systematic expropriations undertaken as part of the socialist project has to involve a different tone and set of premises, seeing them as failed and humanly costly political mistakes but not as crimes. This point holds, I believe, independently of one's preferred normative theory of property.

The only set of premises from which the expropriations' criminality can directly be deduced would be a distorted and dogmatic Lockeanism, one that takes the mere fact of an owner's current legal title to private property as sufficient to exclude any systematic legal change in entitlement. Such a theory is, of course, normatively indefensible (if often defended)—it simply privileges the status quo. A normatively more robust Lockean theory that limits state interference in the private holding and transmission of property requires more of current holders than just that they hold legal title. Their normative standing depends on the desert following from the manner of their original acquisition (typically through the injection of personal labor) and of each successive transfer. It would take excessively strong and historically naive empirical assumptions about these historical processes to think that pre-expropriation baselines were entitled to strong normative deference.[18] In light of the long and undeniable histories of arbitrary feudal privilege, exploitation of actual land workers, and political corruption, there is no reason to think systematic socialization undermines moral desert any more than the status quo ante preserved it. Given the underlying moral indeterminacy of landholding on a Lockean view, there is nothing criminal, much less illegitimate, about the transformation of a private property system.

This point holds a fortiori for more teleological property theories, whether Humean theories maximizing social utility or Kantian or Hegelian theories stressing property's role in assisting self-realization. Such theories need to rest, also on pain of dogmatism, upon a basically empirical foundation in anthropology, psychology, and political economy. Before the communist transformations, there was good reason to doubt whether the existing private property system was doing much to achieve social utility or self-realization, either in absolute terms or as compared with imagined partially or fully socialized alternatives. Collective experimentation with these alternatives was not only consistent with teleological theories but might even have been thought demanded by them. Even taking seriously the costs of disrupted expectations—costs to both efficiency and at least the self-realization of those with property—there was at least an empirical question whether those costs might not be worth bearing. We know now, it seems, the answer to that question: they were not. But the socialist expropriations could only have been condemned *at the time* as criminal, as opposed to being misguided, in the spirit of a kind of moral priggishness, a grossly exaggerated sense of the importance of protocol in political transformation. Such asymmetry derives from the elementary fact that, to paraphrase Kierkegaard, history can only be lived forward and assessed backward.

A further complicating factor in assessing the expropriations is that the patterns of expropriation and of reparative justice have varied significantly from place to place, reflecting the degree of collectivization, the form of privatization policy, the absolute degree of national wealth, inter-ethnic rivalries, and the powers of different political actors, including religious groups.[19] For example, expropriations in communist East Germany occurred in several phases. First were the expropriations commanded by the Red Army during the occupation of 1945–49, nominally a process of de-Nazification, in which "essentially all large business enterprises" were taken.[20] Next came expropriations of agricultural property holdings, in which "more than 7,000 private farms and estates" were taken, ranging from a size of 100 hectares (250 acres) to large Junker estates; roughly 35 percent of all agricultural land in the Soviet zone was taken. This land was then redistributed to individual farmers in small plots, though it would eventually be collectivized over the next decade into state farms. Small businesses, however, remained in private hands until the 1970s, when there was a final expropriations program taking even small businesses.

While the initial agricultural expropriations were uncompensated, under the theory that they were a punishment for fascist complicity, the later expropriations were done through formalistic mechanisms and came with limited compensation.

Like the expropriations, post-unification reparations policy has taken various forms. The initial Soviet occupation expropriations were at first protected from reparations by treaty between West and East Germany, while reparations for property expropriated by the DDR itself were guided by a fundamental principle of reparation in kind (*in natura*) rather than cash repayment, on the view that victims were entitled to as close an approximation as the state could deliver to the status quo ante.[21] The class of eligible claimants was extremely broad, including nonlineal heirs and expatriates, in accordance with a full-throated conception of reparative justice. But this approach also took on a pragmatic cast when it was applied in east-central Berlin, in that it generated funds for renovating a decrepit housing stock that the state could not manage on its own. The idea was that the state should deliver property swiftly into private hands, and the private holders (or new purchasers) could secure independent financing for its rehabilitation. It worked: the result was a fast, thorough, and fairly efficient process of restitution, followed by immediate sale to housing developers who did indeed renovate the properties. The cost, however, was the eviction of long-time tenants and the raising of rental prices generally beyond what former eastern residents could afford.

The principle of reparations in kind was subject to three important exceptions: first, when the property was "needed for urgent investment uses that would yield general economic benefits in eastern Germany"; second, when the property had been developed in such a way that it could not be extracted for return; and third, when the property had been reacquired by a good-faith purchaser.[22] (There were limited opportunities in the DDR for private ownership.) In such cases, former owners would be compensated but would not regain their land. However, many of the occupants of expropriated residential property were not owners but enjoyed some form of long-term lease. Outside Berlin, in a well-studied example, houses leased as rewards to valued members of the socialist state—some collaborators and apparatchiks, undoubtedly, but also members of valued professions, such as teachers—were subject to restoration to original owners and their descendants, again resulting in significant individual dislocation. This dislocation sometimes had dire effects—for example, in 1992 when two eastern Germans, whose homes had been restored to prior owners, hanged themselves in protest.[23] Finally, in 1994 a new "compensation and equalization payments law" added the Soviet-era expropriations to the list, allowing former owners rights of low-cost repurchase or other compensation.[24] The restitutionary program was, on the whole, very efficiently implemented, with nearly 95 percent of all restitution claims resolved by 2001.[25]

In the former Czechoslovakia, the new government instituted a relatively comprehensive program to rectify communist injustices, ranging from political imprisonment to expropriation. Because the scale of state-sponsored injustice was so great, the level of reparations available was quite low and the limitations fairly strict: property claimants must be individuals, as opposed to corporate entities or religious institutions; they or their heirs must be permanent residents of Czechoslovakia, and they had only six months to file; moreover, only undeveloped properties would be returned, and any property that had appreciated in value (an unlikely event) could only be regained by paying into the public treasury the difference between the value at seizure and the appreciated value.[26] As in Germany, a major goal of the ostensibly backward-looking policy of restitution was the forward-looking act of moving state-owned land into private hands quickly, constrained by two more instrumental considerations: keeping the privatization process out of the hands of apparatchiks and preventing extranational capital flight.[27]

In Poland, the process has been even slower and more restrictive, a result of local-national conflicts and administrative and legal confusion. Property was nationalized relatively quickly by the postwar communist government in Poland, the process largely completed by the mid-1950s, and this was done through both formally legal (i.e., in accordance with the regime's law) and illegal means (e.g., state coercion). While other Eastern European nations were able to settle on restitutionary programs within a few years of 1989 (with some adjustments later), the Polish debates continued until the mid-1990s. The position Poland has ended up with, at this writing, generally protects all legal expropriations under communism, thus entrenching the land reform undertaken postwar, which converted large estates into small holdings rather than into collective farms, as in East Germany.[28] Full restitution is available for Catholic Church property (indeed, for such property lost *at any* time in Polish history), Jewish religious property after the German invasion, or for property taken illegally during communism (but showing this involves substantial administrative burdens).[29] Although broader proposals have been introduced as legislation, none has survived.

We have, then, a range of reparative programs: the essentially comprehensive and retrospective (but instrumentally inflected) model of Germany, the fairly restrictive and heavily instrumental model of the Czech Republic and Slovakia; and the highly restrictive, noninstrumental model of Poland. Does any of these do justice to the claimants, and to the rest of the nation? Answering this question involves determining the urgency of the claims for repair that they meet or ignore. I will now turn to this matter and make the following assumptions. First, we should begin with a wide conception of prima facie valid claims, including both formally legal and de facto expropriations as subject to repair. Second, such claims concern the expropriation of real property and structures thereon, including homesteads, commercial properties (factory and residential), and communal or religious structures. Third, the losses inflicted by communism relative to expected levels of welfare under the types of welfare-state capitalism dominant in postwar Western Europe were pervasive and deep. And fourth, no significant identifiable group in the post-communist regime can be singled out as an appropriate target from whom to seek financial repair. True, there are individuals—apparatchiks or zealous collaborators—whose complicity in or principal authorship of state crimes is such that justice demands their eviction from the properties their crimes have provided. But although such cases are useful for motivating a reparative politics, there is no reason to think they are typical. And thus my working hypothesis is that these cases can be handled separately, leaving us with the nub of the problem: what to do with those who do not deserve punishment but who will nevertheless bear the costs of reparations.

12.4. THE CASE AGAINST MONETARY COMPENSATION

I will proceed by distinguishing two cases, one for cash compensation at some objective valuation and one for return in kind, which I will call "subjective compensation," since it seeks to restore former owners to the subjective state they enjoyed before expropriation. I begin with objective compensation, because understanding the reparative justice claim in cash-out terms will help to clarify some of the analytical issues, which are then applicable in the subjective case as well. To fix a point of departure, I will call such claims "maximalist" when they are claims for the total monetized value of the loss suffered by the former property owner.[30] A maximalist claim would entail at least the fair market value of the property at the time of expropriation, plus, for commercial properties, lost income for the property since expropriation, plus lost income on that income.[31] For homestead or communal properties, the maximalist claim would also include imputed income during the expropriated period, as measured by the rental value of comparable properties. This valuation would not capture the subjective value of the property to the resident, and so in that sense is not truly maximalist, but this is inevitable since subjective value is not obviously capable of being fully monetized. Doubtless, there is some amount of money that could persuade virtually anyone to part with even the most sentimental of objects, but sale under these conditions would only indicate voluntariness of the transaction, not a real equivalence in value, since monetary and sentimental values are incommensurable.

The maximalist pole is clearly financially unfeasible, at least in any country with a significant scale of expropriation. It nonetheless remains worth asking whether it is attractive as a regulative ideal. Let us focus first on the difficulties of making the maximalist assessment. It assumes, first, the possibility of specifying a fair market price for the property at the time of expropriation—but, of course, any actual market in land at that time would have been steeply discounted in light of general political unrest or neighboring expropriations. Compensating victims at a generally devalued rate for the particular loss they suffered is ethically awkward, in effect giving the state the benefit of a policy of broad injustice. On the other hand, (somehow) projecting a market value for the property based on an assumption of a stable, private-property-respecting regime would be equally awkward, for that would likely result in victims receiving more for their land than those whose property was not expropriated but who either continued to use it productively under socialism or received some form of compensation under the socialist regime.[32] I see no escape from this dilemma, and splitting the difference between the approaches means giving up on any principled approach to the valuational problem.

Next, even assuming one could identify a market price, consider the difficulty with assessing income on it. One would have to project imaginary rates of interest and taxation back into a counterfactual past. Then there is the worry emphasized by Jeremy Waldron in his discussion of reparations for aboriginal groups: compensating fully for lost investment opportunity assumes that the victims would have been ideal stewards of the investment.[33] Over a relatively short period (say, a decade), or for enduring commercial entities, this assumption may be reasonable. But with five decades' opportunity for financial mistakes, applied across the full spectrum of victims, it becomes clearly unreasonable. It would, again, have the effect of putting the victims of expropriation in a far better position than nonvictims over the same period. If the point were partly punitive, a matter of holding the expropriating regime to the most generous estimate of costs conceivable, then such an assessment might be defensible. But reparations work only in the dimension of corrective, not retributive, justice: though the victims remain, there is no state left to be punished. The very discontinuity between the current regime and the expropriators is what a reparations program is supposed to exemplify.

The passage of time raises a further problem for reparations claims in the European context: the relevant claimants now are, or soon will be, the heirs of the victims of expropriation. Victims will thus not be made whole by the reparations movement; rather, repairing at the maximalist level would give heirs, in effect, the largest conceivable bequest they might have received. But there is no good reason to assume that the victims of expropriation would have bequeathed their property in full to the particular set of claimants. This problem might be finessed, by limiting heirs' claims to the proportions they would receive under default laws governing inheritance (e.g., divided evenly among succeeding generations), thus treating current inheritance law as a proxy for the victims' wishes.[34] If the maximalist aim is to leave heirs in the position they would have enjoyed without the expropriation, then that aim will be frustrated by the variety of possible tax rules, under some of which heirs might be entitled to only a small fraction, if any, of the value of the expropriated property.

These technical questions are daunting. But they raise a yet thornier set of normative issues, one going to the deeper question of the justice of inherited wealth itself. Projecting a baseline of inherited property in effect presumes the legitimacy of what ought to be an open question in principle and has been an open question in history, namely intergenerational wealth transfers. While current populist rhetoric in the United States is deeply hostile to the idea of "death taxes" that in fact only affect the very wealthiest Americans, significant inheritance taxes are a nearly universal constituent of the great range of modern tax systems. As with the basic case for private property, only a dogmatic Lockean could conclude that social experimentation with very onerous estate taxes was per se illegitimate. To the contrary, a legitimate and basically just state could have adopted any of a range of inheritance tax schemes whose net results would have been coextensive with actual expropriation.[35] The normative instability of an inheritance baseline thus dogs the foundation of the maximalist position. (The general problem of shifting normative baselines is the subject of section 12.5.)

The second deep problem with the maximalist position is that it treats the suffering of the expropriated in normative isolation, separate from the claims of other victims of communism. But only the relative suffering of the expropriated, not their absolute claims, can determine whether their claims to the state's limited resources now take priority. Consider the landless compatriots of the reparative claimants. While doubtless some of the landed acquired their lands through effort more than luck, a great many more owned their property by virtue of a fortuitous birth into families already endowed with property or with the social and economic capital that enabled the acquisition of land. As a generalization, then, the landed differed from the unlanded primarily by being luckier—a fact that is, as John Rawls reminds us, without moral significance.[36] Moreover, up until the point of expropriation, the landed were in full enjoyment of the benefits of their luck. They were then deprived of these benefits. But did this make them worse off than the luckless landless? Furthermore, as I mentioned in discussing the putative criminality of the expropriations, many of the expropriated holdings might well have rested on foundations more dubious than mere luck, that is on foundations of economic exploitation, sexist inheritance law, and feudal tradition. If this is so, as it surely was in many cases, the argument for reparations becomes weaker still.

I do not mean to trivialize the moral and human costs of the expropriations. The landed who held their property under reasonable institutional expectations had responsibly planned their lives around those expectations. Such claims ought to and could have been respected and compensated more than they were by the socialist regimes, even in the pursuit of radical social change. But the harm is now done. The fundamental point is that the economic and moral harm done to the victims of expropriation does not dominate the general deprivations suffered by the landed and landless alike. The landless too have been deprived of a substantial fraction of the income they would have received on their capital—human capital—if the socialist regimes had not come to power. But since they likely outnumber reparative claimants, it is they, as a group, who will bear the substantial cost of the reparations program, either now or in future generations, if reparations are paid out of future revenues in the form of bonds. Since they were already worse off than the landed before the expropriation, it seems a double injustice to worsen their position again, once the value of their labor has been restored.[37]

What about other claimants on the public funds that would go to pay off the maximalist claims? Even very wealthy nations would find the maximalist claims difficult to meet without compromising other important claims, and the new capitalist economies of Eastern Europe would find the cost insurmountable. Reparations claims that were reduced in light of strained resources would still be in competition with other claims, and the reparations claims should not rank very high as matters of justice. The victims of expropriation may no longer be among the best off in their nations, but there is no reason to think that they are among the worst off. In terms of distributive justice, then, their claims on public resources rank below those whose claims are grounded in absolute need and deprivation, as well as below general claims for adequate health care, later-life pensions, and other state investments in human capital, particularly education for the young.

12.5. HOW REPARATIVE JUSTICE DEPENDS ON DISTRIBUTIVE JUSTICE

The distinctly normative justification for letting bygones rest, as opposed to the technical failure of the maximalist position I considered above, stemmed from two concerns sounding in distributive justice: the legitimacy of a wide range of rules concerning wealth transfer, and the relative suffering over time of the landless victims of communism. This suggests the priority of distributive justice over reparative justice, and thus over the form of reparative justice specific to property restoration: corrective justice. Justifying this claim requires a detour into the relation between the two. Distributive justice refers to the principles of justice establishing what individuals are entitled to within a legitimate public political ordering: what negative protections they can claim from incursions against their persons and holdings in land and things, and what positive claims they can make on others for assistance in meeting needs for security, shelter, nutrition, and perhaps much more. The negative claims of distributive justice are embodied principally in the criminal law (and in the law of property, which establishes some of the boundaries policed by the criminal law), while the positive claims are embodied in a range of governmental and sub-governmental institutions, including tax, educational, and health systems, typically with some redistributive effect.[38]

Corrective justice refers to principles of justice that aim to rectify wrongful invasions of individual entitlements, particularly entitlements to bodily integrity, mental well-being, and property. In Anglo-American law, these principles are manifested primarily in the institution of tort law, but also in some aspects of contract law—for example, provisions protecting contractors from the costs of breach.[39] Although the typical subject of corrective justice is individual accidents and misadventures, the rubric can also function as a plausible cover for expropriations. The demand that lost property be restored or compensated is, in its object, a claim of corrective justice. Moreover, the kinds of losses under discussion—routine expropriations as opposed to punishments for political disobedience—resemble more misadventures resulting from legitimate activity (here, ordinary politics with a socialist cast) than the malicious harms regulated by retributive justice. Since the principal wrongdoers are now largely off the stage, and with so many pervasive forms of complicitous getting-by during the socialist period, the primary task for the post-socialist state is properly correction, not punishment.

The Central European countries, like all others, faced and face the task of meeting the demands of both corrective and distributive justice. This raises the question of how the two relate to one another, especially when they compete. In the abstract, then, corrective and distributive justice might seem directly related: distributive justice fixes entitlements, and corrective justice protects them against invasion. The simple Lockeanism discussed above would relate them in this way. Assuming that prior holders enjoyed legitimate entitlements, corrective justice demands the restoration of the stipulatively just status quo ante. There will, of course, be a problem about the force of corrective justice claims under non-ideal conditions, when owners do not deserve their holdings because of improper acquisition or transfer. If the status quo ante lacks legitimacy, then no reasons of justice would support its restoration; there is no (Lockean) injustice to correct. Of course, there might be other, instrumental reasons for individuals to regard themselves as owing duties of repair, or for the state to impose such duties—for example, efficiency and deterrence reasons.[40] But the problem with this move, as with any attempt to fuse deontological and utilitarian reasoning, is that the instrumental reasons threaten to devour the Lockean foundations. That is, once efficiency reasons are regarded as sufficient to compel individuals to transfer resources to one another in repair, then they would also be sufficient to motivate a general redistribution of holdings to one with greater social value.

The difficulty a Lockean view has in coping with demands for repair of non-ideal holdings, and thus in generating any coherent normative framework for dealing with the messy world we live in, is one among many reasons for preferring a more robust conception of distributive justice. One such conception is that of a generally egalitarian liberalism, where distributive justice principles require that each person have access to minimally adequate food, shelter, and medical care as well as the opportunity for meaningfully equal participation in social, economic, and political life.[41] I do not mean here to defend such a conception, or to regard it as beyond controversy. I do, however, mean to stipulate it now, because I take it to be sufficiently widely attractive that investigating the relation between it and corrective justice has intrinsic interest. According to the kind of liberal conception I invoke, the justice of prior holdings is fixed both by principles of legitimate acquisition and transfer and also by whether and to what degree extant holdings satisfy the universal demands for minimally decent living conditions and equal participation.[42]

Unlike a Lockean view, which can take only a binary view of the legitimacy of a given holding (as consistent or inconsistent with its underlying principles), a liberal view has conceptual space for questions about the independent force of reparative claims in non-ideal circumstances. Intuitively, it seems that claims of corrective justice have force even when a state's distribution of holdings strays from a full implementation of distributive justice. As Jules Coleman has pointed out, while there is probably no defensible theory of distributive justice under which Bill Gates is entitled to the full holdings he has, he nonetheless has a claim on me in corrective justice when I dent his car.[43] The reason claims of distributive and corrective justice have force is because, on a liberal conception, they have different subjects. Distributive justice regulates the state as such and is a condition of its legitimacy, defining the relations of citizens to the state—or, alternatively, between citizens taken one at a time and the citizenry collectively.[44] Corrective justice, by contrast, orders the relations of individuals to one another (or of individuals to the state, when the state acts as an injurer). Corrective justice thus expresses an interpersonal dimension of justice, not the institutional dimension of distributive justice.

Given their different subjects, corrective and distributive justice could relate to each other in a number of ways.[45] First, corrective justice might be ancillary to distributive justice: its principles seek to maintain or bring about just distributions of holdings, under the recognition that institutional considerations may often make impossible the full realization of distributive justice.[46] On this account, corrective justice claims derive their normative force from distributive justice but retain force despite a significant gap between the actual social state and what distributive justice entails. Second, corrective justice might be seen as normatively independent of distributive justice: corrective justice aims to repair individual invasions of legitimate individual holdings, where "legitimate" is spelled out in terms that do not (or need not) make reference to distributive justice norms—for instance, in terms of reasonable institutional expectations.[47] Even if we conclude that Central European socialism failed as a scheme of distributive justice because of the constraints it imposed on individuals' choices to participate in work and politics, we might still think that the holdings citizens acquired under that system—a car, an apartment lease, a country cottage—merit protection from arbitrary taking. And, of course, similarly for holdings acquired under the flawed ancien régime distribution. Here, the force of corrective justice claims stems from the violation of these expectations per se, not from their underlying relation to distributive justice.

Neither of these views is fully satisfactory. The derivative view fails because it is hard to see how corrective justice might inherit significant normative force from distributive justice without ending up simply subordinated to distributive justice concerns. If distributive justice principles are sufficient to evaluate the post-violation distribution, then any reparative claim is either simply determined or overruled by distributive justice. Alternatively, if distributive justice principles apply only to basic social institutions (as Rawls argues), so that actual distributive shares are a matter of consensual transactions within a just institutional framework, then it is hard to see how their moral force is the ground for claims about disruptions to particular patterns of holdings. Distributive justice principles either matter too much or not enough, on this view.

There remains room for a third, and more plausible, view of the relationship between corrective and distributive justice. Corrective justice principles do represent a distinct normative ground insofar as they express ideals of interpersonal conduct and accountability; but their force presupposes an effective scheme of distributive justice. Two consequences follow. First, a state substantially unable to ensure minimally adequate living standards in its population has no business instead first meeting the historically grounded claims of those whose lives are, or are mainly, already above that minimum.[48] Financial resources should not be drained out of the project of creating social welfare institutions—or, more minimally, meeting claims of material need in an unsystematic way—in order to compensate expropriation victims. In principle, of course, funding ambitious reparations schemes can only be wrong when there are competing claims of need; in the abstract, there is nothing objectionable about paying reparations. If, contrary to fact, reparations programs were designed to pay out slowly enough (or funded through long-term bond issuance), there might also be no stark choice between corrective and distributive justice. But in the fragile moment of the emergence of the new democracies, reparations programs do force a choice, and in the wrong direction.

The second consequence of the dependence of corrective justice on distributive justice is deeper. It goes to why corrective justice is ultimately the wrong framework for considering reparative claims. While corrective justice governs more than just relations among individuals, also including claims by and against firms and governments, it remains individualistic in one important respect: it controls and seeks repair from distortions to a social framework whose normativity is given independently, by distributive justice. In other words, the application of corrective justice principles presuppose an exogenous baseline; they do not themselves construct that baseline. In the department of Anglo-American corrective justice concerning accidents, this is shown through the liability tests of the "reasonable person," whose conduct sets the baseline of noncompensable interaction, and of routine commercial practice, ultra-hazardous variants of which motivate strict liability. In the law of theft, the baseline is set by the norms of property. What happened under communism, however, cannot plausibly be seen as a violation of baseline private property norms. What happened was, rather, a transformation of the baseline itself—a transformation, I argued above, that must be considered within the limits of legitimate political experimentation. The systematic state expropriations cannot be measured against a baseline normatively much richer than either respect for formal legality (as with the Polish reparations program) or a prohibition on religious, ethnic, or political persecution. Those principles arguably form part of any theory of state legitimacy; a private property system does not. Post-socialist claims of corrective justice thus commit a kind of political anachronism, by measuring the expropriations against baselines irrelevant to the expropriation period itself. While the harms from the expropriations are relevant to distributive justice concerns about the relative position of their victims, it follows that formally legal expropriations fall outside the scope of the harms subject to corrective justice.

12.6. THE TROUBLE WITH COMPROMISE

What, then, of programs short of maximalism? In the United States, as I mentioned above, significant but not fully compensatory payments were made to Japanese-American victims of wrongful internment. Similarly, in Eastern Europe, we might reject maximalist claims while endorsing some form of individualized reparation. For example, compensatory reparations could be capped, paid proportionately to the loss, or paid at progressively lower rates of compensation for higher-valued takings, as in Hungary's reparations scheme.[49] Such a compromise might seem to reflect a balance between backward- and forward-looking claims, and between the claims of particular victims of expropriation and the pockets of the many who must pay those claims. Compromise is attractive, whether between adverse positions or between ideals and adverse realities. As Cass Sunstein has argued, it can be socially valuable to avoid resolving principled disagreement by instead constructing a modus vivendi representing a balance of interests.[50]

But the case for pragmatic compromise is unconvincing here. Maximalist compensation, despite its ultimate unfeasibility, would be an expression of principle: original owners are entitled to be restored to the state they would have enjoyed but for expropriation. Say a regime picks a compensatory rate of 75 percent of market value at the time of seizure. Even assuming, contrary to my argument above, that corrective justice claims have force in this context, by hypothesis this compensation rate fails to do corrective justice, for it does not restore a status quo ante but only marks financially the incidence of a loss long ago absorbed. With respect to the expropriation victims, the function of the compensatory scheme is largely symbolic, and there is no good reason for the symbolism to be as expensive as this. One might argue that money is a show of earnest that renders other forms of symbolism—legislative apology, public monuments—as no more than cheap talk. But this claim rests on an assumption about human psychology without much intuitive, much less empirical, support. Partial payment might just as well irritate as salve old wounds in a way that a nonmonetized gesture will not. Of course, money is nice, and some is better than none. But it seems likely that anything short of the maximalist program will leave claimants dissatisfied that justice has been done at all, much less fully. If symbolic, partial payment cannot achieve subjective repair, then one might as well choose a cheaper form of symbolism—saying it with daisies instead of roses.

Equally important, singling out victims of expropriation for symbolic cash payments mistakes both the nature of the harms inflicted by socialism and the form of a proper response. The harms were systemic and universal, in the lack of freedom of movement, political agency, choice of employment, and the flow of information. Symbolic monetary compensation to the single, especially influential, class of the expropriated belies the universality of suffering. Such payments would signal that the new regime is not a community oriented around the future but rather a congeries of interest groups resting in the past.[51] Perhaps cash payments could be given to everyone who suffered under communism, but since this class is pretty nearly coextensive with the current population, funding a universal set of reparations is not even robbing Peter to pay Paul; it is taxing Peter to pay Peter himself. By contrast, a collective gesture of memory—a social and institutional recording of the many different varieties of suffering and waste—stands for the common nature both of social experience and of social hope.

A final reason against symbolic financial compensation is that the comparative justice problem continues to loom. A compensation scheme, even if not maximalist, is a significant draw on the state treasury, and so competes against other urgent claims. To compete favorably as a matter of right, the compensation scheme requires a principled argument that partial payment (as opposed to cheaper symbolism) really is required as a matter of justice. But an argument for expensive but noncorrective justice is precisely what we lack; it cannot be presupposed in the case for compromise without begging the basic question.

Although there is no compelling moral case for reparations, there may be good instrumental arguments for reaching a compromise scheme that combines monetary with nonmonetary reparations. Corrective justice institutions stabilize property arrangements and contribute to a general sense of public order that is itself part of the condition of meaningful collective and individual life. In the special case of post-communist transitions, where cultivating private property ownership is crucial to the emergence of a new economy, selling off state assets and distributing the proceeds to expropriation victims may aggregate social welfare better than the alternative likely uses of those assets.[52] Membership in international organizations may also turn on the effectiveness of a reparations scheme, as may the nation's ability to attract foreign investment capital. All of these considerations may add up to an argument that the social value of reparations exceeds the value of meeting other material needs. Calculating the social value of the reparations scheme is difficult, to be sure, particularly establishing that the value is properly distributed across the whole of the political community. But assuming the claim of social value is sound, then there is nothing to object to in such a program, whatever its expense, as the material for any objections has already been factored into the calculations. Note, however, that this is not an argument for reparative justice at all, but simply a question of optimal social investment.

12.7. A LIMITED CASE FOR LAND REPARATIONS

The argument against cash reparations thus seems clear when the general population of victims greatly outruns the population of those subject to expropriation, and when the latter are not the worst-off of the former. However, my argument so far has treated only the case for compensation for the lost value of land, principally on the ground that others, too, lost or never had things of comparable value. I have argued that the functions of memorialization and recognition can be accomplished better through collective gestures that do not revolve around the problem of finding a monetary equivalent of suffering. My argument leaves room for claims to return of land itself, particularly land invested with sentiment, tradition, and collective meaning—land, in other words, that does not have a monetary equivalence in the first place. So I turn now to consider that question.

Let us begin by setting aside the case of commercial properties: farmlands, factories, apartment complexes, et cetera. Since the function of these properties is income production, the loss to victims is primarily a loss of future income. The argument I offered above controls this issue: the claims of the victims (or victims' heirs) to the future income stream from these properties is no stronger, and perhaps even weaker, than the claims of many other victims. From the perspective of justice and efficiency, it would seem better to auction these properties to their highest-valuing users, with the auction proceeds then allocated through institutions of distributive justice. Moreover, and particularly for foreign-owned businesses, the risk of expropriation was not unreasonably borne by the businesses themselves.[53] To be clear: the initial expropriations may have been unjustified, but the possibility of securing insurance ex ante removes the unfairness of putting priority on distributive justice forty years ex post.

For some businesses—family-owned firms, or others with a particular cultural valence—this will seem a hard doctrine, for the value of the business exceeds the income flow. Even in these cases, however, restitution seems to me inappropriate. The passage of time has ended the symbolic lives of these businesses; restitution would be an exercise in sentimentality. As I argued above, businesses fail for many reasons, and there is no assurance that these particular ones would have succeeded during the intervening years or that alternative tax systems would have permitted their transmission over a generation. I conclude, therefore, that no special claims of repair are generated.

The more compelling case is the family home or family farm, particularly one that has been in a family for generations. Even more so than with the family business, the ratio of sentimental value to (imputed) income value is very high; indeed, it is so high that it undermines the case for money reparations. Such homesteads may be places where children were raised and memories formed, and perhaps were also anchors in local communities. Meaningful return and rehabitation may be possible, even after a generation, even for expatriates. If a homestead can be reinvested with memory and identity, then its real value can be preserved: its role in grounding identity and giving family members a sense of origin, place, and rootedness. This sense of place is what Rawls calls a "primary good": a general resource common across a great range of particular conceptions of ways of living well. Thus, restoring homesteads has an intimate and pervasive connection to the fundamental aim of the state, enabling individuals to live good lives, which distinguishes it from the case of commercial enterprises.[54] Life in a family-owned business is also a way of leading a good life, but only one particular way among many, and so should not be privileged over the many ways of working that inevitably disappear; no doubt some children of carriage makers also pine for the family tradition.

And yet: there are worse misfortunes than to be unable to return to the place of one's childhood. Many of us are members of modernity's deracinated throngs, who have moved many times and whose lives and families' lives have been spent in housing vulnerable to market and landlord vicissitudes. A family homestead would have been nice, to be sure; but what enables such lives to be good nonetheless is not property ownership but adequate housing as such. Ensuring that is the province of the state; happiness is up to us, to attain it in the circumstances in which we find ourselves. Lives without homesteads are, nonetheless, lives with their own myths of origins and memories. The cosmopolitan life, in this thin sense, has its disadvantages; and there are clearly values missing from it, values found only in the concentration of tradition that a particular place makes possible. But it is nonetheless a good life, and one upon which no claims for compensation can generally be grounded. Indeed, as modern Jews can attest, the deep values associated with ancient origin and the underlying myth of autochthony can contribute catastrophically to crimes against those deemed not to belong, to the rootless and the landless. A reparations movement that honors the longstanding resident may end up playing into a politics of otherness and exclusion, fomenting dangerous myths of racial purity and pride.[55] That way Europe must surely not go again.

This danger implies another argument against the restitution of land, which is that such programs create a new class of dispossessed, and among them are many whose claims seem no weaker than the original owners'. True, some of the fancier properties subject to restitution were rewards for party lackeys and collaborators of the nastiest sort. But others were just citizens who performed social roles valued in any state or society, such as artists, scientists, and athletes. Yet others, in the large land estates, were workers whose housing, as well as all other social services—were provided by the collective farms those estates had become. The expectations of those using property under a socialist system deserve as much respect as those of the prior owners. This does not mean the new inhabitants enjoy an absolute right to stay—to claim that would simply be to parallel the dubious position taken by the expropriated, that no change can be justified—but it does mean that their interests in the nature of the restitutionary program must be taken into account, for example in giving them priority in other claims on state resources.

For the many who never had an opportunity to establish or inhabit a transgenerational homestead, devoting scarce resources to ensuring that some can return to theirs will clearly seem less urgent than the provision of other primary goods, notably education and health care. The opportunity cost of restoring homesteads (the auction price of the properties) may not be very great. But if it is, then the issue of priorities of distributive justice looms large, for reparations look again like a program of rewarding the already fortunate at the expense of the unfortunate. Because what is restored is more a repository of particular, relational, concrete meanings than of economic value (despite its shadow economic cost) and thus not fungible, the problem of comparative priorities does not have the same significance as with monetized reparations. But it is a significant countervailing consideration nonetheless. In short, the case for homestead reparation is strong but not decisive, and the balance of considerations suggests that the claims of victims should be met, if they should at all, as a judgment of preferred social policy, and not as a trumping claim of social justice.

12.8. RESTITUTION OF COMMUNAL PROPERTY

I come now to the final and most compelling form of reparations claims: claims to communal properties, which function essentially to make possible a distinct cultural, religious, or intellectual tradition—for example, churches, synagogues, seminaries, museums, performance spaces, and universities. What such institutions provide is a form of public good: an indivisible (and only partially excludable) resource of structure, ritual, and significance in the lives of their members.[56] Reparative claims for these properties cannot in general be monetized; the value comes from the fact of their geography, enabling a kind of crossroads for their members, in whose interactions a common culture is formed. If the confiscation of property destroyed the institution itself in a particular region, and if restoring the property could enable the restoration of the institution in the lives of people to whom it remains meaningful, then restoration has a very great claim on social attentions and resources.

This claim derives partly from the ways these institutions contribute to the lives led by their members. As I argued in the case of homesteads, the alternative to their restoration is not an absence of a common culture but a common culture of a different, less institutionally dependent form.[57] True, the loss of a common culture rooted in a shared history is a very great loss, greater than the loss of home or business, but that loss has happened; the former members of that culture have already necessarily adjusted their lives; and the sentimental resurrection of the institution will differ from naive continuity. Thus, while the argument for restoration on these grounds has weight, it is not decisive. Therefore the stronger argument for reparations in these cases comes from the importance to the nation as a whole of having a range of distinct social institutions, future sources of cultural, intellectual, and religious mongrelization and hybridization. Their sheer existence fosters the tolerance necessary to national (and individual) flourishing. And the destruction of a nation's cultural institutions undermines something crucial to its citizens: a sense of belonging to a collective project whose aims and identity transcend their own. Edmund Burke made a similar point about the destruction of political institutions with a stark image:

> [O]ne of the first and most leading principles on which the commonwealth and the laws are consecrated, is lest the temporary possessors and life-renters in it, unmindful of what they have received from their ancestors, or of what is due to their posterity, should act as if they were the entire masters . . . hazarding to leave to those who come after them, a ruin instead of an habitation . . . By this unprincipled facility of changing the state . . . the whole chain and continuity of the commonwealth would be broken. No one generation could link with the other. Men would become little better than the flies of a summer.[58]

Flies of a summer live and die, just one damn fly after another—not even with the dignity of bees, whose lives contribute to the construction of a hive. We need not agree with Burke's wholesale conservatism to see the force of his claim. Reparation in the case of cultural, intellectual and religious institutions is a diachronic condition of the meaningfulness of collective life as such, analogous to the synchronic condition of access to the material bases of self-respect. If the properties themselves are unreturnable, then a subsidiary claim for compensation will also be justified, provided that compensation will be used for rebuilding the tradition's infrastructure elsewhere. Thus, there is an argument in justice, not just policy, for reparation, but it is an argument in distributive, not corrective, justice.

And it is, I believe, the strongest argument for reparations. Yet it, too, operates only with substantial qualifications. First, the claim for reparations rests on the empirical assumption that the continuity of the institution was seriously threatened by expropriation and could be restored by restitution. The Catholic Church's existence in Eastern Europe, while rendered more difficult under communism, was not seriously imperiled. At the opposite extreme, a community of members or potential members must be available. They cannot all have relocated or scattered diasporically, as in the case of Eastern European Jews, making a restoration of Jewish culture in the region extremely unlikely. Second, the claim of restoration applies only to the properties clearly essential to the cultural life of the institution, principally places of study and worship, but also income-producing properties in whose absence the institution would surely fail. It may well be that some of the institutions had very great holdings of income-producing properties, beyond those necessary to ensure cultural survival. Claims for such extra properties must compete with, and will ordinarily lose to, other claims on social resources. Last, the claim that cultural institutions merit protection and reparative response does not imply that they are beyond any form of political control or interference. Some institutions may have exercised disproportionate social and political power during their heyday, contributing in their own right to unjust policy and custom—for example, by inciting religious intolerance. It is surely consistent with the aim of restoring their distinct cultural contribution to do so in a way that does not give rise to the same imbalances of power. Such considerations would be a further reason to limit the scope of reparative claims.

12.9. CONCLUSION

My argument in this chapter is overwhelmingly negative. Despite the harms flowing from expropriation, reparation by new regimes will usually fail to restore justice and will instead cause yet further injustice. This claim reflects, in two senses, what I have elsewhere called the relationality of responsibility. First, the gesture of repair is owed by injurers, not by the world at large, and certainly not by fellow victims. Say a neighbor breaks a vase at your party. I may not meaningfully apologize for that neighbor's misconduct (assuming he was not somehow under my control). And you cannot demand payment from me for the vase he broke: my apology would be hollow and your demand misapplied. If the injurer has fled the scene, then the unfortunate fact is that no claims to repair in justice can be made. Second, responsibility is relational in the sense that the importance of meeting responsibility claims rests on the importance, and nature, of the underlying social and political relationships such responsibility claims protect.

The claims of repair, and their rejection, need to be understood in terms of the democratic relationships they both presuppose and project among fellow citizens. A central task of Europe's nascent democracies has been to establish the mutual relationships of respect and reciprocity constitutive of common citizenship. Demands by some for compensation for crimes committed, in similar form, against all presuppose instead a different form of relationship: interest-seekers at a common pool, fighting for individual shares of resources. By seeking collective forms of memory and respect for victims and common protections against future crimes, the democratic relationship is far better honored.

NOTES

CHAPTER I. INTRODUCTION: WAR, POLITICS, DEMOCRACY

1. As of 2015, of the Arab democratic revolutions, only Tunisia is on even an uneasy road to success; Egypt is under military control, and Libya is in total chaos.

2. This is a rare Churchill aphorism that he actually said, after being voted out of office. 444 Parl. Deb. H.C. (5th ser.) (1947) 207 (U.K.).

3. The democratic peace thesis was first popularized by Bruce Russett, *Grasping the Democratic Peace: Principles for a Post-Cold War World* (Princeton: Princeton University Press, 1993). Although both North and South were highly imperfect democracies, the decision for war had mass support on both sides.

4. Edward D. Mansfield and Jack Snyder, *Electing to Fight: Why Emerging Democracies Go to War* (Cambridge: MIT Press, 2005).

5. Francis Fukuyama, *The End of History and the Last Man* (New York: Free Press, 1992).

6. See, e.g., Benjamin Barber, *Strong Democracy* (Berkeley: University of California Press, 1984); Drucilla Cornell, *Defending Ideals: War, Democracy, and Political Struggle* (2004).

7. In the phrase of Bernard Williams, this request is the "Basic Legitimation Demand," and in liberal thought extending since Thomas Hobbes, it is a demand every political subject has standing to make. Bernard Williams, *In the Beginning Was the Deed: Realism and Moralism in Political Argument* (Princeton: Princeton University Press, 2005), p. 135.

8. I take the term of spectacle from Jeffrey Green's powerful book, *The Eyes of the People: Democracy in an Age of Spectatorship* (New York: Oxford University Press, 2010).

9. For important discussions of the American self-conception of a wartime democracy, see Mary Dudziak, *Wartime: An Idea, Its History, Its Consequences* (New York: Oxford University Press, 2013); Adam Berlinsky, *In Time of War: Understanding American Public Opinion from World War II to Iraq* (Chicago: University of Chicago Press, 2009).

10. Max Weber, "Politics as a Vocation," in H. H. Gerth and C. Wright Mills (trans. and eds.), *From Max Weber: Essays in Sociology*, pp. 77–128 (New York: Oxford University Press, 1946), p. 78.

11. UN Charter 2(4); Kellogg-Briand Pact [1928]. I have been much influenced by a manuscript by Oona Hathaway and Scott Shapiro, "The Worst Crime of All: The Paris Peace Pact and the Beginning of the End of War."

12. At the domestic level, the ambivalence is reflected not just in the electoral uses of war but also (in the United States, anyway) in the celebration of vindictive violence in the criminal justice system.

13. Protocol Additional to the Geneva Conventions of 12 August 1949, and relating to the Protection of Victims of Non-International Armed Conflicts (Protocol II), 8 June 1977.

14. See my *Complicity: Ethics and Law for a Collective Age* (New York: Cambridge University Press, 2000).

15. Fascinating recent empirical work by Michael Tomasello and his colleagues has pursued the idea that the capacity for complex cooperation is indeed uniquely human, although other primates share some of the relevant capacities.

16. An outstanding collection of sources in the history of Just War Theory is Gregory Reichberg, Henrik Syse, and Endre Begby, *The Ethics of War: Classic and Contemporary Readings* (London: Wiley-Blackwell, 2006).

17. Emer de Vattel, *The Law of Nations; or, Principles of the Law of Nature, Applied to the Conduct and Affairs of Nations and Sovereigns, with Three Early Essays on the Origin and Nature of Natural Law and on Luxury*, ed. Béla Kapossy and Richard Whitmore (Indianapolis: Liberty Fund, 2008), http://oll.libertyfund.org/titles/2246, Bk. III, ch. 4, sec. 66: "Since it is equally possible that either of the parties may have right on his side,— and since, in consequence of the independence of nations, that point is not to be decided by others (§ 40),—the condition of the two enemies is the same, while the war lasts."

18. "Non-international armed conflicts" (NIACs) are conflicts typically between a state and a nonstate actor, such as civil wars and rebellions, or between a state and a nonstate opponent, such as al-Qaeda. They are governed by the Second Additional Protocol to the Geneva Conventions, adopted in 1977. https://www.icrc.org/ihl/INTRO /475?OpenDocument.

19. Mark Osiel, *The End of Reciprocity* (New York: Cambridge University Press, 2010).

20. One need not agree with the policies put in place to see the point in Alberto Gonzales's statement that the Geneva Convention conditions for prisoners of war, such as their right to recreation halls, seem "quaint" in application to al-Qaeda suspects. Obviously, the lesson is to discern a common principle of human treatment. Alberto Gonzales to George Bush, "Decision re Application of the Geneva Convention on Prisoners of War to the Conflict with Al Qaeda and the Taliban," Memorandum of 25 January 2002 (accessible at ww2.gwu.edu/~nsarchiv/NSAEBB/NSAEBB127/02.01.25.pdf).

21. Hugo Grotius, *The Rights of War and Peace, including the Law of Nature and of Nations*, trans. A. C. Campbell (New York: M. Walter Dunne, 1901), http://oll.libertyfund .org/titles/553, Bk. II, ch. 25, sec. 8.

22. Vattel, *Law of Nations*, Bk. II, ch. 4, sec. 54: "It is an evident consequence of the liberty and independence of nations, that all have a right to be governed as they think proper, and that no state has the smallest right to interfere in the government of another."

23. Vattel, *Law of Nations*, Bk. II, ch. 4, sec. 54.

24. See also Grotius, *Rights of War and Peace*, Bk. I, ch. 4, pp. 157–58: "The right to make war may be conceded against a king who openly shows himself the enemy of the whole people . . . for the will to govern and the will to destroy cannot coexist in the same person."

25. The NATO/UN-endorsed intervention in Libya averted an imminent atrocity by Gaddafi, but as of this writing has left Libya in a state of anarchy.

26. Indeed, the nineteenth century is rife with examples of European military adventures under the banner of "preventing atrocities," especially in the Balkans—and it is a

noteworthy feature of almost all the nineteenth-, and indeed twentieth- and twenty-first-century incidents, that the intervened-upon state is non-Christian.

27. See Michael Walzer, *Just and Unjust Wars* (New York: Basic Books, rev. ed. 2006).

28. For an elaboration of this idea of law, see Scott Shapiro, *Legality* (Cambridge, MA: Belknap Press, 2013).

29. H.L.A. Hart, *The Concept of Law*, rev. ed. (New York: Oxford University Press 1997); Carl Schmitt, *The Crisis of Parliamentary Democracy* [1923], trans. Ellen Kennedy (Cambridge, MA: MIT Press, 1988).

CHAPTER 2. DEMOCRATIC SECURITY

1. Amartya Sen and Jean Drèze, *Hunger and Public Action* (New York: Oxford University Press, 1989).

2. Immanuel Kant, "On Perpetual Peace: A Philosophical Sketch" (Königsberg: Friedrich Nicolovius, 1795), available in English at http://www.constitution.org/kant/perpeace.htm; Bruce Russett, *Grasping the Democratic Peace: Principles for a Post–Cold War World* (Princeton: Princeton University Press, 1993).

3. UN Charter, Ch. VII, Art. 39.

4. See chapter 7, "Must Democracies Be Ruthless?"

5. See, e.g., UN Development Programme, *1994 U.N. Human Development Report*, ch. 2, http://hdr.undp.org/en/reports/global/hdr1994/chapters/; Amartya Sen, *Development as Freedom* (New York: Basic Books, 2001).

6. See, e.g., United Nations, *Final Report of the Commission on Human Security* (2003), available at http://www.humansecurity-chs.org/finalreport/index.html; and materials collected in IDEA (Institute for Democracy and Human Security), *Democracy, Conflict, and Human Security* (2006), available at http://www.idea.int/publications/dchs/dchs_vol1.cfm.

7. For a recent review of the democratic peace literature with a region-based explanation, see Erik Gartzke, "The Capitalist Peace," *American Journal of Political Science* 51: 166–91, available at http://dss.ucsd.edu/~egartzke/publications/gartzke_ajps_07.pdf.

8. Contrarily, if groups see democratic competition as hopeless, then democracy will not play this instrumental role.

9. Sen and Drèze, *Hunger*.

10. While theoretical concerns about the rationality of democratic choice date back at least to the Marquis de Condorcet, the modern formal treatment of the insufficiency of democratic institutions to provide a coherent form of social choice is Kenneth Arrow, *Social Choice and Individual Values*, 2d ed. (New Haven: Yale University Press, 1970); see also William Riker, *Liberalism against Populism: A Confrontation between the Theory of Democracy and the Theory of Social Choice* (Prospect Heights, IL: Waveland Press, 1988).

11. This is a theme of Montesquieu, Constant, Herder, and Condorcet in the Enlightenment, and of Isaiah Berlin more recently.

12. Convention against Torture and Other Cruel, Inhuman, or Degrading Treatment or Punishment, Art. 20, http://www.unhchr.ch/html/menu3/b/h_cat39.htm.

13. Indeed, it is patently true that a commission would find this. See Laurel Fletcher and Eric Stover, *Guantanamo and Its Aftermath: U.S. Detention and Interrogation Practices and Their Impact on Former Detainees* (Berkeley, CA: Human Rights Center, 2008).

14. Judith Shklar, *The Faces of Injustice* (New Haven: Yale University Press, 1988).

15. For the claim that EU legitimacy is best conceived in performance terms, see David Beetham and Christopher Lord, *Legitimacy and the European Union* (London: Longman, 1998).

16. True, we may seem to be left with intuitionism in some form if we are pressed for why we concern ourselves with what people want or should want. But a fundamental insistence on this conception of the political good seems a reasonable place to declare one's justificatory spade turned. For example, the current docket of the International Court of Justice reports just twelve pending cases, dating from 1993.

17. See H.L.A. Hart, *The Concept of Law*, 2d ed. (New York: Oxford University Press, 1994), p. 103.

18. *Roper v. Simmons*, 543 U.S. 551 (2005).

19. Scalia, J., dissenting, 543 U.S. __ (2005), at 16.

20. http://www.wto.int/english/tratop_e/sps_e/spsagr_e.htm.

21. See the the Appellate Body Report, EC-Hormones, WT/DS 26, 48/AB/R, http://www.worldtradelaw.net/dsc/ab/ec-hormones(dsc)(ab).pdf.

22. Judgment of the Appellate Body, pars. 208–9.

23. Under US law, federal courts can reject health and safety administrative regulations as "arbitrary or capricious" exercises of delegated judgment, and they can reject health and safety legislation as inconsistent with a limited constitutional mandate.

24. Eric Posner and Jack Goldsmith, *The Limits of International Law* (New York: Oxford University Press, 2005), p. 189–92.

CHAPTER 3. CITIZENS AND SOLDIERS:
THE DIFFERENCE UNIFORMS MAKE

1. Based loosely on *Taylor v. Superior Court*, 3 Cal.3d 578, 477 P.2d 131 (1970).

2. 1949 Geneva Convention relative to the Treatment of Prisoners of War, Art. 118 (hereinafter cited as GPW 118).

3. I draw upon the "facts" offered by the government in the Yasser Hamdi case. See "Declaration of Michael H. Mobbs," Special Advisor to the Under Secretary of Defense for Policy, filed in *Hamdi v. Rumsfeld*, No. 2:02CV439 (E.D. Va). The Supreme Court has since ruled that US citizens taken on foreign battlefields are constitutionally entitled to a legal forum in which they can contest the facts governing their legal status. *Hamdi v. Rumsfeld*, 542 U.S. 507 (2004). This ruling attempted to return US practice with respect to its own citizens to conformity with GPW 5, which requires adjudication of all dubious cases by a "competent tribunal." As of this writing (2015), the US treatment of non-US captures remains dubious under both US constitutional and international law. See *Balul v. United States*, No. 11-1324 (D.C. Cir. June 12, 2015).

4. Raymond Aron, *On War* (New York: W. W. Norton, 1968).

5. GPW 4(A)(2)(b); 1977 Protocol Additional to the Geneva Conventions of 12 August 1949, and relating to the Protection of Victims of International Armed Conflicts (PI), Art. 44(3). Under PI 1(4), only persons involved in interstate conflicts or "conflicts in which peoples are fighting against colonial domination and alien occupation and against racist regimes in the exercise of their right of self-determination" have access to the relaxed standard of combatancy of PI 44(3). In addition, GPW 4(A)(6) extends battlefield privileges to citizens who, as a whole, rise up as a foreign invader arrives. This "*levée en masse*" clause is almost never triggered and would not be triggered by partisans resisting an occupation.

Nonprivileged combatants may be killed on the battlefield as well as be prosecuted after conquest for their belligerency.

6. A "substantial step" is the Model Penal Code's rule for attempt liability, § 5.01(1)(c).

7. The United States calls these "unlawful combatants." See, e.g., *Ex parte Quirin*, 317 U.S. 1, 31 (1942). One of the pernicious features of the term "unlawful combatants" is that it effectively conflates crimes like killing civilians with not wearing a uniform in combat. Another is that it concludes, rather than leaving open, the question of whether they enjoy any privilege to kill.

8. Currently, 146 states have ratified PI, though many have made reservations to Article 44. Given the number of ratifiers, some argue that PI 44 (like Common Article 3 of the Geneva Conventions, which lays down general limits to violence in all conflicts) now has force as a universal, customary (rather than treaty-based) norm. See Antonio Cassesse, "The Geneva Protocols of 1977 on the Humanitarian Law of Armed Conflict and Customary International Law," *Pacific Basin Law Journal* 3 (1985): 55–118, at pp. 72–73. But US noncompliance with that regime undermines the argument for customary force.

9. Special Forces soldiers may have dressed *distinctively*, however, in the garb of the militias with whom they were affiliated. If so, and given a reasonably generous interpretation of the requirement of GPW 4(a)(2), which requires that combatants wear "a fixed distinctive sign," then they would be lawful combatants. Ironically, however, this reading is denied by the United States officially, as part of their grounds for not treating captured Taliban as POWs. See W. Hays Parks, "Special Forces Wearing of Non-Standard Uniforms," *Chicago Journal of International Law* 4 (2003): 493–547, at pp. 496–98. It is unclear whether CIA personnel who took part in the hostilities wore any distinctive garb; since presumably they were already unlikely to gain POW status if captured, they had no reason to.

10. These developments are nicely surveyed by Herfried Münkler, "The Wars of the 21st Century," *International Review of the Red Cross* 85 (2003): 7–22.

11. Civilian contractors, for example, routinely operate surveillance aircraft, provide direct logistical support for weapons systems, operate combat-zone radar equipment, and fly armed drug interdiction efforts in collaboration with the US military. Many of these roles seem close enough to the criterion of "direct participation" in the hostilities to render them combatants under GPW 4. For a survey of this phenomenon, see Peter Singer, *Corporate Warriors* (Ithaca, NY: Cornell University Press, 2003). As Singer points out, the new mercenaries can contribute to social peace (as they did in Sierra Leone, at least until their contract expired) as well as help escalate conflicts between weak states that would not otherwise be able to engage in sophisticated levels of violence.

12. An early, important philosophical discussion of this point is by Thomas Nagel, "War and Massacre," in his *Mortal Questions* (New York: Cambridge University Press, 1979), pp. 53–74. Jeff McMahan's "The Ethics of Killing in Wars," *Ethics* 114 (2004): 693–733, is especially perspicuous in pointing out the puzzles of IHL's normative authority.

13. These norms further proscribe certain disproportionate or indiscriminate killing means, such as poisonous gas. See, e.g., Hague Convention of 1925, Protocol for the Prohibition of the Use in War of Asphyxiating, Poisonous or Other Gases, and of Bacteriological Methods of Warfare; Declaration of 1899 Declaration on the Use of Bullets Which Expand or Flatten Easily in the Human Body.

14. See Michael Walzer: "It is perfectly possible for a just war to be fought unjustly and for an unjust war to be fought in strict accordance with the rules." *Just and Unjust Wars*, 3d ed. (New York: Basic Books, 2000), p. 21. This formulation, of course, leaves it

ambiguous whether any strong substantive normative value attaches to the formal crite-rion of "playing by the rules." See also Gabor Rona, "Interesting Times for International Humanitarian Law: Challenges from the 'War on Terror,'" *Fletcher Forum of World Affairs* 27 (2003): 55–74, at pp. 67–68: "The very essence of *jus ad bellum* is the distinction between just and unjust cause—between entitlement and prohibition to wage war. *Jus in bello*, on the other hand, rightfully recognizes no such distinction. While one party may be a sinner and the other a saint under *jus ad bellum*, the *jus in bello* must and does bind the aggressor and the aggressed equally."

15. See Theodore Meron, *Bloody Constraint: War and Chivalry in Shakespeare* (New York: Oxford University Press, 1998), as well as Allan Rosas, *The Legal Status of Prisoners of War* (Helsinki: Suomalainen Tiedeakatemia, 1976), pp. 44–84.

16. The phrase is from Samuel Scheffler, "Individual Responsibility in a Global Age," *Social Philosophy and Policy* 12 (1995): 219–36, at p. 222.

17. See Jean Bodin, *Bodin: On Sovereignty*, ed. Julian Franklin (New York: Cambridge University Press, 1992), Bk. I, ch. 8, "On Sovereignty."

18. Bodin: "For although one can receive law from someone else, it is as impossible by nature to give one's self a law as it is to command one's self to do something that depends on one's will." *On Sovereignty*, Bk. I, ch. 8, [360–361], p. 12.

19. See Geoffrey Parker, *The Military Revolution: Military Innovation and the Rise of the West 1500–1800* (Cambridge: Cambridge University Press, 1988), pp. 71–72; "Uniforms," in *The Oxford Companion to Military History*, ed. Richard Holmes (New York: Oxford University Press, 2001), pp. 931–35; Toni Pfanner, "Military Uniforms and the Law of War," *International Review of the Red Cross* 86 (2004): 93–130, at pp. 95–99.

20. See Münkler, "Wars of the 21st Century," pp. 14–16.

21. "From all this it is clear that the principal mark of sovereign majesty and absolute power is the right to impose laws generally on all subjects regardless of their consent." Bodin, *On Sovereignty*, Bk. I, ch. 7 (Tooley trans.)

22. Jean Jacques Rousseau, *The Social Contract*, Bk. I, ch. 7, par. 10, in *The Social Contract and Other Writings*, ed. Victor Gourevitch (New York: Cambridge University Press, 1997), pp. 50–51.

23. Ibid., par. 1 (p. 51).

24. Ibid., ch. 4, par. 9 (pp. 46–47).

25. Ibid., par. 10 (p. 47).

26. Ibid.

27. What I have called in other work a "participatory obligation" to do one's part in a collective project to which one is committed. See my "The Collective Work of Citizenship," *Legal Theory* 8 (2002): 471–94.

28. Compare George Fletcher, *Romantics at War* (Princeton: Princeton University Press, 2002). Fletcher argues that Rousseau's conception of war is essentially Romantic, a form of self-expression by an organically united people. While Fletcher is right that Rousseau's thought featured prominently in later Romantic conceptions of peoples and their self-expression (as, for example, in J. G. Herder), his reading ignores the Enlightened and contractarian aspect of Rousseau's own conception of sovereignty, as well as Rousseau's view of the contingent nature of a politically united people.

29. Hence conscripts in authoritarian regimes might be seen as doubly impunible: as in-dividuals they may have a claim of duress, and they lack any collective citizen responsibility.

This does, however, assume that duress is true in fact (i.e., that conscripts will be killed if they do not kill) and that it excuses even killing, which is generally not true in Anglo-American law. See McMahan, "Ethics of Killing," p. 700.

30. McMahan also rejects traditional *jus in bello* principles and argues that individual soldiers in unjust wars bear moral responsibility for what they do. Although, as I elaborate below, I agree that individual soldiers may bear moral responsibility, one still needs to argue for the legitimacy of *punishing* combatants for their (morally) impermissible killings. Impunity, in other words, is not the same as justification or moral permissibility.

31. See, e.g., Gabor Rona, a legal advisor to the ICRC, in "Interesting Times," p. 57: "[H]umanitarian law is a compromise. In return for these protections, humanitarian law elevates the essence of war—killing and detaining people without trial—into a right, if only for persons designated as 'privileged combatants', such as soldiers in an army."

32. They may also have been strategic miscalculations, at least in Europe, where there is little evidence that they made a difference to already quickly declining German power. See, e.g., Michael Sherry, *The Rise of American Air Power: The Creation of Armageddon* (New Haven: Yale University Press, 1987), p. 260.

33. J.J.C. Smart, "An Outline of a Theory of Utilitarianism," in J.J.C. Smart and Bernard Williams, *Utilitarianism: For and Against* (New York: Cambridge University Press, 1973).

34. True, this argument would not work for "robosoldiers." Even so, we would want an argument for the soundness of the battle program we give them.

35. For doubts about its lawfulness, though not about its prudence, see Louis Henkin, "Kosovo and the Law of 'Humanitarian Intervention,'" *American Journal of International Law* 4 (1999), accessible at http://www.asil.org/ajil/kosovo.htm.

36. Problems would arise for humanitarian military intervention by national, as opposed to UN, forces. This is a difficult problem, as arguably only national actors have the will to intervene early enough to make a difference. I think it sufficient here to say that the benefits of expanded permission to engage in such missions have to be offset by the costs that that permission will underwrite clearly unwarranted interventions.

37. This assumes that they do not care independently about civilian casualties, as indeed they may not if fighting on enemy territory.

38. I would guess that real challenges for discrimination come in two settings. The first is urban combat, where discrimination is already difficult even between distinctively marked troops. Second is the long-distance aerial strike, where small arms might not be visible to a target spotter. But since combatants, uniformed or not, might well be camouflaged in buildings or vehicles that require no distinctive marking, the problem of discrimination does not seem to me appreciably greater with PI 44 than without. (This may underestimate the difficulties faced by US troops facing guerrilla warfare in Vietnam, though France, with similar guerrilla experience, ratified PI without reservation to Article 44.)

39. Arguably, protection should also be extended to foreign volunteer groups aiding partisans in struggles for self-determination, or against extermination, so long as the national partisans themselves qualify for protection. (Foreign members of national groups, like Gray, are protected under the current PI criteria.) While there is a cost to this position—it increases instability by making foreign intervention more attractive—it has the corresponding benefit of increasing the likelihood of success in just struggles. The logic is thus parallel to the national group case and ought to be governed by the same deeper

principle, namely, that these volunteer groups have come to joins their wills in the collective struggle as well. (I thank an editor of *Philosophy & Public Affairs* for this suggestion.)

40. I explain and defend this claim extensively in *Complicity: Ethics and Law for a Collective Age* (New York: Cambridge University Press, 2000).

41. [1978] 1 W.L.R. 1350.

42. I develop this argument in "Collective Work of Citizenship," *Legal Theory* 8 (2002): 471–94.

43. This is one of many reasons why "terrorism" cannot be the opponent of a war. If the protean abstraction of global terrorism is the opponent, then anywhere terrorists act is a scene of "battlefield" combat, governed only by the laws of war. This means states might target and kill virtually anyone suspected of terrorism, subject only to constraints of reasonable discrimination and proportionality. For discussion, see Rona, "Interesting Times."

Questions about the proper legal analysis governing the conflict with terrorist groups such as al-Qaeda are very complicated and are beyond the scope of my argument, which concerns unproblematic deployments of the idea of armed conflict and battle. For discussion, see John C. Yoo and James C. Ho, "The Status of Terrorists," *Virginia Journal of International Law* 47 (2003): 207–28.

44. It is even more plausible on a deterrence theory, of course: a state has every legitimate interest in deterring attacks on its soldiers.

45. It is a clear implication of my view that noncombatant citizens are also, in principle, exposed to punishment for the belligerency. However, for the much-discussed consequentialist and slippery-slope reasons of trying to avoid total war, I regard the impermissibility of attacking noncombatants as much easier to defend than the permissibility of intercombatant killing.

46. Bernard Williams, "Moral Luck," in *Moral Luck* (New York: Cambridge University Press, 1981), pp. 20–39. I return to the theme of political luck, with respect to leaders, in chapter 5.

47. This raises the question of the fairness of prosecuting national leaders for waging unjust wars. They too, after all, may be prosecuted long before opinions are clear on the justification for their legitimacy. Nonetheless, a distinction between leadership and line prosecutions is acceptable. Prosecutions of national leaders are likely to be such rare events, involve so few persons, and to be so constrained by the exigencies of international politics that the risk of unfairness is surely lower than that courted by routine prosecutions of enemy combatants. It also seems appropriate to hold national leaders to higher standards of compliance with standards of just conduct than soldiers, whose views about the permissibility of their nation's conduct are likely to be more permeated by jingoistic false consciousness than their leaders'. For a discussion of post-war justice, see chapter 9.

48. As GPW 4(A)(2)(d) requires.

49. Here I extend into politics H.L.A. Hart's argument that the necessary and sufficient conditions of a legal system's existence are the acknowledgment among officials of the normative force of a system's rules and a popular practice of obedience to those rules. *The Concept of Law*, 2d ed. (New York: Oxford University Press, 1994), p. 113.

50. There is, then, an asymmetry for soldiers of egregious regimes: those fighting voluntarily to extend their nations' sway would not be privileged, even though they retain the privilege in defending their states. But since the privilege of killing comes with the correlative privilege of their enemies to kill them, this asymmetry is not such a benefit.

CHAPTER 4. A MODEST CASE FOR SYMMETRY:
ARE SOLDIERS MORALLY EQUAL?

1. David Rodin, "The Moral Inequality of Soldiers: Why *in bello* Asymmetry Is Half Right," in *Just and Unjust Warriors*, ed. Henry Shue and David Rodin (New York: Oxford University Press, 2010), pp. 44–68. I am much indebted to Rodin's discussion.

2. See, among other sources, Convention with Respect to the Laws and Customs of War on Land (Hague II), Sec. II (entry into force 29 July 1899); Protocol for the Prohibition of the Use in War of Asphyxiating, Poisonous or Other Gases, and of Bacteriological Methods of Warfare (entry into force 8 February 1928); Geneva Convention relative to the Treatment of Prisoners of War (entry into force 21 October 1950); Geneva Convention relative to the Protection of Civilian Persons in Time of War (entry into force 21 October 1950). The International Committee of the Red Cross provides a useful compendium, at http://www.icrc.org/ihl.nsf/TOPICS?OpenView#Methods%20and%20Means%20of%20 Warfare.

3. I am grateful to Jeff McMahan for emphasizing the arbitrariness of the baseline and the way in which starting with the status quo distorts investigation into the ideal theory of war.

4. Thomas Nagel, "War and Massacre," in *Mortal Questions* (New York: Cambridge University Press, 1991), pp. 53–74, at 53.

5. The traditional Anglo-American system of domestic violence might be thought to be of this sort, where certain forms of provocation (witnessing an act of adultery, most famously) give one party, but not both, a quasi-permission (in the form of a reduced penalty) to use lethal force.

6. Rodin argues for such a position in "The Ethics of Asymmetric War," in *The Ethics of War*, ed. Richard Sorabji and David Rodin (London: Ashgate, 2006), pp. 153–68.

7. Protocol Additional to the Geneva Conventions of 12 August 1949 and relating to the Protection of Victims of International Armed Conflicts (Protocol 1) (entry into force 7 December 1979).

8. The case is more difficult for the destruction of cultural property: can the destruction of Coventry and Dresden be judged equivalent, on some shared basis? If not, this is reason to suspect a priori that protection of cultural property will be less effective than protection of life.

9. Rodin, "Moral Inequality." John Rawls, *A Theory of Justice*, rev. ed. (Cambridge: Harvard University Press, 1999), esp. secs. 3, 4, 24, 26.

10. More precisely, Rawls argues that his conception of justice ("justice as fairness") is justified in "reflective equilibrium," where that equilibrium is a matter of prior conviction, acceptance of the Original Position argument, and an evaluation of the larger, outside-the-original-position argument from stability. *Theory of Justice*, sec. 9.

11. Rawls, *Theory of Justice*, secs. 29, 76.

12. See, e.g., Judith Lichtenberg, "How to Judge Soldiers Whose Cause Is Unjust," in Shue and Rodin, *Just and Unjust Warriors*, pp. 112–31.

13. See my *Complicity*.

14. Perhaps selective prosecution is not decisively unfair, so long as those actually prosecuted merit prosecution. At the least, however, horizontal unfairness is part of a strong case against asymmetry.

15. This is the major theme of Rawls's *Political Liberalism*, 2d ed. (New York: Columbia University Press, 2005), where Rawls develops the notion of a "political" justification of a theory of justice as one that prescinds from sectarian, "comprehensive" moral grounds and rests instead upon weaker, shared normative notions. Thomas Nagel develops the point in the context of interpersonal relations in "Concealment and Exposure," *Philosophy & Public Affairs* 27 (1998): 3–30.

16. The justifiability of Israel's strike, immediately condemned by the UN Security Council in Resolution 487 (19 June 1981), is still debated by international lawyers, though that debate clearly aims to serve a prospective purpose of rebutting US claims to a right to preemptive war, rather than merely retrospective purposes. Arguing for the justifiability, see John Yoo, "Using Force," *University of Chicago Law Review* 71 (2004): 729–97; arguing cautiously against, see Miriam Sapiro, "The Shifting Sands of Preemptive Self-Defense," *American Journal of International Law* 97 (2003): 599–607. I also think it is hard to define and defend moral criteria for assessing political violence, though I do not wish to defend that point here.

17. This, again, is a major theme of *Political Liberalism*. The point is also developed in compact form by Bernard Williams, in "From Freedom to Liberty: The Construction of a Political Value," in his *In the Beginning Was the Deed* (Princeton: Princeton University Press, 2005), pp. 75–96.

18. Judith Shklar, "The Liberalism of Fear," reprinted in *Political Thought and Political Thinkers*, ed. Stanley Hoffman (Chicago: University of Chicago Press, 1998), pp. 3–20. I do not mean to endorse such modesty in the domestic question of social justice, though current affairs remind us in the United States of the importance of worrying first about governmental oppression and overreaching.

CHAPTER 5. LEADERS AND THE GAMBLES
OF WAR: AGAINST POLITICAL LUCK

1. Leo Tolstoy, *War and Peace*, trans. Constance Garnett (London: Heinemann, 1904), Pt. X, ch. 25, p. 838.

2. Hugo Grotius, *Rights of War and Peace*, Bk. 2, ch. 23 ("On Dubious Causes"). See also James Whitman's history of the idea of war as dispute resolution mechanism, in *The Verdict of Battle* (Cambridge: Harvard University Press, 2012).

3. Thomas Nagel, "Moral Luck," reprinted in *Moral Luck*, ed. Daniel Statman (Albany: SUNY Press, 1993): pp. 57–71, 63.

4. Ibid., p. 62.

5. This equalizing strategy is the heart of a number of responses to Nagel's and Williams's articles. See, e.g., Judith Andre, "Nagel, Williams, and Moral Luck," in Statman, *Moral Luck*, pp. 123–29.

6. Nagel, "Moral Luck," pp. 62–63.

7. Bernard Williams, "Moral Luck," reprinted *in* Statman, *Moral Luck*, pp. 38–55.

8. This formulation of course raises the question, addressed below, of whether betrayal can be justified. Compare E. M. Forster's famous quip in *Two Cheers for Democracy*: "[I]f I had to choose between betraying my country and betraying my friend I hope I should have the guts to betray my country." "What I believe," in *Two Cheers for Democracy* (London: Edward Arnold, 1939), p. 78.

9. Williams, "Moral Luck," p. 41.

10. And one might, as Williams suggests, be happy that if bad people are the price of good art, that there are some bad people in the world. Ibid., p. 38. It should be said that this seems a dubious proposition in both the particular and the general case. Surely there might have been some way Gauguin could have done more for his family while realizing his talents.

11. Williams, "Moral Luck," p. 39. As Williams says, a principle that permits such harms when and only when one believes oneself to be a great artist (or to be capable of becoming such) is a license for fatuous self-delusion.

12. Of course, if the consumption value of gambling itself—the thrill of risk-seeking—is taken into account, then ex ante even a highly improbable gamble can be justified.

13. Ibid., p. 40.

14. I admit that the analogy is not wholly illuminating, since a raffle ticket's not being drawn seems as intrinsic a form of failure as anything else.

15. Ibid., p. 42.

16. The claim that justification is only epistemically available ex post is, I think, consistent with Williams's somewhat puzzling denial that the luck at play is epistemic rather than metaphysical. Williams's point is that it could not be said, at the time of decision, that Gauguin knew that his choice would be justified. That knowledge, if knowledge it is, is only available retrospectively. Ibid., p. 40.

17. Ibid., p. 38.

18. See, e.g., T. M. Scanlon, "Contractualism and Utilitarianism," in *Utilitarianism and Beyond*, ed. Amartya Sen and Bernard Williams (New York: Cambridge University Press, 1982), pp. 103–28. The views of Jurgen Habermas are cognates; see, e.g., his *Moral Consciousness and Communicative Action*, trans. Christian Lenhardt (Cambridge: MIT Press, 2001).

19. Williams, "Moral Luck," p. 38 (I have rearranged the sentential clauses). This sentence rules out one interpretation of the claim of justification, that it is basically consequentialist. If such justifications were adequate in cases like this, then this would be a world in which (consequentialist) morality were respected as well.

20. Bernard Williams, "Internal and External Reasons," in *Moral Luck* (New York: Cambridge University Press, 1981), pp. 101–13.

21. Williams stresses the narrowness of the import of his claim in "Internal Reasons and the Obscurity of Blame," in *Making Sense of Humanity* (New York: Cambridge University Press, 1995), pp. 35–45.

22. Williams, "Moral Luck, p. 51.

23. I also mean to leave open the possibility that we might regard Gauguin's actions as unjustified in any sense, yet still be glad of the outcomes—making the proverbial lemonade. But Williams's rejection of the priority of morality does not encompass this possibility.

24. Immanuel Kant, *Groundwork of the Metaphysics of Morals*, trans. Mary J. Gregor (New York: Cambridge University Press, 1996 [1785]), 4:407.

25. Niccolo Machiavelli, *The Prince*, trans. Luigi Ricci (New York: Modern Library, 1950), ch. 25, p. 94.

26. James Mann, *Rise of the Vulcans: The History of Bush's War Cabinet* (New York: Viking, 2004), esp. p. 351ff.

27. As a quip of the war planners had it at the time, "Everyone wants to go to Baghdad. Real men go to Tehran." Quoted in David Remnick, "War without End," *New Yorker* (April 21, 2003).

28. As President George Bush said in a prewar speech, "Facing clear evidence of peril, we cannot wait for the final proof—the smoking gun—that could come in the form of a mushroom cloud." Speech in Cincinnati, OH (October 7, 2002), available at http://www .narsil.org/war_on_iraq/bush_october_7_2002.html.

29. For a depressing, account of these distortions, see Thomas E. Ricks, *Fiasco: The American Military Adventure in Iraq* (New York: Penguin, 2007).

30. This discussion owes much to Ariel Colonomos, *The Gamble of War* (New York: Palgrave Macmillan, 2013).

31. For a list of relevant biases, see Daniel Kahneman and Amos Tversky, "Judgement under Uncertainty: Heuristics and Biases," *Science* 185 (1974): 1124–31.

32. More specifically, the certainties of war's direct costs must be weighed against the risk that substitute risks or substitute repression will arise.

33. Amy Hagopian et al., "Mortality in Iraq Associated with the 2003–2011 War and Occupation: Findings from a National Cluster Sample Survey by the University Collaborative Iraq Mortality Study," *PLOS Medicine* (13 October 2013), DOI: 10.1371 /journal.pmed.1001533. The study estimates, with a 95% confidence interval, 460,000 "excess" Iraqi deaths, beyond ordinary mortality rates.

34. Moreover, one might think that political actors who have risen high enough to have the authority to make such wagers have already shown themselves to be risk takers in this dimension.

35. Martha Nussbaum's *The Fragility of Goodness* (New York: Cambridge University Press, 2001) remains one of the most eloquent explorations of this ideal, in Greek philosophy and literature.

36. The phrase was meant to characterize the Obama Administration's approach to working with allies in Libya. It was reported in Ryan Lizza, "The Consequentialist," *New Yorker* (2 May 2011).

CHAPTER 6. WAR, DEMOCRACY, AND PUBLICITY: THE PERSISTENCE OF SECRET LAW

1. For an account of the struggles within absolutist theory to work out an account of the king's public, legal, voice, see Ernst Kantorowicz, *The King's Two Bodies* (Princeton: Princeton University Press, 1957).

2. Evan Wallach, "Drop by Drop: Forgetting the History of Water Torture in U.S. Courts," *Columbia Journal of Transnational Law* 45 (2007): 468 (detailing prosecution of waterboarding by the United States).

3. According to former OLC head Randolph Moss, "When the views of the Office of Legal Counsel are sought on the question of the legality of a proposed executive branch action, those views are typically treated as conclusive and binding within the executive branch." Moss, "Executive Branch Legal Interpretation: A Perspective from the Office of Legal Counsel," *Administrative Law Review* 52 (2000): 1303, 1305. To be clear, however, the opinions are, formally speaking, generally advisory rather than binding, in that the president is free to disregard them but usually does not.

4. This is a rough summary of the OLC's current practice. See Moss and other cites in Note, "The Immunity-Conferring Powers of the Office of Legal Counsel," *Harvard Law Review* 121 (2008): 2086.

5. See Moss, "Executive Branch"; Dawn Johnsen, *Guidelines for the President's Legal Advisors*, *Indiana Law Journal* 81 (2006): 1345. According to Johnsen (and echoed in a letter jointly signed by former OLC attorneys, the OLC had a longstanding tradition of maintaining a principled distance in its analysis from the policy goals of the executive branch. Johnsen and Martin Lederman, another harsh critic of the Bush OLC, have now themselves been appointed by President Obama to the OLC.

6. Even then, the withdrawn memoranda may continue to serve as elements of a due process–based advice of counsel defense to any criminal prosecution—a "golden shield," as Jack Goldsmith described the memoranda. Goldsmith, *The Terror Presidency: Law and Judgment inside the Bush Administration* (New York: W. W. Norton, 2009), pp. 144, 162. Such a defense, which is really a species of equitable estoppel (like entrapment), would rest on the reasonableness of the particular opinion, weighing the authority of the source against the controversial nature of the conclusions.

7. Immanuel Kant, "On Perpetual Peace," app. 2, par. 2: "All actions relating to the right of other men are unjust if their maxim is not consistent with publicity." Available online at http://www.mtholyoke.edu/acad/intrel/kant/kant6.htm; and in Harry Reiss, ed., *Kant: Political Writings* (New York: Cambridge University Press, 1991), 93–130.

8. Hearings before the Subcommittee of the Constitution of the Senate Judiciary Committee, April 30, 2008.

9. Perhaps one can conceive of laws generally not known by most subjects, or known only to police or officials. And perhaps such a system might merit the notion of law, if official conduct were sufficiently controlled, though law failed in its usual purposes of interpersonal governance. But little seems informative in pursuing this pathological case.

10. Jean Bodin, *Six Books of the Commonwealth*, Bk. II, ch. 4, available at http://www.constitution.org/bodin/bodin_.htm (trans. M. J. Tooley).

11. Ibid., ch. 2.

12. The Platonic principle of rule by law, and of law's relation to an articulable principle of reason, sits at odds with one of his most famous proposals in the *Republic*, that of the "noble lie," or *gennaion pseudos*, concerning the birthright of the guardians to lead. *Republic,* 414b.

13. Henry Maine, *History of Ancient Law* (New York: Charles Scribner, 1864), p. xvi.

14. *Digests*, Bk. I, ch. 2 (Pomponius); *Institutes of Justinian*, trans. J. B. Moyle (Oxford: Oxford University Press, 1913), Bk. I, title 2; repr., Clark, NJ: Lawbook Exchange, 2004), p. 4.

15. See Bodin, *Commonwealth*, Bk. I, ch. 8, "On Sovereignty," distinguishing between a prince's private contracts and his public statements of the law, pp. 364–66. Oddly for today, for Bodin the publicity of law means precisely that the ruler is not thereby bound (thus not compromising his sovereignty), while private contracts bind the conscience. See, e.g., p. 379: "The prince who swears to keep the civil laws either is not sovereign or else becomes a perjurer if he violates his oath, which a sovereign prince will have to do in order to annul, change, or correct the laws according to the exigencies of situations, times, and persons." Bodin, *On Sovereignty*, ed. Julian Franklin (New York: Cambridge University Press, 1992), p. 27.

16. Thomas Hobbes, *Leviathan*, ed. Richard Tuck (New York: Cambridge University Press, 1996 [1651]), ch. 30, p. 240. I owe this reference to Jeremy Waldron, "Hobbes and the Principle of Publicity," *Pacific Philosophical Quarterly* 82 (2001): 447–74, n. 8.

17. "Les lois sont éxecutoires dans tout le territoire français, en vertu de la promulgation qui en est faite par l'Empereur. Elles seront executes dans chaque partie de l'Empire du moment où la promulgation en pourra être connue." Code Napoléon, Preliminary title, Art. I. For discussion, see John Chipman Gray, *The Nature and Sources of the Law*, 2d ed. (New York: Macmillan, 1921), p. 164. I owe the Gray reference to Lon Fuller, *The Morality of Law* (New Haven: Yale University Press, 1964), p. 49.

18. Jeremy Bentham, "Essay on the Promulgation of the Laws," ch. 1, in *The Complete Works*, vol. 1, ed. J. Bowring (Edinburgh: William Tait, 1843).

19. Bentham, "Codification Proposal," Pt. I, sec. 2, in *Complete Works*, vol. 4.

20. Fuller, *Morality of Law*, pp. 34–35, 43–44. Fuller later qualifies the relevant notion of publicity as publicity with respect to those to whom the law applies. As I will argue, I regard this as too narrow—the inner morality of law stretches even more widely than Fuller thought.

21. Jules Coleman, *The Practice of Principle: In Defense of a Pragmatist Approach to Legal Theory* (New York: Oxford University Press, 2003), p. 194.

22. The strongest statements in the positivist tradition are those of Austin, but reflected in Hart's more polemical positions in his famous debate with Fuller on Nazi law and legality, "Positivism and the Separation of Law and Morals," *Harvard Law Review* 71 (1958): 593. But Hart's own position was more complicated, as reflected in his own account of the truth of the natural law tradition, as in "The Minimum Content of Natural Law," in *The Concept of Law*, 2d ed. (New York: Oxford University Press, 1997), ch. 9. John Finnis's distinction between a "focal," value-rich concept of law and a "penumbral" concept that extends to even hideous law, stakes out a similar ground, although with a different underlying semantics. Finnis, *Natural Law and Natural Rights* (New York: Oxford University Press, 1981), p. ix. There are also echoes of the "double secret probation" of *Animal House*.

23. This is the category of "unknown unknowns," which Donald Rumsfeld famously said are the ones that bite you on the ass. (Of course, unknown knowns, such as the false presence of the WMDs, can also have serious posterior effects.)

24. William Blackstone, *Commentaries on the Laws of England in Four Books* (Oxford: Clarendon Press, 1765), available at http://oll.libertyfund.org/titles/2140, Bk. I, Introduction, sec. 2, *40. The reference is to Dio Cassius's *Roman History* (155–235 CE), available at http://penelope.uchicago.edu/Thayer/E/Roman/Texts/Cassius_Dio/59*.html, Bk. LIX, ch. 28, p. 11: "But when, after enacting severe laws in regard to the taxes, he inscribed them in exceedingly small letters on a tablet which he then hung up in a high place, so that it should be read by as few as possible and that many through ignorance of what was bidden or forbidden should lay themselves liable to the penalties provided, they straightway rushed together excitedly into the Circus and raised a terrible outcry."

25. "Charlie Wilson's War" is a well-known example: the contours of the CIA's program to assist the mujahideen changed dramatically because of the intervention of the legislature.

26. A current species of the category of enforcement secrecy involves "National Security Letters" (NSLs) issued typically by the FBI under authority found in the PATRIOT

Act. Until recently, recipients of these letters—typically librarians or registrars—could not disclose the receipt of the letter to anyone, including legal counsel, on pain of punishment. Under current FBI guidelines, recipients can now discuss compliance with counsel, but not beyond. For discussion of the legal foundations of NSLs, and some of their problems, see the reports by the Department of Justice Inspector General, Report of March 2007 (covering 2003–2005), available at http://www.usdoj.gov/oig/special/s0703b/final.pdf, and Report of March 2008 (covering 2006), available at http://www.usdoj.gov/oig/special /s0803b/final.pdf. The Inspector General found a dramatic increase, post-9/11, in the incidence of NSL requests, from 8,500 in 2,000 to roughly 50,000 annually today. The IG also documented a range of concerns in the issuance of the letters, including problems of accountability.

27. Law enforcement procedures are protected from mandatory disclosure under the Freedom of Information Act (FOIA), 5 U.S.C. § 552(b)(7).

28. See, e.g., Defense Appropriations Bill of 2007, Report of the Committee of Appropriations (2006), p. 305. For a scholarly discussion of the intermittent and frequently ineffectual nature of congressional oversight of intelligence matters, see Loch Johnson, "Supervising America's Secret Foreign Policy: A Shock Theory of Congressional Oversight for Intelligence," in *American Foreign Policy in a Globalized World*, ed. David P. Forsythe, Patrice C. McMahon, and Andrew Wedeman (New York: Routledge, 2006), pp. 173–92.

29. "Dirty Secrets of the Black Budget," *Businessweek* (27 Feb. 2008), available at http://www.businessweek.com/magazine/content/06_09/c3973050.htm.

30. For a catalog of such treaties, see Edward Grosek, *The Secret Treaties of History* (Buffalo, NY: William S. Hein, 2007).

31. President Woodrow Wilson, Address delivered to Joint Session of Congress, 8 January 1918, available at http://wwi.lib.byu.edu/index.php/President_Wilson%27s_Fourteen _Points.

32. See Beth A. Simmons and Richard H. Steinberg, eds., *International Law and International Relations* (New York: Cambridge University Press, 2006).

33. Respectively, Executive Orders 11905, 12306, and 12333.

34. Freedom of Information Act, 5 U.S.C. § 552(B).

35. The NSA directive was reported by the *New York Times* (Risen and Shane) and is explored more fully by Eric Lichtblau in *Bush's Law: The Remaking of American Justice* (New York: Pantheon, 2008); National Security Presidential Directive (NSPD) 51 (9 May 2007).

36. According to Jane Mayer, when an NSA lawyer asked to review the memorandum, he was told by David Addington, "You don't need access. The President decides who sees what, not you." Mayer, *The Dark Side* (New York: Doubleday, 2008), p. 268.

37. Section 152(2) of the British-mandate enacted Penal Code. I owe this discussion to conversation with Meir Dan-Cohen and Alon Harel, "The Rise and Fall of the Israeli Gay Legal Revolution," *Columbia Human Rights Law Review* 31 (1999–2000): 443. Early judicial interpretations of the statute included oral sex and (per dictum, lesbian sex), but subsequent interpretations restricted it to anal penetration.

38. The Combatant Status Review Tribunals (CSRTs) of Guantanamo allow the tribunal to consider any relevant classified evidence, including that not disclosed to the defense. CSRT Procedures G(7) (Admissibility of Evidence), available at http://www

.defenselink.mil/news/Combatant_Tribunals.html. Authoritarian states have also famously made use of the complement of the secret trial: the show trial, where all is public but the verdict is a product of political pressure. Show trials are, of course, no improvement over secret trials, but their vices run along a different spectrum. See Mark J. Osiel, "In Defense of Liberal Show Trials—Nuremberg and Beyond," in *Perspectives on the Nuremberg Trial*, ed. Guénaël Mettraux (New York: Oxford University Press, 2008), pp. 704–26.

39. For a critical overview of the use of secret evidence in criminal and quasi-criminal proceedings, see Note, "Secret Evidence in the War on Terror," *Harvard Law Review* 118 (2005): 1962.

40. Thomas Aquinas, *Summa Theologica*, Q. 90, Art. 4 [1265–74], available at http://www.newadvent.org/summa/.

41. John Austin, *Lectures on Jurisprudence; Or, The Philosophy of Positive Law*, ed. Robert Campbell *(London*: John Murray, 5th ed. 1885), Vol. 2, Lecture 29, p. 526.

42. See the papers collected in Richard Buxbaum and Kathryn Hendley, eds., *The Soviet Sobranie of Laws* (Berkeley: University of California Press, 1991).

43. Clive Parry, "Legislatures and Secrecy," *Harvard Law Review* 67 (1954): 737–85.

44. Charles J. Zinn, "Secret Statutes of the Eleventh Congress," *U.S. Congressional and Administrative News* 156 (1952): 2475.

45. Charles W. Ramsdell, ed., *Laws and Joint Resolutions of the Last Sessions of the Confederate Congress* (Durham, NC: Duke University Press, 1941), pt. 2 ("Secret Laws and Resolutions of the C.S.A.").

46. CIA Inspector General, "Special Review of Counterterrorism Detention and Interrogation Activities," Office of the Inspector General (7 May 2004). Available at http://www2.gwu.edu/~nsarchiv/torture_archive/20040507.pdf.

47. Senate Select Intelligence Committee Study of the CIA's Detention and Interrogation Program (Executive Summary) (released December 2014), pp. 119–26.

48. Ibid., pp. 419–27, 439–52. CIA officers have strongly rejected the claim that Congress was under- or misinformed. See http://ciasavedlives.com/briefed.html.

49. It has become a commonplace in evolutionary accounts of morality that one of the core functions of social norms is to allow us to coordinate our acts and attitudes, stabilizing cooperation across the temptations of free-riding or exploitation. See, e.g., Allan Gibbard, *Wise Choices, Apt Feelings* (Cambridge: Harvard University Press, 1992), ch. 6.

50. To pick a Schmittian form of the claim about the nature of politics.

51. Joseph Raz makes a similar point about the distinctive political value of the rule of law for pluralistic moderns such as ourselves, in "The Politics of the Rule of Law," in *Ethics in the Public Domain* (Oxford: Clarendon Press, 1994), 370–78. See also his "The Rule of Law and Its Virtue," in *The Authority of Law* (New York: Oxford University Press, 1979), ch. 11.

52. Jeremy Waldron, "Torture and Positive Law: Jurisprudence for the White House," *Columbia Law Review* 105 (2005): 1681.

53. I mean to echo Plato's claim in the *Republic* of the relation between intra- and interpsychic equilibria.

54. See Alon Harel, The Rise and Fall of the Israeli Gay Legal Revolution, *Columbia Human Rights Law Review* 31 (2000): 443–71.

55. On the claim that 2004 election vindicated the memoranda, see John Yoo, *War by Other Means* (Boston: Atlantic Monthly Press, 2006), p. 180.

CHAPTER 7. MUST A DEMOCRACY BE RUTHLESS?
TORTURE, NECESSITY, AND EXISTENTIAL POLITICS

1. Bernard Williams, *Shame and Necessity* (Berkeley: University of California Press, 1993), p. 111.

2. I echo here David Luban's claims in his chapter, "Liberalism, Torture, and the Ticking Bomb," in *The Torture Debate in America*, ed. Karen J. Greenberg (New York: Cambridge University Press, 2005), p. 35.

3. The Senate Report on the CIA's Detention and Interrogation Program, discussed in the last chapter, catalogues these techniques in detail. While there is debate over whether some other well-documented techniques (mild assault, sexual humiliation, terrorization with dogs) legally constitute torture or merely "cruel, inhuman, or degrading" treatment, there is no reasonable debate over whether waterboarding (whose point is to introduce fear of death), hanging, and induced hypothermia fit within the definition of torture.

4. See Ronald Dworkin, *Freedom's Law* (Cambridge: Harvard University Press, 1996), ch. 1; John Rawls, *A Theory of Justice*, rev. ed. (Cambridge, MA: Belknap Press, 1999).

5. Memorandum from Jay S. Bybee, Assistant Attorney Gen., to Alberto R. Gonzales, Counsel to the President, and William J. Haynes II, Gen. Counsel of the Dep't of Def. (22 Jan. 2002), p. 11 (discussing the president's plenary authority), available at http://www.washingtonpost.com/wp-srv/nation/documents/012202bybee.pdf; see also Memorandum from Jay S. Bybee, Assistant Attorney Gen., Re: Standards of Conduct for Interrogation under 18 U.S.C. §§ 2340–2340A, to Alberto Gonzales, Counsel to the President (1 Aug. 2002), p. 33 (arguing that the president enjoys complete discretion) (hereinafter cited as Torture Memo), available at http://fl1.findlaw.com/news.findlaw.com/wp/docs/doj/bybee80102mem.pdf. The legal memoranda from this period are collected in Karen J. Greenberg & Joshua L. Dratel eds., *The Torture Papers: The Road to Abu Ghraib* (New York: Cambridge University Press, 2005).

6. The principal Supreme Court decisions are *Hamdan v. Rumsfeld*, 548 U.S. 557 (2006), and *Rasul v. Bush*, 542 U.S. 4667 (2004); the Executive Order is EO 13491, "Ensuring Lawful Interrogations," issued on Obama's first day in office, 22 January 2009.

7. On *Meet the Press*, in response to a question whether the Senate Report's estimated 25% of interrogated prisoners judged to be innocent of terrorist involvement was a concern, Cheney said, "I have no problem as long as we achieve our objective. And our objective is to get the guys who did 9/11 and it is to avoid another attack against the United States." http://www.nbcnews.com/meet-the-press/meet-press-transcript-december-14–2014-n268181.

8. Torture Memo.

9. Carl Schmitt, *Legality and Legitimacy*, trans. Jeffrey Seitzer (Durham: Duke University Press, 2004), pp. 68–74.

10. Convention against Torture and Other Cruel, Inhuman, or Degrading Treatment or Punishment, 26 June 1987, 1465 U.N.T.S. 85. The Convention was ratified by the United States on 18 April 1988.

11. Interview by Tim Russert with Richard Cheney, *Meet the Press* (16 Sept. 2001) (transcript available at www.whitehouse.gov/vicepresident/news-speeches/speeches/vp20010916.html). As Cofer Black, the former director of the CIA Counterterrorist Center, subsequently testified to Congress, "All I want to say is that there was 'before' 9/11

and 'after' 9/11. After 9/11 the gloves come off." Testimony of Cofer Black to Joint House and Senate Select Intelligence Committee, 26 Sept. 2002, available at http://www.fas.org /irp/congress/2002_hr/092602black.html.

12. Douglas Jehl and David Johnston, "C.I.A. Expands Its Inquiry into Interrogation Tactics," *New York Times*, 29 Aug. 2004, at A1; Mark Danner, "Abu Ghraib: The Hidden Story," *New York Review of Books*, 7 Oct. 2004, available at http://www.nybooks.com /articles/17430.

13. 18 U.S.C. § 2340A(a).

14. 18 U.S.C. § 2340(1), (2)(c).

15. Torture Memo.

16. I discuss the Torture Memo at greater length, and the specific role of the OLC lawyers, in two papers: "The Lawyers Know Sin," in Greenberg, *Torture Debate*, pp. 241–46; and "Causeless Complicity: The Case of the OLC Lawyers," Criminal Law and Philosophy 1 (2007): 289–305.

17. Torture Memo, p. 27.

18. Ibid., p. 39.

19. Model Penal Code § 3.02(1), (1)(a) (hereinafter cited as MPC). More exactly, § 3.02(1) provides for a defense whenever a defendant believes, even unreasonably, that he or she is in a situation of necessity. Under § 3.02(2), however, reckless or negligent defendants can still be liable for crimes for which recklessness or negligence suffice for culpability. The net result approximates the position at common law, according to which only a reasonable belief as to the necessity of the act serves as a defense.

20. Model Penal Code and Commentaries § 3.02, cmt. 1, pp. 9–10 (hereinafter cited as MPC Commentaries).

21. Torture Memo, pp. 33–34.

22. MPC § 3.04(1); Wayne R. LaFave and Austin W. Scott, Jr., *Substantive Criminal Law*, vol. 1 (St. Paul, MN: West, 1986 and 2002 Supp.), § 5.7 at 649.

23. Michael S. Moore, "Torture and Balance of Evils," *Israel Law Review* 23 (1989): 280, 323 (cited by the Torture Memo, at p. 44).

24. Torture Memo, pp. 42–43 (citing MPC § 3.04 and LaFave and Scott, *Substantive Criminal Law*, p. 649).

25. Logically, if "ought implies can"—that is, one only has obligations to do what it is possible to do—then "cannot" also implies "not ought." One has no obligation, much less requirement, to do the impossible. My swimming to rescue the drowning swimmer might have been a necessary condition of his being saved, if I am the only one within range; but if I cannot swim, it is not necessary that I try.

26. MPC § 3.02(2) states: "When the actor was reckless or negligent in bringing about the situation requiring a choice of harms or evils or in appraising the necessity for his conduct, the justification afforded by this Section is unavailable in a prosecution for any offense for which recklessness or negligence, as the case may be, suffices to establish culpability."

27. See Wayne R. Lafave, *Criminal Law* (St. Paul: West Academic Publishing, 5th ed. 2010), § 10.1(d)(3).

28. The effect of rendering the justification subjective is to include both objectively unjustified but morally nonculpable actors, and to exclude coincidentally justified but morally culpable actors. The essentially objective character of the justification is evident in LaFave and Scott's treatment, and is manifest in the memo, which discusses the defense as providing a genuine justification, and not just exculpation.

29. As LaFave says, "The rationale of the necessity defense is not that a person, when faced with the pressure of circumstances of nature, lacks the mental element which the crime in question requires. Rather, it is this reason of public policy: the law ought to promote the achievement of higher values at the expense of lesser values, and sometimes the greater good for society will be accomplished by violating the literal language of the criminal law." *Criminal Law*, p. 524.

30. See the famous example of *Regina v. Dudley & Stephens*, 14 Q.B.D. 273 (1884) (upholding rejection of defense of necessity by cannibalistic sailors, in part because the sailors "might possibly have been picked up next day by a passing ship; they might possibly not have been picked up at all.") (Lord Coleridge, C.J.).

31. At common law, self-defenders are not even held to such a high standard. The majority of states do not require defenders to choose to retreat, even when they can do so in safety, and one need never retreat from a home. See LaFave and Scott, *Substantive Criminal Law*, § 10.4(f).

32. Treatises, the MPC Commentaries, and the Torture Memo straightforwardly identify the defense as having utilitarian value. See MPC Commentaries, § 3.02, cmt. 3; LaFave, *Criminal Law*, §10.1(a); Torture Memo, p. 40.

33. HCJ 6536/95 Hat'm Abu Zayda v. The General Security Service [1999] (consolidated with other cases), available at http://www.law.yale.edu/documents/pdf/Public _Committee_Against_Torture.pdf (unofficial translation).

34. Torture Memo, p. 39.

35. Ibid., pp. 36–37 (internal citations omitted).

36. Ibid., p. 39.

37. "The text, structure and history of the Constitution establish that the Founders entrusted the President with the primary responsibility, and therefore the power, to ensure the security of the United States in situations of grave and unforeseen emergencies." Ibid., p. 37.

38. David Luban, "Liberalism, Torture and the Ticking Bomb," *Virginia Law Review* 91 (2005): 1425–61, p. 1455 (referring to a "near consensus that the legal analysis contained in the Bybee memo was bizarre"). See also Jeremy Waldron, "Torture and Positive Law: A Jurisprudence for the White House," 105 Columbia Law Review (2005): 1681. Critics of the Torture Memo ranged from academics to policymakers, and from the left to the (relative) right, including an influential editorial denunciation by former CIA chief James Woolsey (under Bill Clinton) and Ruth Wedgwood, until then a tireless advocate for the post-9/11 policies of the Bush Administration. Ruth Wedgwood and R. James Woolsey, "Law and Torture," *Wall Street Journal*, 28 June 2004, p. A10, available at http://www .benadorassociates.com/article/5500. Senator John McCain's legislative attempts, through the Detainee Treatment Act of 2005 and the Military Commissions Act of 2006, can also be seen as responses to the new policy on interrogation.

39. The Torture Memo treats a statutory definition of pain severe enough to trigger emergency care health benefits, per 42 U.S.C. § 1395w-22(d)(3)(B), as defining the threshold above which the infliction of suffering is criminally punished. Torture Memo, p. 6. Luban, "Liberalism, Torture," in Greenberg, *Torture Debate*, pp. 65–67, notes all the flaws in the analysis summarized in this paragraph.

40. Torture Memo, p. 41 n. 23 ("By leaving Section 2340 silent as to the harm done by torture in comparison to other harms, Congress allowed the necessity defense to apply when appropriate."). It is as though a command "Stop now, right where you are" should

be properly interpreted to mean, "Stop where you are . . . unless you have a good reason to keep going." It is true that speeding laws, for example, also are couched in absolute terms yet support necessity justifications. However, there is no plausible canon of statutory construction according to which an unqualified prohibition on torture can be read as a selective permission, when such prohibition implements a treaty that, by its terms, specifically proscribes torture's deployment for "such purposes as obtaining from [the victim] or a third person information or a confession, punishing him for an act he or a third person has committed or is suspected of having committed, or intimidating or coercing him or a third person." Convention against Torture, Art. I.

41. Luban, "Liberalism, Torture," in Greenberg, *Torture Debate*, pp. 62–65. See also Waldron, "Torture and Positive Law," which also takes up the peculiar and disturbing nature of the memo's interpretive approach to positive law.

42. *Youngstown Sheet & Tube v. Sawyer*, 343 U.S. 579 (1952). *Youngstown* is, of course, the locus of Justice Jackson's famous concurrence, in which he argued:

> When the President takes measures incompatible with the expressed or implied will of Congress, his power is at its lowest ebb, for then he can rely only upon his own constitutional powers minus any constitutional powers of Congress over the matter. Courts can sustain exclusive presidential control in such a case only by disabling the Congress from acting upon the subject. Presidential claim to a power at once so conclusive and preclusive must be scrutinized with caution, for what is at stake is the equilibrium established by our constitutional system. (pp. 637–38 [Jackson, J., concurring])

Jackson's concurring dictum was reasserted, to effect, in *Hamdan*, 548 U.S., n. 23.

43. U.S. Const. Art. 1, § 8, cl. 14 and 16. As Richard Posner notes, the framework of the Torture Memo argument (which he attributes to John Yoo) makes little sense: since the president is commander in chief in peace as well as war, it cannot be that his status as commander in chief precludes congressional regulation of the land and naval forces. Richard A. Posner, *Not a Suicide Pact: The Constitution in a Time of National Emergency* (New York: Oxford University Press, 2006), pp. 67–68.

44. Torture Memo, p. 37 (quoting The Federalist No. 23 [Alexander Hamilton]).

45. On the intellectual sources of the political theory of the Framers, including Montesquieu, see Bernard Bailyn's classic work, *The Ideological Origins of the American Revolution* (Cambridge, MA: Belknap Press, 1967).

46. Jack N. Rakove, "Making Foreign Policy: The View from 1787," in *Foreign Policy and the Constitution*, ed. Robert A. Goldwin and Robert A. Licht (Washington, AEI Press, 1990), p. 16. See also Jack N. Rakove, *Original Meanings* (New York: Basic Books, 1996). Rakove discusses the original conceptions of presidential power in chapter 9 and argues that "[i]n reconstituting the executive, then, Americans paid homage to Montesquieu's principle of separation without allowing his (or Locke's) defense of prerogative to outweigh the lessons of their own history" (p. 250). While the Framers did change a draft version of Congress's authority to "conduct" war to its authority to "declare" war, this is fully consistent with a conception of executive authority to conduct war subject to congressional regulation. U.S. Const. Art. 1, § 8, cl. 11; Rakove, *Original Meanings*, p. 263.

47. Working Group Report on Detainee Interrogations in the Global War on Terrorism: Assessment of Legal, Historical, Policy, and Operational Considerations (4 Apr. 2003), reprinted in Greenberg and Dratel, *Torture Papers*, pp. 241–85. Also available at http://www.gwu.edu/~nsarchiv/NSAEBB/NSAEBB127/03.04.04.pdf.

48. See Memorandum from Daniel Levin, Assistant Attorney Gen., Re: Legal Standards Applicable under 18 U.S.C. §§ 2340–2340A, to James B. Comey, Deputy Attorney Gen. (30 Dec. 2004) (hereinafter cited as Levin memo), available at http://www .usdoj.gov/olc/dagmemo.pdf.

49. Ibid., pp. 11–12. The Levin memo also repudiates another of the more peculiar features of the Torture Memo: its oblique suggestion that only a "precise objective" of inflicting severe pain amounts to torture (rather than a purpose of eliciting information, knowing that pain will be used to produce the result). Ibid., pp. 16–17; Torture Memo, pp. 4–5.

50. The legal justification for the administration's controversial program of warrant-less domestic surveillance by the National Security Agency appears to rest, in part, on the same claim of legislatively untrammeled executive authority in national security matters. *See* Department of Justice White Paper, Legal Authorities Supporting the Activities of the National Security Agency Described by the President (19 Jan. 2006) (hereinafter cited as White Paper), available at http://permanent.access.gpo.gov/lps66493/White%20Paper%20 on%20NSA%20Legal%20Authorities.pdf.

51. Levin memo, p. 2.

52. See Letter from Daniel Levin to William Haynes II, Gen. Counsel at the Dep't of Defense (4 Feb. 2005), available at http://balkin.blogspot.com/Levin.Haynes.205.pdf. The Levin letter refers to an OLC decision announced in December 2003 by OLC to withdraw a still-unreleased memo by John Yoo of 14 March 2003, which apparently incorporated the executive power arguments of the Torture Memo. For discussion, see Lederman's commentary, http://balkin.blogspot.com/2005/07/graham-hearing-on-detainees-progress .html.

53. White Paper, pp. 6–11. The White Paper also argues that the wiretapping was implicitly statutorily authorized by the Authorization to Use Military Force (AUMF), and that it is also permitted by FISA.

54. Detainee Treatment Act of 2005, Pub. L. No. 109–148, Title X, § 1003(a) (2005).

55. See, e.g., Dana Priest and Robin Wright, "Cheney Fights for Detainee Policy," *Washington Post*, 7 Nov. 2005, p. A1 ("Cheney's camp . . . believes the president needs nearly unfettered power to deal with terrorists to protect Americans.").

56. Presidential Statement on Signing the Department of Defense, Emergency Supplemental Appropriations to Address Hurricanes in the Gulf of Mexico, and Pandemic Influenza Act, 2006 (30 Dec. 2005), available at http://www.presidency.ucsb.edu/ws/index .php?pid=65259.

57. This is, I think, a consensus view of what a deontological conception of rights, or of duties grounding rights, is committed to: a claim of right (or duty not to act in some way) overrides whatever instrumental (welfare-based or other) considerations militate in favor of acting contrary to the right. For its sources in the philosophical literature, see, obviously, Immanuel Kant, *Groundwork of the Metaphysics of Morals* Bk. II [1785] (our duties as rational agents to treat others as free and equal agents create in them rights not to be used for our purposes, and to be aided in the pursuit of their ends); Robert Nozick, *Anarchy, State and Utopia* (New York: Basic Books, 1977), pp. 30–34 (the function of rights is to limit, as "side constraints," the pursuit of individual or collective welfare gains); Thomas Nagel, "War and Massacre," reprinted in *Mortal Questions* (New York: Cambridge University Press, 1979), pp. 53–74 (duties to others are deontological constraints that limit the force of consequentialist justifications); Samuel Scheffler, *The Rejection of Consequentialism*, rev. ed.

(New York: Oxford University Press, 1994), pp. 80–83 (duties not to act in certain ways limit the force of consequentialist claims).

Ronald Dworkin's famous metaphor of "rights as trumps," suggests a concept of rights as claims that categorically defeat considerations of general policy. However, Dworkin's particular deployment of the concept of a right relies on a quasi-utilitarian theory, according to which rights claims are justified when determinations of general welfare would be corrupted by what Dworkin styles "nosy" or "external" preferences. Such preferences are ruled out by an underlying individual right to treatment (by the state at any rate) as an equal, entitled to respect. See his *Taking Rights Seriously* (Cambridge, MA: Belknap Press, 1977).

58. On the potential justifiability of killing a nonthreatening individual, see Lafave, *Criminal Law*, § 10.1(a); MPC Commentaries, § 3.02, cmt. 3; Glanville Williams, *Criminal Law: The General Part*, 2d ed. (London: Stevens and Sons, 1961), § 237; Sanford H. Kadish, *Blame and Punishment* (New York: Macmillan, 1987), pp. 122–23. George Fletcher is a rare criminal law theorist who explicitly rejects a much less restrictive necessity test. See his *Rethinking Criminal Law* (New York: Oxford University Press, 1978) § 10.4. J. C. Smith notes that if English law does permit application of the defense to cases of homicide (unclear, given the infamous *R. v. Dudley & Stephens* precedent, 14 Q.B.D. 273 [1884]), the defense does not extend past cases of killing some lest all die. Sir John Smith and Brian Hogan, *Criminal Law*, 10th ed. (Oxford: Oxford University Press, 2003), pp. 271–74.

59. See Richard A. Posner, "An Economic Theory of the Criminal Law," *Columbia Law Review* 85 (1985): 1193–231.

60. 34 Cal. 4th 1, 100 (2004), *cert. denied*, 544 U.S. 1063 (2005) (denying necessity defense in robbery-murder where defendant alleged co-perpetrator had threatened her life and the life of her son) (internal quotation marks omitted).

61. Smith and Hogan, *Criminal Law*, pp. 272–73; *United States v. Holmes*, 26 F. Cas. 360, 1 Wall Jr. 1 (C.C.E.D. Pa. 1842). By contrast, the defense was famously denied in *Dudley & Stephens*, in part on the ground that there was no reason why the cabin boy, rather than any of the others, should have been killed for food, as well as on the ground discussed before, that the court (though not the trial jury) thought they had not waited long enough for rescue before turning to cannibalism. For more discussion of this peculiar case, see A. W. Brian Simpson, *Cannibalism and the Common Law* (London: Bloomsbury Academic Press,1984).

62. MPC Commentaries, § 3.02, cmt. 3.

63. Code Pénal Art. 122-7 (my translation). In principle, the defense covers all crimes, including assault or homicide, but I have found no recorded decisions showing even rejection of the defense in such cases.

64. Jacques-Henri Robert writes that "although one can defend using force against someone posing a threat to the household [patrimoine] . . . necessity will not lie against an innocent." *Droit pénal général* (Paris: Presses Universitaires de France, 5th ed. 2001), p. 272. The defensible cases of necessity he instances are of the familiar Anglo-American variety: sailors jettisoning some of their number lest all die, and surgeons cutting flesh without consent in order to save life.

65. Deutsches Strafgesetz §§ 32–34. German and French criminal law, unlike Anglo-American law, do in principle permit the excuse of duress for killing of the innocent, as does the ICC Statute, § 31(1)(d), although the homicide limitation had been recognized before, e.g., in *Prosecutor v. Erdemovic, ICTY* (Appeals Chamber), IT-26–92, judgment of

7 October 1997. For discussion, see Gerhard Werle, *Principles of International Criminal Law* (The Hague: T.M.C. Asser Press, 2005), p. 146. In German law, interrogatory torture is subject to multiple specific prohibitions, apart from any inherent limitations in the necessity defense. Notwithstanding the prohibitions, in a recent article Winfried Brugger performs interesting interpretive acrobatics to show how torture might be justified under German law. "May Government Ever Use Torture? Two Responses from German Law," *American Journal of Comparative Law* 48 (2000): 661.

66. Fletcher, *Rethinking Criminal Law*, at 784.

67. Because the German court imposed essentially a symbolic sanction for a serious offense, in 2009, the European Court of Human Rights criticized the German court for failing to vindicate the prohibition on torture, thus deepening the rejection of the necessity defense. *Gäfgen v. Germany*, ECtHR (1 June 2010), http://hudoc.echr.coe.int/sites/eng/pages/search.aspx?i=001–99015.

68. Ibid., § 10.2; Robert, *Droit pénal général*, p. 272.

69. Rewards in the afterlife are, in fact, Plato's apparent solution to the conundrum of the good man faced by evil circumstance, in the "myth of Er," in Book X of the *Republic*.

70. Leading claimants of the threshold theory are, e.g., Thomas Nagel, "War and Massacre," in *Mortal Questions* (New York: Cambridge University Press, 1979); Thomas Nagel, "Personal Rights and Public Space," in *Concealment and Exposure* (New York: Oxford University Press, 2002), pp. 31–52, 66; Robert Nozick, *Anarchy, State, and Utopia* (New York: Basic Books, 1975), p. 41; Charles Fried, *Right and Wrong* (Cambridge: Harvard University Press, 1978). But some version of the position is nearly universal among noninstrumental rights theorists.

71. Moore, "Torture and Balance of Evils," p. 332. For discussion, see Larry Alexander, "Deontology at the Threshold," *San Diego Law Review* 37 (2000): 893.

72. William K. Frankena, *Ethics*, 2d ed. (Boston: Pearson, 1973): 116.

73. In Stig Kanger's influential formulation of "deontic logic," or the logic of obligations, all principles can be reduced to statements involving the operator "is required": an act is forbidden if it is required that one not do it; it is permitted if it is not required that one not do it, and not required that one do it. Kanger, "New Foundations for Deontic Logic," in *New Studies in Deontic Logic*, ed. R. Hilpinnen (Dordrecht: D. Riedel, 1971).

74. Kant, *Groundwork*, p. 435. Nagel's conception of moral rights as grounded in "status," something that can be neither redistributed nor increased in quantity, is similarly absolute in form, though he says (without defending the claim) that assertions of right are consistent with thresholds. Nagel, "Personal Rights," pp. 83, 85, 88; F. M. Kamm, "Non-consequentialism, the Person as an End-in-Itself, and the Significance of Status," *Philosophy & Public Affairs* 21 (1992): pp. 354, 381–89. Both are interpretations of Kant's claim in the *Groundwork* that the value of rational agency can only be captured by the concept of "dignity" rather than "price" (*Groundwork* 4:434). For still the most acute discussion of the paradox, which insists on its puzzling character, see Samuel Scheffler, *The Rejection of Consequentialism* (New York: Oxford University Press, 2d ed. 1994).

75. T. M. Scanlon, *What We Owe to Each Other* (Cambridge, MA: Belknap Press, 2000), pp. 83–85. More precisely, Scanlon says that the reason not to violate an agent-centered restriction could be grounded on a principle whose justification itself lies on the contractarian footing that no one searching for principles to provide a fair basis for regulating common life could reasonably reject; this is not, in his view, a "teleological" (or maximizing) conception of value.

76. Nozick, *Anarchy, State, and Utopia*, p. 33.

77. Henry Shue, "Torture," *Philosophy & Public Affairs* 7 (1978): 124, 142–43.

78. John Langbein quotes Sir James FitzJames Stephen's *A History of the Criminal Law of England*, concerning "the proclivity of the native police [in India] for torturing suspects. 'It is far pleasanter to sit comfortably in the shade rubbing red pepper in some poor devil's eyes than to go about in the sun hunting up evidence.'" John H. Langbein, "The Legal History of Torture," in S. Levinson, ed., *Torture: A Collection* (New York: Oxford University Press, 2004), pp. 93, 101. Notably, Justice Frankfurter also quotes Stephen in *McNabb v. United States*, 318 U.S. 332, 343 (1943), an important coerced-confession case in which the court asserted its inherent authority to regulate federal investigatory authority.

79. There is no way to institutionalize any principle of permissible torture without falling into the swamp of Abu Ghraibs and Bagrams, in which innocents are routinely subjected to abuse for the amusement of sadists playing "intelligence" games. On the abuses at Bagram, see Tim Golden's exposé, "In U.S. Report, Brutal Details of 2 Afghan Inmates' Deaths," *New York Times*, 20 May 2005, at A1.

80. I defend these claims in "The Lawyers Know Sin," p. 241. Briefly, there exists a basis for accomplice liability for any purposefully abetted acts of assault or torture, and for purposefully abetting acts, in reckless disregard of the risks, that through recklessness or negligence led to the deaths of some of the detainees.

81. 124 N.W. 221, 222 (Minn. 1910) (holding that the boat operator acted justifiably but was still liable for damage to dock incurred during unconsented use during storm); 81 Vt. 471, 474–75 (1908) (plaintiff had right to compensated use of defendant's dock during storm).

82. Arguably, this is not quite right. If one accepts a right to be free from certain degrees of ex ante risk, then a speeding driver on the way to the hospital may be violating the rights of those he endangers. French criminal law explicitly treats the issue in this way and deems it a matter of justified necessity. Robert, *Droit pénal général*, pp. 273–77 (citing CA Metz, 8 mars 1990, Dr. pén., 1991, comm. 49).

83. Apart from the Convention against Torture, torture is categorically prohibited by the International Covenant on Civil and Political Rights, 999 U.N.T.S. 171 (Dec. 16, 1966); by all four Geneva Conventions, through both Common Article 3 and through specific articles: Geneva Convention for the Amelioration of the Condition of the Wounded and Sick in Armed Forces in the Field, 75 U.N.T.S. 31; Geneva Convention for the Amelioration of the Condition of Wounded, Sick and Shipwrecked Members of Armed Forces at Sea, 75 U.N.T.S. 85; Geneva Convention Relative to the Treatment of Prisoners of War, 75 U.N.T.S. 135 (hereinafter cited as GC III); Geneva Convention Relative to the Protection of Civilian Persons in Time of War, 75 U.N.T.S. 287 (hereinafter GC IV). All were signed 12 August 1949. The rule against torture is also seen as a nonderogable, *jus cogens* norm of customary international law. See, e.g., *Restatement (Third) of Foreign Relations Law of the United States* (Philadelphia: American Law Institute, 1987), § 702, and Reporter's Note 5.

84. I borrow the idea of the institutional vs. pre-institutional distinction from John Rawls, though he uses it to discuss the related issue of desert. Rawls, *Theory of Justice*, § 48.

85. In the United States, of course, intellectual property is instrumental and conventional as a matter of constitutional text: "To promote the Progress of Science and useful Arts, by securing for limited Times to Authors and Inventors the exclusive Right to their respective Writings and Discoveries." U.S. Const. Art. 1, § 8, cl. 8.

86. These are, roughly, the "personality theory" views of Kant and Hegel, well discussed by Jeremy Waldron in *The Right to Private Property* (New York: Oxford University Press,1990); Margaret Jane Radin is a modern inheritor of these views—see her *Contested Commodities* (Cambridge: Harvard University Press, 1991).

87. In these paragraphs I have oversimplified grotesquely, but I expand my discussion in chapter 10.

88. These are familiar points, found most easily in J.J.C. Smart's "An Outline for a System of Utilitarian Ethics," in J.J.C. Smart and Bernard Williams, *Utilitarianism: For and Against* (New York: Cambridge University Press, 1973). Contrary to Smart, I do not want to claim that rule-utilitarianism "collapses into"—is extensionally equivalent to—act-utilitarianism. As Donald Regan has shown, rule-based forms of utilitarianism can promote utility in a way that individualistic act-utilitarianism cannot, by solving coordination problems. Regan, *Utilitarianism and Cooperation* (New York: Oxford University Press, 1980). But the case at issue here is not coordination dependent.

89. Note that while the point of the "just compensation" requirement is to push takings in the direction of Pareto-efficiency, given that actual compensation is frequently less than the owner's subjective value, the actual normative justification is more Kaldor-Hicks than Pareto. A different version of the same principle is at work in the *Vincent* cases: there will be no criminal liability, assuming Kaldor-Hicks efficiency, and then ex post compensation to bring the transfer to "objective" Pareto standards.

90. *Kelo v. New London*, 545 U.S. 469, 125 S. Ct. 2655 (2005).

91. Testimony of Thomas A. Merrill to Senate Committee on the Judiciary, 19 Sept. 2005, available at http://judiciary.senate.gov/testimony.cfm?id=1612&wit_id=4661.

92. What is puzzling is Justice Thomas's dissenting argument that the Framers, by changing what appears to be Blackstone's prohibition on takings even for "public necessity" into a permission to take for "public use" provided that just compensation is paid, somehow meant to capture the restrictiveness of Blackstone's own view. 125 S. Ct. at 2677 (Thomas, J., dissenting).

93. See, e.g., GC IV, Art. 147. "Military necessity" is an extraordinarily plastic term. According to one classic statement, "Military necessity permits a belligerent, subject to the laws of war, to apply any amount and kind of force to compel the complete submission of the enemy with the least possible expenditure of time, life, and money." *United States v. List*, in *Trials of War Criminals before the Nuremburg Military Tribunals Under Control Council Law No. 10* (1949), available at http://www.loc.gov/rr/frd/Military_Law/NTs_war-criminals .html, pp. 1253–54. The regime of military necessity is more like egoism than utilitarianism, albeit constrained by protection of the innocent from deliberate targeting.

94. The figures for US or coalition-caused deaths come from the "Iraq Body Count" project, which is regarded as very credible. It consolidates all reports by news agencies of civilian deaths, and claims to triple-check all of them. The project counts 154,000 Iraqi direct deaths from violence by any actor (coalition or Iraqi). See http://www.iraqbodycount .net/press/pr12.php (accessed 1 March 2015). The total count of excess deaths attributable to the war derives from an epidemiological study, discussed in the previous chapter and published in *PLOS Medicine*, http://journals.plos.org/plosmedicine/article?id=10.1371 /journal.pmed.1001533.

95. GC III, Art. 17(1) (prohibits coercive interrogation, including torture, of any lawful combatant taken prisoner of war); GC IV, Art. 32 (prohibits torture of any "protected person"—civilian citizen of a contracting party); Protocol Additional to the Geneva

Conventions of 12 August 1949, and Relating to the Protection of Victims of Non-International Armed Conflicts, Art. 4 (Protocol II) (7 Dec. 1978) (prohibits torture of prisoners taken in civil insurgencies).

96. Memorandum to the Vice President from President George Bush, Re: Humane Treatment of al Qaeda and Taliban Detainees (7 Feb. 2002), reprinted in Greenberg and Dratel, *Torture Papers*, p. 135.

97. These are rights against murder, cruel or degrading treatment or other "outrages upon personal dignity," being taken hostage, or summary execution. Common Art. 3(1)(b). While POW rights to facilities for "sports and games" (GC III, Art. 39) might be an instance, it is hard to imagine what else Attorney General Gonzales had in mind by labeling as "quaint" the provisions of the Convention.

98. For an excellent discussion, see David Sussman, "What's Wrong With Torture?" *Philosophy & Public Affairs* 33 (2005): 1.

99. Of course, from the perspective of the interrogators, it is this scene that renders the victim least human, as Hannah Arendt observed of WWII refugees in *The Origins of Totalitarianism* (Cleveland: Meridian Publishing, 1958), p. 299.

100. I want to put aside the very different case of knowingly running ex ante risks of statistical deaths, even risks up to a moral certainty. Such risks can, I think, be justified on a basis consistent with individual rights. I discuss this briefly in "Self-Defense and Political Justification," *California Law Rev*iew 88 (2000): 751–58.

101. See, e.g., Kadish, *Blame and Punishment*, p. 122.

102. Williams, *Shame*, pp. 101, 116–17.

103. Aristotle, *Politics* 26 (1252a30), trans. Benjamin Jowett (Oxford: Oxford University Press,, 1967).

104. Williams, *Shame*, p. 114. Aristotle, *Politics*, 1252a33–b5: "For he who can foresee with his mind is by nature intended to be lord and master, and he who can work with his body is a subject, and by nature a slave. . . . For [nature] is not niggardly, like the smith who fashions the Delphian knife for many uses; she makes each thing for a single use, and every instrument is best made when intended for one and not for many uses."

105. Williams, *Shame*, pp. 110–12.

106. This is true even if, as some critics have charged, Williams understates the degree to which "ordinary" Greek thought was infected by a less sophisticated version of Aristotle's racism, seeing "barbarians" as naturally fit for slavery. See, e.g., Nick Fisher, "Shame and Necessity," *Classical Review* 45 (1995): 71.

107. Torture Memo, pp. 31–38; see also White Paper, p. 3.

108. Torture Memo, p. 38 ("In wartime, it is for the President alone to decide what methods to use to best prevail against the enemy.").

109. John Ferejohn and Pasquale Pasquino, "The Law of the Exception: A Typology of Emergency Powers," *International Journal of Constitutional Law* 2 (2004): 210, 213.

110. The Romans in fact had both forms: the dictatorship and the enhanced powers of the consulate. Rousseau and Machiavelli agree that true emergency (but only true emergency) calls for the time-limited dictatorship. Jean-Jacques Rousseau, *The Social Contract*, ed. Victor Gourevitch (New York: Cambridge University Press, 1997 [1762]), pp. 138–40; Niccolo Machiavelli, *Discourses on Livy*, ed. Julia Conway Bondanella and Peter Bondanella (New York: Oxford University Press, 1997 [1517]), pp. 84–96; see also Ferejohn and Pasquino, "Law of the Exception," p. 213.

111. 1958 Const. 16 (Fr.), available at http://www.oefre.unibe.ch/; Cost. Art. 77, cl. 2 (1948) (Italy), available at http://www.oefre.unibe.ch/; U.S. Const. Art. I, § 9, cl. 2.

Germany's Basic Law provides for exceptional powers wielded by a joint committee in a "state of defense" (an envisioned invasion by the Soviet Union). GG Art. 115 (FRG), available at http://www.iuscomp.org/gla/statutes/GG.htm#115k.

112. Clinton L. Rossiter, *Constitutional Dictatorship: Crisis Government in the Modern Democracies* (Princeton: Princeton University Press, 1948).

113. Torture Memo, p. 36.

114. Ibid., p. 38. The memo itself refers to no checks on the president's wartime authority, although John Yoo, in his academic identity, does argue for the power of the congressional purse as a sufficient check. See Yoo, *Powers of War and Peace* (Chicago: University of Chicago Press, 2006).

115. Jules Lobel's article, "Emergency Power and the Decline of Liberalism," 98 *Yale Law Journal* 1385 (1989), has a useful survey of emergency powers invocations, as does Sanford Levinson, "Constitutional Norms in a State of Permanent Emergency," *Georgia Law Review* 40 (2006): 699.

116. Lobel, "Emergency Power," pp. 1392–93; Daniel Farber, *Lincoln's Constitution* (Chicago: University of Chicago Press, 2004), pp. 192–95. I am indebted to Farber's valuable book.

117. Torture Memo, p. 34; Posner, *Not a Suicide Pact*, p. 68. See also Levinson, "Constitutional Norms," pp. 742–43 (arguing for the radicalism of the Bush administration view of executive power).

118. Rakove argues persuasively in "Making Foreign Policy" that such a broad view of executive power clearly postdates ratification and is instead a product of Alexander Hamilton's controversial view of 1793, voiced in the Helvidius-Pacificus debates, concerning the extent of President Washington's authority to proclaim US neutrality in the European wars.

119. Carl Schmitt, *Political Theology*, trans. George Schwab (Chicago: University of Chicago Press, 1985 [1922]). For broader discussion, see Giorgio Agamben, *State of Exception*, trans. Kevin Attell (Chicago: University of Chicago Press, 2005); Peter C. Caldwell, "Controversies over Carl Schmitt: A Review of Recent Literature," *Journal of Modern History* 77 (2005): 357; Peter C. Caldwell, *Popular Sovereignty and the Crisis of German Constitutional Law* (Durham, NC: Duke University Press, 1997). A fascinating discussion of the value of Schmitt for making sense of American executive power in general is Eric Posner and Adrian Vermeule, *The Executive Unbound* (New York: Oxford University Press, 2011).

120. Schmitt, *Legality and Legitimacy*.

121. This history is summarized by Agamben, *State of Exception*, pp. 14–16.

122. Weimar Const. of 1919, Art. 48: "In case public safety is seriously threatened or disturbed, the Reich President may take the measures necessary to reestablish law and order, if necessary using armed force. In the pursuit of this aim he may suspend the civil rights described in articles 114, 115, 117, 118, 123, 124 and 154, partially or entirely." Available at http://www.zum.de/psm/weimar/weimar_vve.php.

123. Schmitt, *Legality and Legitimacy*, pp. 68–74; see also the helpful introduction by John P. McCormick in ibid., pp. xxxvi–xxxix.

124. Schmitt, *Political Theology*, p. 15.

125. See Hans Kelsen, *The Pure Theory of Law*, trans. Max Knight (Berkeley: University of California Press, 1967 [1934]).

126. Schmitt, *Political Theology*, p. 5.

127. Ibid., p. 33.

128. Carl Schmitt, *The Concept of the Political*, trans. George Schwab (Chicago: University of Chicago Press, 1996 [1932]), p. 26.

129. Ibid., pp. 26–28.

130. The remainder of the paragraph summarizes *Concept of the Political*, pp. 28–32.

131. Schmitt, *Legality and Legitimacy*, pp. 28, 60. In later work, especially Schmitt's controversial interpretation of Hobbes, Schmitt argues that the sovereign is not a creator of national identity out of chaos, but rather forms a post-national cultural identity out of pre-national cultural materials. Thus, in his view, Hobbesian "liberalism," which pretends to be culturally neutral for the sake of preserving life, actually makes its own cultural stand. For discussion, see Victoria Kahn, "Hamlet or Hecuba: Carl Schmitt's Decision," *Representations* 83 (2003): 67.

132. Carl Schmitt, *On the Three Types of Juristic Thought*, ed. Joseph W. Bendersky (New York: Praeger, 2004 [1934]).

133. Schmitt's concept of sovereignty as decisional, but rooted in pre-legal ordering, reflects his longstanding cultural and political conservatism. But Schmitt's increased emphasis on this concept coincides both with his joining of the Nazi party and with the Nazis' claim to root their authority not just in response to Weimar's chaos (inflicted by themselves), but in their capacity to represent and defend real Germanness. There is a lively debate whether Schmitt's move reflects intellectual conservatism as much as political opportunism. Certainly he offered the Nazis a theoretical grounding they could, and did, make use of. Schmitt also became a prominent anti-Semite, in both writing and deed—for example, purging academic ranks of Jewish scholars. As with Martin Heidegger, there is also considerable debate whether Schmitt was merely a deplorable opportunist or a sincere Nazi. See Caldwell, "Controversies over Carl Schmitt."

134. Note that I am not claiming that Bush administration policy deliberately reflected Schmitt's theories. While some of the administration's executive power theorists may have had some acquaintance with Schmitt, and certainly with Schmitt's colleague, Leo Strauss (who also saw Hobbes as one of the preeminent political theorists), there is no reason to suppose any direct derivation from his views.

135. Schmitt, *Political Theology*, p. 65. This view of the legislative process is implicit in official arguments for executive supremacy, but it is highly visible in contemporary work in positive political theory, and in the normative lessons drawn therefrom, as in Seventh Circuit Judge Frank Easterbrook's influential theory that statutes ought to be interpreted as arms-length deals between self-interested parties. See Frank H. Easterbrook, "Statutes' Domains," *University of Chicago Law Review* 50 (1983): 533.

136. See Farber, *Lincoln's Constitution*, pp. 115–43.

137. The conservative view for the need for a constrained executive is discussed in Rossiter, *Constitutional Dictatorship*. For a prominent example of such recognition by avowedly liberal constitutionalists, and suggestions for coping in a structural way with emergency, see Bruce Ackerman, "The Emergency Constitution," *Yale Law Journal* 113 (2004): 1029, expanded as *Before the Next Attack* (New Haven: Yale University Press, 2006). For valuable discussion to which I am much indebted, see David Dyzenhaus, "Schmitt v. Dicey: Are States of Emergency Inside or Outside the Legal Order?" *Cardozo Law Review* 27 (2006): 2005.

138. Rousseau, *Social Contract*, p. 138.

139. This is, roughly, the position staked out by Posner in *Not a Suicide Pact*.

140. Ackerman, "Emergency Constitution," pp. 1047–49.

141. Rousseau, *Social Contract*, p. 138.

142. It would equally be a mistake to pay no heed to the powerful psychological dimension of the ticking-bomb and national-emergency hypotheticals. The fantasies of being the leader on the white horse, the secret agent saving the city, are surely as tempting to those in power as they are to the Hollywood imagination.

CHAPTER 8. HUMANITARIAN INTERVENTION AND THE NEW DEMOCRATIC HOLY WARS

1. See David Rodin, *War and Self-Defense* (New York: Clarendon Press, 2002); Jeff McMahan, *Killing in War* (New York: Oxford University Press, 2009).

2. Or, rather, it is a necessary and not a sufficient ingredient: the legitimacy of intervention turns on a host of factors.

3. UN Security Council Resolution 1674 (2006), par. 4.

4. As of this writing (March 2015), Libya is in chaos, controlled by local warlords and ISIS. The Syrian conflict is effectively a slow victory for President Assad, with more than 200,000 estimated as killed. Rick Gladstone and Mohammad Ghannam, "Syria Deaths Hit New High in 2014, Observer Group Says," *New York Times* (1 Jan. 2015).

5. For a quick but informative discussion of post-intervention Kosovo, see Gerry Knaus's contribution to his volume with Rory Stewart, *Can Intervention Work?* (New York: W. W. Norton, 2011).

6. And in a form calibrated to the prospects of success.

7. Notably David Rodin, *War and Self-Defense*, p. 130ff; see also Richard Norman, *Ethics, Killing, and War* (New York: Cambridge University Press, 1995).

8. For cosmopolitanism in general, see K. Anthony Appiah, *Cosmopolitanism: Ethics in a World of Strangers* (New York: W. W. Norton, 2006); and Kok-Chor Tan, *Justice without Borders* (New York: Cambridge University Press, 2004).

9. Cicero, *De Officiis*, Bk. III, par. 6 (Peabody trans., 1883, open source, available via Google Books).

10. J. S. Mill, "A Few Words on Non-Intervention" (1859), p. 5, available at http://www.libertarian.co.uk/lapubs/forep/forep008.pdf, p. 5 (accessed 3 July 2013).

11. A note about the special case occupation: as I use it, Mill's test applies to the threshold decision whether to intervene in a state, not to the nature of intervention. If an intervening state is an occupier (perhaps because it has exercised its own right of self- or other-defense), it has a duty to establish democratic and just institutions, and to impose a system of social order until the occupied state can do so itself—so long as its occupation is not itself a degrading processes of order and democratization, through backlash effects. Thus, whether or not 1945 Germany or Japan had civil societies exercising something resembling democratic agency, the duty of their occupiers was to establish the conditions under which it could flourish. I take up the issue of victors' rights in chapter 11.

12. I recognize that most actual processes of working out ethno-sectarian divisions have involved covert interventions by outside actors. But the fact of such interventions, no more than the fact of the divisions being exploited, does not itself vitiate the right of self-defense.

13. Michael Walzer, "The Moral Standing of States: A Response to Four Critics," *Philosophy & Public Affairs* 9 (1980): 209–29.

14. Charles R. Beitz, "Nonintervention and Communal Integrity," *Philosophy & Public Affairs* 9 (1980): 385–91; David Luban, "The Romance of the Nation-State," *Philosophy & Public Affairs* 9 (1980): 392–97. See also Charles Beitz, "The Moral Standing of States Revisited," *Ethics & International Affairs* 23 (2009): 325–47.

15. Walzer, "Moral Standing," p. 211.

16. Walzer follows Mill in linking his normative point to an epistemic one: the question of whether a state and its culture are sufficiently integrated is one that outsiders are presumptively poorly placed to assess. Luban, "Romance," is correct in noting the limits of the epistemic claim (p. 395).

17. John Rawls, *The Law of Peoples* (Cambridge, MA: Harvard University Press, 1999), sec. 9.

18. J. J. Rousseau, *The Social Contract*, ed. Victor Gourevitch (New York: Cambridge University Press, 1997 [1762]), Bk. 1, ch. 6.

19. This is an awkward point—but it has, I think, a legal analogue: there are frequently situations in US federal law in which a law has apparently been violated, but no litigant has standing to enjoin the violation. (Environmental cases often take this form.) The lack of an opponent provides no vindication for the violator. We must also take care to distinguish Gaddafi's (and his military's) personal criminal responsibility in international criminal law, under the Rome Statute, from the state's liability to attack.

CHAPTER 9. DEMOCRATIC STATES IN VICTORY: *VAE VICTIS?*

1. Vol. I, trans. Rev. Canon Roberts, Everyman's Library (London: J. M. Dent, 1912), accessible at http://etext.virginia.edu/toc/modeng/public/Liv1His.html, sec. 5.48.

2. See, e.g., Hague Convention (IV) of 1907 respecting the Laws and Customs of War on Land, Geneva Convention IV of 1949, esp. Sec. III.

3. See, e.g., Protocol I Additional to the Geneva Conventions, Art. 51(5)(b).

4. Gary Bass, "Jus Post Bellum," *Philosophy and Public Affairs* 32 (2004): 384–412.

5. I take this up in the following chapter, on reparations.

6. See chapter 4, "A Modest Case for Symmetry."

7. Grotius, *Rights of War and Peace* ((Indianapolis: Liberty Fund, 2005 [1625]), Bk. III, ch. 6, par. 2; see also chs. 5–7.

8. Plato, *The Republic*, trans. B. Jowett (Oxford: Oxford University Press, 1888), Bk. I, 338B, p. 17.

9. Fulgosius, *Im primam Pandectarum partem Commentaria*, ad *Dig.*, 1, 1, 5, trans. Peter Haggenmacher, quoted in Gregory Reichberg, Henrik Syse, and Endre Begby, *The Ethics of War* (London: Wiley-Blackwell, 2006), p. 228. Fulgosius was writing in the 1420s.

10. See Peter Haggenmacher, "Just War and Regular War in Sixteenth Century Spanish Doctrine," *International Review of the Red Cross* 32 (1992): 434–45.

11. See Emer de Vattel, *The Law of Nations*, Bk. III, ch. 3, sec. 38.

12. See Joel Feinberg, "On Desert," in *Doing and Deserving* (Princeton: Princeton University Press, 1974).

13. Michael Walzer, *Just and Unjust Wars*, 4th ed. (New York: Basic Books, 2006), p. 53ff.

14. Thomas Vio de Cajetan, writing shortly before Fulgosius, represents the idea of war as punitive justice in its fullest flower, who treats the power to impose punishment

as a necessary attribute of the perfect commonwealth. See his Commentary to *Summa Theologiae* II-II, q. 40.

CHAPTER 10. DRONES, DEMOCRACY, AND THE FUTURE OF WAR

1. Barack Obama, Speech to the Woodrow Wilson International Center, August 2007, available at http://www.cfr.org/us-election-2008/obamas-speech-woodrow-wilson-center /p13974 (accessed 30 May 2012).

2. Numbers in this arena are extremely difficult to defend, because of restrictive governmental policies and other dangers to independent reporters and researchers. The numbers compiled by the Bureau for Investigative Journalism use the most inclusive methodology, and I use them here, but they are only for drone strikes, not for raids. See http:// www.thebureauinvestigates.com/category/projects/drone-data/. The numbers cited above are current as of March 2015. For a good summary of targeted-killing policies, see http:// www.cfr.org/counterterrorism/targeted-killings/p9627; see also "Report of the Special Rapporteur on extrajudicial, summary or arbitrary executions, Philip Alston." Report of the Human Rights Council, United Nations (28 May 2010), available at http://www2.ohchr .org/english/bodies/hrcouncil/docs/14session/A.HRC.14.24.Add6.pdf; and Philip Alston, "The CIA and Targeted Killings beyond Borders," *Harvard National Security Journal* 2 (2011): 283–446.

3. Department of Defense, "Sustaining US Global Leadership: Priorities for 21st Century Defense" (January 2012), p. 4. Available at http://www.defense.gov/news /Defense_Strategic_Guidance.pdf.

4. Jo Becker and Scott Shane, "A Secret Kill List Proves a Test of Obama's Principles and Will," *New York Times*, 29 May 2012. Daniel Klaidman, *Kill or Capture: The War on Terror and the Soul of the Obama Presidency* (New York: Houghton Mifflin, 2012).

5. White House Press Secretary, "Fact Sheet: U.S. Policy Standards and Procedures for the Use of Force in Counterterrorism Operations outside the United States and Areas of Active Hostilities" (released 23 May 2013).

6. See Charlie Savage and Scott Shane, "Memo Cites Legal Basis for Killing U.S. Citizens in Al Qaeda," *New York Times*, 5 February 2013), available at http://www.ny-times.com/2013/02/05/us/politics/us-memo-details-views-on-killing-citizens-in-al-qaeda .html?_r=0. The white paper is available at http://msnbcmedia.msn.com/i/msnbc/sections /news/020413_DOJ_White_Paper.pdf.

7. During the Bush administration's experiments with routinized torture, its apologists claimed that, if it would be permissible to kill identified terrorists, it was permissible to torture them, since any rational person would prefer to be nonlethally waterboarded than killed. This was dismissed as sophistry: the question is not the desirability of the choice to the victim, which is a Hobson's choice among forms of suffering, but the permissibility of torture from the point of view of the state. No doubt many legitimate combat targets would be prefer to be raped than killed as well, but it does not follow that it is permissible to rape enemy soldiers, whether or not that would secure a military advantage. The case for torture is weaker yet if there exist, as many intelligence professionals say, nonbrutal methods of interrogation that achieve at least as good rates of success. Indeed, according to former FBI investigator Ali Soufan, Abu Zubaydah revealed nothing in his eighty-three sessions of waterboarding that he had not already revealed in noncoercive

interrogations. See Ali Soufan and Daniel Freedman, *The Black Banners: The Inside Story of 9/11 and the War against al-Qaeda* (New York: W. W. Norton, 2011), pp. 423–24.

8. According to the *New York Times*, deaths of military-age males are counted as combatant deaths unless there is strong individualized evidence to exonerate them.

9. An excellent discussion of the difference between a spectatorial and a participatory public is Jeffrey Green, *The Eyes of the People* (Oxford University Press, 2010).

10. Somewhat less democratic Britain controlled roughly half the earth's landmass during the same period.

11. See Richard Norman, *Ethics, Killing and War* (New York: Cambridge University Press, 1998).

12. The assumption of better discriminatory capacities is one I will question below, especially as the focus of inquiry shifts from inquiry in specific attacks to discrimination in drone campaigns that do not substitute for conventional attacks, because the conventional attacks would never have occurred.

13. In one sense, all traditional battlefield targeting makes use of a signature—namely that the targeted person is wearing a uniform and/or engaged in hostilities. The concern about signature strikes in the drone area is the use of targeting criteria that neither involve uniforms or obvious combat activity, nor individually specific behavior, but instead rely on such vague criteria as bearing a gun in the vicinity of known militants. The CIA appears to have been the primary agency making use of vague signature criteria, as opposed to specific intelligence, to the concern of others in the administration. The *Times* quotes a State Department official as saying that "[t]he joke was that when the C.I.A. sees 'three guys doing jumping jacks,' the agency thinks it is a terrorist training camp." Becker and Shane, "Secret Kill List"; Klaidman, *Kill or Capture*, p. 41. President Obama has denied using vague criteria and instead said that strikes are undertaken only when there is "near-certainty" that no civilians would be killed. See Scott Shane, "Drone Strikes Reveal Uncomfortable Truth: U.S. Is Often Unsure about Who Will Die," *New York Times* (23 April 2015).

14. According to the Senate Foreign Relations Committee, traffickers within the "battleground" of Afghanistan may be targeted for killing, consistent with the laws of war. Senate Prt. 111–29 (10 Aug. 2009). Of course, everything depends on the interpretation of "battleground."

15. Unnamed members of the Obama administration have been reported as acknowledging that this is in response to domestic difficulties in incarcerating and trying captives. See, e.g., Klaidman, *Kill or Capture*, p. 125.

16. See Alston's "Study on Targeted Killings", sec. 30.

17. See Klaidman, *Kill or Capture*.

18. We must not imagine that risk to the innocent can be eliminated through capture missions. First, many capture raids will end in the death of the target; second, as the roll call of Guantanamo shows, innocents can be held in custody, in terrible conditions, for very long periods. That said, as a comparative matter, capture raids no doubt provide better security.

19. See Alston, "CIA and Targeted Killings," pp. 341–43. The number of names on so-called kill lists is, of course, undisclosed and varies with intelligence and geopolitical concerns. The lists compiled by different agencies, including NATO, JSOC, and the CIA, have now apparently been aggregated into a unified "disposition matrix" database, which lists individuals targeted for both killing and for capture. Reports suggest each agency

contributing a few dozen names. Final authority for inclusion on the "kill list" rests with the president. See Greg Miller, "Plan for Hunting Terrorists Signals U.S. Intends to Keep Adding Names to Kill Lists," *Washington Post* (Oct. 23, 2012).

20. Strictly speaking, Article 51 permits force only as authorized by the Security Council, or for self-defense (and only until the council resolves the problem). It has been understood since the Kosovo intervention to permit regional defenses of others, whether or not endorsed by the Security Council. See Kofi Annan, "The Effectiveness of the International Rule of Law in Maintaining International Peace and Security," https://www.globalpolicy .org/component/content/article/190-issues/38833.html, distinguishing between NATO's (in his view) "legitimate" use of force and the legality of it under the Charter. See also Louis Henkin, "Editorial Comments: Kosovo and the Law of 'Humanitarian Intervention,'" *American Journal of International Law* 93 (1999): 824.

21. See the speech by former US State Department Legal Advisor Harold Koh, "The Obama Administration and International Law," arguing that "strategic" and international law-respecting multilateralism is at the heart of the Obama-Clinton foreign policy (25 March 2010), http://www.state.gov/s/l/releases/remarks/139119.htm.

22. Gabriella Blum and Philip Heymann, "Law and Policy of Targeted Killing," *Harvard National Security Journal* 1 (2010): 145–70; Herb Keinon, Janine Zacharia, and Lamia Lahoud, "UN, US: Stop Targeted Killings," *Jerusalem Post*, 6 July 2001, p. A1.

23. See P. W. Singer, *Wired for War* (New York: Penguin, 2009).

24. Becker and Shane, "Secret Kill List."

25. Indeed, as a matter of strict, if contested, international law, non-uniformed combatants are protected from targeting when not engaged in combat, unlike most uniformed combatants, who are targetable regardless of their function. They are liable to capture and arrest, and to lethal force only if capture is not possible. (That is, they are entitled to a law-enforcement model of the use of force.)

26. See Klaidman, *Kill or Capture*, p. 214ff.

27. For discussion, see Alston, "Report by the Special Rapporteur," pars. 28–36.

28. See Barbara Herman, *The Practice of Moral Judgment* (Cambridge, MA: Harvard University Press, 1999); Jeff McMahan, *Killing in War* (New York: Oxford University Press, 2009); Frances Kamm, *Ethics for Enemies* (New York: Oxford University Press, 2013). As Kant's own ethics are oriented chiefly around the problem of free-riding in conventional morality, problems of response to one-off violent aggression don't have a determinate response within his system. To be sure, a rule prohibiting attacks is easily derived, as a condition of equal freedom. But a personal right of reprisal, which involves substituting the destruction of someone else's invaluable dignity for one's own, is not obviously derived.

29. The exception, relevant later in our discussion, would be if the state has an adequately successful deterrence policy, such that overall welfare would be increased by prohibiting individual self-defense.

30. See Avery Plaw, Matthew S. Fricker, and Brian Glyn Williams, "Practice Makes Perfect? The Changing Civilian Toll of CIA Drone Strikes in Pakistan," *Perspectives on Terrorism* 5 (December 2011): 51–69.

31. See cases collected by the Center for Investigative Journalism. While there is no reason to think noncombatants have been deliberately targeted in Pakistan, it is an open question whether some of the errors fall within the "reasonable" bounds of the fog of war.

32. International Human Rights and Conflict Resolution Clinic at Stanford Law School and Global Justice Clinic at NYU School of Law, "Living under Drones: Death,

Injury and Trauma to Civilians from US Drone Practices in Pakistan" (September 2012), p. 57ff. Available at livingunderdrones.org.

33. See generally ibid., ch. 3.

34. We thus far have no evidence that drone pilots, or the officials who order those pilots to fire their missiles, are abnormally detached. For some discussion, see Singer, *Wired for War*, p. 326ff. Recent news reports, released apparently in response to concerns about drones, suggest at least normal levels of post-traumatic stress among drone operators. Indeed, it is hard to imagine how a targeter, watching a target over hours or days to identify the ten minutes between his sending off his children and his rejoining his wife, could not be psychologically affected. See James Dao, "Drone Operators Are Found to Get Stress Disorders Much as Those in Combat Do," *New York Times*, 25 Feb. 2013, http://www.nytimes.com/2013/02/23/us/drone-pilots-found-to-get-stress-disorders-much-as-those-in-combat-do.html?_r=0.

35. There are many reasons to think that the popular images of the warrior's courage, which do much to sustain the legitimacy of combat, and transitively the legitimacy of war itself, are at odds with war's grimier and much more collective reality. This is not to deny acts of individual bravery, or to imply cowardice as a routine matter, but merely to note, as honest writers about war explain, that war's chaos, even in limited engagements, limits our observation of individual achievement and responsibility.

36. Immanuel Kant, "Perpetual Peace: A Philosophical Sketch" [1795], sec. II.

37. Paul Kahn, "The Paradox of Riskless Warfare," *Philosophy and Public Policy Quarterly* (Summer 2002), http://digitalcommons.law.yale.edu/fss_papers/326.

38. See Garry Wills, *Lincoln at Gettysburg* (New York: Simon and Schuster, 2006).

39. *The History of the Peloponnesian Wars* (trans. B. Jowett), Bk. I, par. 121. Pericles then responds to the danger of for-profit warriors, not reassuringly: "Suppose, again, that they lay hands on the treasures at Olympia and Delphi, and tempt our mercenary sailors with the offer of higher pay, there might be serious danger, if we and our metics embarking alone were not still a match for them. But we are a match for them: and, best of all, our pilots are taken from our own citizens, while no sailors are to be found so good or so numerous as ours in all the rest of Hellas." Bk. I, par. 143. For further discussion, see Josiah Ober, *Fortress Attica: Defense of the Athenian Land Frontier* (Leiden: Brill, 1985), p. 47ff.

40. See P. W. Singer, *Corporate Warriors* (Ithaca, NY: Cornell University Press, 2003). By "mercenaries" I mean individuals carrying weapons and deploying lethal force. The use of ancillary personnel—for logistics, for example—raises interesting problems of cost-monitoring and safety, but not the same issues.

41. Of course, courage is also an ethical value, and there is an important ethical dimension to the warrior's virtue. But while the lack of displayed courage affects its courageousness (tautologically), it does not make the act impermissible so long as it is not also perfidious. And indeed, a protective act displays other virtues.

42. Kahn, "Paradox," p. 5.

43. For a brilliant discussion of policing from the perspective of democracy, see David Sklansky, *Democracy and the Police* (Stanford: Stanford University Press, 2006).

44. See Carl Schmitt, *The Nomos of the Earth* (New York: Telos Press, 2003), ch. 3, "Freedom of the Sea."

45. There is no reason to think the moral mathematics of proportionality are actually linear, either in the sense of applying to single, larger attacks, or to aggregates of attacks,

regardless of how it is implemented by military lawyers; to the contrary, it is clear that the proportionality criterion can only be applied contextually. For discussion, see Judith Gardam, *Necessity, Proportionality, and the Law of War* (New York: Cambridge University Press, 2004), ch. 1; Thomas Hurka, "Proportionality in the Morality of War," *Philosophy & Public Affairs* 33 (2005): 34–66.

46. The DOJ White Paper on targeted killings describes the standard as involving an assessment that the target is a continuous and imminent threat. However, imminence is a term of art in the memorandum, since imminence may be inferred from a target's having engaged in attacks in the past, with no evidence of having renounced his participation. While the two terms are logically compatible, they tend to stand in tension: imminent threats are rarely continuous. White Paper, p. 8ff.

47. Klaidman, *Kill or Capture*, p. 216: "[Koh] had set his own legal standard to justify the targeted killing of a US citizen: evil, with iron-clad intelligence to prove it."

48. Sandra Dieterich, Hartwig Hummel, and Stefan Marschall, "Parliamentary War Powers: A Survey of 25 European Parliaments," Occasional Paper No. 21, Geneva Center for the Democratic Control of the Armed Forces (DCAF) (2010); French Constitution of 1958, Art. 35.

49. "United States Activities in Libya," US Departments of State and Defense, 15 June 2011, available at http://www.nytimes.com/interactive/2011/06/16/us/politics/20110616_POWERS_DOC.html?ref=politics.

CHAPTER 11. DEMOCRACY AND THE DEATH OF NORMS

1. The debut of the contemporary literature is Martha Finnemore and Kathryn Sikkink, "International Norm Dynamics and Political Change," *International Organization* 52 (1998): 887–917. See also Thomas Risse and Kathryn Sikkink, "The Socialization of International Human Rights Norms into Domestic Practices: Introduction," in Thomas Risse, Stephen C. Ropp and Kathryn Sikkink, eds., *The Power of Human Rights: International Norms and Domestic Change* (New York: Cambridge University Press, 1999), pp. 1–38; Ellen Lutz and Kathryn Sikkink, "The Justice Cascade: The Evolution of Human Rights Trials in Latin America," *Chicago Journal of International Law* 2 (2001): 1. An important and recent examination of the propagation of human rights norms is Beth Simmons, *Mobilizing for Human Rights* (New York: Cambridge University Press, 2009).

2. Changes in norms (especially norms concerning preventive war) have been part of the important work of Ariel Colonomos. See his *The Gamble of War: Is It Possible to Justify Preventive War?* (New York: Macmillan, 2013).

3. My argument here differs from that of Vaughn Shannon, in his "Norms Are What States Make of Them: The Political Psychology of Norm Violation," *International Studies Quarterly* 44 (2000): 293–316. Shannon argues that states violate vague or incompletely specified norms through motivated reasoning that rationalizes violation as the triggering of an excepted condition. As I will argue, the norms concerning torture and assassination cannot plausibly be seen as vague. Their violation is best understood, by the actors themselves, as the replacement of restrictive norms by permissive ones.

4. Executive Order 13491 (22 Jan. 2009), restricted interrogation methods to those consistent with the *Army Field Manual*, hence those consistent with international human rights standards. http://www.whitehouse.gov/the_press_office/EnsuringLawfulInterrogations/.

5. Definitions vary in their particulars with their authors, but the definition I use here, as distillation of social practice and judgment whose objects include acts, dispositions, and feelings, keeps with both philosophical and political science traditions. Compare, for example, Jepperson, Wendt, and Katzenstein's definition of norms as "collective expectations about proper behavior for a given identity" with Jon Elster's negative definition of (social) norms as shared judgments of approval and disapproval that are not "outcome-oriented." Ronald Jeppersen, Alexander Wendt, and Peter Katzenstein, "Norms, Identity and Culture in National Security," in Peter J. Katzenstein, *The Culture of National Security: Norms and Identity in World Politics* (New York: Columbia University Press, 1996), pp. 33–78, p. 54; Jon Elster, "Norms of Revenge," *Ethics* 100 (1990): 862–85, p. 863.

6. See Michael Bratman, *Intentions, Plans and Practical Reason* (Cambridge, MA: Harvard University Press, 1987), ch. 2. In Bratman's account, filters are part of the intricate structure of complex plans, commitments, goals and constraints that together constitute our identity and give shape to our lives.

7. Williams's point was that some norms must be fully internalized to count as being held at all; see his *Ethics and the Limits of Philosophy* (Cambridge, MA: Harvard University Press, 1986), p. 185. But this is, I think, too strong: a norm can affect ex post reactions in a given instance, and thereby have future effects, without being fully internalized.

8. Immanuel Kant famously thought that actors themselves could not be sure whether they were guided by the norm (the categorical imperative) or by concerns about social costs and benefits. Kant, *Groundwork of the Metaphysics of Morals* [1785], sec. 2, par. 2.

9. In positivist legal philosophy, which focuses on the definition (positing) of norms, the Austinian tradition sees sanctions as integral to legal norms; the Hartian tradition regards the sanction as fully separable.

10. Shannon, "Norms Are What States Make of Them."

11. See David Kahn, *The Codebreakers: The Comprehensive History of Secret Communications from Ancient Times to the Internet*, rev. ed. (New York: Simon and Schuster 1996), p. 360.

12. This description of norm dynamics draws on Lutz and Sikkink, "Justice Cascade." On policy entrepreneurs in particular, see Michael Mintrom and Phillipa Norman, "Policy Entrepreneurship and Policy Change," *Policy Studies Journal* 37 (2009): 649–67. See also the important related discussion of "acculturation" in human rights in Ryan Goodman and Derek Jinks, "How to Influence States: Socialization and International Human Rights Law," *Duke Law Journal* 54 (2004): 621–703.

13. Finnemore and Sikkink, "International Norm Dynamics," p. 887.

14. Heather Timmons and Sruthi Gupati, "Woman Dies after a Gang Rape That Galvanized India," *New York Times* (28 December 2012).

15. The story of how US media interests have struggled to acculturate individuals to respect IP norms is well told in Peter Menell, "This American Copyright Life for the Internet Age," UC Berkeley Public Law Research Paper No. 2347674, http://papers.ssrn.com/sol3/papers.cfm?abstract_id=2347674 (4 April 2014).

16. Given the very low degree of legitimacy accorded to US economic interests in intellectual property, this outcome is unlikely.

17. Compare John Dower's account of the behavior of WWII American soldiers in the Pacific theater with even the most critical accounts of conduct by American soldiers in Iraq. While individual soldiers have acted wrongly, none would write home to a village chaplain, promising him a trophy ear from a dead enemy soldier. Dower, *War without Mercy* (New York: Pantheon, 1987), pp. 64–65.

18. See Jerry Skolnick, "American Interrogation: From Torture to Trickery," in Sanford Levinson, ed., *Torture: A Collection* (Oxford, 2004), pp. 105–28.

19. Common Geneva Convention Art. 3 (adopted 1949); Universal Declaration of Human Rights, Art. 5 (adopted 1948); International Covenant on Civil and Political Rights (ICCPR), Art. 7 (1966). The International Criminal Tribunal for the former Yugoslavia (ICTY)'s Judgment in *Prosecutor v. Kunarac, Kovac and Vukovic* (Trial Chamber Judgment), Case Nos. IT–96–23–T and IT–96–23/1–T (22 Feb. 2001), holding a nonstate actor liable for torture, rests on the claim that the ICCPR prohibition itself rests on a customary norm prohibiting torture.

20. Darius Rejali, *Torture and Democracy* (Princeton: Princeton University Press, 2009).

21. For discussion of the jurisprudence of torture, see Jeremy Waldron, "Torture and Positive Law: A Jurisprudence for the White House," *Columbia Law Review* 105 (2005): 1681–750.

22. Pub. L. 103–236, Title 5, sec. 506(a), 30 Apr. 1994, 108 Stat. 463.

23. See the account of former military interrogator Matthew Alexander in *Kill or Capture* (New York: Macmillan, 2010), and of former FBI interrogator Ali Soufan, in *The Black Banners* (New York: W. W. Norton, 2011).

24. Ward Thomas, *Ethics of Destruction* (Ithaca, NY: Cornell University Press, 2001), ch. 2; Thomas, "The New Age of Assassination," SAIS Review 25 (2005): 27–39; Michael Schmitt, "State-Sponsored Assassination in Domestic and International Law," *Yale Journal of International Law* 17 (1992): 609–85. See also the useful historical survey produced for the US Army Command and Staff College by Major Matthew Machon, *Targeted Killing as an Element of the War on Terror* (2006), available at http://www.fas.org/irp/eprint/machon.pdf.

25. Hans Morgenthau, *Politics among Nations (New York: Alfred Knopf, 1948)*, p. 225 (quoted in Thomas, *Ethics of Destruction*, p. 54).

26. Alberico Gentili, *De Jure Belli Libre Tres* (1612), trans. John C. Rolfe, Classics of International Law no. 16 (Oxford: Clarendon Press, 1933) , 168.

27. Hugo Grotius, *The Rights of War and Peace* (1625), ed. Richard Tuck, from the edition by Jean Barbeyrac (Indianapolis: Liberty Fund, 2005), vol. 3. , ch. 4, sec. 18, par. 2; http://oll.libertyfund.org/title/1427/121224.

28. Ibid., par. 5.

29. See Asa Kasher and Amos Yadlin, "Assassination and Preventive Killing," *SAIS Review* 25 (2005): 41–57. Kasher and Yadlin use the term "preventive" rather than "targeted" killing.

30. As discussed below, Executive Order 12333 states: "No person employed by or acting on behalf of the United States government shall engage in or conspire to engage in, assassination." 46 F.R. 59941, 3 C.F.R, 1981, Comp. "Executive Order 12333: United States Intelligence Activities," accessed online at http://www.cia.gov/cia/information/eo12333.html, sec. 2.11.

31. Instructions for the Government of Armies of the United States in the Field (Lieber Code), 24 April 1863, Art. 148, available at http://avalon.law.yale.edu/19th_century/lieber.asp#sec9.

32. It conforms thus with the definition offered by Philip Alston, Special Rapporteur for the U.N. Human Rights Council: "[In targeted killing] lethal force is intentionally and deliberately used, with a degree of pre-meditation, against an individual or individuals specifically identified in advance by the perpetrator." "Study on Targeted Killings" (28 May 2010), A/HRC/14/24/Add.6.

33. President Ford's order was superseded by Carter Order 12306 and Reagan Order 12333; all preserved the assassination ban. Order 12333 removed 11905's qualifier "political" from its restriction on assassination.

34. See Stephen David, "Fatal Choices: Israel's Policy of Targeted Killing," Begin-Sadat Center for Strategic Studies, Bar-Ilan University Mideast Security and Policy Studies No. 51 (2002) (also published as chapter 9 of Efraim Inbar, ed., *Democracies and Small Wars* (London: Frank Cass, 2003)). David suggests that the easy acceptance of assassination by Israeli policymakers lies partly in approving descriptions in the Torah. Of course, Israeli security officers had purely pragmatic reasons to favor the strong statement made by its deployment of assassination squads. See also Michael Gross, *Moral Dilemmas of Asymmetric War* (New York: Cambridge University Press, 2010), ch. 5.

35. Adam Stahl, "The Evolution of Israeli Targeted Operations: Consequences of the Thabet Operation," *Studies in Conflict & Terrorism* 33 (2010): 111–33, DOI: 10.1080 /10576100903487065. In 2001, *USA Today* reported that "Since late September, at least 60 suspected militants have been blown up by cellphones or car headrests packed with explosives, shot by undercover agents disguised as Arab beggars or killed by laser-guided missiles launched from helicopters." Jack Kelley, "We're Going to Get Them," *USA Today*, 21 August 2001.

36. Between 2009 and July 2014 (before the Gaza operations), the Israeli human rights organization B'Tselem reports that another 16 civilians were killed collaterally in targeted killing operations specifically, and an additional 204 were killed who did not take part in hostilities or were not known to have taken part. B'Tselem, "Statistics—Fatalities," http:// www.btselem.org/statistics/fatalities/after-cast-lead/by-date-of-event.

37. A 2001 poll put support at 90% of the public. David, "Fatal Choices," p. 7. There have been many philosophical discussions within Israeli circles of the morality of targeted killing, but virtually all analyses by Israeli philosophers conclude its acceptability. See, e.g., Gross, *Moral Dilemmas*.

38. *Public Committee against Torture in Israel v. Government of Israel* (2006), HCJ 769/02. The decision is relatively permissive because it rejects the narrow interpretation of "taking direct part in hostilities," urged, for example, by Professor Antonio Cassesse, according to which civilians are attackable when, and only when, they are actually engaged in hostilities. According to the narrow understanding, civilians planning future attacks, or otherwise preparing for them, are not direct participants in hostilities. The court instead accepts that civilians who have made their "home" in a terrorist organization can be treated like military staff, as engaged in a continuous combat function, and so are attackable at any time, and not merely when giving specific instructions for attack (par. 39). More generally, civilians are to be treated as attackable whenever they play the same functional role as uniformed combatants (pars. 34–35). There is a further empirical broadening of the criterion, stemming from the difficulty of attributing such a function to a civilian, without the aid of the bright lines provided by a military hierarchy. While the court emphasizes the need for clear intelligence asserting the pervasive role of civilians who play leading roles, and places the burden of proof on the Army, it is hard to evaluate how tightly the proof process is controlled.

39. David, "Fatal Choices," p. 11; Joel Greenberg, "Israel Affirms Policy of Assassinating Militants," *New York Times*, 5 July 2001.

40. Kelley, "We're Going to Get Them." I do not wish to overstate the evidence of US public concerns with assassination in general, as opposed to concerns with Israel's

management of its relations with Palestinians. It is notable that polling databases contain no queries on assassination in general before September 2001.

41. David Johnston and David Sanger, "Yemen Killing Based on Rules Set by Bush," *New York Times*, 6 Nov. 2002.

42. See Schmitt, "State-Sponsored Assassination," p. 639ff; Machon, *Targeted Killing*; W. Hays Parks, Memorandum of Law: Executive Order 12333 and Assassination, Army Law (Dec. 1989), available at https://www.law.upenn.edu/institutes/cerl/conferences /targetedkilling/papers/ParksMemorandum.pdf. That said, and whatever the analytic or tactical merits of the distinction, however, it is clear that the official US military position hewed largely, before 2001, to the broader Lieber Code understanding of assassinations as including individualized killing off the hot battlefield.

43. See generally Philip Alston, "Report of the Special Rapporteur on Extrajudicial, Summary or Arbitrary Executions," UN HCR (28 May 2010).

44. For an account of the immediate post-9/11 policy atmosphere, notably the panic engendered by unfiltered intelligence reports of a variety of terrorist plots at work, see Jane Mayer's *The Dark Side* (New York: Doubleday, 2008).

45. Chapter 7 discusses the legal arguments in more detail.

46. Although the Bush administration halted the harshest forms of interrogation, including waterboarding, by 2004, the last reported interrogation using techniques that would generally be found illegal under the Convention occurred in late 2007, when a detainee was subjected to six straight days of sleep deprivation. See Pamela Hess and Devlin Barrett, "Memos: CIA Pushed Limits on Sleep Deprivation," 27 August 2009, Associated Press, available at http://6abc.com/archive/6985308/. Sleep deprivation, among other techniques, had been approved by Steven Bradbury, head of the Office of Legal Counsel, in the Memorandum for John A. Rizzo, Acting General Counsel, Central Intelligence Agency, Re: Application of the War Crimes Act, the Detainee Treatment Act, and Common Article Three of the Geneva Conventions to Certain Techniques that May Be Used by the CIA in the Interrogation of High Value al Qaeda Detainees, 20 July 2007, available at http://www .justice.gov/olc/docs/memo-warcrimesact.pdf. (I am grateful to an anonymous referee for this information.)

47. "CIA Launches Drone Attack," CNN (5 Nov. 2002).

48. For Pakistan and Yemen, http://www.thebureauinvestigates.com/category/projects /drones/drones-graphs/ (accessed March 2015). Some of the Afghan drone strikes, about which little is known, were conducted by Britain.

49. Remarks of John Brennan, Woodrow Wilson Center, 30 April 2012, available at http://www.lawfareblog.com/2012/04/brennanspeech/.

50. See James Cavallaro, Stephan Sonnenberg, and Sarah Knuckey, *Living under Drones: Death, Injury and Trauma to Civilians from US Drone Practices in Pakistan* (Stanford, CA: International Human Rights and Conflict Resolution Clinic, Stanford Law School; New York: NYU School of Law, Global Justice Clinic, 2012).

51. CBS News/New York Times poll (27 Feb. 2014). Polling after 9/11 put public support of CIA "assassination" of terrorists at between 60% and 80%. See *Polling the Nations* database, http://www.orspub.com/index.php.

52. Mayer, *Dark Side*, ch. 1 ("Panic"). The lag time in US condemnations of Israeli targeted killings shows a slower policy process at work.

53. See also the very interesting article of Ryder McKeown, "Norm Regress: US Revisionism and the Slow Death of the Torture Norm," *International Relations* 23 (2009):

5–25. McKeown interprets the story of the disappearance of the torture norm as a case of successful destructive norm entrepreneurialism by, principally, Vice President Dick Cheney and other neoconservative elements of the executive branch. While I agree with McKeown that the efforts by these norm dissenters were necessary conditions of the norm's disappearance, my argument concerns the deeper conditions for the success of these efforts: the transformation of the deliberative institutional environment in which the entrepreneurs' arguments took hold. It was by silencing or sidelining the institutional voices favoring dignitary norms, and making use of pragmatic or utilitarian justifications, that these entrepreneurs were successful.

54. Two important accounts of the harm of torture are David Luban and Henry Shue, "Mental Torture: A Critique of Erasures in U.S. Law," *Georgetown Law Journal* 100 (2012): 823–63; and David Sussman, "What's Wrong with Torture?" *Philosophy & Public Affairs* 33 (2005): 1–33.

55. It is, strictly speaking, a domain-limited form of consequentialist moral deliberation, in which only negative direct and indirect consequences for US citizens appear to be counted. And it applies a maximin rather than maximizing principle to choice, setting priority on avoiding the worst-case scenario of large-scale US deaths. But it fits within a broader conception of the utilitarian family.

56. Less charitably, one could see the reaction not as a utilitarianism of fear at all, but simply as a revenge reaction, in which there were no calculations apart from giving to the terrorists what they deserved. But the continued public references by Bush administration figures to a "one percent" doctrine of avoiding catastrophic risk, and the reporting by Jane Mayer mentioned above, suggest that fear-engendered calculation was a large part of the deliberative frame. See Ron Suskind, *The One Percent Doctrine* (New York: Simon and Schuster, 2006).

57. Pew Center, http://www.people-press.org/2011/09/01/united-in-remembrance -divided-over-policies/1/; Investor's Business Daily/Christian Science Monitor/TIPP poll, 14 Nov. 2001 (available from *Polling the Nations*).

58. One can say that the ultimate ethical justification is a national duty of self-defense, understood categorically. But in the context of drone strikes, with few possible exceptions, this duty is not best characterized as an immediate need to self-defend. It is, rather, a broader duty to maximize US interests and minimize harms.

59. I thus disagree with the view of Diana Panke and Ulrike Petersohn, "Why International Norms Disappear Sometimes," *European Journal of International Relations* 18 (2012): 4719–42. Panke and Petersohn argue that norm death is best explained by the lack of enforced sanctions. In my view, lack of enforcement is neither necessary nor sufficient in general to explain norm collapse, since many norms can be sustained so long as there are other symbolic indicia of a community's seriousness about the norm, as embodied, for example, in recent enactment or in formal instruction. In the case of the torture and assassination norms, the prohibitions were rarely enforced or strongly observed.

60. Mark Mazzetti and Mark Landler, "Despite Administration Promises, Few Signs of Change in Drone Wars," *New York Times*, 2 August 2013.

61. I allude to the famous Nelson Goodman "riddle of induction," which draws on the impossibility of distinguishing the correctness of applying two different predicates versus one discontinuously applied predicate to the same phenomenon, of a mineral that changes color. Goodman, "The New Riddle of Induction," in *Fact, Fiction and Forecast*, 4th ed.

(Cambridge, MA: Harvard University Press, 1993). Ludwig Wittgenstein's rule-following paradox is a close kin.

62. Pew Research Center Polls, July 2004, November 2009, and January 2015, available at http://www.people-press.org/question-search/. Most strikingly, public acceptance of torture shifted dramatically upward, between February 2009 (when rejection stood also at 32%) and November 2009, following VP Cheney's public defenses of torture. No facts emerged in the interim to show that torture was a wiser policy.

CHAPTER 12. LOOKING BACKWARD: DEMOCRATIC TRANSITIONS AND THE CHOICE OF JUSTICE

1. See the valuable discussion by Eric Posner and Adrian Vermeule, "Transitional Justice as Ordinary Justice," *Harvard Law Review* 117 (2003): 761–825.

2. A demand for reparative payment may also mask a demand for punishment and so not genuinely count as reparative. I leave open whether the infliction of punishment can itself be reparative. In the peculiarities of US politics, capital punishment is now frequently justified by its purported contribution to victims' and survivors' healing, or "closure." There is, to my knowledge, no psychological or sociological evidence for its making any such contribution.

3. See, e.g., Marcel Mauss, *The Gift: Forms and Functions of Exchange in Archaic Societies*, trans. Ian Cunnison (Glencoe, IL: Free Press, 1954).

4. That punishment (in the sense of institutionally inflicted suffering) should have reparative functions does not preclude its having retributive and compensatory functions as well. Reparative justice need not be viewed as a competitor theory of punishment, in the sense of claiming to offer a privileged justification of punishment. As I am deploying it here, it is just an account of a possible function or range of functions of certain social practices.

5. Roughly speaking, reparative justice may effectively compel empathy when the crime is relatively minor (and so forgivable) and the offender feels some connection to the community calling him to account. For discussion of this question, see Geoffrey Sayre-McCord, "Criminal Justice and Legal Reparations as an Alternative to Punishment," in *Legal and Political Philosophy*, ed. Enrique Villanueva (New York: Editions Rodopi, 2002), pp. 307–38; and John Braithwaite, *Crime, Shame and Reintegration* (New York: Cambridge University Press, 1989).

6. See, e.g., M. L. Cohen et al., "The Psychology of Rapists," in *Forcible Rape*, ed. Duncan Chappell et al. (New York: Columbia University Press, 1977), pp. 291–314, which distinguishes as "types" of rapes (a) rape motivated by overwhelming sexual impulses; (b) rape as a defense against homosexual wishes; (c) rape as sexual and sadistic expression; and (d) rape as expression of a more generally predatory disposition (p. 296). Of course, many forms of rape do involve an absolute failure to acknowledge the victim's humanity.

7. For a general discussion of the slavery reparations issues, see Eric Posner and Adrian Vermeule, "Reparations for Slavery and Other Historical Injustices," *Columbia Law Review* 103 (2003): 689–747, and citations therein.

8. This is not true in all cases. Military intervention in Kosovo and the international criminal tribunals in Rwanda and former Yugoslavia followed the atrocities for which

they were formed by only a few years. But justice has been much slower with the fall of Eastern European communism.

9. Their descendants may be compensated, however, and their reputations may be repaired through posthumous review and vacating of criminal convictions or discharges.

10. "L'oubli, et je dira même l'erreur historique, sont un facteur essentiel de la creation d'une nation. . . ." Ernest Renan, "Qu'est-ce qu'une nation?" reprinted in *Qu'est-ce qu'une nation?* (Paris: Pocket, 1992), p. 42.

11. See Charles Taylor, *Multiculturalism: Examining the Politics of Recognition*, ed. Amy Gutmann (Princeton: Princeton University Press, 1992), pp. 30–37.

12. "I have seen, in my life, French, Italians, Russians, etc.; I even know, thanks to Montesquieu, that one can be Persian: but when it comes to mankind, that I have never encountered in my life." Joseph de Maistre, *Considérations sur la France*, 2d ed. (London: Bale, 1797), p. 102 (quoted in K. Anthony Appiah, "Identity, Authenticity, Survival," in Taylor, *Multiculturalism*, pp. 149–63, at 150).

13. Expropriation as part of a genocidal program is a different matter, and this is why I do not consider here the proper treatment of claims by Holocaust survivors or victims' descendants. Those claims are, I think, substantially stronger than the purely political claims I examine in this chapter.

14. I do not mean that there were no indigenous socialist movements but that, as one leading historian has written, they "never had a chance"—they were crushed by Stalin and his satellite parties, working with the Red Army at their backs. See Norman M. Naimark, "Revolution and Counterrevolution in Eastern Europe," in *The Crisis of Socialism in Europe*, ed. Christiane Lemke and Gary Marks (Durham, NC: Duke University Press, 1992), pp. 61–83.

15. The fact that the transition to socialism was not a Pareto improvement is no reason on its own to condemn it; any even minimally redistributive transition from a state of massive inequality and grinding poverty to one of even meager protection of the poor fails the Pareto criterion.

16. The Nazi party, and hence Hitler, famously came to power through roughly democratic means; his regime's illegitimacy is due more to the substance of its policies than the vehicle of their implementation. Retrospective assessment is a matter of both process and substance.

17. It may also include much else—for example, regret at one's (or one's nation's) complicity in the crimes, depending on the position of the theorist.

18. This point is, of course, very familiar, from criticisms of Robert Nozick's Lockean theory in *Anarchy, State and Utopia* (New York: Basic Books, 1977).

19. Elazar Barkan, *The Guilt of Nations* (Baltimore: Johns Hopkins University Press, 2001), ch. 6.

20. Peter Quint, *The Imperfect Union* (Princeton: Princeton University Press, 1997), p. 125. The rest of my discussion of East Germany draws heavily on ibid., pp. 125–26.

21. Nazi-era expropriations were also treated this way.

22. Quint, *Imperfect Union*, pp. 129–30.

23. Commission on Security and Cooperation in Europe, "Human Rights and Democratization in Unified Germany," excerpted in, *Transitional Justice*, vol. 3, ed. Neil J. Kritz (Washington, DC: United States Institute of Peace Press, 1995), 595–602, p. 600.

24. Quint, *Imperfect Union*, 142.

25. Grazyna Skapska, "Restitutive Justice, Rule of Law, and Constitutional Dilemmas," in Adam Czarnot, Martin Krygier, and Wojciech Sadurski, *Rethinking the Rule of Law after Communism* (Budapest: Central European University Press, 2005).

26. Michael Neff, "Eastern Europe's Policy of Restitution and Property in the 1990's," *Dickinson Journal of International Law* 10 (1992): 357–81, p. 368–73.

27. Vojtech Cepl, "A Note on the Restitution of Property in Post-Communist Czechoslovakia," excerpted in Kritz, *Transitional Justice*, pp. 581–85.

28. The greater economic viability of the Polish small farm lots, by contrast to the economically disastrous collective farms of the DDR, is another reason Poland has been reluctant to engage in agricultural sector reparations; there would be no efficiency gain but only transaction costs from reparations.

29. See Neff, "Eastern Europe's Policy," pp. 376–80, for discussion of the early Polish discussions of restitution, and Skapska, "Restitutive Justice."

30. I am grateful to Stephen Williams for correspondence discussing this model.

31. Strictly speaking, the fair market value is a function of either the actual lost income or the income that would have been lost by a more profitable alternative use of the property.

32. There is a further, conceptual point: since land markets are activities grounded in and hence relative to particular social, political, and legal institutions and practices, it makes no sense to stipulate a market price based on a purely hypothetical and idealized regime. On the other hand, it is true that some Central European countries (notably Poland) maintained some markets in private property. Although such market prices would presumably be too low (given constrained surplus earning) to satisfy expropriation victims, they might serve as an defensible value marker. The arguments below in the text against paying any significant valuation still control the issue.

33. Jeremy Waldron, "Superseding Historical Injustice," *Ethics* 103 (1998): 4–28. See also Gregory Alexander, "The Limits of Property Reparations," http://scholarship.law.cornell.edu/lsrp_papers/24/ (paper presented at Conference on Political Transformation, Restitution, and Justice at Jagiellonian University, Krakow, Poland, 6–8 June 2002) for arguments drawn from cognitive psychology that also impugn our ability to judge counterfactuals.

34. But if default inheritance provisions are unjust—for example, sexist—then the case for recourse to this formula is very weak.

35. My own view is that a confiscatory estate tax is justified, with some sort of sentimental exemption for limited transfers of property. But matters are obviously complex: for example, spousal inheritance presumably ought to be untaxed; and provisions for minor dependents would need to be made. More complicated yet is the proper treatment of a family home. I cannot defend my view here, and it is anyway irrelevant to the argument, which rests only on the claim that second-generation claimants cannot plausibly maintain that they would have inherited the property under any set of just state policies. For more discussion of some of these issues, see Liam Murphy and Thomas Nagel, *The Myth of Ownership* (New York: Oxford University Press, 2002).

36. John Rawls, *A Theory of Justice*, rev. ed. (Cambridge, MA: Harvard University Press, 1999), p. 87.

37. Jon Elster makes a similar point, in "On Doing What One Can: An Argument against Restitution and Retribution as a Means of Overcoming the Communist Legacy,"

East European Constitutional Review 1 (1992): 15–17. Even if the landless were to receive compensation for the wasting of their human capital, they would still be relatively worse off, since the previously landed would be entitled to the same claim, on top of the claim for their land. And even if the claims of the landed were limited, then reparations would seem largely a matter of taking in each other's wash.

38. The realization of negative claims, of course, depends on the existence of positive institutions: criminal law provides no protection without a police force and court system, and those will be undersupported without a coercive tax system.

39. This characterization of corrective justice is meant to be neutral between libertarian conceptions, which focus on individual duties to repair harms caused by individual action (see, e.g., Richard Epstein, "A Theory of Strict Liability," *Journal of Legal Studies* 2 (1973): 151–204) and moralized conceptions, which focus on violations of individual moral duties to take care with others' entitlements (see, e.g, Jules Coleman, *Risks and Wrongs* [New York: Cambridge University Press, 1992], or Stephen Perry, "Responsibility for Outcomes, Risk, and the Law of Torts," in *Philosophy and the Law of Torts*, ed. Gerald Postema [New York: Cambridge University Press, 2002]). I discuss the relation of corrective and retributive justice to underlying notions of responsibility in "Responsibility," *Oxford Handbook of Jurisprudence and Philosophy of Law*, ed. Jules Coleman and Scott Shapiro (Oxford University Press, 2002), pp. 548–87.

40. Showing the relevance of such reasons is, roughly, the program of law and economics. See, e.g., Richard A. Posner, *The Economic Analysis of Law* (New York: Aspen Publishers 2003).

41. I mean to invoke a familiarly Rawlsian view, although Rawls's Difference Principle is more stringent than a demand for a social minimum; the view in the text also has much in common with (but may be weaker than) the conceptions of, for example, Ronald Dworkin, Jeremy Waldron, Brian Barry, or Bruce Ackerman. More stringent theories of distributive justice yet, either strict egalitarian or act-utilitarian, might require the full subordination of corrective justice principles to the realization of their distributive goal. The argument I make in the text, therefore, presumes a theory of distributive justice that allows some play at the level of particular distributions of holdings. (I owe this point to Seana Shiffrin.)

42. Alternatively, extant holdings are evaluated by reference to the institutional principles of acquisition and transfer that flow from an underlying conception of distributive justice.

43. Coleman, *Risks*, p. 304. Coleman's main discussion of the relation of corrective to distributive justice is at pp. 350–54.

44. In Rawls' formulation, the subject of distributive justice is the "basic structure" of society: "the political constitution and the principal economic and social arrangements." Rawls, *Theory of Justice*, p. 6.

45. For discussion, see Stephen Perry's valuable article, "On the Relationship between Corrective and Distributive Justice," in *Oxford Essays in Jurisprudence, Fourth Series*, ed. Jeremy Horder (New York: Oxford University Press, 2000), pp. 237–63. James Gordley defends a more sophisticated variant of the derivative view as an Aristotelian conception of corrective justice, in "Tort Law in the Aristotelian Tradition," in *Philosophical Foundations of Tort Law*, ed. David Owen (New York: Oxford University Press, 1995), pp. 131–58.

46. One such view is presented by Coleman and Arthur Ripstein, "Mischief and Misfortune," *McGill Law Journal* 41 (1995): 91–131. On their view, corrective justice protects distributively just (or "political") allocations of responsibility and agency.

47. This is Stephen Perry's view, in Horder, *Oxford Essays*. One could construct a similar account from Thomas Scanlon's contractualist theory of the pre-institutional wrong involved in promise-breaking; see Scanlon, *What We Owe to Each Other* (Cambridge, MA: Harvard University Press, 1998), ch. 7.

48. Poor states may still devote resources to ensuring that current corrective justice claims are met—for example, compensating new property takings or injuries. Such payments are a crucial part of fostering the rule of law and a regime of private property. Provided that the benefits of the rule of law and a private property system redound to all as public goods—a significant condition in Eastern Europe—then the interests of all, including the destitute, are thereby served.

49. See Neff, "Eastern Europe's Policy," pp. 373–74; and for further discussion, Posner and Vermeule, "Transitional Justice."

50. See, e.g., Cass R. Sunstein, *One Case at a Time: Judicial Minimalism on the Supreme Court* (Cambridge: Harvard University Press, 2001).

51. This point holds a fortiori for the maximalist position, which puts hard as well as symbolic capital behind the victimhood of the expropriated.

52. This will not be true when the victims are foreign businesses and expatriates, who will play no continuing role in the nation's new economic or political life.

53. Of course, the new regimes will want to reduce the future risk as much as possible if they hope to attract foreign capital; and as I suggest in the text above, restoring properties taken by the previous regime's acts may also be necessary to attract that investment. But moving down that path may entail discriminating against domestic victims who lack the bargaining power of foreign firms. I therefore worry about efforts by foreign nations to condition aid and investment on property restitution.

54. For the same reasons, it also seems to me a requirement of a just tax policy that there be an exemption, up to some reasonable threshold, for bequests of homesteads; the parallel claim in justice for family businesses seems to me far weaker, though perhaps advisable as a matter of economic policy, given the deadweight and efficiency costs of ownership transfers to those less familiar with the business.

55. To clarify: my argument here is not that reparations might be "bad for the Jews," as the expression goes, for Jewish victims of expropriation are among the claimants. Rather, it is that any movement that privileges national belonging is dangerous to any group deemed an outsider or newcomer. In today's world of increasingly easy movement across borders, such worries may abate—or the conflicts may intensify.

56. I say "partially excludable," for cultural and religious institutions do, of course, exclude nonmembers, and the benefits to members may be allocated on the basis of sex, age, and family status. But, putting aside the issue of nonmembers, to the extent that the life such institutions enable is a good at all for their members, its goodness comes by virtue of members' general participation in them. My argument here is indebted to Will Kymlicka, *Multicultural Citizenship* (New York: Oxford University Press, 1996).

57. For an analogous argument on which I have drawn, see Jeremy Waldron, "Minority Cultures and the Cosmopolitan Alternative," in *The Rights of Minority Cultures*, ed. Will Kymlicka (Oxford: Oxford University Press, 1995), pp. 93–119.

58. Edmund Burke, *Reflections on the Revolution in France*, ed. C. C. O'Brien (New York: Viking, 1982), pp. 192–93. The first sentence does not parse even without ellipses, but the meaning is reasonably clear.

INDEX

Abu Ghraib, 238, 240, 298n79
accomplice liability, 37–38, 40–43, 54–61.
    See also complicity
accountability, 98–100, 198–205, 217–22,
    224–28, 244–45. *See also* justification;
    morality
Ackerman, Bruce, 156, 318n41
active political community, 161
Addington, David, 237, 289n36
Afghanistan, 14, 37, 42, 61–62, 174, 177,
    195–96, 202, 209, 219, 232, 237–42
agency (political), 171–78, 198–201
agentic democracy, 4, 6–8, 12–14, 16,
    159–61, 168, 171–78, 198–201. *See
    also* collective memory; democracy
al-Awlaki, Anwar, 206–7, 215
Algeria, 195
Al-Haraethi, 205
al-Qaeda, 9–10, 16, 42, 136, 155–56, 196,
    203, 215–17, 237–43, 276n18
API 44, 40, 42, 44, 53, 59, 67–68, 279n8
APII, 6, 276n18
Aquinas, Thomas, 118
Arab League, 162
Arab Spring, 2, 11–12, 246–47, 275n1
area bombing, 9, 230, 283n8
Arendt, Hannah, 300n99
Aristotle, 148–49
Aron, Raymond, 39
Arrow, Kenneth, 277n10
Article 51, 79, 204, 235–36, 307n20
assassination, 16–17, 202–3, 232–43, 309n3,
    311n30, 312n33, 312n40
Augustine (Saint), 191
Austin, John, 118, 310n9
autonomy (national), 166–71

Bahrain, 161
Barry, Brian, 318n41
Bass, Gary, 180, 191
Battle of Marathon, 212
Bay of Pigs, 113–14
Beitz, Charles, 171–72
Bentham, Jeremy, 109–10, 138
bin Laden, Osama, 195, 215
biological weapons, 9, 201, 203–4
Black, Cofer, 291n11
Blackstone, William, 110–12, 118, 144
Blair, Tony, 220
Blutgeld, 213
Bodin, Jean, 45–49, 108, 280n18,
    287n15
Boucher, Richard, 236
Bratman, Michael, 226
Brennan, John, 238, 240
Brugger, Winfried, 296n65
B'Tselem, 235, 312n36
Burke, Edmund, 271
Bush, George H. W., 235
Bush, George W., 2, 16, 104–6, 125–28,
    136, 146, 161, 165, 237–38, 286n28
Bybee, Jay, 104, 129, 135, 151

Caligula, 112
Cambodia, 113
capitalism, 1, 3, 20–21, 35–36, 246–47. *See
    also* democracy; reparations
Cassesse, Antonio, 312n38
Castro, Fidel, 234
Catholic Church, 256, 272
challenge terms, 28–29
Chamberlain, Neville, 101
chemical weapons, 9, 201, 203–4

mercenaries, 210–12, 279n11, 280n29,
308n40
mere secrets, 113–14
Merrill, Thomas, 144
meta-secrecy, 112–21
micro-necessity claims, 128–33, 137–38,
144–45, 147–48
Mill, John Stuart, 45, 161, 169–70, 172, 176,
191, 303n11
mission civilisatrice, 191, 194, 200. *See also*
colonialism
Mitchell, James, 237
monetary compensation, 257–61
Montesquieu, Charles de Secondat, baron
de, 294n46
Moore, Michael, 140
morality: collective will and, 171–78;
combat privileges and, 41–50, 65–69;
cynicism and, 2, 26, 183, 248; democracy's shape and, 23–24, 106, 217–22;
deontological approaches to, 90–99,
128, 140–49, 207, 215, 239, 242–43,
295n57; evaluation and, 84–88, 93–97,
102–3, 224–28, 244–45; humanitarian
interventions and, 161–66, 169–71;
international politics and, 11–12; moral
luck and, 57, 83–103, 169, 285n19,
285nn10–11; national selves and,
159–61, 171–74; necessity claims and,
137–47; psychology and, 33, 85, 87,
93, 182–83, 225–30, 239–42, 254,
303n142; reparative justice and, 248–
52, 265–67; rights claims and, 125–28,
137–47, 155–57; risk assessments
and, 209–15; secret law and, 106–24;
targeted killing and, 197–98, 201–5,
232–36; utilitarianism and, 91–97,
100, 128–37, 150–57, 190, 207–8,
239–43, 295n57, 314n55; victor's rights
and, 178–94; war's conduct and, 9,
15, 63–65, 77–82, 201–5. *See also* democracy; justification; norms and the
normative
"The Moral Standing of States" (Walzer),
171–74
Morgenthau, Hans, 233

Moss, Randolph, 286n3
MPC (Model Penal Code), 130–32, 138–39

Nagel, Thomas, 66, 84–88, 98, 102–3,
279n12, 297n74
Napoleon Bonaparte, 83–84, 100, 109, 111
National Security Directives, 116
NATO (North Atlantic Treaty Organization), 11, 52, 57, 162, 175, 213
natural legitimacy, 29
natural right, 143, 183, 190, 253–54, 259–60
necessity (military): drone warfare defenses and, 238; IHL and, 38–39;
macro-necessity and, 133–37, 149–57;
micro-necessity and, 128–33, 137–38,
144–48; rights' abrogation and, 125–37;
as routine practice, 147–49, 157–58,
299n93. *See also* democracy; emergency
rule; legitimacy; wars
neoconservatives, 2, 103, 160, 313n53. *See
also specific people*
neoliberalism, 229
New York Times, 196
NGOs (non-governmental organizations),
229
Nicaragua, 113
9/11 attacks. *See* September 11th
no-difference (ND) model, 184–86, 189–90
noninterference principle, 11
norm death, 228, 236–45
norm entrepreneurs, 228–29, 310n12
norms and the normative: agentic democracy and, 14–16, 78–82; definitions of,
224–28, 310n5; democracy's special duties and, 2, 12–13, 217–22, 224; deontological positions and, 90, 94–95; human
rights paradigm and, 9–11, 18–19,
21–23; international law and, 27–35,
44–45, 159–61, 166–71; *jus ad bellum*
and, 2, 7–8, 15, 48, 63–82; *jus in bello*
and, 2, 37–40, 43–45, 50–61; law's
publicness and, 106–24; necessity
claims and, 130–37, 147–49; political
luck and, 84–88, 93–97; psychology
and, 33, 85, 87, 93, 182–83, 225–30,
239–42, 254, 303n142; reasons and,

GPSR Authorized Representative: Easy Access System Europe - Mustamäe tee 50, 10621 Tallinn, Estonia, gpsr.requests@easproject.com